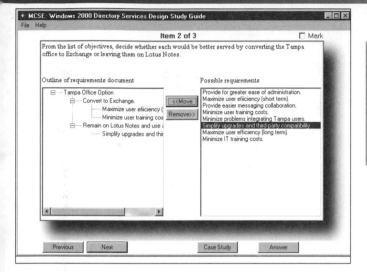

Test the depth and breadth of your knowledge with our exclusive Case Study program that simulates the case studies you'll encounter on all Windows 2000 Design exams. New question formats are covered, including:

✔ Build, List, and Reorder

✔ Create a Tree

✔ Drop and Connect

Search through two complete books in PDF– MCSE: Windows 2000 Directory Services Design Study Guide *and the* Dictionary of Networking!

✔ Access the entire *MCSE: Windows 2000 Directory Services Design Study Guide*, complete with figures and tables, in electronic format.

✔ Search the *MCSE: Windows 2000 Directory Services Design Study Guide* chapters to find information on any topic in seconds.

✔ Look up any networking term in the *Dictionary of Networking*.

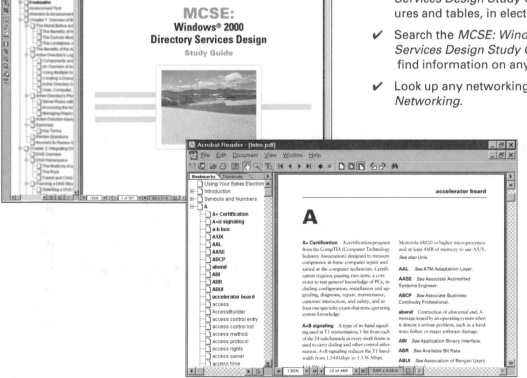

SYBEX®

MCSE: Windows 2000 Directory Services Design Study Guide

Exam 70-219

SYBEX

OBJECTIVE	PAGE

NOTE Exam objectives are subject to change at any time without prior notice and at Microsoft's sole discretion. Please visit Microsoft's Training & Certification Web site (www.microsoft.com/trainingandservices) for the most current listing of exam objectives.

SYBEX

MCSE:
Windows 2000
Directory Services Design
Study Guide

MCSE:
Windows® 2000
Directory Services Design
Study Guide

Robert King

Gary Govanus

San Francisco • Paris • Düsseldorf • Soest • London

SYBEX

Associate Publisher: Neil Edde
Contracts and Licensing Manager: Kristine O'Callaghan
Developmental Editor: Dann McDorman
Editor: Judy Flynn
Production Editor: Elizabeth Campbell
Technical Editors: Joshua Konkle, Steve Wisniewski
Book Designer: Bill Gibson
Graphic Illustrator: Tony Jonick
Electronic Publishing Specialist: Bill Gibson
Page Layout: Jeff Gammon
Proofreaders: Amey Garber, Laurie O'Connell, Nancy Riddiough, Jennifer Greiman, Andrea Fox
Indexer: Matthew Spence
CD Coordinator: Kara Eve Schwartz
CD Technician: Keith McNeil
Cover Design: Archer Design
Cover Photograph: Natural Selection

SYBEX

To Our Valued Readers:

In recent years, Microsoft's MCSE program has established itself as the premier computer and networking industry certification. Nearly a quarter of a million IT professionals have attained MCSE status in the NT 4 track. Sybex is proud to have helped thousands of MCSE candidates prepare for their exams over these years, and we are excited about the opportunity to continue to provide people with the skills they'll need to succeed in the highly competitive IT industry.

For the Windows 2000 MCSE track, Microsoft has made it their mission to demand more of exam candidates. Exam developers have gone to great lengths to raise the bar in order to prevent a paper-certification syndrome, one in which individuals obtain a certification without a thorough understanding of the technology. Sybex welcomes this new philosophy as we have always advocated a comprehensive instructional approach to certification courseware. It has always been Sybex's mission to teach exam candidates how new technologies work in the real world, not to simply feed them answers to test questions. Sybex was founded on the premise of providing technical skills to IT professionals, and we have continued to build on that foundation, making significant improvements to our study guides based on feedback from readers, suggestions from instructors, and comments from industry leaders.

The depth and breadth of technical knowledge required to obtain Microsoft's new Windows 2000 MCSE is staggering. Sybex has assembled some of the most technically skilled instructors in the industry to write our study guides, and we're confident that our Windows 2000 MCSE study guides will meet and exceed the demanding standards both of Microsoft and you, the exam candidate.

Good luck in pursuit of your MCSE!

Neil Edde
Associate Publisher—Certification
Sybex, Inc.

SYBEX Inc. 1151 Marina Village Parkway, Alameda, CA 94501
Tel: 510/523-8233   Fax: 510/523-2373   HTTP://www.sybex.com

Software License Agreement: Terms and Conditions

As always, to Suze.
   Bob King

To Bobbi, my very best friend in the whole world.
   Gary Govanus

Acknowledgments

It's funny how life throws you curveballs from time to time. When I accepted this project, I was living just north of Tampa, was self-employed, and planned to use the traditional slow period at the beginning of the year to write. By the time we started working, I was moving to Grand Rapids, had a new job, and ended up using all of my free time trying to keep up! Special thanks go to my little girls, Katie and Carrie, with whom I missed a lot of bedtime stories and Disney videos! And special thanks go to my wife, Susan, who (because of the business I'm in) has experienced single parenting for the last few months (I'll take some time off now—I promise!), and to the management of The Ziemba Group, who have cut a new employee some slack so he could finish a prior commitment.

I'd also like to thank my partner Gary Govanus (this is starting to feel like one of those Oscar acceptance speeches that gets cut off in the middle). Gary is a true friend, a true professional, and someone whom I respect deeply. He also recommended me to Sybex in the first place—thanks Gary.

Thanks also go to the guys at Ingram Micro, who donated a couple of killer Everest computers to my home lab so I could test my theories before I committed them to print! Ingram Micro doesn't sell to the public, but if you're a reseller, I give them two thumbs up for service! (You can visit them at www.ingrammicro.com.)

—Bob King

I think Bob will agree that whenever we take on these projects, they sure sound good. It should be really easy to knock these books out. It usually takes about two weeks before the enormity of the task hits and we start looking at the page count and thinking we may never finish. And then, someone is asking us for our dedications and acknowledgments. My how time does fly.

Because Bob and I live so far apart (I live in Minnesota, and at last check, he lived in Michigan), I can't tell you what he is like during the book-writing process. I do know that I am not the most fun person in the world to live with. I am never the most fun person in the world to live with, but while writing a book, I can be an absolute bear. So, I really have to thank all those people closest to me.

Thanks to my wife Bobbi; the best daughters a guy can have, Dawn and Denise; my three grandchildren, Brandice, CJ, and Courtney; and finally, to my dear and loving parents, Dolly and Jack Govanus. Thanks all for sticking by me.

—Gary Govanus

We'd both like to thank everyone at Sybex who helped us put this book together: developmental and acquisitions editors Dann McDorman and Neil Edde. Thanks to technical editors Joshua Konkle and Steve Wisniewski, production editor Elizabeth Campbell, electronic publishing specialist Bill Gibson, editor Judy Flynn, and graphic artist Tony Jonick. Without your hard work and dedication, this project could never have happened. Thanks also go to Dan Newland for contributing to the case study questions.

Contents at a Glance

Contents

Introduction

Microsoft's new Microsoft Certified Systems Engineer (MCSE) track for Windows 2000 is the premier certification for computer industry professionals. Covering the core technologies around which Microsoft's future will be built, the new MCSE certification is a powerful credential for career advancement.

This book has been developed, in cooperation with Microsoft Corporation, to give you the critical skills and knowledge you need to prepare for one of the core requirements of the new MCSE certification program for Windows 2000 Server. You will find the information you need to acquire a solid understanding of designing an Active Directory structure; to prepare for Exam 70-219: Designing a Microsoft Windows 2000 Directory Services Infrastructure; and to progress toward MCSE certification.

Why Become Certified in Windows 2000?

As the computer network industry grows in both size and complexity, the need for *proven* ability is increasing. Companies rely on certifications to verify the skills of prospective employees and contractors.

Whether you are just getting started or are ready to move ahead in the computer industry, the knowledge, skills, and credentials you have are your most valuable assets. Microsoft has developed its Microsoft Certified Professional (MCP) program to give you credentials that verify your ability to work with Microsoft products effectively and professionally. The MCP credential for professionals who work with Microsoft Windows 2000 networks is the new MCSE certification.

Over the next few years, companies around the world will deploy millions of copies of Windows 2000 as the central operating system for their mission-critical networks. This will generate an enormous need for qualified consultants and personnel to design, deploy, and support Windows 2000 networks.

Windows 2000 is a huge product that requires professional skills of its administrators. Consider that Windows NT 4 has about 12 million lines of code, while Windows 2000 has more than 35 million! Much of this code is needed to deal with the wide range of functionality that Windows 2000 offers.

Windows 2000 actually consists of several different versions:

Windows 2000 Professional   The client edition of Windows 2000, which is comparable to Windows NT 4 Workstation 4, but also includes the best features of Windows 98 and many new features.

Windows 2000 Server/Windows 2000 Advanced Server A server edition of Windows 2000 for small to mid-sized deployments. Advanced Server supports more memory and processors than Server does.

Windows 2000 Datacenter Server A server edition of Windows 2000 for large, wide-scale deployments and computer clusters. Datacenter Server supports the most memory and processors of the three versions.

With such an expansive operating system, companies need to be certain that you are the right person for the job being offered. The MCSE is designed to help prove that you are.

As part of its promotion of Windows 2000, Microsoft has announced that MCSEs who have passed the Windows NT 4 core exams must upgrade their certifications to the new Windows 2000 track by December 31, 2001, to remain certified. The MCSE Study Guide series, published by Sybex, covers the full range of exams required for either obtaining or upgrading your certification. For more information, see "Exam Requirements" later in this introduction.

Is This Book for You?

If you want to acquire a solid foundation in Active Directory design issues, this book is for you. You'll find clear explanations of the fundamental concepts you need to grasp.

If you want to become certified as an MCSE, this book is definitely for you. However, if you just want to attempt to pass the exam without really understanding Windows 2000, this book is *not* for you. This book is written for those who want to acquire hands-on skills and in-depth knowledge of Windows 2000.

If your goal is to prepare for the exam by learning how to use and manage the new operating system, this book is for you. It will help you to achieve the high level of professional competency you need to succeed in this field.

What Does This Book Cover?

This book contains detailed explanations, hands-on exercises, and review questions to test your knowledge.

Think of this book as your complete guide to designing an Active Directory structure. It begins with a review of directory services, covering the key concepts that are considered prerequisite knowledge for the Active Directory Design exam. Next, you will learn how to analyze various aspects of a given environment with an emphasis on issues pertinent to designing an Active Directory structure, including the following:

- The physical infrastructure
- The business environment
- The current IT environment

You will also learn the key issues involved in designing an overall Windows 2000– and Active Directory–based environment:

- Naming strategies
- Planning a domain and OU structure
- Planning for desktop management
- Planning for Active Directory connectors
- Creating an Active Directory customization strategy

Last, you will be presented with a guide to creating an implementation strategy to roll out your AD design in your environment.

Throughout the book, you will find design scenarios that will help to solidify the concepts discussed in each chapter. At the end of each chapter, you'll find a summary of the topics covered in the chapter, which also includes a list of the key terms used in that chapter. The key terms represent not only the terminology that you should recognize, but also the underlying concepts that you should understand to pass the exam. All of the key terms are defined in the glossary at the back of the study guide.

Finally, each chapter concludes with 10 review questions and one case study that test your knowledge of the information covered. You'll find an entire practice exam, with 35 additional questions and two more case studies, in Appendix A. Many more questions, as well as additional case studies, are included on the CD that accompanies this book, as explained in "What's on the CD?" at the end of this introduction.

The topics covered in this book map directly to Microsoft's official exam objectives. Each exam objective is covered completely.

How Do You Become an MCSE?

Attaining MCSE certification has always been a challenge. However, in the past, individuals could acquire detailed exam information—even most of the exam questions—from online "brain dumps" and third-party "cram" books or software products. For the new MCSE exams, this simply will not be the case.

To avoid the "paper-MCSE syndrome" (a devaluation of the MCSE certification because unqualified individuals manage to pass the exams), Microsoft has taken strong steps to protect the security and integrity of the new MCSE track. Prospective MSCEs will need to complete a course of study that provides not only detailed knowledge of a wide range of topics, but also true skills derived from working with Windows 2000 and related software products.

In the new MCSE program, Microsoft is heavily emphasizing hands-on skills. Microsoft has stated that, "Nearly half of the core required exams' content demands that the candidate have troubleshooting skills acquired through hands-on experience and working knowledge."

Fortunately, if you are willing to dedicate time and effort with Windows 2000, you can prepare for the exams by using the proper tools. If you work through this book and the other books in this series, you should successfully meet the exam requirements.

This book is a part of a complete series of MCSE Study Guides, published by Sybex, that covers the five core Windows 2000 requirements as well as the new Design electives you need to complete your MCSE track. Titles include the following:

- *MCSE: Windows 2000 Professional Study Guide*

- *MCSE: Windows 2000 Server Study Guide*

- *MCSE: Windows 2000 Network Infrastructure Administration Study Guide*

- *MCSE: Windows 2000 Directory Services Administration Study Guide*

- *MCSE: Windows 2000 Network Security Design Study Guide*

- *MCSE: Windows 2000 Network Infrastructure Design Study Guide*

- *MCSE: Windows 2000 Directory Services Design Study Guide*

There are also study guides available from Sybex on additional MCSE electives.

Exam Requirements

Successful candidates must pass a minimum set of exams that measure technical proficiency and expertise:

- Candidates for MCSE certification must pass seven exams, including four core operating system exams, one Design exam, and two electives.

- Candidates who have already passed three Windows NT 4 exams (70-067, 70-068, and 70-073) may opt to take an "accelerated" exam plus one core design exam and two electives.

If you do not pass the accelerated exam after one attempt, you must pass the five core requirements and two electives.

The following tables show the exams a new certification candidate must pass. *All* of these exams are required:

All of these exams are required

Exam #	Topic	Requirement Met
70-216	Implementing and Administering a Microsoft® Windows® 2000 Network Infrastrucuture	Core (Operating System)
70-210	Installing, Configuring, and Administering Microsoft® Windows® 2000 Professional	Core (Operating System)
70-215	Installing, Configuring, and Administering Microsoft® Windows® 2000 Server	Core (Operating System)
70-217	Implementing and Administering a Microsoft® Windows® 2000 Directory Services Infrastructure	Core (Operating System)

One of these exams is required

Exam #	Topic	Requirement Met
70-219	Designing a Microsoft® Windows® 2000 Directory Services Infrastructure	Core (Design)
70-220	Designing Security for a Microsoft® Windows® 2000 Network	Core (Design)
70-221	Designing a Microsoft® Windows® 2000 Network Infrastructure	Core (Design)

Two of these exams are required

Exam #	Topic	Requirement Met
70-219	Designing a Microsoft® Windows® 2000 Directory Services Infrastructure	Elective
70-220	Designing Security for a Microsoft® Windows® 2000 Network	Elective
70-221	Designing a Microsoft® Windows® 2000 Network Infrastructure	Elective
Any current MCSE elective	Exams cover topics such as Exchange Server, SQL Server, Systems Management Server, Internet Explorer Administrators Kit, and Proxy Server (new exams are added regularly)	Elective

For a more detailed description of the Microsoft certification programs, including a list of current MCSE electives, check Microsoft's Training and Certification Web site at www.microsoft.com/trainingandservices.

The Designing a Microsoft Windows 2000 Directory Services Infrastructure Exam

The Designing a Microsoft Windows 2000 Directory Services Infrastructure exam covers concepts and skills required for the design of an Active Directory structure. It emphasizes the following areas of Active Directory design:

- Analysis of the business environment
- Analysis of the physical environment
- Planning for the use of Active Directory and Windows 2000 features
- Creating an optimized Active Directory environment

This exam differs from the core MCSE examinations in that there are no objectives that represent physical tasks. The test objectives involve your ability to analyze a given situation and suggest a solution that meets the business needs of that environment. System analysis is not a skill that can be quantified into a series of facts or procedures to be memorized. Because of the emphasis on providing business solutions, much of this book (and most of the exam objectives) revolve around your ability to create an Active Directory structure that is stable, optimized, *and* designed in such a way that if fulfills true business needs (as opposed to being technology for technology's sake).

Microsoft provides exam objectives to give you a very general overview of possible areas of coverage of the Microsoft exams. For your convenience, we have added in-text objectives listings at the points in the text where specific Microsoft exam objectives are covered. However, exam objectives are subject to change at any time without prior notice and at Microsoft's sole discretion. Please visit Microsoft's Training and Certification Web site (www.microsoft.com/trainingandservices) for the most current exam objectives listing.

Types of Exam Questions

In the previous tracks, the formats of the MCSE exams were fairly straight-forward, consisting almost entirely of multiple-choice questions appearing in a few different sets. Prior to taking an exam, you knew how many questions you would see and what type of questions would appear. If you had purchased the right third-party exam preparation products, you could even be quite familiar with the pool of questions you might be asked. As mentioned earlier, all of this is changing.

In an effort to both refine the testing process and protect the quality of its certifications, Microsoft has introduced adaptive testing, as well as some new exam elements. You will not know in advance which type of format you will see on your exam. These innovations make the exams more challenging, and they make it much more difficult for someone to pass an exam after simply "cramming" for it.

Microsoft will be accomplishing its goal of protecting the exams by regularly adding and removing exam questions, limiting the number of questions that any individual sees in a beta exam, limiting the number of questions delivered to an individual by using adaptive testing, and adding new exam elements.

Exam questions may be in multiple-choice or case study–based formats. You may also find yourself taking an adaptive format exam. Let's take a look at the exam question types and adaptive testing so you can be prepared for all of the possibilities.

Multiple-Choice Questions

Multiple-choice questions include two main types of questions. One is a straightforward type that presents a question followed by several possible answers, of which one or more is correct.

The other type of multiple-choice question is more complex. This type presents a set of desired results along with a proposed solution. You must then decide which results would be achieved by the proposed solution.

You will see many multiple-choice questions in this study guide and on the accompanying CD, as well as on your exam.

Case Study–Based Questions

Case study–based questions first appeared in the Microsoft Certified Solution Developer program (Microsoft's certification program for software programmers). Case study–based questions present a scenario with a range of requirements. Based on the information provided, you need to answer a series of multiple-choice and ranking questions. The interface for case study–based questions has a number of tabs, each of which contains information about the scenario. At present, this type of question appears only in the Design exams.

Adaptive Exam Format

Microsoft presents many of its exams in an *adaptive* format. This format is radically different from the conventional format previously used for Microsoft certification exams. Conventional tests are static, containing a fixed number of questions. Adaptive tests change, or "adapt," depending on your answers to the questions presented.

The number of questions presented in your adaptive test will depend on how long it takes the exam to ascertain your level of ability (according to the statistical measurements on which the exam questions are ranked). To determine a test-taker's level of ability, the exam presents questions in increasing or decreasing order of difficulty.

WARNING   Unlike the previous test format, the adaptive format will *not* allow you to go back to see a question again. The exam only goes forward. Once you enter your answer, that's it—you cannot change it. Be very careful before entering your answer. There is no time limit for each individual question (only for the exam as a whole). Your exam may be shortened by correct answers (and lengthened by incorrect answers), so there is no advantage to rushing through questions.

How Adaptive Exams Determine Ability Levels

As an example of how adaptive testing works, suppose that you know three people who are taking the exam: Herman, Sally, and Rashad. Herman doesn't know much about the subject, Sally is moderately informed, and Rashad is an expert.

Herman answers his first question incorrectly, so the exam presents him with a second, easier question. He misses that, so the exam gives him a few more easy questions, all of which he misses. Shortly thereafter, the exam ends, and he receives his failure report.

Sally answers her first question correctly, so the exam gives her a more difficult question, which she answers correctly. She then receives an even more difficult question, which she answers incorrectly. Next, the exam gives her a somewhat easier question, as it tries to gauge her level of understanding. After numerous questions of varying levels of difficulty, Sally's exam ends, perhaps with a passing score, perhaps not. Her exam included far more questions than were in Herman's exam, because her level of understanding needed to be more carefully tested to determine whether or not it was at a passing level.

When Rashad takes his exam, he answers his first question correctly, so he is given a more difficult question, which he also answers correctly. Next, the exam presents an even more difficult question, which he also answers correctly. He then is given a few more very difficult questions, all of which he answers correctly. Shortly thereafter, his exam ends. He passes. His exam was short, about as long as Herman's test.

Benefits of Adaptive Testing

Microsoft has begun moving to adaptive testing for several reasons:

- It saves time by focusing only on the questions needed to determine a test-taker's abilities. An exam that might take an hour and a half in the conventional format could be completed in less than half that time when presented in adaptive format. The number of questions in an adaptive exam may be far fewer than the number required by a conventional exam.

- It protects the integrity of the exams. By exposing a fewer number of questions at any one time, it makes it more difficult for individuals to collect the questions in the exam pools with the intent of facilitating exam "cramming."

- It saves Microsoft and/or the test-delivery company money by reducing the amount of time it takes to deliver a test.

We recommend that you try the Edge Test Adaptive Exam, which is included on the CD that accompanies this study guide.

Exam Question Development

Microsoft follows an exam-development process consisting of eight mandatory phases. The process takes an average of seven months and involves more than 150 specific steps. The MCP exam development consists of the following phases:

Phase 1: Job Analysis   Phase 1 is an analysis of all of the tasks that make up a specific job function, based on tasks performed by people who are currently performing that job function. This phase also identifies the knowledge, skills, and abilities that relate specifically to the performance area to be certified.

Phase 2: Objective Domain Definition   The results of the job analysis provide the framework used to develop objectives. The development of objectives involves translating the job-function tasks into a comprehensive set of more specific and measurable knowledge, skills, and abilities. The resulting list of objectives—the *objective domain*—is the basis for the development of both the certification exams and the training materials.

Phase 3: Blueprint Survey   The final objective domain is transformed into a blueprint survey in which contributors are asked to rate each objective. These contributors may be past MCP candidates, appropriately skilled exam development volunteers, or Microsoft employees. Based on the contributors' input, the objectives are prioritized and weighted. The actual exam items are written according to the prioritized objectives. Contributors are queried about how they spend their time on the job. If a contributor doesn't spend an adequate amount of time actually performing the specified job function, their data is eliminated from the analysis. The blueprint survey phase helps determine which objectives to measure, as well as the appropriate number and types of items to include on the exam.

Phase 4: Item Development   A pool of items is developed to measure the blueprinted objective domain. The number and types of items to be written are based on the results of the blueprint survey.

Phase 5: Alpha Review and Item Revision   During this phase, a panel of technical and job-function experts reviews each item for technical accuracy, then answers each item, reaching a consensus on all technical issues. Once the items have been verified as technically accurate, they are edited to ensure that they are expressed in the clearest language possible.

Phase 6: Beta Exam   The reviewed and edited items are collected into beta exams. Based on the responses of all beta participants, Microsoft performs a statistical analysis to verify the validity of the exam items and to determine which items will be used in the certification exam. Once the analysis has been completed, the items are distributed into multiple parallel forms, or *versions*, of the final certification exam.

Phase 7: Item Selection and Cut-Score Setting   The results of the beta exams are analyzed to determine which items should be included in the certification exam based on many factors, including item difficulty and relevance. During this phase, a panel of job-function experts determines the *cut score* (minimum passing score) for the exams. The cut score differs from exam to exam because it is based on an item-by-item determination of the percentage of candidates who answered the item correctly and who would be expected to answer the item correctly.

Phase 8: Live Exam   As the final phase, the exams are given to candidates. MCP exams are administered by Sylvan Prometric and Virtual University Enterprises (VUE).

Microsoft will regularly add and remove questions from the exams. This is called item *seeding*. It is part of the effort to make it more difficult for individuals to merely memorize exam questions passed along by previous test-takers.

Tips for Taking the Designing a Microsoft Windows 2000 Directory Services Infrastructure Exam

Here are some general tips for taking the exam successfully:

- Arrive early at the exam center so you can relax and review your study materials. During your final review, you can look over tables and lists of exam-related information.

- Read the questions carefully. Don't be tempted to jump to an early conclusion. Make sure you know *exactly* what the question is asking.

- Answer all questions. Remember that the adaptive format will *not* allow you to return to a question. Be very careful before entering your answer. Because your exam may be shortened by correct answers (and lengthened by incorrect answers), there is no advantage to rushing through questions.

- Use a process of elimination to get rid of the obviously incorrect answers first on questions that you're not sure about. This method will improve your odds of selecting the correct answer if you need to make an educated guess.

Exam Registration

You may take the exams at any of more than 1,000 Authorized Prometric Testing Centers (APTCs) and VUE Testing Centers around the world. For the location of a testing center near you, call Sylvan Prometric at 800-755-EXAM (755-3926), or call VUE at 888-837-8616. Outside the United States and Canada, contact your local Sylvan Prometric or VUE registration center.

You should determine the number of the exam you want to take and then register with the Sylvan Prometric or VUE registration center nearest to you. At this point, you will be asked for advance payment for the exam. The exams are $100 each. Exams must be taken within one year of payment. You can schedule exams up to six weeks in advance or as late as one working day prior to the date of the exam. You can cancel or reschedule your exam if you contact the center at least two working days prior to the exam. Same-day registration is available in some locations, subject to space availability. Where same-day registration is available, you must register a minimum of two hours before test time.

You may also register for your exams online at www.sylvanprometric.com or www.vue.com.

When you schedule the exam, you will be provided with instructions regarding appointment and cancellation procedures, ID requirements, and information about the testing center location. In addition, you will receive a registration and payment confirmation letter from Sylvan Prometric or VUE.

Microsoft requires certification candidates to accept the terms of a Non-Disclosure Agreement before taking certification exams.

What's on the CD?

With this new book in our best-selling MCSE study guide series, we are including quite an array of training resources. On the CD are numerous practice exams and flashcards to help you study for the exam. Also included are the entire contents of the study guide. These resources are described in the following sections.

The Sybex Ebook for *MCSE: Windows 2000 Directory Services Design Study Guide*

Many people like the convenience of being able to carry their whole study guide on a CD. They also like being able to search the text to find specific information quickly and easily. For these reasons, we have included the entire contents of this study guide on a CD in PDF format. We've also included Adobe Acrobat Reader, which provides the interface for the contents as well as the search capabilities.

The Sybex MCSE Edge Tests

The Edge Tests are a collection of multiple-choice questions that can help you prepare for your exam. There are three sets of questions:

- Bonus questions specially prepared for this edition of the study guide, including 34 questions that appear only on the CD

- An adaptive test simulator that will give the feel for how adaptive testing works

- All of the questions from the study guide presented in a test engine for your review

A sample screen from the Sybex MCSE Edge Tests is shown below.

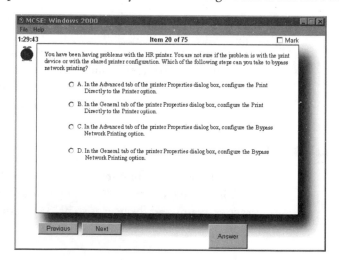

Sybex MCSE Flashcards for PCs and Palm Devices

The "flashcard" style of exam question offers an effective way to quickly and efficiently test your understanding of the fundamental concepts covered in the Designing a Microsoft Windows 2000 Directory Services Infrastructure exam. The Sybex MCSE Flashcards set consists of 150 questions presented in a special engine developed specifically for this study guide series. The Sybex MCSE Flashcards interface is shown below.

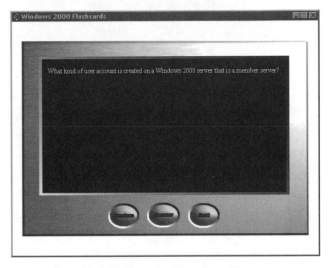

Because of the high demand for a product that will run on Palm devices, we have also developed, in conjunction with Land-J Technologies, a version of the flashcard questions that you can take with you on your Palm OS PDA (including the PalmPilot and Handspring's Visor).

How Do You Use This Book?

This book can provide a solid foundation for the serious effort of preparing for the Designing a Microsoft Windows 2000 Directory Services Infrastructure exam. To best benefit from this book, you may wish to use the following study method:

1. Study each chapter carefully. Do your best to fully understand the information.

2. Answer the review questions at the end of each chapter. If you would prefer to answer the questions in a timed and graded format, install the Edge Tests from the CD that accompanies this book and answer the chapter questions there instead of in the book.

3. Work through the cases studies, referring back to the information presented in the chapter to guide you. After you have decided on a course of action, read through the suggested answer. Reread the chapter to clarify any differences.

4. Note which questions you did not understand and study the corresponding sections of the book again.

5. Make sure you complete the entire book.

6. Before taking the exam, go through the training resources included on the CD that accompanies this book. Try the adaptive version that is included with the Sybex MCSE Edge Test. Review and sharpen your knowledge with the MCSE Flashcards.

To learn all of the material covered in this book, you will need to study regularly and with discipline. Try to set aside the same time every day to study and select a comfortable and quiet place in which to do it. If you work hard, you will be surprised at how quickly you learn this material. Good luck!

Contacts and Resources

To find out more about Microsoft Education and Certification materials and programs, to register with Sylvan Prometric or VUE, or to get other useful information, check the following resources.

Microsoft Certification Development Team
www.microsoft.com/trainingandservices

Contact the Microsoft Certification Development Team through their Web site to volunteer for one or more exam development phases or to report a problem with an exam. Address written correspondence to the following address:

> Certification Development Team
> Microsoft Education and Certification
> One Microsoft Way
> Redmond, WA 98052

Microsoft TechNet Technical Information Network
www.microsoft.com/technet/subscription/about.htm

(800) 344-2121

Use this Web site or number to contact support professionals and system administrators. Outside the United States and Canada, contact your local Microsoft subsidiary for information.

Microsoft Training and Certification Home Page
www.microsoft.com/trainingandservices

This Web site provides information about the MCP program and exams. You can also order the latest Microsoft Roadmap to Education and Certification.

Palm Pilot Training Product Development: Land-J
www.land-j.com

(407) 359-2217

Land-J Technologies is a consulting and programming business currently specializing in application development for the 3Com PalmPilot Personal Digital Assistant. Land-J developed the Palm version of the Edge Tests, which is included on the CD that accompanies this study guide.

Sylvan Prometric
www.sylvanprometric.com

(800) 755-EXAM

Contact Sylvan Prometric to register to take an MCP exam at any of more than 800 Sylvan Prometric Testing Centers around the world.

Virtual University Enterprises (VUE)
www.vue.com

(888) 837-8616

Contact the VUE registration center to register to take an MCP exam at one of the VUE Testing Centers.

Assessment Test

1. Which of the following are primary functions of the security infrastructure of Windows 2000?

   A. It stores security policies and account information.

   B. It implements and enforces security models for all objects.

   C. It authenticates access requests to AD objects.

   D. It stores trust information.

2. Which of the following business models is usually the most dynamic?

   A. Departmental

   B. Project based

   C. Product/service based

   D. Cost center

3. The AD schema defines _____ .

   A. The structure of the AD database

   B. Naming standards for user objects

   C. A structured limit (1,024) to the number of objects that can exist in any given container

   D. The connections available to foreign systems, such as Novell's NDS

4. You are beginning an AD planning project for a company in St. Paul, Minnesota. The company has offices throughout Wisconsin, Minnesota, Illinois, and western Michigan. Each office connects to the headquarters facility with a dedicated line appropriate to its needs. They occasionally have bandwidth issues on some of these lines in remote areas—often these lines are unavailable for hours at a time. To combat this, each remote site has a dial-up connection available to use during these periods. Which geographic models best describes this environment?

A. Simple

B. Regional

C. National

D. International

5. Which of the following can have GPOs associated with them?

A. Forest

B. Domain

C. Organizational unit

D. Site

6. OverAll, Inc. is a holding company for a group of firms involved in the manufacture and distribution of computer peripherals. Each of the firms is autonomous and responsible for its own financial well-being. During your investigation of the company, you discovered a database that tracks invoices between the various firms; for instance, the marketing firm bills the sales firm for any collateral produced. Which of the following business models would best describe OverAll, Inc.?

A. Departmental

B. Project based

C. Product/service based

D. Cost center

7. Which of the following describe the three main steps in network analysis? Organize your answer in the order that they are performed.

   A. Re-create

   B. Monitor

   C. Isolate

   D. Extrapolate

8. Which two of the following are true about partitions?

   A. A partition is a section of a distributed database such as AD.

   B. A partition is an attribute of a server object.

   C. Each domain represents a partition of the AD database.

   D. A partition is a segment of wire.

9. The time it takes for a system change (such as the upgrade to a new operating system) to pay for itself (for example, through lowered support costs) is know as the _____ .

   A. Time To Live (TTL)

   B. Return on investment (ROI)

   C. Pay Back Period

   D. Cost Investment Quotient

10. You are beginning an AD planning project for a company in St. Paul, Minnesota. The company has offices throughout Wisconsin, Minnesota, Illinois, and western Michigan. Each office connects to the headquarters facility with a dedicated line appropriate to its needs. (The company has a contract with a local provider of dedicated lines, which means that bandwidth is never an issue.) Use of the network is limited to printing, file access, and e-mail. Which of the geographic models best describes this environment?

    A. Simple

    B. Regional

    C. National

    D. International

11. Which of the following actions should be included in the definition of the change-management strategy for an IT department?

    A. A description of how NIC drivers will be kept up-to-date on workstations

    B. A description of how funding will be acquired to pay for the upgrade to Windows 2000

    C. A description of how software upgrades will be delivered to end users

    D. A description of how the Web site will be updated with new content

12. Golf Stuff, Inc., established in 1924, manufactures golf-related accessories. During your interviews with staff members, you discover that each business function is managed by a vice president, is overseen by a director, and is responsible for specific business needs. Which of the following business models would best describe Golf Stuff, Inc.?

    A. Departmental

    B. Project based

    C. Product/service based

    D. Cost center

13. Your analysis of the current change-management processes for a company should accomplish which two of the following?

    A. Provide you with a list of persons who are responsible for specific IT tasks.

    B. Provide a list of NIC drivers needed within a given environment.

    C. Give you an idea of the current state of the IT environment.

    D. List which users utilize each software package managed by the IT department.

14. Which of the following would be a good name for an HP printer located in Grand Rapids, in building A, on the second floor, and reserved for marketing personnel only? Choose all that apply.

A. Use the printer's serial number, such as AG506Z.

B. Combine the printer's date of purchase and serial number, such as 02/10/99_AG506Z.

C. Identify its physical location, such as GRA2.

D. Identify its users, such as GR_Marketing.

15. You are beginning an AD planning project for a company in St. Paul, Minnesota. The company has offices throughout Wisconsin, Minnesota, Illinois, western Michigan, and parts of Canada. Each office connects to the headquarters facility with a dedicated line appropriate to its needs. They occasionally have bandwidth issues on some of these lines in remote areas—often these lines are unavailable for hours at a time. To combat this, each remote site has a dial-up connection available to use during these periods. The Canadian offices are managed by a separate branch of the IT department, and all software is installed using the French versions. Which geographic models best describes this environment?

A. Simple

B. Regional

C. National

D. International

16. Frosty's Snow Shovels is a regional manufacturer of snow removal equipment located in St. Paul, Minnesota. It has four manufacturing sites, three distribution sites, and four retail outlets spread out over six states in the north central region of the United States. Its IT staff consists of 14 people: 1 in each of the 3 distribution sites (who also support the retail outlets) and 11 in the St. Paul facility. The support personnel in the distribution sites are responsible for hardware maintenance and end-user support for a specific region. All companywide data and resources are located in St. Paul. Into which management model would this environment fit?

    A. Centralized

    B. Decentralized

17. Which of the following are functions that can be performed by an LDAP connection?

    A. Compare

    B. Search

    C. Abandon

    D. Modify

18. The user account Ggovanus is located within the Education OU, which is within the Persistent-Image.com domain of an Active Directory structure. Which of the following is the distinguished name of this object?

    A. CN=Ggovanus.OU=Education.O=Persistent-Image

    B. CN=Ggovanus

    C. CN=Ggovanus, OU=Education, DC=Persistent-Image, DC=com

    D. Ggovanus@Persistent-Image.com

19. Which of the following IT positions usually requires the least amount of technical skill?

    A. AD expert

    B. Server specialist

    C. Application expert

    D. IT manager

20. The user account Ggovanus is located within the Education OU, which is within the Persistent-Image.com domain of an Active Directory structure. Which of the following is the user principal name of this object?

    A. CN=Ggovanus.OU=Education.O=Persistent-Image

    B. CN=Ggovanus

    C. CN=Ggovanus, OU=Education, DC=Persistent-Image, DC=com

    D. Ggovanus@Persistent-Image.com

21. The server responsible for generating a unique SID for each domain that joins the forest is known as the _____ .

    A. Domain naming master

    B. Relative ID master

    C. Schema master

    D. SID master

22. Which of the following is true about group policies?

    A. A policy created in the Computer Configuration node will be executed as a user logs on to the network.

    B. A policy created in the Computer Configuration node will be executed as the operating system boots.

    C. A policy created in the Computer Configuration node will be executed as the user accesses a network resource, such as a shared directory.

    D. A policy created in the Computer Configuration node will be executed when a remote user tries to access a local share point.

23. True/False: DNS is required in a Windows 2000 Active Directory environment.

    A. True

    B. False

24. The first domain created in an AD environment is known as the

    _____ .

    A. First domain

    B. Root domain

    C. Parent domain

    D. Top object

25. New Age Art is a medium-sized firm that specializes in inspirational office décor. During your interviews with the staff, you discovered that there are groups of "content experts" who specialize in, and are responsible for, specific types of art: motivational, therapeutic, and even aromatic influencers. These groups find artists, negotiate purchase prices, and bring the articles to market. Which of the following business models would best describe New Age Art?

    A. Departmental

    B. Project based

    C. Product/service based

    D. Cost center

26. Your company, XYZ (a well-known chain of motorcycle accessories outlets) is going to merge with ABC (a well-known manufacturer of motorcycle outlets). Each company has a well-established Internet presence, will maintain autonomy, and will share sales, inventory, and marketing data. Which of the following AD designs would best fit this situation?

A. Create a root domain named motorcycle and have a separate OU to hold the resources of each company.

B. Create a single tree with two top-level domains, one for each company.

C. Create a tree for each company and join them in a single forest.

D. Merge both companies into a single domain.

27. Which of the following roles are forestwide?

A. Schema master

B. Domain naming master

C. Infrastructure master

D. PDC emulator

28. Intrasite replication is _____ .

A. Active Directory replication between domain controllers defined within the same site

B. Active Directory replication between domain controllers defined in different sites

C. The traffic generated within a domain to keep the global catalog servers up-to-date

D. An Active Directory process that controls versions of content on an IIS server

29. The replication topology is designed in a ring format to increase fault tolerance. This means that it is possible for a domain controller to receive the same update from multiple sources. The process used to prevent this from happening is known as _____ .

   A. Poison Reverse

   B. Propagation dampening

   C. Cyclical Redundancy Control (CRC)

   D. Originating write control

30. If your goal were to control Bob's ability to change video settings on his desktop, which of the following would be appropriate?

   A. In the Computer Configuration node for Bob's desktop computer, create a group policy that limits the ability to change display settings.

   B. In the User Configuration node for Bob's computer, create a group policy that limits Bob's ability to change display settings.

   C. In the User Configuration node, create a group policy that limits Bob's ability to change display settings.

   D. In the Computer Configuration node, create a group policy that limits the ability to change display settings.

31. To install an application that has been published to them, a user needs to _____ .

   A. Do nothing; the application that was published to the user was automatically installed when they logged on to the network.

   B. Click the icon that automatically appears on their desktop to start the installation process.

   C. Use the Add/Remove Programs applet in Control Panel to install the application.

   D. Access the shared folder on the network that stores the application and run the `setup.exe` program.

32. Your client's environment consists of four NT domains named East, Central, West, and International and six Exchange sites named East, Central, West, Europe, Pacific Rim, and South America. Which of the four connector models would best describe this environment?

A. Model 1

B. Model 2

C. Model 3

D. Model 4

33. Which of the following is not a option when determining where object management should occur in an Exchange connector strategy?

A. Windows Active Directory only

B. Exchange Server 5.5 Administrator only

C. Both Windows 2000 and Exchange Server 5.5 administration tools

D. User Manager for Domains

34. Which of the following best describes the overall function of a connection agreement?

A. It defines which WAN links will be used for synchronization traffic.

B. It is the protocol used when one directory service logs in to another for the purpose of synchronization.

C. It holds the communication configuration between two directory environments.

D. It defines the three-way handshake used during authentication for the purpose of synchronization.

35. In most cases, which of the following objects should be moved to Windows 2000 first?

A. Users and groups

B. Computer accounts

C. Member servers

D. Domain controllers

36. What is contained within LDAP://rootDSE?

    A. The name of the root domain and a list of all of its domain controllers

    B. A list of all changes made to the default schema

    C. A series of subcontainers that hold the schema of the AD database

    D. A pointer to the LDAP Web site

37. Which of the following would suggest a pristine installation method of migration?

    A. The business needs indicate that a fast move to Windows 2000 is required.

    B. All servers are being replaced with newer hardware.

    C. A major restructuring of the company is expected soon.

    D. The company has a low risk tolerance.

38. You have decided to create a new object class, temp worker. During your implementation, you start with the basic user class and add a few new attributes. The end result is known as _____ .

    A. A subclass object

    B. An auxiliary class object

    C. A well-defined class object

    D. A child class object

39. In the Performance tool, which of the following would indicate that it is safe to remove WINS from your network?

    A. Windows Internet Name Service Server: Total number of registrations/sec = 0

    B. Windows internet Name Service Server: Total number of registrations/sec = 10

    C. Windows internet Name Service Server: Queries/sec = 0

    D. Windows internet Name Service Server: Queries/sec = 100

40. The server that is responsible for creating and maintaining connection objects is known as the _____ .

   A. Connection Master

   B. CommOp

   C. InterSite Topology Generator

   D. KCC Master

41. True or False: Intersite replication occurs between domain controllers within a domain.

   A. True

   B. False

42. You are attempting to add the Schema Manager snap-in to the MMC. On the Add/Remove Snap-in dialog box, you do not see it listed as an option. What is the most probable cause?

   A. You do not have permission to change the attributes of the MMC.

   B. You have not installed the Schema Manager.

   C. You must have the Windows 2000 CD-ROM in the drive for this snap-in to be installed.

   D. The schema has been locked at the root domain and must be unlocked first.

43. Which of the following tools can be used for inter-forest domain restructuring only?

   A. ATDM

   B. ClonePrincipal

   C. Netdom

   D. MoveTree

44. Which of the following are true of the Active Directory database?

  A. It is located only on the first AD server promoted to the status of domain controller in the AD tree.

  B. It is broken into partitions defined by domains, and the partitions are replicated to each domain controller within a given domain.

  C. It uses a single-master replication process to avoid conflicting changes to the database.

  D. It uses a multi-master replication model to allow changes to any replica of a partition.

45. The KCC maintains a replication topology that allows no more than _____ hops between any two domain controllers.

  A. 3

  B. 8

  C. 16

  D. 32

46. Which of the following would suggest a post upgrade method of restructuring?

  A. The business needs indicate that a fast move to Windows 2000 is required.

  B. All servers are being replaced with newer hardware.

  C. A major restructuring of the company is expected soon.

  D. The company has a high risk tolerance.

Answers to Assessment Test

1. **A, B, C, D.** The security infrastructure of Windows 2000 controls all internal security mechanisms of the Active Directory database. For more information, see Chapter 1.

2. **B.** In a project-based environment, resources are constantly being moved from one project to another. This results in frequent changes to the Active Directory database. For more information, see Chapter 3.

3. **A.** The schema defines the types of objects and their properties that are available in the AD database. For more information, see Chapter 1.

4. **C.** The addition of variable quality WAN links and dial-up connections moves this example from a regional to a national model. For more information, see Chapter 2.

5. **B, C, D.** Group policies are used to define user or computer settings for an entire group of users or computers at one time. The settings that you configure are stored in a Group Policy object (GPO), which is then associated with Active Directory objects such as sites, domains, or organizational units. See Chapter 8 for more information.

6. **D.** Because each of the child firms is an autonomous business, assuming its own fiscal responsibilities, the cost center model would be the best fit. For more information, see Chapter 3.

7. **C, A, D.** When performing a network analysis, it is important to understand the various types of traffic that will be generated by various network services. To perform this analysis, you first isolate the process so that traffic from other services will not influence your data; second, re-create the traffic by using the service; and third, extrapolate the traffic produced by users to that of whatever number of users will use the service in your environment. For more information, see Chapter 3.

8. A, C. Domains act as the boundaries of sections of the overall AD database. These sections are known as partitions. See Chapter 6 for more information.

9. B. Justifying the costs of a technical upgrade can be difficult. The ROI can be used to show upper management that a change is really an investment that will pay for itself over time. For more information, see Chapter 4.

10. B. In most respects, this company could be a simple model, except that it includes wide area links. For this reason, it is best described as a regional model. For more information, see Chapter 2.

11. A, B, D. Anything that involves the management of IT resources falls within the realm of the change-management strategy. For more information, see Chapter 4.

12. A. Most long-established firms will be managed along traditional departmental guidelines. The clue here is the strict chain of command (VPs and directors) and the function-specific areas of responsibility. For more information, see Chapter 3.

13. A, C. Your analysis of the current change-management processes should not include specific changes; it should revolve around getting an understanding of the current environment so that you can make constructive suggestions. For more information, see Chapter 4.

14. C, D. Answers A and B are not user friendly in any way. Remember that object names are used by end users to find resources. Either C or D identify the printer in a manner that would have meaning to the average end user. For more information, see Chapter 5.

15. D. Because this network crosses international boundaries, one would assume that this would qualify as an international model. Although the answer is correct, the reason is wrong. Given the limited boundaries of the network, this could be considered a regional or national network. What sets it apart (and moves it to the international model) is the fact that different languages are in use across the network and different laws and regulations might apply at various locations. For more information, see Chapter 2.

16. A. Even though there are support persons located outside of the corporate office, those individuals do not seem to be involved in the decision-making process of the IT department. For more information, see Chapter 4.

17. A, B, C, D. Depending upon the configuration of the directory, (1) the Compare function allows you to compare object attributes to match a given criteria, (2) the Search function allows you to query the database (or a portion of the database) for matches to a given set of values, (3) the Stop, or Abandon, function stops a given query, and (4) the Modify function allows you to modify the contents of the directory database. Also available are options to add new records to the database, delete objects from the database, and modify the RDN (relative distinguished name) of an object (rename objects). For more information, see Chapter 5.

18. C. The distinguished name of any object is the relative name of the object plus the names of the containers that make up the path to that object. For more information, see Chapter 5.

19. D. In many companies, the IT manager is more responsible for the budget and the use of resources than for technical know-how. For more information, see Chapter 4.

20. D. The user principal name is the object's relative name combined with the name of the domain tree in which it exists. For more information, see Chapter 5.

21. A . The domain naming master generates a SID that uniquely identifies each domain in the AD forest. This SID is added to the identifier of each object within a domain to ensure that all object SIDs are also unique. For more information, see Chapter 5.

22. B. For Computer Configuration options, the policy is applied as the operating system boots. This means that the configuration options set in the Computer Configuration area will affect *any* user who logs on at the specified computer. See Chapter 8 for more information.

23. True. DNS is required for locating Windows 2000 domain controllers. The Netlogon service uses the DNS database to register the domain controllers on your network. DNS is then used by clients when requesting a list of domain controllers during the logon process. See Chapter 5 for more information.

24. B. The first domain created becomes the root domain. The root domain acts as the top of the structure and determines the beginning of the AD namespace. See Chapter 6 for more information.

25. C. Because each group appears to be totally responsible for a different product line, it is safe to assume that the management philosophy is product based. For more information, see Chapter 3.

26. C. Because both companies have a well-established Web presence, you will probably want to retain their original registered DNS domain names. To accomplish this, you will need to create separate AD trees for each company. To ease the sharing of data, tie the two domains together in a forest. See Chapter 6 for more information.

27. A, B. There can be only one schema master and one domain naming master within an AD forest. See Chapter 6 for more information.

28. A. Intrasite replication occurs between domain controllers within a site. See Chapter 7 for more information.

29. B. Although a loop topology increases fault tolerance and can increase performance, it can also result in a domain controller receiving the same update from two different domain controllers. To prevent this, Active Directory uses a propagation dampening scheme. Propagation dampening is the process of preventing unnecessary replication of directory changes. See Chapter 7 for more information.

30. C. Answer C is the best answer in this case because it will limit Bob's ability to change display settings at any computer from which he logs on to the network. See Chapter 8 for more information.

31. C. Programs that are published appear in the application list of the Add/Remove Programs applet in Control Panel. See Chapter 8 for more information.

32. D. Model 4 is defined as multiple Windows 2000 domains and multiple Exchange Server sites. See Chapter 9 for more information.

33. D. AD objects cannot be managed through User Manager for Domains. See Chapter 9 for more information.

34. C. The connection agreement holds the communication configuration between two environments. See Chapter 9 for more information.

35. A. In most cases, you will want to move your users and groups into Active Directory as soon as possible to give administrators access to the improved management capabilities of Windows 2000. See Chapter 11 for more information.

36. C. At the top of any LDAP-compliant directory service (such as Microsoft Active Directory), there is a special container known as rootDSE. When referring to this container, the appropriate syntax is to refer to LDAP://rootDSE. The rootDSE container contains a number of entries, including the definition of the namespace of the LDAP structure and the schema of the database. The schema itself is stored in the subcontainer that follows this naming context: CN=schema, CN=configuration, DC=*domain_name*, DC=*domain_root*. See Chapter 10 for more information.

37. B, D. A pristine installation migration involves creating a new AD structure on nonproduction equipment and moving to it after everything has been tested. Because the company is replacing hardware, this would be the best choice. Changes are made to a nonproduction network, so this is also the safest migration method. See Chapter 11 for more information.

38. B. An auxiliary class acts as a shortcut—rather than starting from scratch to create a new class, you can start with an existing set of attributes and work from there. See Chapter 10 for more information.

39. A, C. You use Performance to determine if anything on your network is still using WINS for name resolution. If the WINS values are constantly at zero, it is safe to assume that WINS is not longer in use. See Chapter 11 for more information.

40. C. The KCC on one domain controller in each site is given the task of reviewing the intersite topology and creating connection objects for incoming traffic on all bridgehead servers within the site. To put that another way, the KCC on each bridgehead server does *not* create the connection objects for the local server—this task is off-loaded to another server within the site (which does not even have to be a bridgehead server itself). This server is known as the InterSite Topology Generator (ISTG). See Chapter 7 for more information.

41. True. This one catches a lot of students. Remember, replication is always traffic between domain controllers within the same domain. *Intersite* just means that the two servers are in different AD-defined sites. See Chapter 7 for more information.

42. B. If you do not see an entry for Active Directory Schema in the Add/Remove Snap-in dialog box, you need to install the Schema Manager. The Schema Manager is part of the Windows 2000 Administration Tools Package in Add/Remove Programs in the Control Panel. The option pack is located on the Windows 2000 Server Installation CD as `adminpak.msi`. See Chapter 10 for more information.

43. B, D. ATDM and Netdom are used to facilitate both intra- and inter-forest domain restructuring. ClonePrincipal and MoveTree can be used only for restructuring between forests. See Chapter 11 for more information.

44. B, D. The AD database is broken into partitions (defined as domains), and each partition is replicated to all domain controllers within a given domain. Using a multi-master replication model avoids having a single point of failure—all domain controllers can accept changes to the database and replicate those changes to their peer domain controllers. For more information, see Chapter 1.

45. A. The KCC will configure the replication ring so that there are no more than three hops between any two domain controllers within the domain. See Chapter 7 for more information.

46. A, D. Performing a post upgrade method of migration moves users, groups, and computers to Windows 2000 as quickly as possible. After the upgrade has taken place, the objects are moved around within the forest to match the proposed AD design. This method has the highest risk factor because all changes are made on the production network. See Chapter 11 for more information.

Chapter

1

An Overview of Active Directory Service in Windows 2000

Active Directory (AD) service is the flagship component of Windows 2000 Server and Advanced Server. Just about everything that happens on your Microsoft Windows 2000 network will rely upon AD being installed, configured, and managed properly. Everything from the logon process to application installations can be managed through the Active Directory database. This means that, if you intend to master the techniques involved in "good" AD design, you had better have a firm grasp on the basics of Windows 2000 and Active Directory. The folks at Microsoft were quite aware of this fact when they wrote the various exams for the Microsoft Certified Professional (MCP) program. Each test builds upon the last—it is expected that you have mastered the prerequisites for each exam before you move on to the next one in the series. Nowhere is this more apparent than in the three Design tests used to achieve Microsoft's highest certification—MCSE.

If you've taken other Microsoft examinations, the Design tests can come as quite a surprise. Gone are the "Where do you click?" and "How much memory do you need?" questions. These tests require that you have the knowledge necessary to use Microsoft products to solve real-world business needs. You'll need to be able to analyze a given business environment and come up with a business solution utilizing the strengths of Microsoft Windows 2000 and other Microsoft products. This change in testing philosophy mandates a few changes in the layout of any study guides designed to prepare you for the exams.

First, as authors, we have to rely upon you being prepared for the topics discussed. This means that you must master the prerequisites for the exam. We are not going to discuss the procedures involved in installing or administering Windows 2000 or its components—you should already have that knowledge. What we will discuss is how those components work together to provide business solutions.

Second, we must discuss the philosophy behind much of the technology so that you understand not only how to do something, but why and when as well. A good AD design relies upon your ability to integrate the directory with the numerous tools available in Windows 2000. When we discuss Windows 2000 components, we'll have to relate them back to Windows 2000 as a whole.

Last, we will have to discuss AD in relation to real-world business solutions. This exam requires you to analyze case studies and come up with the best solution for a given set of needs. This is probably the hardest part of the Design tests because many business problems have more than one "correct" answer. You'll need to know how all of the pieces work together and how Microsoft views their place in business networks.

In this first chapter, we introduce the basic concepts necessary to understand how AD works, why it works the way it does, and how it fits into the overall Windows 2000 networking realm. Most of this material should be a review for you; if it's not, you might want to prepare a bit more before tackling the AD Design exam.

 If you need more review than is presented in this chapter, we suggest that you read *MCSE: Windows 2000 Directory Services Administration Study Guide,* by Anil Desai (Sybex, 2000).

The Purpose of Directories

The computer industry, especially in the networking arena, generates more acronyms, terms, phrases, and buzzwords than any other business in the world. The phrase for the late '90s is "network directories." Directories are nothing new—they have been around in one form or another since the late '60s. Now, however, they are about to enter the mainstream with the release of Microsoft's long-awaited Active Directory service in Windows 2000 Server. To get the most from this technology, you must have a firm understanding of what directories are, what they are not, and how they can be used to ease the management of your network. That is the goal of this book—to give you the knowledge necessary to design an Active Directory structure that takes into account what we call the four principals of network design: cost, security, reliability, and performance.

Cost Business decisions are made with an eye on return for investment, even decisions regarding something as critical as the network itself. Each choice made reflects an expected result at a given cost. When implementing a directory, we have to ensure that the perceived value outweighs the actual costs.

Security The old maxim "Money is power" has changed to "Information is power." For many companies, the data stored on a network is their edge against the competition. This information *must* be secure or companies will not trust it to their networks.

Reliability *Uptime* is the keyword for business networks. It does not matter what information a company obtains—if that information is not available due to a network problem, it is of no value.

Performance A good network design, both in the physical layout of resources and in the configuration of software, can produce a system in which performance is optimized. A bad design, on the other hand, can greatly impact a user's ability to perform their job.

PC-based networks have become an integral part of the business world. They started out as simple solutions for sharing a few physical resources—hard disk space, printers, and so on. Over time, though, networks have become quite complex—often spanning multiple sites, connecting thousands of users to a multitude of resources. Today, networks control everything from payroll information to e-mail communication, from printers to fax services. As networks offer more services, they also demand more management. Easing the use and management of networks is the real goal of a directory service.

An Introduction to Directories

To understand and appreciate the power and convenience of a directory-based solution, you must have an understanding of the technologies that it will replace. Before the advent of directories, most network operating systems (NOSs) were server based. In other words, most account management was done on a server-by-server basis. With older NOS software, each server maintained a list of users who could access its resources (the *accounts database*) and a list of the users' permissions (the *access control list*, or ACL). If a system had two servers, each server had a separate accounts database, as shown in Figure 1.1.

FIGURE 1.1 A server-based NOS

As you can see, each server in Figure 1.1 maintains its own list of authorized users and manages its own resources. Although this system is simple and easy to understand, it becomes unwieldy once it grows beyond a certain point. Imagine trying to manage 1,000 users on 250 servers—the user and resource lists would soon overwhelm you! To get around this limitation, some NOS software, such as Microsoft NT 4, was configured so that small groups of servers could share one list of users (called a *central accounts database*) for security and authentication purposes, as shown in Figure 1.2. This central accounts database gave administrators a single point of management for a section of their network, known as a *domain*. Once again, however, this solution becomes cumbersome after the network reaches a certain size.

FIGURE 1.2 An NT 4 security accounts database

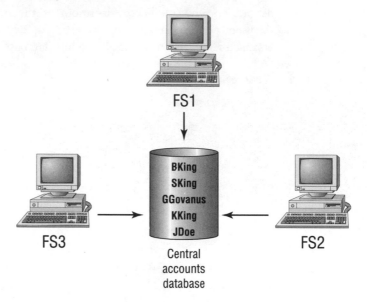

The shift from server-based to domain-based networks was the first step in creating an environment where all users and resources are managed through a single database. In a domain, all user information is stored in a single place and managed with a single set of tools, and users can access the network via a single account (no more having to remember multiple account names and passwords). Network directories take this approach to the next phase: a single database to hold *all* user and resource information across your entire network.

We're using the phrase "user and resource" to refer to the records within a directory database because that is how traditional administrators see their world: users accessing resources. In a directory-based environment, however, users become nothing more than another resource. This subtle shift in philosophy is critical in understanding the strengths of a directory-based network. This distinction should become clear as you become more familiar with directory concepts.

Network directories are just databases that hold network information. They can contain many different types of information:

- User account information (logon names, passwords, restrictions)

- User personal information (phone numbers, addresses, employee ID numbers)

- Peripheral configuration information (printers, modems, faxes)

- Application configuration (Desktop preferences, default directories)

- Security information

- Network infrastructure configuration (routers, proxies, Internet access settings)

Once this information is stored in a centrally controlled, standards-based database, it can be used in many different ways. Most commonly, administrators will use such information to control access to the network and to the network's resources. The directory will become the central control point for many different network processes. Here are examples of some of these processes:

- When a user attempts to log on to the network, the client software will request authentication from the directory. The directory service will ascertain whether the account name is valid, check for a password, validate the submitted password, and check any restrictions on the account to determine if the logon request should be granted.

- Once a user has logged on to the system, the directory will be queried each time that user tries to access a network resource. The directory will authenticate the request to determine if the user has the appropriate permissions to use the resource. The directory will also return the resource's physical address to the client.

- Individual users can use directories to store personal preferences. Each time a user logs on to the network, his Desktop settings, default printer, home directory location—even his application icons—can be downloaded to whatever computer he happens to be at. Users will no longer have to re-create their environment each time they use a new computer. All of their settings will be centrally located to ensure a "universal environment" and, if you desire, centrally controlled to lock them down.

Back to the Future

The simplest definition of a *directory* would be a database used to store and organize data. According to this definition, we all use directories on a daily basis. Perhaps the most common directory would be the plain old phone book. The first step in understanding Active Directory should be to discuss the directories that are already in use.

Paper-Based Directories

The telephone directory acts as a repository of information, storing the names, addresses, and telephone numbers of the residents of your town (or state or nation, depending on the book you are using). This information is presented in an easy-to-use format—in most cases, as a paper-based book that can be used by anyone with a basic level of literacy. The book's information is organized in an easily understood manner: an alphabetical listing. All in all, as a directory, the telephone directory fulfills its purpose admirably, as evidenced by how long it's been around and how little its design has changed.

The telephone directory has become a standard piece of our culture: Consider how many companies now offer such directories to the public. Many of these offerings are specialized—business-to-business listings, neighborhood directories, and even restaurant listings organized by type of food. Having such specific directories means that you don't have to search through page after page of information in order to find that great Mexican restaurant or a pizza parlor near your home.

An example of a common directory that is specific in scope would be the list of physicians—and their specialties, their locations, and sometimes even their office hours—in a particular health-care system. This is an example of a directory that is a little more "directed." The information targets a specific audience. If you do not participate in the appropriate health-care plan, the information would be of no use to you. If, however, you belong to the plan, the information is critical to the health of your family. Once again, this information is presented in a manner that is appropriate for its use: usually a paper-based solution where the physicians are listed alphabetically by specialty.

The biggest problem with both of these examples—the telephone directory and the physician directory—is that a paper-based solution is usually out-of-date before you receive it. Think about the number of times you have dialed the listing for a local pizza parlor only to find that it has gone out of business. Although the list of physicians might be correct and current, wouldn't it be nice to have a list of physicians who are currently accepting new patients? Better yet, wouldn't you prefer to have a list that is so up-to-the minute that you could check to see how far behind schedule the doctor is running today?

Computer-Based Directories

Paper-based directories illustrate the kinds of services a network directory can provide, but they fall short of explaining the true benefits of a real-time, software-based solution.

A better example of a directory would be a personal information manager (PIM), such as Microsoft Outlook. PIMs store, organize, and display information that is specific to an individual. You can use a tool like Outlook to hold your addresses and keep track of appointments; it can even warn you about important dates such as birthdays or anniversaries. PIMs are starting to take the place of paper-based address books because they store more information, they can display that information in more convenient ways, and they can be customized (and all without forcing you to write really small in the margin).

It is not unusual for someone to use a PIM to organize a day's activities, add a list of friends' birthdays to their to-do list, send a copy of a good joke to all their friends, and automatically fax a sales announcement to their clients. A good PIM not only stores information, it also makes information usable in real-world applications. With Outlook, for instance, you can use your contacts list (which contains names, addresses, telephone numbers, and other information about people) as the data list for a mail merge into a document created in a word processor.

PIMs are convenient, but they do have their drawbacks. To retrieve the information in your PIM, you must have access to both the software and a computer. Also, stand-alone PIMs, such as PalmPilots, are not convenient for sharing information because their information is not stored on a central server. If your schedule is stored on your laptop or sitting in your pocket, your colleagues can't access it to find out whether you can attend an important staff meeting.

These limitations are being overcome by moving PIMs from the status of stand-alone applications to groupware products. *Groupware* can be defined as an application that is specifically designed to allow users to share and/or collaborate on projects or data. Most of today's groupware packages started out as e-mail applications and have grown from there. This makes sense; e-mail is a basic way to share information, and most collaboration is just that—shared information.

Microsoft has entered the groupware market in a big way with Microsoft Exchange Server. As an e-mail package, Exchange is about par for the course, although some might argue that Microsoft's traditional graphical interface makes it easier to configure and manage than many others on the market, such as Lotus Notes and Novell's GroupWise. Exchange really shines, though, in its collaborative tools. In an Exchange system, the administrator (or any user with the appropriate permissions) can create *public folders* that hold data. That data can be in just about any form you desire—from traditional e-mail messages to form-based, threaded conversations to executables. All of this data can be made available to users of the system based upon an internal security system.

The Exchange system is managed through a series of containers and sub-containers, just like most network directories. Its access features include the following:

- It has an internal security system so that only specific individuals can access certain data.

- It can be accessed from various types of clients (from mail clients like Outlook, using Internet browser software, and even from LDAP-enabled applications).

Although all of these examples—the telephone directory, a listing of physicians, a personal information manager, and even Microsoft Exchange Server—indicate the kinds of services a network directory can provide, none exemplifies the true depth of the service that such a system can provide. A network directory encompasses all of these examples—and offers even more.

Network Directories

A *network directory* is a database that contains information used to access, manage, or configure a network. As thus defined, network directories have been in use for quite some time. Some examples of mature network directories would include the following:

- Domain Name System (DNS)

- Windows Internet Name Service (WINS)

- Novell Directory Services (NDS)

We'll wait until Chapter 5, "AD Naming Strategies," for an in-depth discussion of DNS. The other two examples, however, warrant some discussion. Understanding what they do, and how they do it, can give you some insight into how network directories can be used to provide services to your environment. Because Active Directory expands on the workings of WINS and NDS, a basic understanding of how they work will be extremely helpful in evaluating Windows 2000 design issues (and in passing the exam).

Windows Internet Name Service (WINS)

Windows Internet Name Service (WINS) is used to resolve NetBIOS names into IP addresses. *NetBIOS names* are the unique identifiers, or computer names, given to resources on an NT network. Because these names identify computers on the network, each computer must have a unique NetBIOS name assigned to it.

Registering a Name

NetBIOS is a *broadcast-based protocol*. As each client is initialized, NetBIOS sends out a broadcast announcing the name it intends to use. If another station is already using the intended name, that station will return a negative acknowledgment to the newcomer. Basically, this boils down to the first station yelling, "I intend to join the network as WS1—anyone mind?" If no response is returned, the station will assume that the name is unique on the network and will continue its initialization.

Using NetBIOS to register a name sounds like a simple but effective technique, but it is of limited use in a routed network. Most of today's routers are configured so that they do not pass broadcast packets. In effect, this means that the NetBIOS station is limited to confirming the uniqueness of its name to the local network. Conceivably, there could be another station with the same name on a different network.

The first function of a WINS server is *name registration*. In a WINS environment, clients are configured with the IP address of a WINS server. Instead of using the broadcast method to announce itself (and determine if its name is unique), each client sends a registration request directly to the WINS server. The WINS server builds a database of the names of those workstations that have registered themselves. When the server receives a new request, it compares the requested name to those that have been registered. If the name is unique, it sends back a positive response; if not, it sends back a negative response. Because all of the traffic is made up of directed packets, routers will pass the request to a WINS server on another network.

The WINS server builds the database dynamically, adding records as workstations register with the service. The net effect is that the database is updated without intervention from a network administrator, greatly reducing the administrative overhead for networking staff.

Figure 1.3 depicts the four steps in the name registration process:

1. The client sends a message to the WINS server requesting registration.

2. The WINS server checks its database to ensure that the name is unique.

3. The WINS server sends a positive response to the client and adds the client's name and IP address to the database.

4. The WINS server adds the NetBIOS name and IP address to its database.

FIGURE 1.3 WINS name registration

Name Resolution

Once a station has determined that its name is unique, it can begin to communicate on the network. In a traditional NetBIOS-based network, *broadcast packets* are used to resolve names to IP addresses. Basically, a workstation yells on the wire, "Hey! I'm looking for a station named WS2—are you out there?" If WS2 is on the wire, it will respond with a packet that contains its IP address. Once again, though, because this process is broadcast based, most routers will not forward the packets to other networks. In effect, this limits communication to the workstations within a single network segment.

The WINS server also provides a name-resolution service. Instead of using the broadcast method, clients send their request to the WINS server. The WINS server checks the requested name against its database of registered names. If the name is available, the WINS server will return the IP address to the requesting workstation. Once again, because this communication is performed using directed packets rather than broadcast packets, routers do not interfere with the process. Figure 1.4 shows how the name resolution process occurs in a WINS environment:

1. The client queries the WINS server for the IP address assigned to a NetBIOS name.

2. The WINS server checks the database for a matching record.

3. The WINS server returns the requested information or an error indicating that the requested resource is unavailable.

FIGURE 1.4   WINS name resolution

Lastly, WINS clients send a notification to the WINS server when they are about to go offline. This notification tells the WINS server to remove the record corresponding to the client from its database. (If a client shuts down without sending this notification, WINS has a mechanism that will delete the record automatically if it hasn't heard from the client in a specified period of time.) From an administrative perspective, this means that the WINS database is both built *and* maintained dynamically—without intervention from the network administrators.

WINS across a WAN

WINS includes one last mechanism that warrants discussion here. Imagine a WINS network that includes wide area network (WAN) links, as shown in Figure 1.5. Because WINS uses directed rather than broadcast-based communication, the router can pass the requests across the WAN from City 2 to the WINS server in City 1.

FIGURE 1.5   WINS across a WAN link

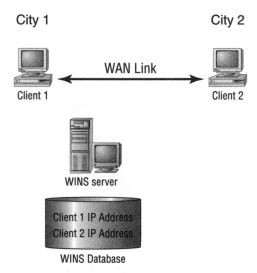

Although this configuration is possible, it might not be appropriate to send all of the WINS registration and resolution traffic across the WAN link. Bandwidth is usually limited (and expensive) across this kind of line. WINS gives you the ability to set up a partnership between WINS servers, overcoming this limitation. With a configuration like the one in Figure 1.6, there is a lot less traffic across the WAN link.

FIGURE 1.6 WINS partnership

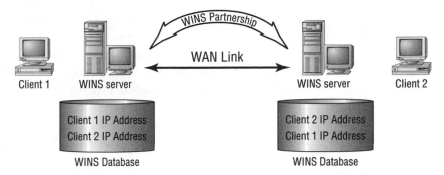

When two WINS servers are configured as partners, they exchange their databases on a regular basis. They can be configured to exchange information based on the number of changes to the database or on a timed basis. In either case, there will be less traffic across the link, and the administrator has more control over when that traffic is generated.

WINS in Short

WINS was Microsoft's first attempt at implementing an enterprise-capable directory service. Considering this fact, WINS is surprisingly stable and efficient. Unfortunately, WINS alone cannot provide the level of service demanded of a true network directory (although much of the WINS technology can be found in AD).

Novell Directory Service (NDS)

With the release of NetWare version 4, Novell introduced what is arguably the most commercially successful network directory to date. *Novell Directory Services (NDS)* was intended to act as the central point of control for *all* network services in a NetWare environment. NDS is a fully functional, mature, and stable example of the kind of services that a network directory can provide. As such, it merits close examination here—if for no other reason than to serve as an example of a well-designed directory.

Although Microsoft would probably deny it, NDS is also worth discussing because a feature sheet of AD reads just like a feature sheet of NDS. In other words, Microsoft watched Novel struggle with the earlier releases of NDS and has learned from Novel's mistakes. If you're coming from a Novell background, this can be good or bad, depending on your attitude. NetWare 4 CNEs have a distinct advantage because the design principles are pretty much the same in both environments. On the flip side, though, you might have to relearn a few of the details to ensure that you don't give the Novell answer on a Microsoft test.

The NDS Structure

The NDS database is critical to the proper functioning of a NetWare network. NDS is queried each time a network resource is accessed. When a user attempts to log on to the network, for instance, the client software submits the user's name to NDS for authentication. Later, this user might try to access some resource, such as a printer, and NDS would again be queried: first to determine whether the user had the necessary permissions and then to find the physical location of the resource. NDS is accessed during all network functions.

The best way to understand NDS (or any network directory) is to think of it as a database. Many administrators are intimidated by the "network" functions of a directory and forget that a network directory is nothing more than a database. The NDS database contains records, or *objects*, that represent network resources. There are many different types of resources that can be managed through the NDS database; these are called *object classes*. The record type for each class of object has a different set of fields, or *properties*. You wouldn't, for example, need a logon name property for a printer object because printers do not log on to the network. Table 1.1 lists a few of the more common classes of objects that exist in an NDS database.

TABLE 1.1   NDS Object Classes

Class	Description of Object
User	Holds information specific to a user, such as logon name, password, account restrictions, telephone numbers, and addresses.

TABLE 1.1   NDS Object Classes *(continued)*

Class	Description of Object
Printer	Holds information about a network printer. This object class contains properties such as network address, name, and amount of printer memory.
Group	Represents a set of users with similar resource needs. All members inherit permissions assigned to the group.
Volume	Acts as a pointer to a discrete portion of storage space (hard disk, optical, CD-ROM, and so on). This object has properties that pertain to storage devices: network address, the server upon which it resides, and certain permission information.
Print Queue	Represents a directory used to store print jobs until the system is ready to release them to a printer.
Alias	Acts as a pointer to an object that exists elsewhere in the NDS structure.

There are many other classes of objects that can exist in the NDS database. NDS is also *extensible*: custom object classes can be created to store information specific to a particular environment. The definition of the object classes contained within a directory is known as its *schema*. The ability to extend the schema to include new or custom object classes is critical for any directory to remain viable in the future.

Global Distributed Replicated Database

NDS is marketed as a "global distributed replicated database" used for the management of network resources on a NetWare network. Most marketing phrases are more hype than substance, but this phrase actually does a fairly good job of describing how NDS works on a network. By breaking down the phrase into its components, we can understand the basic functionality of the directory.

"Global"

In earlier versions of NetWare, each server held its own "accounts database" known as the *bindery*. When a user accessed a given server, this bindery (a flat database) would be queried to determine if the username and password submitted were valid. From an administrative perspective, this meant that a user account had to be created at each server that the user might need to access. Users were often required to submit to the logon process multiple times as they accessed different resources on different servers.

One of the many functions of any network directory is to centralize control of network functions. In an NDS-based system, there are no bindery files. Instead, the NDS database is used for all authentication processes. Notice that this implies that there is only one database for the network—no matter how large or geographically dispersed the network. This is what is meant by the term "global database." When user Wu in Tokyo logs on to the network, he accesses the same database as user Bob in Chicago.

"Distributed"

Given that an object represents each network resource and each object is really only a record in a database, the NDS database in a global environment could grow into a large file. The next logical question is, "Where is NDS stored?"

Because NDS is critical to most network functions, it might be best to place it in a central location, as shown in Figure 1.7. Placing the database in the middle of your environment seems to put it in the "fairest" location. This placement actually mirrors other kinds of corporate access—it always seems that the offices farthest from the center are the last to know anything.

FIGURE 1.7 A centrally located NDS database

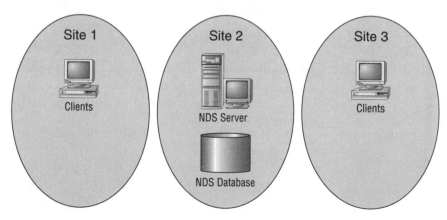

This arrangement might look good on paper, but what if Site 1 is in Tokyo, Site 2 is in Chicago, and Site 3 is in London? Do we really want users in Tokyo accessing a server in Chicago every time they need to utilize a network resource? Probably not! This configuration would not only be inconvenient for the user (imagine how long it would take to log in across the WAN link), it would also generate an unacceptable amount of traffic on what is probably an expensive link.

Because a centrally located database is not a good idea, another design would be to place the database on *all* servers in the network, as shown in Figure 1.8.

FIGURE 1.8   NDS on all servers in the network

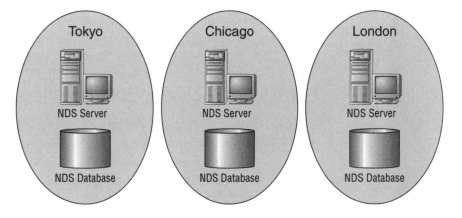

This configuration would ensure local access to NDS for authentication, but it is still not a viable solution. Imagine the traffic that would have to be generated to keep the multiple copies synchronized!

These two scenarios demonstrate the value of a distributed database. NDS can be divided into chunks—the technical term is actually *partitions*—that can be located on servers throughout the network, as shown in Figure 1.9. A good design would be to place the partition that contains records for Tokyo resources (including user accounts) on a server near those resources. This design has the added benefit of distributing the workload of maintaining the database across multiple servers so that no single server is overworked.

FIGURE 1.9   A distributed NDS database

"Replicated"

Although the design shown in Figure 1.9 does solve the problem of where NDS should be located, it does not provide any fault tolerance for the critical information stored in the database. Suppose Server 1 were to go offline. Because the server that contains her authentication information is not available, user Susan in Chicago would be unable to access *any network resources*.

To solve this "single point of failure" problem, each partition of the database can be copied, or replicated, to multiple servers, as shown in Figure 1.10. The *replication* process ensures that in the event that Server 1 becomes unavailable, the system can still authenticate user Susan because her account information is still available on Server 2.

FIGURE 1.10   Replication of partitions to multiple servers

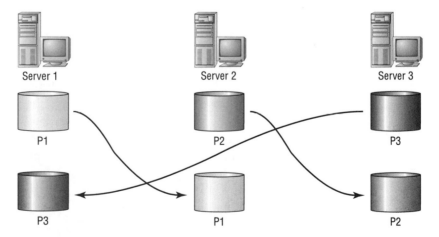

Scalability

Figure 1.10 shows another important feature of NDS. Notice that we now have complete fault tolerance of the database: each partition exists on more than one server. To provide this fault tolerance, though, no server has to hold more than two-thirds of the database. As a network grows, each server will have to hold less and less of the database—and therefore spend less and less time managing NDS—but we will still have complete fault tolerance. This is known as *scalability*. As the number of servers increases, the amount of overhead placed on each server decreases. In other words, NDS becomes more efficient as the network becomes larger.

NDS in Short

NDS is a mature, stable, and efficient network directory. It can be used as the measuring stick for all other directories. The only real weakness of NDS is its proprietary nature. When NDS was released, there were no other viable directories on the market, thus no industry standards were in place to guide Novell's development team. This resulted in a directory that is not as accessible to non-Novell environments as administrators might like. Given the track record of Windows NT and Microsoft, in the long run it is more likely that developers will be working on AD add-ons than NDS add-ons.

Active Directory as a Database

So far, we've discussed a directory as a database of information. We've also looked at how directories have been used to provide various types of functionality. Now let's take a closer look at Microsoft's implementation of Active Directory service. The name Active Directory refers to both the physical database itself *and* to the service that it provides to the network.

The AD Schema

Once again, a directory is a device used to store and organize information. Now that we've looked at a few different examples of directories, it is time to limit the scope of our discussion a bit. Active Directory is a specific type of directory—a network directory. A *network directory* can be defined as a central database used to manage network resources. Like any other database, it contains the equivalent of records—distinct units of information. Each record is divided into fields—specific pieces of data within a record. Records within the Active Directory database are known as *objects*. The fields associated with an object are known as *properties* or *attributes*.

The definition of how those records are formed and what properties are available is stored in the *schema*. The schema of the Active Directory database defines a very complex database. It's easier to understand the function of the schema if you first look at the form of a simpler database. For our example, we'll use the customer contact and billing database that we built for our consulting firm.

The King Technologies Customer Database

As a small company, King Technologies doesn't need a complex (and expensive) piece of software. All we wanted was a database that would track customer information and tie it into billable time—so that we could create invoices, quarterly reports, and all of the other stuff that comes with running a small business. Because we truly believe in the K.I.S.S. principle (Keep It Simple, Stupid), we decided to build it ourselves using Microsoft Access. When you are building any database, no matter how large (or in this case, small), there are certain tasks you must complete.

First, you must decide what information you wish to store. In our case, we wanted to store the following three types of data:

- Customer information. This will consist of customer name, customer address, and customer telephone number.

- Billable items. Here, we'll want a list of the types of work we do and the charges for each. For example, when we teach, we charge a daily rate, but when we consult, we charge an hourly rate.

- Invoice line items. This will consist of the various jobs we have done and the time we've put into them.

The next step is to analyze how the data needs to be related to produce the output you require. In our example, for instance, we'll want to relate the billable items to the invoice line items so that we can pick our rates from a drop-down list. We'll also want to relate the invoice line items to the customer information. This means we'll need a couple of new fields to use as the point of connection between the three separate database files. When we're done, our database structure should look something like the one shown in Figure 1.11.

FIGURE 1.11 The structure of the King Technologies database

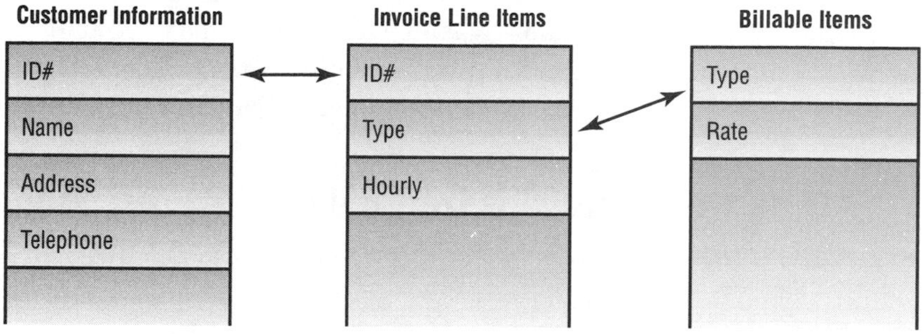

Notice how each database definition contains a list of the fields for each record and the records used to tie the three files together. This structure is known as the schema of the database. The schema is not the actual data that a database stores, but rather a definition of how that data is formatted within the database.

The schema of the Active Directory database is quite a bit more complex than that of our simple example. It performs the same basic function, though. The schema defines how the information stored within the Active Directory database will be formatted. The database engine used to manage the Active Directory is quite a bit more sophisticated than the one used for our simple example. Here are some of the differences:

- Active Directory is a hierarchical database. We'll discuss this concept in more detail in later chapters, but for now just be aware that the relationships between information are handled in a completely different manner. The information is organized in a different manner as well. Instead of multiple files, related by common fields, the Active Directory database is one logical structure that uses a series of containers and subcontainers and a set of rules for naming objects to organize the data that it contains.

- The Active Directory is one big logical file, and that file has to store information about dissimilar resources, so there are different types, or *classes*, of records defined in the same database. Notice that, in our example, the records in each database file are exactly the same. In the Active Directory database, there are multiple classes of objects defined within the single database.

- Because some of the information stored within the Active Directory database will be sensitive and some should be available to the general public, the Active Directory database must have a built-in security mechanism. We'll discuss both the different classes of objects and the security system in later chapters.

AD as the Central Database of Network Resources

The primary function of the Active Directory database is to hold information about network resources. *Network resources* can be defined as anything that attaches to, accesses, or serves your network. By this definition, users, printers, and even routers are just network resources whose configuration information can be stored in the AD database. Here's where the flexibility of the AD schema comes in handy—each of these object classes will have properties pertaining to its function. A user object, for instance, has properties that would represent information about a person—name, logon name, address, telephone number, or even assigned applications. A router object, on the other hand, would probably not need a logon name but would need properties for its various configuration parameters.

Moving information about *all* network resources to a single database provides numerous benefits to both network administrators and end users. Administrators can manage their environment through a single interface, thus reducing the learning curve and any of the redundant management that was common in earlier network operating systems. Critical to the concept of "one management database" is the extensible nature of the Active Directory database. The AD schema can be extended to include object classes and properties that are not in the default installation. This allows application developers or local administrators the option of designing new objects or modifying existing object classes to better fulfill their business needs. We'll discuss the modification of the AD schema in more detail in Chapter 12, "Customizing the AD Schema." For administrators, some of the benefits include the following:

- Administrators will have to create only one user account per user no matter how diverse their environment. With complete control over the AD schema, it should be fairly easy to include the objects and properties necessary to manage multiple environments through Active Directory. Imagine a world where you manage your mainframe connectivity, Novell NDS permissions, and Macintosh computers through a single set of tools.

- Hardware setup should be quite a bit easier. If your environment includes several identical printers, for instance, you will be able to configure the first and then copy that configuration to all of the others. It is conceivable that this capability will carry forth to *all* hardware. If you've ever had to reconfigure a router at 2:00 A.M., you'll appreciate the ability to copy the configuration of some other router on your network!

- Actually, reconfiguring hardware might not be necessary at all. The Active Directory is replicated to multiple servers. This configuration provides automatic fault tolerance to the database. If one server crashes, a complete copy of the portion of the AD database is probably on another server. (We'll discuss the replication and how to control it in more detail in later chapters.)

End users will also benefit from the power of AD in many ways:

- End users need only remember one username and one password to access resources across multiple environments. This is a big change over earlier networks, where users were expected to remember one name and one password to log in to the NT network, another name and password to access the mainframe, and yet another set for dial-in access.

- Because applications can be assigned by computer, user, or security group, users will be presented with the same software choices no matter where they are physically located. Applications controlled through Active Directory are also self-managing. If a user accidentally deletes a file necessary to run an application, the file will be automatically restored. Managing the user's environment through Active Directory is one of the more exciting new technologies available in Windows 2000. We'll discuss it in detail in Chapter 5, "Desktop Management in Active Directory."

- The Active Directory structure is modeled after the company business structure. This reduces the learning curve for end users ramping up to new technologies.

Each of these benefits is made possible by Active Directory. Access to all resources is managed through a single database—the Active Directory database. Anytime a user needs to access a resource—from the point of initial logon to using a printer—the process is controlled through the AD database.

The resource object is found in the directory, permissions to use the resource are controlled through the directory, and the physical location is gathered from the directory. This philosophy of a central management database allows you to view the network as a single system rather than a series of connected resources. Moving your mind-set from server- or domain-based management to network-based management is the first step in creating a well-designed Active Directory environment (and passing the exam!).

Active Directory as a Service

The name Active Directory can also be used to refer to a service running on a Windows 2000 server. The Active Directory service uses the Active Directory database to provide functionality—without the service, Active Directory would serve no purpose!

AD in the Windows 2000 Architecture

No matter what Microsoft's marketing machine might imply, Windows 2000 is based upon technology developed in earlier versions of Windows NT. That might sound like a negative statement, but it is not. The reality is that Windows NT as an operating system was a stable platform upon which to base services. Most of the complaints about earlier versions had to do with security, hardware compatibility, specific add-on services, and ease of management in larger environments—issues that have been dealt with by adding new services such as AD to Windows 2000. The basic architecture of the operating system has not changed. If you were familiar with Windows NT 4, then you will be comfortable with Windows 2000. Understanding how the components that make up AD work together with the rest of the operating system can help with the design of some of the nitty-gritty parts of an Active Directory environment.

Operating System Basics

Windows 2000 still uses the two-part structure—user mode and kernel mode. Most of the same rules apply, but there are some differences:

- User mode operations do not have direct access to system resources; kernel mode operations do.

- User mode operations can be moved to virtual memory; kernel mode operations run in a non-paged pool (they cannot be paged to virtual memory).

- User mode operations run at a lower priority than those running in kernel mode.

The kernel mode is still divided into three main areas:

Executive Services   This area is made up of small, separate pieces of software that provide specific services to the operating system.

Kernel   This is the core code of the Windows 2000 operating system. It is analogous to `command.com` in DOS or `server.exe` in NetWare.

HAL (hardware abstraction layer)   The HAL contains all of the hardware-specific directions to run a particular chip set. There is, for instance, a HAL that allows Windows 2000 to run on an Intel-based computer and another to run it on an Alpha-based computer.

Figure 1.12 shows the kernel mode components.

FIGURE 1.12   Kernel mode components

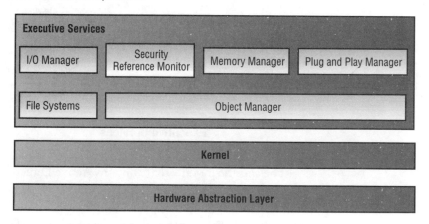

None of the preceding information should be new to you (and if it is, you're probably reading the wrong book!). What might be new are the additional components that make up the Active Directory service and how they interact with other components of the Executive Services.

AD Components

As you can see in Figure 1.13, the Active Directory subsystem is contained within the security subsystem of NT—more specifically, within the *Local Security Authority (LSA)* subsystem of the security environment. Microsoft probably won't like this description, but AD is really just a bunch of domains tied together—and the LSA was responsible for security on the domain database in earlier versions of NT (and, as you can see, is still handling the same basic responsibilities in Windows 2000). The bottom line is that the folks at Microsoft didn't have to rewrite the entire security module—they just added functionality to a subsystem that had already been tested over years in the field.

FIGURE 1.13 AD in the Windows 2000 Server architecture

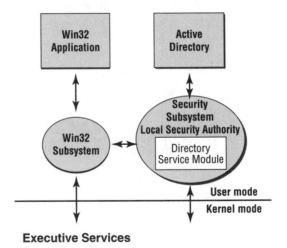

The specific module that contains Active Directory within the LSA is the *Directory Service module*. Understanding how these modules are organized can help when designing your AD network for optimal efficiency and performance. For example, we've determined that AD is a bunch of domains tied together (okay—that's a simplification, but it's adequate for our discussion here), so you can see that you might not want to have a user access resources across domains on a regular basis. You can also see that when you are designing AD sites and site boundaries (a couple more exam objectives, covered in Chapter 7, "Planning an Efficient AD Design"), you will want to ensure that the partition that contains a user's most used resources is located on a server near that user.

NOTE   Designing a Windows 2000 network is not much different (at the basic levels) than designing any other network—keep resources close to the users that use them.

The modular design of Windows 2000 Server means that each component is a separate and distinct piece that is responsible for a particular function. These components work together to perform operating system tasks. Active Directory is a part of the component called the security subsystem, which runs in *user mode*. Applications running in user mode do not have direct access to the operating system or hardware; each request for resources must be passed through various components to determine whether the request is valid. One such component is the security subsystem. *Access control lists (ACLs)* protect objects in the Active Directory structure. ACLs list who or what has been given permission to access the resource. Any attempt to gain access to an AD object or attribute is validated against the ACL by Windows 2000 Server access validation functions.

The Windows 2000 Server security infrastructure has four primary functions:

- To store security policies and account information

- To implement and enforce security models

- To manage authentication requests to AD objects

- To store and manage trust information

The security subsystem for Windows NT is a mature, stable component. Using this subsystem to manage AD ensures that the information stored within the AD database will be secure against unauthorized access.

The Security Subsystem

Active Directory is a subcomponent of the LSA, which is in turn a subcomponent of the security subsystem. The LSA is a protected module that maintains the security of the local computer. It ensures that users have system access permissions. The LSA has four primary functions:

- It generates tokens that contain user and group information, as well as the security privileges for that particular user.

- It manages the local security policy.

- It provides the interactive processes for user logon.

- It manages auditing.

The LSA itself is made up of various components, each of which is responsible for a specific function. These components are shown in Figure 1.14.

FIGURE 1.14 LSA components

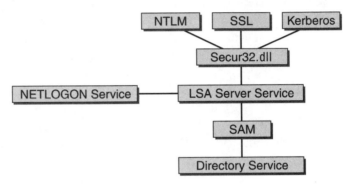

The following files make up the LSA:

NETLOGON Service (Netlogon.dll) Maintains the secure connection to a domain controller. It passes the user's credentials to a domain controller and returns the domain security identifiers and user rights for that user. (In Windows 2000 Server, the NETLOGON service uses DNS to locate the domain controller.) If the environment is a mix of NT 4 and Windows 2000 servers, the NETLOGON service also controls the replication process between the PDC and BDCs.

NTLM (Msv1_0.dll) The Windows NT LAN Manager authentication protocol.

SSL (Schannel.dll) The Secure Sockets Layer authentication protocol.

Kerberos (Kerberos.dll) The Kerberos v5 authentication protocol.

Kerberos (Kdcsvc.dll) The Kerberos Key Distribution Center, which grants security tickets to clients.

LSA Server Service (`Lsasrv.dll`)   The LSA server service enforces security policies.

SAM (`Samsrv.dll`)   The Security Accounts Manager (SAM) enforces stored policies.

Directory Service (`Ntdsa.dll`)   The Directory Service module, which supports LDAP queries and manages partitions of data.

`Secur32.dll`   The multiple authentication provider that manages the rest of the components.

The Directory Service Module

The Directory Service module is itself made up of multiple components that work together to provide directory services. These modules are arranged in three layers:

- Agents layer (with many components that access the database in different manners)

- Directory System Agent layer

- Database layer

These three layers (shown in Figure 1.15) control access to the actual database itself, which is known as the *Extensible Storage Engine (ESE)*. Notice that these three layers are not actually the "Active Directory," as in the thing that stores information. They are simply components that control access to that "thing"—the ESE, to use the technical term. Once again, from an exam perspective, these service components define how the directory database is accessed. An understanding of them (or at least knowledge of what is available) can help you chose a design that is accessible from a diverse set of clients or foreign systems. For instance, in Chapter 9, "Planning for Active Directory Connectors," we discuss components that allow you to connect to, and share information with, foreign directories. The components of the agents layer (shown in Figure 1.15) define the communication methods that can be used to communicate with AD.

FIGURE 1.15 Directory Service components

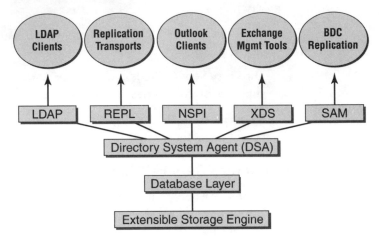

Agents Layer

There are five interface agents that gain access to the directory through internal functions:

- Lightweight Directory Access Protocol (LDAP)

- Intersite and intrasite replication (REPL)

- Name Service Provider Interface (NSPI)

- Exchange Directory Service (XDS)

- Security Accounts Manager (SAM)

Each of these interfaces uses a different method to access the information stored within the database.

Directory System Agent (DSA) Layer

The DSA is responsible for creating a hierarchical treelike namespace from an existing flat namespace. This allows you to view objects in a more logical manner rather than as a flat list. The database itself is not really a tree—the DSA uses the information found for containers to create the logical structure that we see in the various management tools. The DSA has the following responsibilities:

- Enforce all Directory Service semantics

- Process transactions

- Enforce the common schema

- Support replication between AD servers

- Provide global catalog services

- Propagate security descriptors

Database Layer

The database layer provides the functionality needed to access and search the directory database. All database access is routed through the database layer. It controls the ways in which the data is viewed.

Extensible Storage Engine

The ESE is the actual database used to store the Active Directory database. It is an enhanced version of the database used in Microsoft Exchange versions 4 and 5. The ESE allows you to create a 16-terabyte database that (theoretically) can hold up to 4 billion objects. The practical limit is about 10 million.

The Jet database engine has been used for Microsoft Exchange Server for quite some time. The version used by AD comes with a predefined schema (the definition of object classes and their attributes). ESE reserves storage only for the space actually used. If you create a user object, for example, which *could* have 50 predefined attributes, but you only give values to 4 of them, then ESE will use only as much storage space as needed for the 4 attributes. As you add values to other attributes for that user, ESE will dynamically allocate space for the growth in record size. ESE can also store multiple values for a single attribute (such as telephone numbers). It will allocate space as needed for each telephone number added to a user object.

The Internal Architecture of the Directory Service Module

In the preceding sections, we discussed the components that control access to the directory database. The database itself has numerous components to control its form and function—for instance, the rootDSA object is inside the DSA in the Directory Service module. It is the top of the logical namespace defined by the AD database and, therefore, at the top of the LDAP search tree, as shown in Figure 1.16.

FIGURE 1.16 AD internal architecture

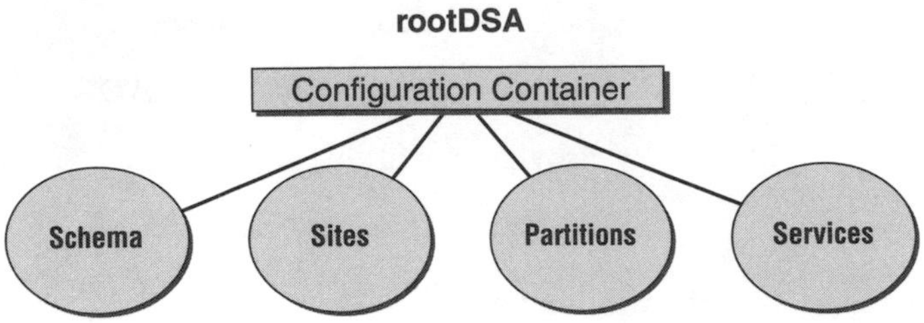

The rootDSA object contains a configuration container, which in turn holds data about the entire AD network. The information stored in the configuration container provides the data necessary to replicate the directory database and to define how this server relates to the overall namespace and how the database is partitioned. This information is known as the *name context* for the various types of information. There are four name contexts described under the configuration container:

Schema   Contains the definitions of all object classes and their attributes

Sites   Contains information on all of the sites in the Enterprise network, the domain controllers in those sites, and the replication topology

Partitions   Holds pointers to all of the partitions of the directory database

Services   Holds the configuration information for network-wide services such as Remote Access Service (RAS), system volumes, and DNS

The Active Directory Structure

The phrase "Active Directory structure" refers to the manner in which the information stored within the AD database is presented within the various tools. We have discussed network directories as repositories for network information. For this information to be of any use, it must be organized in a manner that makes it easy to access and secure. There are many different types of databases on the market and just as many different ways to organize them. For network directories, however, various design specifications will determine the type of database you'll use and how you'll organize it.

A *flat-file database*, for instance, would not work for a large directory. Imagine how large the file would be in a global network. The size limitations would confine its usefulness to networks so small that they don't really need a directory. Beyond even the physical limits, imagine trying to define a record type that could manage everything from user accounts to router configuration.

A *relational database* also would not handle the needs of a full-fledged network directory. Given the diversity of the information that a network directory must store, the number of related files would grow so large that just the index of relationships would soon overwhelm even the fastest computers on the market.

Based on the specialized needs of a network directory, the industry has developed the *X.500 recommendations* for organizing directories. Microsoft has adopted these recommendations in its design of the AD database. A firm understanding of these recommendations is necessary before any discussion of AD can continue. Because X.500 is a recommendation and not a standard, incompatibilities exist between its implementations. For example, Microsoft's implementation differs from Novell's, but because the namespace is consistent, the information stored in the directory can be accessed from either implementation.

What Is X.500?

Before we discuss what X.500 *is*, we should define what it is *not*. X.500 does *not* define the implementation of network directories. X.500 is instead a model upon which vendors can build their own products. In this, it resembles the seven-layer Open Systems Interconnection (OSI) networking model, which simply defines the functions that must be performed by networking software at each layer without defining direct implementation techniques.

The X.500 Recommendations

The X.500 specifications were originally developed in conjunction with the OSI networking model (the same seven-layer model that many of us learned, and then forgot, while studying for various networking certifications). The goal of the specification was to provide a mechanism that would give products from different vendors the capability to access and share information. Exactly what type of information is not defined; that is left up to the implementation of the vendor. What *is* defined is a common method of organizing, naming, and accessing that information—in other words, a standard definition of the format the directory will take to facilitate interoperability. Two international standards organizations—the International Standards Organization (ISO) and the International Electrotechnical Commission (IEC)—created a joint committee, the International Telecommunications Union (ITU), to oversee a set of technical documents with this goal in mind. The documents that make up the X.500 recommendations are listed in the sidebar "X.500 Technical Resources."

X.500 Technical Resources

If you are overly curious or suffer from insomnia, the following nine documents make up the core of the X.500 technical suite. Although most administrators will not need this level of expertise, these documents do give a wonderful feel for the goals of the international committee. It's interesting to note that, if you read these documents and then work with any product on the market, you will have a firm understanding of the difference between compatible and compliant (the documents can be purchased at www.itu.int).

ITU-T Recommendation X.500 (1993) ISO/IEC 9594-1:1993, *Information Technology—Open Systems Interconnection—The Directory: Overview of Concepts, Models, and Services*. This is probably the best read of the bunch. It provides a great overview of what a directory is all about.

ITU-T Recommendation X.500 (1993) ISO/IEC 9594-2:1993, *Information Technology—Open Systems Interconnection—The Directory: Models*. Provides a series of models to be used in the other documents.

ITU-T Recommendation X.500 (1993) ISO/IEC 9594-3:1993, *Information Technology—Open Systems Interconnection—The Directory: Abstract Service Definition*. Defines, in an abstract way, the externally visible services provided by a directory (such as Read or Write services to the data).

ITU-T Recommendation X.500 (1993) ISO/IEC 9594-4:1993, *Information Technology—Open Systems Interconnection—The Directory: Procedures for Distributed Operations*. Specifies ways in which the distributed components of a directory can interoperate.

ITU-T Recommendation X.500 (1993) ISO/IEC 9594-5:1993, *Information Technology—Open Systems Interconnection—The Directory: Protocol Specifications*. Defines various protocols used by or to access the directory.

ITU-T Recommendation X.500 (1993) ISO/IEC 9594-6:1993, *Information Technology—Open Systems Interconnection—The Directory: Selected Attribute Types*. Defines various attributes for the data stored in a directory, such as the naming of objects.

ITU-T Recommendation X.500 (1993) ISO/IEC 9594-7:1993, *Information Technology—Open Systems Interconnection—The Directory: Selected Object Classes*. Defines a series of common types of data that might be stored. These classes can act as the starting point for vendors when creating their products.

ITU-T Recommendation X.500 (1993) ISO/IEC 9594-8:1993, *Information Technology—Open Systems Interconnection—The Directory: Authentication Framework*. Defines two methods of authentication:

- *Simple*, in which passwords are exchanged

- *Strong*, which can take advantage of credentials formed using cryptographic techniques

ITU-T Recommendation X.500 (1993) ISO/IEC 9594-9:1993, *Information Technology—Open Systems Interconnection—The Directory: Replication*. Defines methods for replication of the data within the directory to various directory servers and provides for automatic updates.

General Hierarchical Structures

X.500 presents a method of organizing the data stored within a directory that is easy to manage and that also makes it easy for users to access the information they need. The recommendations define the model as a hierarchical structure, often referred to as the *directory tree*. For some reason, many experienced network administrators have a hard time with the concept of a directory tree structure. For years, networks have had a server-centric design: each server was an island of services in a sea of connectivity.

The X.500 recommendations present a new paradigm for network management that can take some getting used to. Although it *is* different, the concept is nothing new. Computer professionals have been working with a hierarchical system for quite some time—DOS! Both DOS and an X.500 directory tree are based upon a hierarchical structure, so they are managed similarly. Let's review a few simple DOS basics before we look at the X.500 structure—basics that will help you understand a hierarchical network directory structure. We know that comparing Microsoft's latest technology to DOS might seems a little strange—after all, even though this section is about X.500, we're actually laying the groundwork for discussing AD, right? The bottom line here is that a hierarchy is a hierarchy, and because DOS is one of the simplest hierarchical systems, it is also a great place to start. When we get to Chapter 6, "Planning a Domain and OU Structure," you'll be surprised at how many correlations there are between a good hard drive layout and a good AD layout.

Default Directory

The first term to review is *default directory*. In DOS, the default directory is the directory in which you are currently working. Here's another way of looking at it: If you were to save a file (without specifying a path), it would be placed in your default directory. This is quite a bit different from Windows 98 and NT, which hold a default "save" location (usually a directory named My Documents) in the Registry. Because many DOS activities revolved around the default directory, we often configured our prompt to display the default directory. (Remember the C:\ prompt?) Figure 1.17 shows a common DOS directory structure. Let's review a few more basic DOS recommendations before we go on.

FIGURE 1.17 DOS directory structure

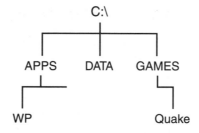

Naming DOS Files

First, let's review how DOS files are named. Most of us are probably used to simply typing in just the filename to start a program. For instance, we would probably start a game of Quake by typing **Quake.** In reality, though, that is not the full name of the file. The full name of the file includes the path back to the root of the drive: in this case, the full name of the file would be `C:\games\quake\quake.exe`. As a convenience, DOS includes the path function so that we don't have to type in the complete name to start a program.

Moving Around in DOS

In DOS, you use the CD (Change Directory) command to move around the structure. If your default directory were `C:\` and you wanted to move to the Quake directory, you would enter the following command:

CD games\quake

In the background, DOS would perform an append action, adding what you typed to your default directory to end up with your destination. If the named destination exists, you are moved there. If not, DOS will return an error.

If your default directory were `C:\apps\wp` and you wished to move to the `C:\data` directory, you would enter the following command:

CD \data

The backslash character (\) indicates the root in this command. DOS moves to the root and appends the path you have entered. Once again, if you have entered a correct path, you will be moved there.

For most of us, moving around a DOS file system is second nature. Luckily, this means that moving around an X.500 directory structure is also second nature!

The X.500 Hierarchical Structure

The structure of a directory specifies how the information within the directory will be organized. There are two main goals for the design of any network directory structure:

- Object identification
- Object organization

Both goals are critical to the proper functioning of any directory.

Object identification ensures that each object within the structure has some sort of unique identifier. Each unique identifier must map directly to some resource. Think of it this way: Without some unique name, you would be unable to ask for information about a particular resource. At best, you could ask for information about all similar objects. Imagine that you needed to print a document. Instead of identifying the printer near your desk, you would have to present a request for all "HP printers in my building" or some other, less-specific grouping. In this case, you wouldn't know whether your job would print at the nearest printer or at some HP printer on another floor. The unique identifier allows you to specify a particular object within the directory database.

AD is often referred to as a *namespace* because the database defines the structure that makes each object name unique. Think of a namespace as a database in which all object names contain similar structures but also contain enough differences to remain unique. The best example would be your family. Your family defines a namespace—in the case of the example family, the King namespace. Each name in this family ends with a similar component—King. Each family member has a unique first name so that others can differentiate them from one another. For example, everyone knows that *Katherine* and *Caroline* refer to the King daughters; *Susan* refers to Mrs. King, and *Kodiak* refers to the family dog. Outside of the family and friends, though, you would have to add the King family name to differentiate Mrs. King from all of the other Susans in the world.

Object organization allows the data within the directory to be broken into subsets for administrative purposes. Suppose you wanted a local administrator at the Tampa office to be able to create new user objects within a certain area of your structure. Without some sort of organizational plan, it would be difficult to limit the access of the administrator.

The X.500 recommendations not only fulfill these two requirements quite well (as you'll see in a few pages), they actually exceed them. The X.500 structure defines a uniform way to uniquely name objects and provides a framework that can be used to organize those objects once they are created. It also provides for other necessary services: distribution of the database to multiple servers, replication of pieces of the database to more than one server, and various protocols to be used when accessing the directory.

The X.500 Tree

As stated earlier, there are many similarities between the DOS file structure and the X.500 directory structure. In DOS, you organize your files by creating directories and subdirectories. In an X.500 structure, you have the equivalent of directories, called *containers*. Instead of using containers to organize files, you use them to organize the objects within your database.

You may have heard the DOS structure referred to as a tree because of the way subdirectories branch off from the root of the drive. Because the X.500 structure acts in much the same way, we refer to it as the *tree*. You use the tree to organize your objects for ease of management or ease of access (just as you'd use directories to organize files in DOS for the same reasons). In an X.500 tree, we refer to the objects as *leaves*. A leaf object can be defined as any object that does not contain any other object. This can get complicated, so let's start with the container objects and ignore leaf objects for now.

In DOS there is no real difference between a directory and a subdirectory, except that subdirectories are beneath some directory in the structure. Unlike DOS, the X.500 structure does define different types of container objects. Each has a specific purpose and certain limits on placement within the tree.

There are four types of containers:

Country Represented as a C object. The highest container object in the schema as defined by the X.500 committee. It can only exist at the top, or root, of the tree.

Organization Represented as an O object. These containers can only exist off the root of the tree or below a country.

Location Represented as an L object. It is a grouping object that can exist at any level of the tree except directly below the root.

Organizational unit Represented as an OU object. Another grouping object. Basically, this is the equivalent of a subdirectory in DOS. OUs can exist under Os or other OUs.

Figure 1.18 presents a graphical representation of an X.500 structure for the company King Technologies. King Technologies has offices in Tampa, Florida, and Berlin, Germany.

FIGURE 1.18   The directory tree structure for King Technologies

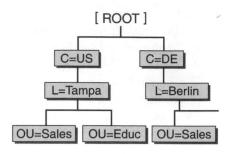

As with a DOS disk, there is no *right* way to organize a network directory. Many of the principles are the same, though. In DOS, you create a directory for one of two reasons: to ease access or to ease management. The same holds true when creating containers in a network directory. Unnecessary levels only add to users' confusion and to management overhead.

Once you have planned the structure, the next step is to populate it with leaf objects. Within the directory, leaf objects are represented by CN, as shown in Figure 1.19.

FIGURE 1.19   A populated directory

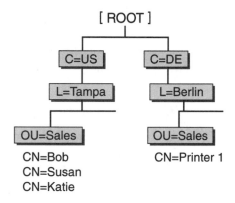

Partitioning the Database

Because Active Directory is critical to network functionality (all access to network resources is controlled through AD), its placement becomes an important design issue. If you take some time to think about it, there were basically three choices for the Microsoft engineers:

- Put the AD database on a centrally located server.

- Place a copy of the entire database on every server.

- Split the database into pieces, distribute those pieces to multiple servers, and build a mechanism to tie them together.

The third option is the choice they made, but analyzing the other two can help to explain why AD is designed the way it is. Let's look at the two choices they did *not* implement first.

Theory: Central Location

At first glance, this might seem like a feasible design. Placing the AD database on a centrally located server, as shown in Figure 1.20, would reduce the average distance from end users to the information they need.

FIGURE 1.20 AD on a single server

Upon further consideration though, two weaknesses become apparent. First, remember that all requests for network services pass through the Active Directory service. This means that, when a user in Tokyo needs to log in, the logon request will be handled by the server in Chicago—not only is this going to take too much time, think of the network traffic generated across the slow and expensive WAN links.

The second weakness is even more critical. The AD server in Chicago is a single point of failure. If the link between London and Chicago goes down, users in London will not be able to authenticate to local resources. In the event of server failure, no one can be authenticated to *any* network resource.

Based upon these weaknesses, a single, centrally located AD server would not be a good design choice.

Theory: All Locations

In this theory, each Windows 2000 server would contain a complete copy of the Active Directory database, as shown in Figure 1.21. Using this type of design, we eliminate the weakness of the single-server design. Users can be authenticated to network resources from *any* Windows 2000 server to which they can attach. This certainly eliminates the single point of failure and should decrease the amount of time that network processes take to finish (because they could be handled by the closest server).

FIGURE 1.21 AD on all servers

Unfortunately, there are two major drawbacks to this design as well. First, think of the amount of traffic that would be generated by keeping all of these copies of the database synchronized. If user Caroline in Chicago changed her password, that change would have to be replicated to servers around the world. The overhead of keeping all of the copies of the directory database synchronized would clog even the biggest of WAN links!

The second weakness would be the overhead this would place on every server in the network. The overhead of keeping the database up-to-date, especially in a large environment, would certainly mandate some serious horsepower at every server.

Once again, based upon these two weaknesses, placing a complete copy of the entire AD database on every server would not be a good design choice.

Reality: A Distributed, Replicated Directory Database

When all is said and done, the final form of the AD database looks quite a bit like the Novell NDS database described earlier—AD is a distributed, replicated database. This type of design offers good performance by allowing administrators to break the database into pieces and place those pieces near the users who will need them; it offers fault tolerance by replicating those pieces to multiple servers.

The Active Directory is broken into pieces, which are sometimes referred to as *partitions*, using the domain technologies from earlier versions of the Windows NT network operating system. In many ways, this approach looks much like the manner in which Novell partitions the NDS database, as described earlier in this chapter. This approach, using technologies that existed in earlier versions of Microsoft operating systems, has two major advantages:

- Because the domain structure has been around since the first release of Windows NT, most of the problems have been resolved. The major complaint made about Windows NT was that the trust relationships between domains were difficult to manage in larger environments. This issue is exactly why the Active Directory service was created. We'll discuss trusts in Windows 2000 in detail in Chapter 6, "Planning a Domain and OU Structure."

- Incorporating older technologies guarantees backward compatibility. It is fairly easy to mix earlier versions of NT into your Windows 2000 environment.

A *domain* can be defined as a logical grouping of users and computers managed through a single database. In many ways, a domain can be thought of as a directory on a limited scale. In earlier versions of Windows NT, each domain defined a Security Accounts Manager (SAM) database that held limited (when compared to the AD database) information about the users, groups, and computers in an environment. The SAM database was stored on domain controllers. In each domain, there was one primary domain controller (PDC), which held the master copy of the database, and an unlimited number of backup domain controllers (BDCs) that each held a copy of that database. Because all changes to the database occurred at the PDC and were then replicated to the BDCs, this system was known as a *single-master environment*.

In Windows 2000, the domain structure still exists. Each domain defines both a specific portion of the overall AD database and a set of security boundaries used to control aspects of network management. Rather than using the outdated single-master method of replication (one PDC and multiple BDCs), though, each AD server is able to accept changes to the database and initiate changes to all other copies. This is known as a *multiple-master environment*.

The trust relationships are handled in a completely different manner from those available in Windows NT. We'll save that discussion for Chapter 6!

Summary

In this chapter, we laid the groundwork for the technical discussion to come later in the book. We've discussed directory technology in general, looked at a couple of examples of other directories in use today, seen how AD fits into the overall structure of the Windows 2000 architecture, and looked at how the Windows 2000 network uses the technology of earlier Windows products to both maintain backward compatibility and capitalize upon the network components that have been tested on production systems.

This is probably a good time to discuss the rest of the book—how it's organized and why we made the choices we made. When you're writing a study guide, you have to be sure to cover all the objectives that Microsoft has defined for the exam. After all, people buy study guides because they want to pass the exams. (If you're reading this standing in the bookstore while you wait for the geek to put down the latest Dilbert calendar—we hope this first chapter was enough to entice you!) As an author, you also hope to present your information in a logical manner and with a new perspective (otherwise any old study guide would do).

When we started thinking about this book, the first thing we did was take the Microsoft Exam objectives and put them on index cards. We then tried to place them in logical groupings (not always the easiest thing to do with Microsoft objectives). When we were finished, we found that we had four basic groups of objectives:

Business Objectives concerned with the analysis of the business environment into which AD will be placed

Structure   Objectives concerned with the actual design of the AD database structure

Services   Objectives concerned with various add-on services that AD can provide to a network

Implementation   One objective concerned with planning for the implementation of your design

As we looked at the list of objective "groups," we realized that this was exactly the order of steps we have used to design the various networks we have worked on. We always begin by getting to know the environment. Based on this knowledge, we can then move to laying out the basic structure. Once the structure is in place, we can add the various services and applications that are unique to the business of our client. Once this is done, we can manage the implementation based upon our design. We've organized this study guide to match that real-world design effort. Chapters 2 through 4 discuss the research phase of design (getting to know your client's business), Chapters 5 through 7 discuss the structure of the AD tree, Chapters 8 through 10 are concerned with additional network functionality available in Windows 2000, and Chapter 11 discusses planning an AD rollout.

With that said, we can now move into the first phase of any good design process—getting to know your client's business environment. In Chapter 2, "Analyzing the Physical Environment," we'll discuss the types of information you'll want to gather about the physical layout of the network.

Key Terms

Before you take the exam, be sure you're familiar with the following terms:

access control lists (ACLs)

broadcast packets

directory

domain

extensible

network directory

Novell Directory Services (NDS)

object classes

partitions

properties

replication

schema

Windows Internet Name Service (WINS)

Review Questions

1. The function(s) of WINS (Windows Internet Name Service) includes which of the following?

   A. NetBIOS name registration

   B. URL resolution

   C. NetBIOS name resolution

   D. Host name resolution

2. In Novell NetWare Directory Services (NDS), the directory database is _____ .

   A. Stored on a centrally located NDS server

   B. Stored on all NetWare servers

   C. Broken into partitions and distributed across multiple servers

   D. A group of bindery-like files managed by a third-party database engine

3. The schema is _____ .

   A. A database that contains the IP addresses of all AD servers

   B. A definition of the records and fields in the AD database

   C. Another name for Active Directory service

   D. Software used to import user information into the AD database

4. Records in the AD database are known as _____ .

   A. Resources

   B. Objects

   C. Records

   D. Addresses

5. The specific information stored about an object (name, address, telephone number, etc.) is known as the object's _____ .

   A. Properties

   B. Attributes

   C. Fields

   D. Segments

6. The X.500 specifications define _____ .

   A. A protocol to be used for managing network devices

   B. An implementation of a network directory

   C. Guidelines that can be used during the design of a network directory

   D. 500 methods of network management

7. Which of the following are directories?

   A. Telephone book

   B. Outlook contacts list

   C. Rolodex

   D. Active Directory

8. Which of the following statements is true about domains within the Windows 2000 environment?

   A. A domain defines a discrete subset of the overall AD database.

   B. A domain defines a set of AD servers.

   C. Domains act as security boundaries.

   D. Domains cannot communicate.

9. Which of the following are valid X.500 container classes?

   A. Country

   B. Organization

   C. Location

   D. Organizational unit

10. Which three of the following are components of the kernel mode?

   A. Executive Services

   B. Kernel

   C. Hardware abstraction layer (HAL)

   D. WIN32 Subsystem

Answers to Review Questions

1. A, C. WINS clients submit their name to the WINS server during initialization. Name registration takes place during client initialization. WINS clients submit their NetBIOS name to the WINS server. The WINS server determines if the name is already in use and, if not, adds the name and associated IP address to a database. During name resolution, WINS clients query the WINS server for the IP address of a particular NetBIOS name.

2. B. NDS is a global, distributed, replicated directory.

3. B. The schema defines the object classes and properties in the directory database.

4. B. An object represents a network resource and is defined through a record in the directory database.

5. A, B. Although *fields* might be technically correct (after all, properties are just fields within the database), the Microsoft terminology is *properties* or *attributes*.

6. C. The X.500 specifications in and of themselves do *not* define a network or any other specific component of networks. They are an industry-accepted model for how directory databases should be designed.

7. A, B, C, D. Anything that holds information is a directory—some are just more technical in nature than others.

8. A, C. A domain acts as a partition of the AD database and also as a boundary for security (such as Group Policy objects or administrative privileges).

9. A, B, C, D. Each of these is a valid X.500 container.

10. A, B, C. The three components of the kernel mode are Executive Services, kernel, and the HAL.

Chapter

2

Analyzing the Physical Environment

✓ **Analyze the existing and planned business models.**

- Analyze the company model and the geographical scope. Models include regional, national, international, subsidiary, and branch offices.

- Analyze company processes. Processes include information flow, communication flow, service and product life cycles, and decision-making. (This topic will be covered in Chapter 3.)

✓ **Evaluate the company's existing and planned technical environment.**

- Analyze company size and user resource distribution.

- Assess the available connectivity between the geographic location of worksites and remote sites.

- Assess the net available bandwidth.

Historically, Microsoft exams have always favored the software fix rather than the "screwdriver approach." The perfect example would be the correct Microsoft fix for the failure of the boot disk in a mirrored pair. The Microsoft answer was to create a boot floppy, edit the `Boot.ini` file (which means understanding ARC paths), and then boot to the floppy. In real life, as opposed to the testing room, using a screwdriver and switching the drive cables (and maybe a few jumpers) was the quicker fix.

In the Design exams, Microsoft has decided that the physical aspects of your network are important considerations when designing an overall Active Directory solution. This chapter introduces the concept of analyzing the network infrastructure and existing technologies before installing the first Windows 2000 server.

This chapter includes a discussion of the objective, Analyze the existing and planned business models. However, the discussion will cover only the first subobjective, Analyze the company model and the geographical scope. We'll cover analyzing company processes in Chapter 3.

The chapter will begin with a discussion of the various types of locations that exist in businesses (as defined by Microsoft) and then will move on to a look at the physical variables you will need to analyze in order to propose a good AD design.

Analyzing the Company

Every time a marketing person talks about an X.500 directory (no matter what the brand—Novell, Banyan Vines, or Microsoft AD), they always explain that the "directory allows users and administrators to see their network as a logical set of resources." What they really mean is that resources are organized so that the user doesn't have to understand the physical layout of the network. A fax server object in the directory is all the user needs to see; they don't need to know where that fax server is physically located or its network address. The basic premise of many directory sales pitches is that the physical nature of the network is secondary to the logical organization of network resources.

As "network guys," we always find that pitch absurd. No matter how much you pretty up the interface, no matter how easy you make it for the end user or the day-to-day administrator, the bottom line of networking is moving bits from place to place. Those bits are ground zero for network design. The "plumbing" (or connectivity) between computers, buildings, and sites is usually an expensive part of your network, and preserving the bandwidth on those connections is a big consideration of any good network design.

We sometimes get a little preachy about network bandwidth issues. Technologists often think that adding more, better, or faster hardware will solve any performance issue. These types of fixes cost money—often a lot of money (which explains why they are the preferred fix of many consulting firms). Many times, performance issues can be solved by analyzing the physical layout of a network and then adjusting the placement of services to optimize traffic patterns.

That's exactly what this chapter, and these exam objectives, are about. The first step in *any* network design project is gathering information about the physical network, also known as the *infrastructure*. (We call it the plumbing.) We'll discuss the types of information you'll want to gather and have at hand during the rest of the design process. Think of this as the first phase of network design—the physical analysis phase.

The goal of this analysis is to gather the information necessary to make good decisions when planning the domain and OU structure for, and placement of services within, your Windows 2000 network. During this phase of the design process, you should not even consider AD issues—what you want is a picture of the current layout of the network infrastructure.

Evaluating the Scope of a Project

As a consultant, or even as an IT professional within a company, the first thing you need to do for any contract is get a feel for the size, or *scope*, of the project. This helps you to estimate certain criteria:

- The number of person-hours that will be involved

- The types of expertise that will be needed

- How much ongoing support will be involved

- What types of software will be needed

- What types of hardware will be needed

- Whether you have the skill sets necessary or will need to subcontract certain aspects of the job

- What telecommunication companies, if any, you will have to deal with (This makes a big difference, especially on international networks.)

Lastly, getting a feel for the size of the job will allow you to estimate the number of complications you can expect and the amount of Maalox you should purchase.

Based upon these estimates, you can answer the most important question in the first phase of design—is the project feasible? You may think this sounds strange, but there will be times when the best business solution will be to *not* move to Windows 2000 and AD. The usual constraint will be funding. Knowing the scope of the project should allow you to give a rough estimate of both the time and money involved.

Microsoft ✓ *Exam Objective*

Analyze the existing and planned business models.

- Analyze the company model and the geographical scope. Models include regional, national, international, subsidiary, and branch offices.

- Analyze company processes. Processes include information flow, communication flow, service and product life cycles, and decision-making. (This topic will be discussed in Chapter 3).

The scope of a project can be considered an educated guess of its complexity. When you are determining the scope of a design project, there are certain aspects of the environment that you can use to rate the network. For exam purposes, Microsoft has defined a set of standards that can be used as a yardstick when determining the scope of a design project. There are two sets of standards, or models, mentioned in the examination objectives:

Geographic model   The *geographic model* of a company is determined by the number of physical locations that make up the network and the connectivity between them. There are three levels of geographic models—regional, national, and international. The differences between them will be examined a little later in this section.

Business model   The *business model* refers to the business relationship between sites and services. In other words, you'll look at each location and determine its relationship to the company. You might, for instance, have a research site that is technically part of your network but is in reality a completely separate entity, using none of the corporate resources and not requiring complete access to the company infrastructure. On the other hand, you might have a location that is the central distribution point for all order processing for your company. Employees at this site might need to read data or use other resources at every location within the company. Each of these two examples would require a different level of access and would be handled differently in your final AD design.

Understanding the Geographic Model

One of the most expensive components of any network consists of the connections between physical locations (hereafter known as *sites*). With this in mind, one of the first design goals for any network should be to reduce, or at least control, the network traffic that crosses any expensive wide area links. The bigger the network, or the larger the number of links in the network, the more important this first goal becomes! Microsoft defines three "sizes" of networks based upon the amount of wide area connectivity inherent in the geographic layout of facilities—regional (small), national (medium), and international (large). We're going to add one more class of network—the simple-network model, which often consists of just a single site. Microsoft doesn't include this as a design model because a simple-network environment shouldn't take a whole lot of planning. For testing purposes, though, you'll need to know when to plan and when to go with the defaults.

Simple-Network Model

Remember, you're not going to see this name on the exam, but you might see a case study or question that revolves around a network that really doesn't take much planning. The definition of a simple network would be an environment in which all resources are connected over fast, reliable lines that have ample available bandwidth. In most cases, the simple network will be made up of a single site, and the company will have no need to create network relationships with outside vendors, customers, or other foreign systems. A simple network will not require any extensive planning—it will be a single domain, it will contain no special connectivity issues, and the existing network traffic will not push the limits of whatever topology (Ethernet, Token Ring, etc.) is currently in place. To tell the truth, the simple network will be the most common environment in the market—very few of us will be able to work on the design of large networks.

Don't get scared by the number of users involved in a given project. As of Technology Week 2000, Microsoft has tested a single-domain environment with 160 million (yes, million!) users in a single Windows 2000 domain. It imported the entire United States white pages into a single database. The interesting thing to note is that the tests showed no significant loss of performance with this large sample set.

We won't go into great deal about the simple network, but you should be aware that systems so small that they do not fit into one of Microsoft's defined environments are probably simple networks. It's important to remember the following distinctions about a simple network:

- No wide area links, unless those links are high speed, reliable, and have plenty of available bandwidth

- No special relationships with outside systems

- Single NT domain

Regional Model

A *regional model* would be one in which all sites are contained within a well-defined geographic area. Although this definition is vague, it works well in conjunction with the other two models defined by Microsoft. To make it a bit more specific, we would add that, in most cases, a regional network will be made up of connections that travel through a single vendor's lines. If, for instance, all of a company's lines are purchased through one of the regional Bells, then it follows that the network itself is regional in scope. The network in Figure 2.1 is a perfect example of a regional environment.

FIGURE 2.1   A regional network

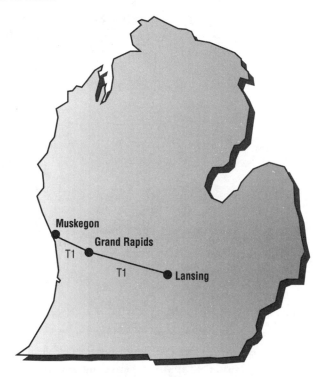

In this example (shown in Figure 2.1), the network consists of two wide area links: one from Grand Rapids to Muskegon and another from Grand Rapids to Lansing. In this case, the region can be defined as western Michigan, and both wide area lines are probably provided by the same vendor.

Notice that no time zones are crossed, nor are any state boundaries. You will not have to be concerned with the time differences on any scheduled processes, and you will not have to be knowledgeable about more than one set of legal issues. Unfortunately, there is no definitive description of a regional network. The network depicted in Figure 2.2 is considerably larger in area (but no more complex) than the first example, and it too qualifies as a regional environment.

FIGURE 2.2 A larger regional network

As you can see from Figure 2.2, geographic dispersion is not the only criterion for ranking an environment as a regional network. You will also have to take into account the relative complexity of the environment. Take, for example, the network depicted in Figure 2.3. Outwardly, it appears almost identical to the network presented in Figure 2.2, with one additional site.

FIGURE 2.3 A more complex network

The reality is, though, that this network is much more complex than the preceding example. Here you will have to consider an unreliable dial-up connection and a potential bottleneck on the 64K line. You also need to note that all traffic from both the Atlanta and the Boston sites must travel across a single T1 line to reach Grand Rapids. There is also a straight-line path for data to travel from one end of the network to another. If either Grand Rapids or Boston becomes unavailable, the continuity of communication will be broken. This would not qualify as a regional network based upon the additional complexity of the environment. It would more likely fit into the next category—the national model network. The important distinctions to remember about a regional model are as follows:

- Simple infrastructure design

- Well-defined geographic boundaries

- No complex setup issues

National Model

A *national model* environment is one that, as the name implies, covers an entire country. The network infrastructure is complex, it crosses time zones, rules and regulations might differ from site to site, complex services are part of the mix, and/or in general, it services a larger number of users. If any one of these conditions is met, it *might* be a national network. Sound confusing? Welcome to the world of Microsoft testing. Let's start our discussion by breaking down each of these points to get a clearer understanding of what each represents:

Complex infrastructure   If the network in question is made up of fast, reliable links that have plenty of available bandwidth, you don't *really* have to take them into account for your design. You could assume that the WAN links would not have an appreciable impact on network performance. Luckily for consultants, few networks match these specifications. A typical national network will be made up of the following components:

- Different speed dedicated lines (T1, 256K, 64K, etc.)

- Dial-up connections

- Different network topologies (ATM, Frame Relay, etc.)

- Different connectivity vendors

- Different hardware configurations (switches, routers, etc.)

- Different levels of available bandwidth

When a network becomes a heterogeneous mix that fulfills some of the bulleted items above, it is probably a national network. Each of these considerations will add complexity to the design and length to the design process.

Time zones   Multiple time zones in and of themselves would not mandate a national network design (although crossing time zones is almost a given in any national network in the United States). Crossing them can, however, add complexity to such issues as scheduled over-the-Net back-ups, time-sensitive database entries, and any other process that relies on a timed function. If your environment includes time-sensitive processes, you might be a national network.

Laws and regulations   What is acceptable in one community might not be acceptable in *every* community. If your network crosses cultural boundaries, it should probably be considered national in scope.

A great example of this type of issue is offering gambling services across the Internet. Consider Reno, Nevada—a place where gambling is just another business. Consider also Provo, Utah—a place where gambling is frowned upon. If you had a business that included services for gamblers, you would have to be aware of the legal ramifications of offering services in both states. As the network administrator for a business with offices in both locations, you would have to be aware of the laws in both communities and design your network services accordingly.

Complex services   Most of today's networks offer a complex set of services to end users. Networks still provide the basics, such as file and print services, but are now also expected to support advanced messaging systems (such as Exchange Server 5.5), Internet Web servers (such as Internet Information Server), and even voice-over-IP phone service. The more complex the services, the more complex the design to support those services will have to be.

Larger number of users   This is the most subjective of the considerations. Because Windows 2000 and Active Directory can support a million objects in a single domain, "large" is hard to define in straight numbers. It would be more likely be defined as a large number of users with diverse business needs. A group of accountants might need to download large amounts of investment information from the Internet, another group might need large amounts of bandwidth to support a streaming video application, and yet another group might need to access only the e-mail servers. If you stop to think about these three examples, you will find that they each demand different physical capabilities of the network. Add them together in the same business, and you'll have to control your network traffic patterns carefully.

The bottom line is that a network will be national in scope if it is more complex than a regional network but does not cross any international boundaries.

International Model

The name of the *international model* sums up the definition—international networks cross international borders. In many respects, the makeup of most international networks will be much the same as most national networks. Their size alone mandates a certain amount of complexity. Like national networks, they will usually have the following characteristics:

- They have a complex infrastructure.
- They cross time zones.
- They move through areas with different laws and regulations.
- They offer complex services to their end users.
- There are language differences between sites.

From a design standpoint, there are two major differences between a national network and an international network:

- Laws and regulations of two (or more) different countries will have to be taken into account.
- There will usually be multiple providers for connectivity services, and those services will probably vary in quality and reliability.

Laws and Regulations

Understanding the laws and regulations involved in a multicountry environment can be a full-time job. You will have to stay up-to-date on the export laws of each country (the U.S., for instance, is very careful about the technology that it allows to be exported), the acceptable content for each area (many parts of the Pacific Rim, for instance, do not allow full access to the Internet), and even standard worker's compensation customs (Germany, for instance, has a standard 37.5-hour work week for all employees). Knowledge of these items allows you to plan for implementation of technology, person-hours available, and tariffs that might affect your environment.

Multiple Providers

A typical international network, like the one shown in Figure 2.4, will span the territories of multiple providers of communication services. A working knowledge of the reliability of services and the cost of those services is critical when you are planning the budget for your design project.

FIGURE 2.4   An international network

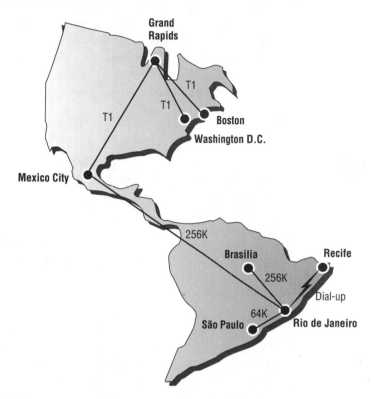

The costs involved in international connectivity can be astronomical! It is important that you fully understand how those costs are applied when designing your network. We once, for instance, saved a client 40 percent/month by changing which side of a WAN link initialized the line. The client had an office in Los Angeles and another in the Pacific Rim. When our company looked over the client's wide area connectivity, we noticed that the Pacific Rim site called the U.S. site every evening to download production information. After looking over the rates for the two telecommunication companies involved, we discovered that it was 40 percent less expensive to have the U.S. site call the Pacific Rim site than the other way around. This one change saved (and is still saving) the client over $12,000.00 per year!

Geographic Scoping

Now that we've discussed the variables involved in determining the scope of an environment, we can take a look at a few examples. Remember that determining the scope of a project is not an exact science. We tend to always err on the side of conservatism—if a network could conceivably be one of two scopes, we will always chose the more complex of the two. From a consultant's perspective, this ensures that we will never underestimate the amount of work (and therefore, money) in a project. If you are on a staff that is designing an AD structure, this ensures that your budget will be large enough to accomplish your goal.

In business, it's usually better to ask for more than you need and come in under budget than to ask for less than you need and have to ask for more money later.

Design Scenario: The Whole-Bottle Milk Company

The Whole-Bottle Milk company encompasses a series of collection/distribution sites and production facilities in Minnesota, Wisconsin, Illinois, and Michigan. Whole-Bottle Milk (WBM) acts as a cooperative with hundreds of locally owed farms. "We represent the last bastion of independent farming in America," the CEO often says. "We offer small farmers a chance to work together to compete with the large corporate farms that seem to be taking over the business." Each farm is provided with Internet access, a computer and modem, and specialized software that allows them to connect to the WBM network to download the latest milk prices as well as a slew of other services (everything from investment services to free Web pages).

Whole-Bottle Milk owns 14 distribution centers that act as collection points for local farms. These centers control between 25 and 40 truck routes for the collection of milk. Each day, the local farmers access the company databases through the Internet and upload their production figures. This information is fed to specialized software that then plans daily pickup routes based upon the amount of milk waiting at each farm and the capacity of each truck.

WBM also owns eight production facilities. The local distribution centers truck the milk to these facilities for processing. From there, it is trucked to grocery stores throughout the area.

Whole-Bottle Milk is headquartered in Geneva, Wisconsin. All deliveries to grocery outlets are managed through a real-time database that accepts input from the production facilities at 10-minute intervals. At any given point in time, management can access real-time information about stock on-hand and current deliveries and probable production and sales information forecasts.

The network infrastructure, provided by AT&T, consists of 56K lines from the distribution centers to the closest production facility. The production facilities all have T1 lines to the company headquarters in Geneva. No recent bandwidth problems have been logged, and the IS staff seems happy with the network service and support they are receiving from their provider.

You've been asked to bid on a project to upgrade the company network to Windows 2000. Before you begin any actual work, you will need to scope the project so as to give the company a preliminary bid for your services.

Based upon this description, which of the three scopes would best describe this environment—regional, national, or international?

First eliminate the obvious—this is not an international company. No international boundaries are crossed, and no "international" considerations are necessary. This leaves two choices—regional and national. Because this company spans a very specific (and bounded) physical area, and because all connections are provided by a single vendor, this would be scoped as a regional project.

Design Scenario: GG Funtime Imports, Inc.

GG Funtime Imports, Inc. is a company that imports party favors used in most of the major festivals in the United States. Its headquarters is in New Orleans (home of the largest festival of the year, Mardi Gras). It has warehouses and distribution centers throughout the United States—27 facilities in all. These facilities are connected to the home office in a variety of ways, everything from dedicated 256K lines to dial-up connections. GG also has a large Internet presence, both for retail business and to facilitate connections to its various vendors.

Purchasing and sales staff members connect to vendors throughout Central and South America and the Pacific Rim to place orders and check vendor inventories.

The CEO of GG Funtime Imports has hired your company to do a feasibility study on upgrading to a Windows 2000 environment. Your job is to analyze the current network and justify the expense of the upgrade.

Based upon the description, what scope of project would this upgrade be—regional, national, or international?

First eliminate the obvious. This is most definitely not a regional project. The company has facilities that span the United States and business concerns that span the globe. The next question is whether the project is national or international. Surprisingly, an argument could be made either way. Remember, the goal of these new Design exams is to push for total business solutions. In the actual exam, Microsoft would probably provide you with a little more detail, but what you want to look for is hints toward more advanced uses of its software. In this example, the company is described as a company that is national in its physical environment but international in its business. GG Funtime Imports *imports* from Central and South America and the Pacific Rim. This is a great opportunity to build a Windows 2000 forest. The details say that its staff accesses vendors around the globe; if those vendors are also using Windows 2000 and Active Directory, you could easily tie those environments together. Based upon the description, you should go for an international scope.

This is also probably the best choice for the consulting firm. Rather than underbidding the project and sticking to a national network, you can bid a true business solution that encompasses the entirety of the actual environment.

The GG Funtime Imports design scenario is the perfect segue into the next section—analyzing the business model of your company. With the release of Windows 2000 and Active Directory and the changes to the MCSE program, Microsoft has changed the scope of your responsibilities. You are no longer allowed to focus solely on the technology. As network administrators, you are being asked to understand the business side of the equation. You are going to have to learn how companies do business, why they do business as they do, and how Microsoft software can improve the business environment. Detailed analysis of the environment and the ability to integrate technology and business to provide a solution are the keys to success in the new MCSE program!

Understanding the Business Model

You've seen how the physical infrastructure of a company can affect the scope of the upgrade or migration process, but this is only half of the equation. To fully scope a project, you must have a good understanding of the relationships between the components that make up that infrastructure. This requires an analysis of more than just network bandwidth. It requires you to analyze at least these three issues:

- The political relationships between sites, departments, and individual managers

- The uses to which the connections will be put (just e-mail versus real-time database access, for instance)

- The similarities and differences between the sites, both in physical makeup and in management philosophy

As you can see, this is where real-world business experience and knowledge come in handy!

We were recently at a Microsoft convention and were talking with a high-ranking member of the Microsoft Official Curriculum (MOC) vision team. During our discussion, he said a couple of things that enlightened us about the philosophy of these new Design tests. Most important, he said that in a perfect world, MCSE candidates would take the first four core exams and then spend a year implementing technology in real-world solutions before attempting the Design tests. We all know that this is an unrealistic goal—many of us are required by our bosses or clients to have the certification for our careers—but it *does* exemplify the direction of Microsoft certification.

The exam objectives mention two different business models to consider at this point in the design project: subsidiary offices and branch offices. As a measure of comparison, we're going to add one more type of facility: corporate offices. Once you have finished the geographic scoping of the environment—in other words, after you have gathered the information necessary to fully understand the physical infrastructure of the network—you must take a good look at the end points of that structure. The end points represent the physical locations where "work" is done—be it administrative, production, research, or what have you. The geographic models help you map the network infrastructure; the business models help you map the business infrastructure. Remember that the goal of the Design exams is to produce MCSEs who can suggest whole-business solutions, so the ability to analyze the underlying business processes of a company is critical to successfully passing these tests.

We'll discuss the detailed information that you will need to have at hand to scope a project later in this chapter.

Corporate Offices

Remember, the designation "corporate office" is our own creation. We'll use the definition that follows as a comparative value to determine which type of location any given site represents. A *corporate office* represents a full-blown business site—a location in which the company has invested heavily in facilities, information services staff, and hardware or a location that is heavily staffed. Some or all of the following statements will describe a corporate office environment:

- It has a diverse environment made up of varying client types, hardware, software, and supporting staff.

- It has multiple servers or specialized servers.

- It acts as a hub for the network infrastructure.

- It provides company-wide access to data or services.

- It has large (relative to the overall size of the company) numbers of employees.

- It houses the management staff of the company.

- It represents a key location in the company political structure.

- It has the "feel" of a permanent facility.

- It is fully controlled by the company (as opposed to a partner relationship).

We know that a few of the characteristics of a corporate office environment are rather subjective—what can we say? Many of the decisions you'll be making during an AD design project will indeed be subjective. For testing purposes, though, you should get enough of a feel for each location from the text to be able to categorize it.

The bottom line for corporate office sites is that they feel like permanent facilities. They will act as a central point for something within the company—management, production, delivery, and so on. If the company as a whole could not continue without a particular location, that location can be considered a corporate office.

"Why," you might ask, "did they bother adding this definition of a business model to this discussion?" For the simple reason that, for testing purposes, anything that does not fit into the corporate office class of location will be defined as one of two other classes of sites: branch or subsidiary. By knowing what *not* to include, you can eliminate some of the variables in the case studies you see on the exam.

Branch Offices

A *branch office* can be defined as a wholly controlled facility that does not meet the criteria to be a corporate office. Although this definition is not very descriptive in and of itself, when you compare a location to the list of attributes for a corporate site, it becomes fairly straightforward to make the distinction. The following list includes statements that do *not* describe branch offices:

- They have a diverse client base.

- They have multiple or specialized servers. (Often, branch offices do not contain any servers.)

- They usually act as a hub for the network infrastructure.

- They provide access to company-wide data or services.

- They usually house the company's management staff.

- They act as a key location for the company.

The following statements *do* describe branch offices:

- They are fairly permanent facilities.

- They are fully controlled by the company.

Although these distinctions allow you to classify locations fairly easily, there are also a few desirable design factors that you would like to find in the branch offices for your company. Most of the time, companies that have branch offices will set them up in a fairly standard fashion. These similarities allow you to set up standard management strategies, or policies, that can be applied to all branch office sites. As an example, let's look at the facilities in the Last National Bank of Michigan (LNB). The network for LNB is shown in Figure 2.5.

FIGURE 2.5 The network for the Last National Bank of Michigan

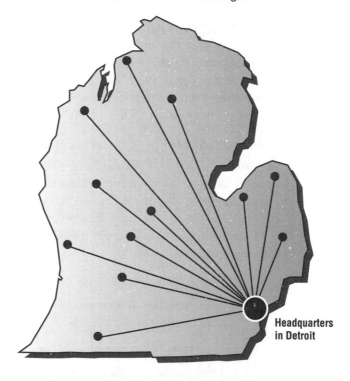

Headquarters
in Detroit

The LNB office in Detroit houses the corporate IS department, the legal staff, the CEO, the CIO, the CFO. It processes all transactions with the Federal Reserve Bank, provides a central database of client and account information, and houses the corporate marketing department. All other offices have dedicated lines that link to Detroit, so it also acts as the hub of the network infrastructure. As you have probably already guessed, the Detroit facility qualifies as a corporate office. The question remains: "Are any of the other sites also corporate offices?"

The outlying sites represent actual community banks. Each site is connected to the Detroit office by either a 56K or 256K dedicated line (depending upon the volume of business generated at the facility). All sites have between four and eight computers used by the bank tellers, between two and four computers used by loan officers, one or two computers used by the bank's management staff, and two to four printers. Each facility also contains a BDC that belongs to the single domain defined for the current NT 4 implementation (this prevents a complete loss of functionality in the event of the WAN link going down).

The other sites are fairly similar in their environment. None is critical to the continued functioning of the company as a whole. In other words, all other sites can be classified as branch offices. The branch offices all have fairly consistent environments, provide no company-wide services, and can be managed in a similar manner.

These similarities between sites within a company are not unusual. Granted, most companies are not as "clean" as LNB, but many have consistent layouts. Take, for example, KMK, Inc. in Minnesota. KMK is a large grocery company headquartered in Hutchinson. Its headquarters meets all of the criteria for a corporate office designation—all other sites are managed there, inventory databases are kept there, all deliveries to retail outlets are dispatched from there, and so on. It also has three other types of facilities: central distribution warehouses, KMK grocery stores, and KMK convenience stores.

The central distribution centers act as warehouses for the retail facilities within a region. They house inventory database servers (that connect to the corporate databases in Hutchinson), complete shop floor management software to control order fulfillment and truck routing (connected to a cool global-positioning system that allows real-time rerouting of trucks), and local accounting personnel who control billing for the region. Based upon this description, we can safely assume that the distribution centers are *not* branch offices and can therefore be considered corporate offices.

The KMK grocery stores also have inventory control software that is connected to their point-of-sale bar-code scanning system. Local inventory is stored on a local database that uploads changes to the local distribution center each evening. The IS environment consists of 5 to 10 networked cash registers and 2 to 3 computers used by store management. Because the computer environments are fairly simple and no single store is critical to the company as a whole, we can classify the grocery stores as branch offices.

The KMK convenience stores can best be described as smaller versions of the grocery stores with a few additional considerations. The convenience stores also sell gasoline and so have a complete inventory control system built in to the gas pumps. Typical stores have two to three cash registers that are tied into a bar-code scanning package used for inventory control. Each store has one server (although the computers are usually old and out-of-date) that stores local sales information and connects to the local distribution center each night to update the central database. Because the computer environments are fairly simple and no single store is critical to the company as a whole, we can classify the convenience stores as branch offices.

Are you seeing a pattern yet? The easiest way to determine if a site is a branch office is to first determine if it is *not* a corporate office!

You are probably asking yourself why this is important. Take another look back at Figure 2.5. At first glance, this network looks fairly complex. There are 10 to 20 sites connected over a regional network infrastructure. Based solely upon the physical network, you might classify this as a complex project. The reality is that the Last National Bank of Michigan would be a fairly easy system to work with—only one site contains any complex technology. Without looking at the business model, you would overbid the project and probably lose the job, or if you were on the LNB staff, you might decide that the upgrade would cost too much in dollars and time and cancel or delay your upgrade plans.

From a design perspective, you should look at all of the sites, determine how many corporate offices are involved and treat them as a separate design component, and then group branch offices into management clusters that can be seen as a single design element. (You will have to design only one consistent plan for each type of branch office instead of each separate office.)

Subsidiary Offices

Subsidiary office locations are sites that are part of the overall business but are not controlled by the company. Partner companies, franchise sites, and separate business divisions are the best examples of true subsidiary offices, but any office that is beyond the control of corporate management can qualify. As you can imagine, gathering information from such entities can be difficult.

Unfortunately, the business relationships with subsidiary offices are often more complex than those with corporate-owned facilities. Complex business relationships usually imply complex IS relationships. You might, for instance, need to access sales information from an independently owned franchise, but its IS department might want complete control over the transfer for information. Take, for example, the Mom's Apple Pie (MAP) company shown in Figure 2.6.

FIGURE 2.6 Mom's Apple Pie company

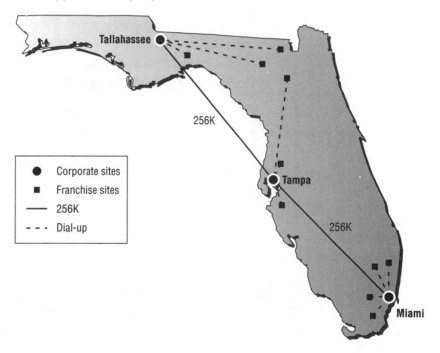

Mom's Apple Pie sells pies, cakes, and cookies. It started with one small location in Tampa, Florida, and soon expanded to three sites (marked as corporate sites in Figure 2.6). A few years ago, the company decided to franchise its name, and it has been going strong ever since. Each franchise is independently owned and managed but reports sales figures and orders supplies through the parent company.

When a person or company buys a franchise license from MAP, they attend a month-long training session during which they are brought up to speed on the computer software and hardware used to connect to MAP's corporate system for placing orders and reporting sales figures.

Designing an AD environment (or any other operating system, for that matter) that includes autonomous entries is quite a bit more complicated than putting together a system controlled by a single IS department. In our Mom's Apple Pie example, you will have to write new training materials for the management course, talk to each franchise owner to gather information about their interaction with MAP's system, and plan for additional security to control the access that the franchisees have when they connect.

Now that we've looked at the criteria used to scope a design project, let's run through a design scenario to drive the information home (see the sidebar "Design Scenario: Carrie's Books, Inc.").

Design Scenario: Carrie's Books, Inc.

Carrie's Books, Inc. (CBI) specializes in children's reading material, both educational and recreational. It has a large network of stores—some owned by CBI, some franchise, and some independently owned stores that order from CBI. The layout of its network is shown below.

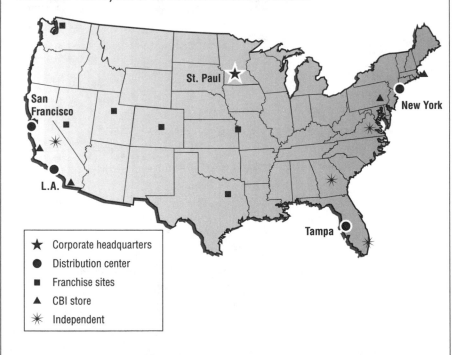

The company headquarters is located in St. Paul, Minnesota. At the head-quarters facility are 250 employees, 17 servers, and a full-blown distribution center. The corporate IS provides e-mail servers, manages a company e-commerce Web site, manages connectivity to all other sites, and provides dial-in services for connecting to this information remotely.

Each of the five distribution sites (St. Paul, New York, Tampa, San Francisco, and Los Angeles) consists of a warehouse and its supporting personnel. They each also house an inventory database that uploads information to the corporate headquarters each night.

Each CBI store has between 6 and 12 cash registers and uses a real-time, point-of-purchase database to control inventory. They are all connected to the closest distribution center by a dedicated 56K link.

Franchise sites log in each night to report sales and update their weekly order (based upon what was sold during the day). Most have a dedicated line, although some are using dial-up connections.

Independent bookstores ally themselves with Carrie's Books in order to benefit from the discounts associated with large corporate orders. Each independent site is run a little differently from all the rest and does not share real sales figures with anyone. All of the independent stores use a dial-up connection to connect to the corporate servers.

Into which of the geographic models does Carrie's Books, Inc. fit? Based upon the diversity of the network infrastructure and its distribution throughout the United States, this would qualify as a national environment.

Is each site a corporate, branch, or subsidiary office? This one is fairly easy. The five distribution centers are the only locations that Carrie's Books actually controls, and because they are critical to the company's day-to-day business, they would qualify as corporate sites. The CBI stores do not meet the criteria for corporate office status, but they are managed by the company's IS staff, so they should be considered branch offices. All other locations are controlled by outside management and would therefore qualify as subsidiary locations.

Scopes in Short

Knowing the complexity of a project, or its scope, will help you make decisions during the entire design process. First, you can make intelligent (and hopefully accurate) estimates of the costs and time involved. Second, an accurate picture of the environment can help you chose the personnel you will need on your project team. The design process has numerous phases (as were discussed earlier), and this physical and business model information forms the foundation upon which later decisions are made.

Gathering the Information

In the beginning of this chapter, we discussed the process of scoping a design project. What we didn't discuss is the information that you will need to gather to make your decisions. The rest of this chapter revolves around the types of information, the methods of gathering that information, and the analysis of the information needed to continue the design process. The information described in the next few sections acts as the foundation upon which the rest of the design process relies. As such, it is imperative that you spend the time to collect, collate, and analyze the physical and business environment before implementing Windows 2000 and Active Directory in any but the most basic of networks.

Microsoft
✓ *Exam*
Objective

Evaluate the company's existing and planned technical environment.

- Analyze company size and user resource distribution.

- Assess the available connectivity between the geographic location of worksites and remote sites.

- Assess the net available bandwidth.

Bandwidth Issues

One of the biggest issues facing wide area networks is limited bandwidth. The costs of connecting two (or more) locations can be outrageous. Knowing the physical limitations of your network infrastructure is the first step in a good AD design. Many, if not most, of the decisions you will make later will be based upon your knowledge of the wide area infrastructure.

The first step in "learning" the environment is to put together a wide area network map. This map should show all of the locations in your company and the links between them. Find out which vendor provides the lines, how much they cost, and how reliable they have been in the past. Talk to the network gurus to determine which vendors have provided the best service. A major change to the network, such as the upgrade or migration to Windows 2000, might be the perfect opportunity to optimize the network infrastructure.

When you are done, you should have an overall picture of how the network is laid out, as shown in Figure 2.7.

FIGURE 2.7   Infrastructure map

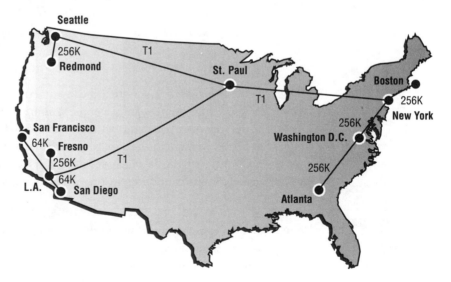

Over the years, we've all used all kinds of maps—everything from electronic atlases to hand-drawn "cocktail napkin" versions. The most intuitive for most people are probably paper-based maps. Almost every major city in the world has a map store—we buy new maps for every project and hand-draw the links on them. This is an opportunity for us to learn the environment (unlike using the auto-mapping software that does the work for you).

Once you've got an overall picture, if appropriate, break the network into regions. On the regional maps, label each link as shown in Figure 2.8.

FIGURE 2.8 Detailed WAN map

A map like that shown in Figure 2.8 can sometimes lead to an optimization of the WAN environment before implementation of the migration plan. One of the best services you can offer a client is to redesign the WAN links to provide better performance, more reliability, or lower costs. As consultants, we've found that it is in our best interest to have a general idea of the costs of various links from different providers in various regions.

No one (that we know anyway) has in-depth knowledge of every provider in every area. As consultants, though, we make it our business to know which vendors provide the best service at the lowest costs. There have been a few occasions when our suggestions for changing vendors has saved clients enough ongoing connectivity costs to pay for our design services—a win-win situation!

Bandwidth vs. Available Bandwidth

Once you've gotten your maps together, the hard work starts. The next step is to determine the available bandwidth on each link. *Available bandwidth* is the amount of bandwidth left after current traffic has been taken into account. There are many tools available on the market that can be used to measure the amount of traffic actually being placed on a network. If you are upgrading from an earlier version of Windows NT, tools such as Performance Monitor and Network Monitor are available. If you are migrating from some other operating system, you will have to determine what tools that OS has available. In some cases, you will need to purchase or lease hardware and software to gather this information. The easiest method by far is to use the services of your connectivity vendor. Almost every major provider in the market has the ability to give monthly, weekly, or daily reports that detail the network traffic crossing its lines. The biggest mistake you can make, though, is to trust this information implicitly. When you are measuring bandwidth, make sure that you do the following:

- Measure bandwidth at different times of the day. Bandwidth utilization often fluctuates throughout the business day. A wide area link that is carrying minimal traffic at 9:00 A.M. might be saturated during the across-the-wire backup being performed at 7:00 P.M. each day.

- Measure bandwidth at different points in the business cycle. A network that is saturated during the month-end reports might be underutilized during the rest of the month. Add information about network bottlenecks and periods of congestion to the detailed maps you made earlier, as shown in Figure 2.9.

FIGURE 2.9   Detailed Information

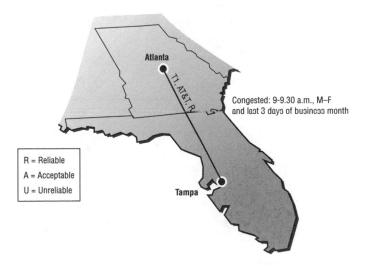

The information you gather during this design phase will help you make decisions about server placement, AD replication, AD sites and site bridges, and other services that the network will provide.

Analyze Each Location

Once you've got a handle on the bandwidth issues, you can turn your eye toward gathering site-specific data. At a minimum, you should know the following information about each location:

- Number of users
- Number and configuration of servers
- Number and configuration of client computers
- Specification of computers
- Network services utilized

We usually put together two sets of documents at this point in the design process: a general information sheet and a detailed listing for each location. A sample general information sheet is shown in Table 2.1.

TABLE 2.1   General Information for Company XYZ

Location	Number of users	Number of Client Computers	Number of Servers
Grand Rapids, MI	200	148	4
Tampa, FL	145	152	3
St. Paul, MN	53	40	1
Reno, NV	27	5	0
Payson, UT	12	17	3

We then put together a detailed analysis of each location. The following example shows the kind of information we include. Provide this kind of detailed list for each site in the company.

Grand Rapids, MI

Users   200
Client computers   148
Servers   4

Current implementation. This site represents a resource domain in the company's Windows NT 4 network. All user account information is managed by the central IS department in the corporate headquarters.

Users. The Grand Rapids location consists of a manufacturing plant and a distribution warehouse. Most of the staff is made up of non-knowledge workers. Any changes to the environment will be have to made slowly with adequate training to prevent downtime. There is no on-site IS staff for support during the migration process. The office staff (approximately 25 users) is connected to the Internet through an ISDN router.

Computers. Two basic configurations: manufacturing line and office staff. The manufacturing computers are older Pentiums with an average of 32MB of RAM. The office staff has newer, but not high-end, equipment. The average computer is a Pentium 166 with 64MB of RAM. All are currently using Windows 95 as their operating system and Office 95 as their productivity suite. No specialized software in is use.

Servers. One BDC of the master domain, one PDC of the local resource domain, two database servers that provide services to both manufacturing and administrative departments.

Other issues. The site has five HP5 printers, shared using Windows 95 printer sharing. Recently the target of a hostile workplace lawsuit based upon inappropriate material downloaded from the Internet. The database servers place a heavy load on the WAN link to corporate headquarters every evening. Backups are sporadic at best.

Suggestions for Grand Rapids before the upgrade:

- Ideally:
    - Upgrade all client computers to minimum Pentium 233 with 128MB of RAM.
    - Increase bandwidth on wide area link.
    - Purchase direct connect cards for all printers.
    - Provide one-day training to all users regarding the migration and its effects.
- Minimum:
    - Upgrade clients to Windows 98 for added stability. Begin purchasing higher-end computers that will support Windows 2000 Professional.
    - Merge resource domain with the master domain.
    - Apply latest service packs to all servers and applications running on them.

Analyze the Existing Use of Technology

So far, the information you have gathered for your design project has concentrated on the physical aspects of the existing network—WAN links, number of users, number of computers, available bandwidth, and so on. The next step is to take a look at the business process that uses this physical structure. This involves a lot of what we call "face time." You'll need to sit down with the IS staff and discuss their current environment. Be sure to include these topics in your discussion:

- IP addressing.

- Use of DHCP servers. Are they being used? Where are they? To whom do they lease addresses? Who manages them?

- Current DNS implementation. Has a domain name been registered on the Internet? Who manages DNS? What software is being used?

- Network and local operating systems in use. What are their versions? What service packs have been applied? Who manages them?

- Software distribution and update management processes.

- What server-based applications are currently being used? What are their versions? Who manages them?

- What client-based applications are being used? What are their versions? Who manages them?

- Current support staff, their experience and training levels.

- Review of all troubleshooting logs to determine current problems.

- What hardware standards are in place for client computers, servers, and other peripherals (including network components)?

In other words, find out what technology is currently in place, how it is managed (and by whom), and if it is working to their satisfaction. This is where you learn the environment. Take your time to get a good picture of what's in place.

Exam (and Real-Life) Hint: At this point, *fix all existing problems*! Microsoft—and our experience—suggests that you make sure everything is working before you make any major changes to a network.

Analyze the Future Technology Plans

For the MCSE Design exams, Microsoft is stressing your ability to analyze an environment and provide the best solution to the business needs of the company. Listening to what the company plans for the future can make this task quite a bit easier! If your client plans to open an e-commerce site on the Internet, for instance, you should certainly take that into account when planning network bandwidth needs, the number of servers, and any security policies you put in place.

This is one of the more difficult tasks in a design project. You must not only listen to their ideas, you must come up with ideas of your own that can improve their business. If, for instance, your client/company is currently using statically assigned IP addresses, you might want to suggest (and then justify) a move to DHCP services. If your client/company has a limited budget for hardware upgrades, you might want to suggest using terminal services to save money on client computer upgrades.

Unfortunately, there is no crystal ball approach to this process. Because every situation is different, you will have to take a different approach to each project. This is where your interpersonal communication skills will come into play. The most successful consultants we know are the ones who can sit down and talk to a client for a while and walk away with an idea of where the company wants to be three years in the future.

For the MCSE exams, you will be presented with case studies. The real skill needed for these kinds of questions is the ability to separate the important information from the fluff. The case study will describe a company and have quotes from various key personnel. Your job is to extract the business needs of the company out of the text and decide which technologies you would implement to fulfill those needs. (Basically, this is the same job that any good consultant does on a daily basis.)

Summary

In this chapter, we laid the groundwork for the rest of the design process. First we discussed the process of "scoping" the project to determine its complexity. There are three physical models and two business models used during this process: regional, national, and international geographic models and the branch office and subsidiary office business models.

We then looked at the information that you will want to gather before moving any further into the process of designing the Active Directory structure for the environment. The basic premise here is that the more knowledge you have about the existing network, the easier it will be to plan for the upgrade or migration to Windows 2000 and Active Directory.

Now that we've gathered the information necessary to fully understand the physical nature of the existing network, in the next chapter we will look at the business environment and its effect on Active Directory design.

Key Terms

Before you take the exam, be sure you're familiar with the following terms:

available bandwidth

branch office

business model

corporate office

geographic model

infrastructure

international model

national model

regional model

scope

subsidiary office

Review Questions

1. Which of the following best defines the purpose of scoping a project?

   A. To determine the exact number of servers that will need to be purchased

   B. To determine the complexity of a project to help in forecasting time and costs

   C. To determine exactly which service packs have been placed on each server

   D. To determine the training that will be necessary for each employee in the company

2. Which of the following aspects of a network would indicate a national rather than regional or international scope?

   A. Well-defined physical boundaries

   B. Dial-up connections

   C. Different connectivity vendors

   D. Language differences

3. Which of the following aspects of a network would indicate a regional rather than national or international scope?

   A. Well-defined physical boundaries

   B. Simple infrastructure design

   C. Language differences

   D. Mixed topology for WAN connections

4. Which of the following best describes the term "business model" as it pertains to AD design?

   A. An analysis of the marketplace for the company's products

   B. An analysis of the business relationships between locations

   C. A chart of the administrative strategy for the IS department

   D. A listing of the executive staff and their relationships to internal departments

5. Which of the following criteria would indicate that a location should be defined as a corporate office?

   A. It has a diverse client base.

   B. It contains multiple or special purpose servers.

   C. It acts as a hub for the network infrastructure.

   D. All business functions will continue normally if the site is unavailable.

6. Which of the following criteria would indicate that a location should be defined as a branch office?

   A. It does not have a diverse client base.

   B. It does not contains multiple or special-purpose servers.

   C. It acts as a hub for the network infrastructure.

   D. All business functions will continue normally if the site is unavailable.

7. Which of the following best describes the criteria used to classify a location as a subsidiary office?

   A. The office is defined as a subcontainer in the AD structure.

   B. The office is not controlled by the corporate headquarters.

   C. The office is a subset of the resources of an internal department.

   D. The office is subject to internal auditing on a regular basis.

8. Available bandwidth is best defined as _____ .

   A. The total bandwidth that the line is capable of carrying

   B. The amount of bandwidth available after current traffic has been accounted for

   C. How much bandwidth the connectivity provider is willing to sell you

   D. The cost per bit transferred on any given line

9. Which of the following are reasons to consider future technology plans when designing an Active Directory structure?

   A. Server placement could be impacted by user access patterns.

   B. Changes to your current technology could increase network traffic.

   C. It is easier to plan ahead than to redesign at a later time.

   D. Your design must include room for any growth to the environment.

10. The first thing to do when starting a design project is _____ .

   A. Address current problems and fix them

   B. Arrange for payment

   C. Install Windows 2000 and implement AD

   D. Discuss future plans for expansion with the IS staff

Answers to Review Questions

1. B. The scope of a project is a basic rating of its complexity. Knowing this helps you to accurately forecast the costs and time that will be involved in the project.

2. B, C. The criteria for a national scope are as follows:
   - Different speed dedicated lines (T1, 256K, 64K, etc.)
   - Dial-up connections
   - Different network topologies (ATM, Frame Relay, etc.)
   - Different connectivity vendors
   - Different hardware configurations (switches, routers, etc.)
   - Different levels of available bandwidth

3. A, B. The three criteria for a regional scope are as follows:
   - Simple infrastructure design
   - Well-defined geographic boundaries
   - No complex setup issues

4. B. The business model describes the relationship between sites in the network—corporate offices, branch offices, and subsidiary offices.

5. A, B, C. A corporate office is a permanent, business-critical location that has the following characteristics:
   - It has a diverse client base.
   - It usually houses multiple or specialized servers. (Often, branch offices do not contain any servers.)
   - It usually acts as a hub for the network infrastructure.
   - It provides access to company-wide data or services.
   - It usually houses the management staff of the company.
   - It acts as a key location for the company.

6. A, B, D. Branch offices are simple and do not offer services that are critical to the functioning of the rest of the company.

7. B. Subsidiary offices are not a part of the overall corporate resources. Usually, they will represent a partner company, a separate business division within the company, or a franchise site. The bottom line is that the corporate headquarters does not have complete control of the site.

8. B. Available bandwidth is the amount of bandwidth left after current traffic is accounted for.

9. A, B, C, D. Your design must include room for growth so that it is scalable to future needs of the company.

10. A. Microsoft suggests that all current issues be addressed *before* upgrading to Windows 2000. This helps to avoid bringing your problems with you during the upgrade.

Case Study: Rugged Gear

Take about 10 minutes to look over the information presented and then answer the questions at the end. In the testing room, you will have a limited amount of time; it is important that you learn to pick out the important information and ignore the "fluff."

Background

Rugged Gear is headquartered in Bozeman, Montana. It started out as a single store selling high-end camping equipment and supplies. In the 10 years it has been in business, it has grown to 8 storefronts (including the Bozeman site) and a growing catalog sales division. The owner, Tom, has developed a loyal base of customers from around the world—people who visit Montana on a regular basis to take advantage of the great outdoor activities. You've been hired to analyze the company's current system and suggest some alternatives to help it grow. Tom is open to technology and ready to expand his market.

Current System: Bozeman

Overview   The Bozeman facility covers three stories of one of the oldest buildings in the city. The administrative offices on the third floor have a 100MBps Ethernet network. Most of the desktop computers are Pentium-class computers with adequate RAM and disk space (Tom has just recently decided to move into the computer age). There are two NT 4 servers—one is dedicated to running the point-of-sale software (the inventory control database running on SQL Server), and the other handles all other network functions (printing, domain activities, and file server functions). There are 20 users on the system during normal working hours.

Owner   "The building itself has been designated an historical site, which limits the amount of physical changes that can be made."

CIO   "The store itself has four networked cash registers that feed sales information to an inventory control system running on an NT 4 server."

Current System: Butte, St. Regis, Helena

Butte, St. Regis, and Helena are the three biggest retails stores, and each has an identical IS configuration: one NT server that handles local functions and acts as a RAS server for a nightly dump of sales information to the inventory control system in Bozeman. All connections are made with 56K modems over normal phone lines. All cash registers dump their data into the local database, which is dumped to the headquarters database each night. Technology has never really been an issue with the retail stores. The recent addition of a catalog sales division has forced Tom to purchase new equipment and software.

Current System: The Four Other Locations

The four other retail locations (Paradice, Billings, Great Falls, and Missoula) are located within and managed by other retail stores. In Paradice, for example, the local hardware store has set aside a corner of its floor space for hunting and camping gear. Rugged Gear keeps these facilities stocked but does not manage pricing, employees, or any other aspect of the business.

Current Issues

Owner   "I'm hearing a lot of requests from customers who like our products but don't live anywhere near our stores. We're losing business to the big catalog and Web-based retailers."

CIO   "The dial-up solution was fine when we were smaller, but now we need better control over inventory and purchasing. The modem pool just isn't handling our needs."

Goals

Owner   "I know that we're going to have to spend some money on this project; I just want to know how much and when I can expect to see a return on our investment." (The company is looking for an estimate of the costs and time involved in upgrading its environment. Its major goals are to address the issues discussed earlier. After this is taken care of, the company would like to expand its business into the national or even international market.)

Security

Overview   At this point, Rugged Gear has no set security policies in place. Once it develops a presence on the Internet, though, Tom is worried about hackers entering his system illegally.

Owner   "These recent hacks into the big Web sites are really making me nervous. If we start doing business over the Net, I want my customers to rest assured that their orders, and especially their credit card information, is secure."

Fault Tolerance

At this point, Rugged Gear is small enough that a little downtime is acceptable. As it grows, Tom would like the Web site to be available 24-7.

Maintenance

Tom has no on-site support staff. Currently, all computer support is done by local "experts"—regular employees who understand technology—and a few consultants (these consultants are chiefly responsible for the SQL Server–based inventory program).

Performance

Owner   "No one dies if a sale takes a few extra minutes. We are people oriented here, and our customers don't even notice when our computers are down.

CIO   "In today's market of order-on-demand, a company cannot afford to be unaware of its inventory. We don't order items too far in advance, preferring to keep just a few of an item available. This helps us keep our inventory seasonal and made up of the latest gadgets available."

Funding

Tom sees the move to the Internet as the most important function for the next 12 to 18 months. He is ready to expend as many resources (within reason) as necessary to be successful in this new market.

Questions

1. What is the scope of this project?

A. Regional

B. National

C. International

D. Subsidiary

2. As what business model would the Paradice store be categorized?

A. Corporate office

B. Branch office

C. Subsidiary office

D. Regional office

3. How would you rate the complexity of this design project?

A. Straightforward

B. Medium

C. Difficult

D. Bring in the whole team—this one's going to take months!

4. Place the following tasks in the correct order.

Task	Task
	Replace the dial-up connections with dedicated (and more reliable) lines.
	Set up company-wide security policies.
	Install and configure a Web site.
	Purchase, install, and configure Windows 2000 Server.

5. To simplify the design process, you will try to group similar environments together. There are three types of offices in the Rugged Gear company structure: corporate, branch, and subsidiary. Move each location to the correct category.

Categories	Locations
Corporate	Billings
Branch	Bozeman
Subsidiary	Paradice
	Butte
	St. Regis
	Missoula
	Helena
	Great Falls

Answers

1. A. Although Rugged Gear plans to add Web-based services, the current environment is fairly simple and exists within a well-defined set of boundaries.

2. C. Because another company manages the Paradice location, it would be considered a subsidiary location.

3. A. There is nothing complex about Rugged Gear's physical business model. Most of the locations are either branch offices with similar layouts or subsidiary offices where the only concern is inventory control.

4. See table.

Task
Set up company-wide security policies.
Replace the dial-up connections with dedicated (and more reliable) lines.
Purchase, install, and configure Windows 2000 Server.
Install and configure a Web site.

Your first order of business is always to secure existing data. (It isn't mentioned in the case study, but you should also ask about backups at this point.) Once the environment is secure, you can move to improvements, such as better connections between locations. Installing Windows 2000 before creating the Web site makes sense because IIS is part of the OS.

CASE STUDY ANSWERS

5. See table

Categories
Corporate
Bozeman
Branch
Butte
St. Regis
Helena
Subsidiary
Billings
Paradice
Missoula
Great Falls

Based upon the fact that all ordering and inventory control happens in Bozeman, you can assume it is a corporate site. Based upon the amount of control Rugged Gear has over each of the other locations, you can divide them as shown in the answer.

Chapter

3

Analyzing the Business Environment

MICROSOFT EXAM OBJECTIVES COVERED IN THIS CHAPTER:

✓ **Analyze the existing and planned business models.**

- Analyze the company model and the geographical scope. Models include regional, national, international, subsidiary, and branch offices. (This topic is covered in Chapter 2.)

- Analyze company processes. Processes include information flow, communication flow, services and product life cycles, and decision-making.

✓ **Analyze the existing and planned organizational structures. Considerations include management model; company organization; vendor, partner, and customer relationships; and acquisition plans.**

✓ **Analyze factors that influence company strategies.**

- Identify company priorities.

- Identify the projected growth and growth strategy.

- Identify relevant laws and regulations.

- Identify the company's tolerance for risk.

- Identify the total cost of operations.

Coauthor Bob King relates this experience:

"Years ago, long before I discovered my 'inner geek,' I was working as a bartender/bouncer to put myself through school. I looked around me at the people having fun, the cash register overfilling, and the great music I got to listen to every night and said, 'This is what I want to do!' So when I got out of college, I took two full-time jobs and saved my money. It wasn't long before I had enough for a down payment on a little tavern/restaurant in Ladysmith, Wisconsin. I named it Bobbers and thought I was set for life.

"That tavern was my introduction into the life of a small business. I was really good at the basics of my job; I mixed a mean cocktail, chatted a great small talk, and even put together pretty good pool, dart, and softball teams. Unfortunately, I wasn't so good at managing cash flow, monitoring inventory, or counting the pennies for tax time. (That's what accountants are for, right?) The more I learned about being a tavern owner, the more I realized that business skills are key to success."

Guess what? The same holds true for what we do today (although we like to think that we're a bit better at it). Even though we're "technologists" at heart and make our living consulting on technical issues, the need for business skills keeps creeping back into our daily lives. When a client asks us what the best solution is for their environment, we immediately know that we can't make a recommendation without fully understanding their company's business environment. If, for instance, Company XYZ wants to create a Web site, we can't just say, "Sure, we'll install IIS and have you up and running in no time!" We need to gather a little more information first. We need answers to a lot of questions before we can give any kind of suggestions (let alone estimate the cost). These questions are among some of the first we'll ask:

- *Why do you want a Web site?* You'd be surprised at the number of clients who can't answer this question. The CEO read some article about the Web changing the way business is conducted and decided to get in on the action.

- *What should your Web site accomplish?* Is it just going to be used to inform potential customers about your products, or are you going to sell your widgets online?

- *How big is the market in which you do business?* How big are you in comparison to that? Are any of your competitors on the Web?

- *Are there any regulations that need to be taken into account when you promote or sell your product?*

- *What is your product's life cycle? In other words, how often will content need to be updated?*

- *Who will be responsible for long-term maintenance?*

- *What are your plans for growth?*

- *Do you have any business relationships with vendors or partners that we can take advantage of?*

- *Within the company, what is the priority of this project? Are there any budget constraints?*

NOTE We've actually had clients who got defensive about the number of questions we asked about the internal processes of their companies. We often ask questions that seem "personal" or "irrelevant to the project." The reality is that, the more information we have about the business, the better we can serve our clients. We now have a standard nondisclosure contract that we sign in front of our clients and give to them (explaining that we will be asking for information that shouldn't be made public). Getting that out in the open early in the process seems to help.

All these questions for the simple decision to move to the Web? Imagine the number of questions we'd ask if this were a major operating system upgrade—no, don't imagine, we'll be talking about that in this chapter! We once had a college professor who said, "Anyone can make decisions, but good decisions are only made by the well informed." Now that we've covered the physical side of the environment, we're going to move our discussion to the business side of the coin.

We'll start with a general discussion of the classic business models most commonly found in today's companies. After our discussion of the business models, we'll move to a discussion of the common business processes that influence an AD design. Understanding these models and processes can allow you to make some "cookie cutter" solutions that will work in most situations (with a few modifications to meet the specific needs of a client). The first few sections of this chapter will be a crash course on how businesses work. This information isn't taught in any of the Microsoft courses (although a few of the software developer courses come close), but it should be considered a prerequisite to the Design exams.

 This chapter includes a discussion of the objective, Analyze the existing and planned business models. However, the discussion will cover only the second subobjective, Analyze company processes. Analyzing the company model and geographic scope is covered in Chapter 2.

Once we've covered our "Business 101" information, we'll move on to a discussion of some of the specific business-related factors and management philosophies that will influence the design of an Active Directory structure.

Business 101

If you take a few courses in business management, you'll soon discover that no matter how diverse the economy, no matter how varied the products and services that are available, most successful businesses are organized along one of a few management philosophies. These philosophies, or *business models*, define the internal structures used to manage the complex interrelationships between the functions necessary to successfully conduct business. To put it more simply, a business model defines how work gets done. From a design perspective, knowing how work gets done allows you to design an Active Directory structure that matches (and maybe even enhances) the company's management structure.

Microsoft
Exam
Objective

Analyze the existing and planned organizational structures. Considerations include management model; company organization; vendor, partner, and customer relationships; and acquisition plans.

NOTE   Remember that one of your major design goals is to design an environment in which technology matches business rather than one in which business must change to match technology. If you ever utter the words "You *can't* do it that way because the system won't allow it," you need to reevaluate your design.

Microsoft defines four major business models:

- Departmental
- Project based
- Product/service based
- Cost centers

Each of these models represents a different way of looking at the same thing—the structure of a business. In reality, most businesses do pretty much the same stuff—accounts payable, accounts receivable, marketing, sales, and so on. What differs from company to company is the way these functions interrelate. The relationships between functions are what business models are all about.

When you're trying to determine the business model used by a company, a great place to start is with the company's organizational chart. Look at how branches of the chart are named and look at the chain of command. For each model, we'll provide a sample organizational chart to try to drive home the differences. Another great way to determine the business model is to listen to how management refers to processes, personnel, or projects. We'll also include a few examples of how management will refer to internal processes with each model.

In the case study exam questions, Microsoft will often include quotes from staff. Read these quotes carefully—not only do they give you clues about the company's business needs and goals, they also give hints toward the management philosophy of the environment. Knowing how the business is managed can help you determine which solution would be the best answer for the case study company.

Understanding the Departmental Model

The *departmental model* is the traditional method of managing a business. The basics of the departmental model are quite simple—look at the tasks that make up the business processes of a company, group them according to function, and manage each group. For any company (from a small tavern to a large international corporation) to be successful, certain tasks must be completed. These tasks can be grouped into departments. Some of the traditional departments include (but are not limited to) the following:

Accounting   Manages the money—both incoming and outgoing. They are usually also responsible for ensuring that the former outpaces the latter!

Marketing   Ensures that the public (or some portion thereof) knows about the company and its goods or services.

Sales   Convinces someone to actually buy a product or service.

Research and development   Defines the goods or services offered by the company.

Production   Makes the goods or performs the service.

Information services   Manages the hardware and software the computer environment comprises.

Most of us are quite comfortable with the functions performed by these traditional departments. This is what makes it an attractive business model—familiarity with function is built in. If you hire Katie to be a salesperson, you don't have to teach her what the accounting department does—she already knows (at least superficially).

Some businesses have departments that are specific to their function. If you were designing an AD structure for a city, for instance, your departments would probably include the standards *and* a few that are specific to city management, such as the following:

- Water works

- Sanitation

- Fire control

- Health and welfare

- Law enforcement

- Animal control

- Road construction and repair

Once again, though, the power of this business model is that the overall function (if not the specific tasks) for each department is well known. If there's a big pothole in the street in front of your house, you instinctively know which city office to call.

Understanding the departments a city government would have is a good example of the extra knowledge required to design an international network. The list of departments will often differ by culture.

The organizational chart for a company managed using the departmental model will be familiar to anyone who has worked for a large corporation, as shown in Figure 3.1.

FIGURE 3.1 A departmental organizational chart

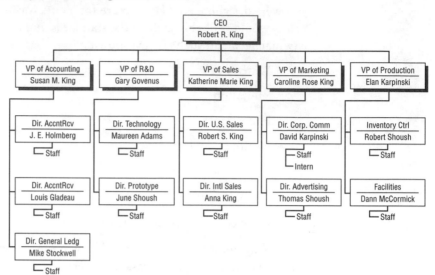

Discovering the management model in use for a company usually involves talking to upper management. You'll listen for clues in the way they reference business procedures. Ask for the organizational chart and then ask a few questions about the interrelationships between areas of functionality. If the chain of command is straightforward and it is easy to explain who reports to whom, the odds are the company is using a departmental management model.

Exam Hint: Many of the case study questions include quotes from different people within the sample company, but very few of the questions will include an organizational chart. You'll have to read the material carefully, looking for clues to these internal relationships.

Understanding the Project-Based Model

For quite some time, the *project-based model* was considered the "new age" of management. In it, the company is broken into small groups, or teams (to use the vernacular). Each team contains all of the resources necessary to support a company project. At first glance, this might seem like the same as the departmental model, but in the case of a project-based model, teams are "cross-discipline." In other words, a team might consist of research and development staff, accountants, marketers, and salespeople. For many years, this was seen as wasteful because you lose the advantages of centralized staff. (Think of it this way—if every project needs an accountant, you will probably need more personnel than if you had a centralized accounting group.) What has been discovered over the last few years, though, is that this management strategy is the fastest way to get goods or services to market. The advantages of having "content experts" working on a project often outweigh the additional costs. To put that another way, a company will often see faster results by putting together a team of individuals that are dedicated to a single project as opposed to having departmental staff that have to split their time among all projects.

From a management perspective, this is the most dynamic business environment. The project teams are constantly forming, reforming, and breaking up as projects are created, finished, or dropped. The chain of command is often disjointed—people report to project heads who often report to other project heads or upper management. These kinds of companies are often in industries in which the ability to make instant decisions is critical (many companies in the computer industry use the project-based business model).

To a consultant or inside staff administrator trying to create an AD structure, the project-based model can often be a nightmare to design for. The same dynamics that make this model good for cutting-edge businesses can make it difficult to design a stable directory structure. Your AD structure must be designed to take into account the constant reassignment of personnel and other resources.

As consultants, we will usually avoid a project-based directory structure for companies that do not have on-site IS support. The dynamic nature of the business model mandates regular changes to the AD structure—moving people from container to container, reassigning physical resources, and even constantly adding and removing OUs for projects. Because our major career is teaching, not consulting, we don't have the time to spend on-site performing these tasks.

Organizational charts for companies using a project-based management model usually follow one of two forms: matrix or free-flow. The matrix chart is basically just a spreadsheet that crosses references to projects and personnel, as shown in Table 3.1. Most such charts will also include a column (as shown) to indicate each person's skill set. This view is handy when individuals might be assigned to multiple projects.

TABLE 3.1 A Project-Based Organizational Matrix

Name/ Project	Expertise	Beef Dog Food	Tuna Cat Food	Dog Treats	Cat Treats	Pet Toys
Susan K.	Accounting	X				
Bob K.	Project Lead					X
Katie K.	Packaging	X				
Carrie K.	Design					X
Kodiak K.	Product Tester	X		X		X
Fluffy	Product Tester		X		X	X
Tom S.	Project Lead	X				
Robert S.	Project Lead		X			
June S.	Accounting		X			
Anna K.	Production	X	X	X	X	X
Elan K.	Purchasing	X		X		

As you can see, this type of organizational matrix is great for seeing who is working on what project, but it's not too good at portraying who reports to whom. The free-flow organizational chart is better at this, as shown in Figure 3.2.

FIGURE 3.2   A project-based free-flow organizational chart

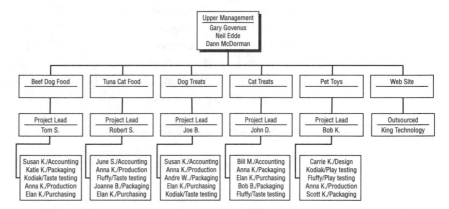

During your interviews with management, you will hear a few key words that will indicate a project-based model. If you hear things like the following, then it's probably a project-based model (we've made the key words bold):

- "Joe is working on the new widget **team**." (As opposed to Joe is "in production.")

- "Jane is **doing accounting for** the support **group**." (As opposed to Jane is "in accounting.")

- "Accounting **data is spread out** over multiple projects." (One of the worst aspects of the project-based model is that, because resources are dedicated to each group, information is often disjointed and distributed across multiple locations.)

Exam Hint: Watch for statements that contain key words in the case study questions—they'll clue you in to the management philosophy of the company.

Understanding the Product/Service-Based Model

The *product/service-based model* is quite similar to the project-based model. Once again, resources are dedicated to specific functions, but in this model, those groups are specifically organized to support whatever products or services the company sells. Companies that start out using the project-based model often mature into the product/service-based model. The organizational chart will look exactly like that of a company using the project-based approach except that the groupings will be by product or service rather than internal projects.

In Figure 3.3, we see a part of the organizational chart for a product-based environment. The only real difference between this and a project-based company is that the product lines might include product-based projects.

FIGURE 3.3 A product-based organizational chart

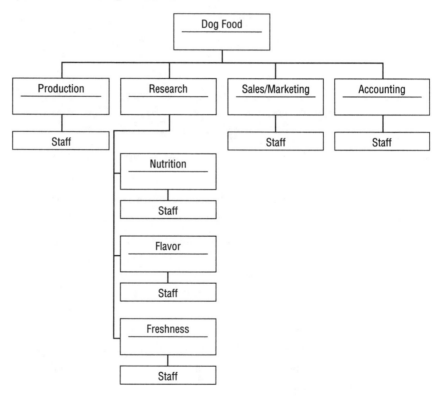

The biggest clue you'll get when interviewing management is that all references are made specific to a product or service. You might hear, for instance, something like the following:

- "Joe's working on the dog food team."

- "Our network integration division...."

Understanding the Cost Center Model

The *cost center model* is usually a hybrid of all of the other models. In this model, the functions of business are once again divided into groups—based on projects, products/services, or traditional departments—just as they are in the other models we have discussed. The big difference is in how those groups interact. Each group is seen as a separate business entity within the company. Groups charge each other for the services they provide. The IS department, for instance, might charge the sales department for server disk space usage or e-mail functionality.

We've found that this model is great for departments that provide intangible internal services, such as the IS department. No longer do these groups have to rely on the whims of upper management for their budget; they build their budget based upon the services they provide to other departments within the company.

From an Active Directory design perspective, this business model mandates some specific functionality—the most important is the ability to track and control the use of resources. The organizational chart can follow the format of any of the other models (departmental, project, or product/service). The clues to a cost center model will come during your analysis of information flow, funding, priorities, and growth strategies. (We'll discuss these topics later in this chapter.)

Analyzing Business Relationships

So far, we've concentrated on the internal business structure of a company. Because no business survives in a vacuum, we'll now expand our discussion to include the various forms of relationships that exist with "outside" entities—vendors, partners, customers, and acquisitions. In many legacy operating systems, you really don't have to worry about outside relationships because their focus is limited to internal resources. In Windows NT 4, for instance, whether a company has close ties with its vendors would have little (if any) impact on the domain structure. But in Windows 2000 (and Active Directory), these outside entities can have a large impact on AD design.

Analyzing Vendor Relationships

A few years ago, the term *vendor* really only referred to an outside company that provided services or goods to a company. Today, markets have shifted, and this shift has resulted in much closer relationships with vendors than existed even five years ago. In Bob's current position with Progressive Education Services (`www.ProgressiveEd.com`), he does business with a particular vendor; let's call it XYZ. The vendor has worked hard to build a relationship with his company because of the volume of hardware and software that he orders. Although this situation is great (it's nice to call a vendor and say "It's Bob" and have them know who you are and what company you represent), it would be nicer to have a closer relationship. Right now, Bob can access XYZ's Web site (with an authenticated logon) and access its part numbers and inventory. Its system is so advanced that Bob can access its inventory database through its Web page and find pricing and availability on its products. Progressive Education has built such a strong relationship with this vendor that they get faxes, e-mails, and phone calls for daily specials and new technologies. The point here is that the vendor has almost become another department of Progressive Education.

During your design considerations, you will have to consider ways to increase the effectiveness of the vendor relationship. Remember that the vendor is trying to sell to you (or your client), not the other way around. This puts you in the position of power. Any administrative work that can be placed at the other end will be good for your company. With this in mind, consider giving your vendors access to some of the information on your network. If, for instance, your company builds widgets and you purchase some of the widget parts from company ABC, why not give company ABC access to some of your shop floor data? It could be responsible for checking your production schedule to ensure that you have enough stock on hand. Active Directory is the perfect tool for granting access to some resources while protecting others.

From an examination perspective, Microsoft is pushing the cooperative aspects of AD. If your vendors are also using Windows 2000, it is easy to add their AD trees to your forest. If not, it is easy to set up a certificate server to allow secure access to resources across the Internet. Don't forget to consider other Microsoft products for your complete business solution. You might, for instance, want to use Exchange Server to create a series of public folders that can be used as a communication channel with vendors. Or you might think about using the filtering capabilities of Proxy Server to control access from certain IP subnets.

Exam Hint: The bottom line for analyzing vendor relationships is access to information. The more your vendors know about your needs, the better they will be able to serve them. Use the capabilities of Windows 2000 and Active Directory to grant that access!

Analyzing Partner Relationships

One of the keys to success in today's competitive markets is to partner with other companies. A *partner* can be defined as another business entity that exists as a separate company but works with your company to achieve a mutual goal. The biggest problem (until the release of Windows 2000) was controlling the flow of information between the two companies. Windows 2000 and Active Directory make it easy to tie two systems together and control access to confidential information while still allowing access to the information or resources that are necessary for the partnership to work. Once again, the analysis of the partner relationships should concentrate on shared resources. Consider all of the ways that Windows 2000 allows outside entities to access internal resources and use those capabilities to facilitate the partnership.

Analyzing Customer Relationships

Among the most important relationships that a business can build are those with its customer base. There are many ways to foster these relationships, and our job in IS is to offer technological solutions that help to sustain these relationships (one of the most important statistics in business is the number of customers who would do business with a company again or recommend the company to friends). When analyzing the customer relationships of a company, there are two questions you need to answer:

- What is the nature of the relationship with the customer base?
- What technologies can be used to increase these relationships?

There are as many types of relationships with customers as there are types of businesses. You need to analyze the amount of customer contact—both before and after the sale—the nature of those contacts (technical support, installation support, reordering supplies, etc.), and the frequency of contact. A dietary consultant, for instance, is in constant contact with his client base.

Those contacts would probably be either to ask a series of questions (How many calories are in a candy bar? Which vegetable has the vitamins I need?) or to purchase additional items such as books or packaged meals.

The nature of the contact will directly affect the technologies you might suggest to the client. A company in which the contact is mostly "conversation," such as a psychic hot line, would probably love a telephony product that ties into a contact database (something that would read the incoming caller ID and automatically bring up any information about the customer's former calls). A company that offers technical support, on the other hand, would probably benefit from a full-blown help desk package. In either case, match the technology to the type of customer contact.

You will also want to consider the technical sophistication of the customer base. It makes no sense to offer Internet support, for instance, if the demographics show that most of the customers do not own a computer.

Analyzing Acquisition Plans

If your company has plans to acquire or merge with other companies, you will want to ask some very specific questions. Your overall design strategy can be affected by the results of this type of growth. Ask about the process of integration between the two companies. Will the two companies be merged into one or will both companies continue to function as separate business units? Does the newly acquired company have a registered domain name? If so, will it continue to use it? (Remember that the Active Directory root domain name defines the scope of the name space—if the two companies need separate identities, you might be forced to create two AD trees and tie them together in a forest.) What new physical locations will be added to the WAN? (Don't forget to include them in the material you gathered during your analysis of the network infrastructure.) Is the new company using Windows 2000? If not, can you suggest a migration or will you have to deal with a heterogeneous environment? Which IS staff will be responsible for merging the two networks?

The bottom line for analyzing business acquisitions or mergers is to remember that you are, in effect, dealing with two separate companies. There will be political, cultural, and philosophical differences between the two businesses. Your job will be to wade through all of that and come up with the best technical and business solution available.

Design Scenario: Acme Shoe

The Acme Shoe company is headquartered in St. Paul, Minnesota. It has hired your consulting firm to design its move to Windows 2000—everything from installation and configuration to ongoing maintenance. Because you have the most business experience, you have been chosen to analyze the business environment so that the final AD design matches the way Acme Shoe does business. You've interviewed most of the upper- and middle-management employees and are now required to analyze the information you gathered and present it to the rest of the design team. Excerpts of the interviews include the following:

CEO   "Since we're not Nike or some designer label, we face a lot of challenges in the shoe market. We basically watch what the big guys are doing, design something close, and rush it to market. We've got a few traditional shoe designs that sell well year after year, but most of our market is in the trendy stuff that changes constantly. If you can't keep up with the fashion trends, you'll never make in our business."

CFO   "Each of our models has to stand on its own in the marketplace. Any shoe that doesn't sell well (and quickly) is yanked from our production line to make room for the next designer trend. We need a daily record of sales, both of our own products and of our competitors', to help us manage internal resources. If our running shoe, for instance, isn't selling, we need to immediately reassign those resources to another design team."

Manager of the running shoes line   "My guys have to watch the big companies constantly. Remember that shoe with the pump? We had a team together and a design in production within three weeks of their product hitting the market."

Accountant   "The hardest part of my job is keeping track of the profitability of whatever shoe I'm tracking. I not only have to track sales, I have to track production costs, design costs, returned products, everything that affects the bottom-line profits from a line of shoes. If a design is doing badly, I have to be able to know that immediately, and vice versa, if a product is doing well, I need to know that too. That's the fun part, since I get to push for additional production facilities."

Shoe designer   "We all make bonuses for the success of the shoe we are working on. If we design a shoe that sells like hotcakes, we make pretty good money. If you get stuck working on something that doesn't sell, though, you aren't going to get those year-end bonuses. I've been lucky so far—I've always been assigned to products that sell."

Based upon these remarks, what would you tell your consulting staff about the internal management of this company?

When determining the management model in use by a company, first eliminate the obvious. Notice that, in this example, no one mentioned any of the traditional business departments. We heard *about* accounting and *about* production, but we didn't talk to anyone *from* the accounting or production departments. Based upon this, we would remove the departmental model from the list of possibilities.

There are some key phrases used in these quotes that you will have to be able to pull out of a Microsoft exam question. The accountant says he keeps "track of the profitability of **whatever shoe** [he's] working on." The shoe designer says, "**We** all make bonuses for the success of the **shoe we are working on**." The CFO says, "Each of our models has to stand **on its own** in the marketplace."

You could argue for the project model, product/services model, or even the cost center model. In real life, any of these would probably work, but the best answer is the product model. The clues point to each individual working on one (and only one) product at a time—and that indicates a product-based management philosophy!

Analyzing the Internal Business Processes

Once you have gotten a clear picture of the general management model used within a company, you are ready to begin the in-depth investigation that is required to provide a true business solution. To do this, you'll have to analyze every aspect of the company's business—from funding to production and everything in between.

Analyze the existing and planned business models.

- Analyze the company model and the geographical scope. Models include regional, national, international, subsidiary, and branch offices. (This topic is covered in Chapter 2.)

- Analyze company processes. Processes include information flow, communication flow, services and product life cycles, and decision-making.

Exam Hint: Keep the ultimate goal—providing a complete business solution—in mind during your examination. The biggest problem people have with all of the Design exams is an inability to look at the big picture. Don't get so caught up in the technology that you forget to look for the customer's needs. (This advice helps in the real world too!)

Microsoft defines five main business processes that will have major impacts on AD design:

- Information flow

- Communication flow

- Services

- Product life cycles

- Decision-making

Achieving an in-depth understanding of each of these issues is critical to a good AD design. The analysis process itself is mostly a matter of interviewing key personnel and surveying groups of employees. On a large project, this process can take quite a bit of time and effort, but it pays off in an AD design that functions flawlessly!

Analyzing Information Flow

Information flow refers to the actual access of data. A typical company has numerous sources and types of information that is critical to the functioning of the business. For our purposes, let's define *information* as anything that crosses the network. Using this definition expands the analysis process but gives you a more detailed look at network traffic patterns—and *that* is what this section is really about. Most companies will have one or more of the following:

- Customer database(s)
- Sales information
- Marketing material
- Inventory database(s)
- Accounting data

Along with this "hard" data, most companies also have we call "soft information." *Soft information* is data that is not easily quantified or qualified. This would include the following:

- E-mail
- Web site content
- Call logs
- Contact information
- Miscellaneous documents (including everything from legal contracts to templates for marketing material)

Another type of "information" that is often handled by the network is software. Installations and upgrades are easier to perform across the network, and standards are easier to enforce. Many companies are moving back to the old school of moving applications from the desktop and storing them on the server (thus making upgrades, patches and fixes, and version control easier to manage). Another form of "information" that is becoming quite popular is the use of terminal services. Because terminal services are built in to Windows 2000 Advanced Server, it is safe to assume that more and more companies will be looking at this option.

The ultimate design goal of analyzing the information flow of an environment is optimizing the placement of that data and minimizing its effect on the network. To accomplish this, you'll have to gather a list of all of the information sources within a company, its current location, and who accesses it. From there, you can begin to think about moving data so as to reduce its impact on the rest of your network. From our experience, the best way to accomplish this is to build a set of matrixes, as shown in Table 3.2, that cross-reference information sources with users. This helps later, because it helps to define the group objects you'll want to create to within AD. Unfortunately, the process of gathering this information can be long and tedious.

One of the best parts of being an outside consultant is that you often get to skip the "tedious" stuff. Rather than paying the exorbitant hourly rate for a consultant to gather this information, most companies will have an internal employee do the legwork.

TABLE 3.2 Information Flow Matrix

	Customer List	Inventory Database	Sales Database	Accounting Information	Document Templates	Office 2000
Bob	X		X		X	X
Susan		X		X		X
Katherine	X		X		X	X
Caroline		X	X	X		X

For a large company with hundreds of users, this process is not feasible. For these types of environments, analyze the data access of a few key people in each department and then be prepared to deal with any issues during implementation. It can also be helpful to survey all employees a few times during this process—once at the beginning as you build your list of information sources and again when you are trying to see who uses which source. We've run across numerous examples where a large number of people are using a data source (such as a shared contact list or custom-made database) that management didn't even know existed.

Exam Hint: What you learn from your analysis of information flow can be used to provide a business solution. If the analysis shows redundant data entry, for instance, your solution might include a consolidation of data. (Microsoft loves this type of answer, especially if it involves the sale of a copy of SQL Server or Exchange Server!) Taking multiple Access databases, for instance, and moving them to a central SQL Server database can reduce traffic and provide central management.

It's always important to keep your goal in mind during each step of the design process, so let us reiterate—the goal of analyzing information flow is to control network traffic. You'll use this information when planning your server placement, when planning the placement of various services (PDC emulator, DNS services, DHCP services, etc.), when designing your site boundaries for AD replication, and even during design (or redesign) of the network infrastructure. Once you're done with the AD design, this information can be used to help choose and configure routers and other network components, purchase new servers, and even implement new software. In other words, in a real-life scenario, having a good grasp on information flow is critical to good administration, not just good design.

Exam Hint: If a Microsoft exam question starts discussing data sources and their location on the network, you can bet you'll be asked to analyze and optimize the information flow. All of the design issues listed in the preceding paragraph might be involved in the final answer.

It's been said that the phrase "Money is power" has changed to "Information is power." In any consulting work, whether it is an AD design or just an optimization of an existing network, one of the first questions we ask is, "Can you give us a list of all of the data sources on your network?" You'd be surprised at the number of times we get an answer from upper management and the IS staff (sometimes even they don't match), and then after investigation, we supply them with an entire list of information they didn't even know existed on their network. Or worse, we'll be talking with someone from marketing and they'll describe an information source that they would like to have created, and we'll inform them that accounting already has that data available. The latter problem is really one of communication flow (which is our next topic), but its roots start in information management. You can only manage information if you know what you have and where it is located—in other words, you have to analyze the information flow.

Analyzing Communication Flow

Once you have analyzed the information flow for a company, the next step is to analyze how that information is used. Here, once again, business knowledge rather than technical knowledge is key. First we should define the difference between information flow and communication flow. As we discussed in the last section, information flow refers to the actual access of data. *Communication flow*, on the other hand, refers more to the sharing of information and the free flow of ideas within a company. As such, it is both a physical aspect (who talks to whom) and a philosophical aspect (how much freedom of information exists) of AD design.

During your analysis of the information flow, you gathered a list of all of the data sources within the company. To analyze the communication flow, you must now start asking about how that data is used as information. The word *data* refers to a bunch of facts; *information*, on the other hand, refers to useful (and usable) facts. To visualize the difference, think about all of the databases and documents on the Internet. If there were no way of linking those resources, it would be data—good facts, but no real context. Now add a search engine and the HTML protocol. Suddenly, all of those documents and databases become useful—and the moment they become useful, they become information.

Start the analysis of communication flow by asking questions about who uses what data for what purposes. Create another matrix that lists all of the data sources, who maintains them, and who uses them, as shown in Table 3.3.

TABLE 3.3 Communication Flow Matrix

Data Source	Maintenance	Users
Inventory database	Purchasing	Purchasing, Production, Sales, Accounting
Customer database	Sales	Sales, Marketing

TABLE 3.3 Communication Flow Matrix *(continued)*

Data Source	Maintenance	Users
Sales figures	Sales	Sales, Accounting
Document templates	Marketing	Marketing, Sales
Price list	Accounting	Sales, Accounting
Vendor list	Purchasing	Purchasing, Production
Marketing material	Marketing	Marketing, Sales
Product designs	Research and Development	R&D, Production, Purchasing, Accounting
Software	IS	All departments

Once you've got a list of what we call the "hard" facts—who uses what—you must continue your investigation into communication flow by analyzing the "soft" facts. You need to ask about other types of information: Who uses the Web and what kind of content do they access? Who uses e-mail and how much mail is sent and received? Who uses the printers, what do they print, and how often? Is there a fax server, and if so, who uses it and how much? In other words, now you have to look at anything that might generate network traffic. For each of these "soft" network uses, you need to gather three pieces of information:

- Who generates it?

- How frequently?

- How much traffic does it create?

Once again, the goal of analyzing communication flow is controlling network traffic—what is generated and where it goes on the network. You'll be using this information extensively later in your design process.

Analyzing Services on the Network

By this time in your quest for the MCSE, you should be quite familiar with the various network services Windows 2000 can provide. You should understand the installation, configuration, and maintenance of DHCP, DNS, WINS, and all of the other network services available. Don't forget some of the "hidden" services, such as user authentication, AD replication, and proxy services. There are also numerous add-on services available—e-mail, system management, software distribution, and remote management. Each of these components provides a valuable service to your network. Each also comes with a price—in dollars, time, and/or network traffic. Those costs are what network design is all about.

This phase of the design process begins with an analysis of each service your network provides. The process can be divided into three steps:

- Isolate

- Re-create

- Extrapolate

First, isolate a test network so that your analysis isn't affected by other traffic on the wire. Second, re-create the traffic generated by the service. Use one of the tools provided by Microsoft (Performance, Network Monitor, Replication Monitor, etc.) to measure the amount of traffic the service generates. From this information, you can then extrapolate the impact of the service for as many users as necessary.

As an example, let's look at the traffic generated during the initialization of a DHCP client. The DHCP process generates four packets during initialization—Discovery, Offer, Selection, and Acknowledgment. Knowing this, you can then determine the amount of traffic that would be generated by 100 clients initializing—4 packets each times 100 clients equals 400 packets. You could get even more detailed if necessary, measuring the number of bytes involved and dividing your available bandwidth by that number. This should give you the number of computers that can initialize simultaneously. Of course, this isn't the whole picture yet. DHCP traffic is not the only traffic generated during client initialization. You will have to measure *all* traffic generated and extrapolate from that figure to see the true impact of client initialization.

Once again, the goal in analyzing the traffic generated by services on your network is to control that traffic. Knowing how many bytes or packets are generated by a given process might seem a bit extreme, but in the long run, you can use that information to control network traffic, decreasing the chance that network congestion will adversely affect network performance.

Product Life Cycles

Unfortunately, there are two ways to define the phrase "product life cycles": with an internal perspective and with an external perspective. When using the internal definition, it is the length of time the company's products or services are valid—in other words, the amount of time its products remain viable in the marketplace. Using the external definition, "product life cycle" can be defined as the length of time the environment is valid—in other words, the amount of time the environment will remain static (no hardware or software upgrade required). Both definitions are valid considerations during an AD design.

Remember the quotes from Acme Shoe company (presented in the design scenario earlier in this chapter)? For Acme, the short life span of its products created a very dynamic network. Each time a new shoe went to market, a slew of resources got assigned to that product. In the quick world of fashion, when the shoe was no longer selling, all of those resources had to be reassigned to other projects. This meant that objects within the AD structure would be moving from container to container on a regular basis—not the kind of AD structure you would want to design for a company with no internal IS staff (unless you are a consultant who sells hourly support). If, however, Acme has an adequate and experienced IS department, then a dynamic structure might be the best business solution.

We know that the Microsoft party line is that the AD design should *always* match or complement the internal processes of the business environment. This is a great theory, but it is not always possible in the real world. In our Acme Shoe company example, if Acme didn't have an adequate IS staff, we would probably go with a more geographic design, thereby limiting the number of changes to the AD database (people or physical resources might change projects, but they will probably stay in the same physical location).

More germane to our discussion is the external definition of product life cycles. We recently read that the average life span of software is down to about 18 months. That means that 18 months (on average) after you install a piece of software, an upgrade will be available, which in turn means that, if Microsoft follows the industry average, a significant change to Windows 2000 can be expected around July 2001. Scary, isn't it? Luckily, two factors influence this estimate:

- Operating systems usually have a longer life span than applications.

- Microsoft was years late in releasing Windows 2000, so maybe it'll be late with its next one as well.

Applications, on the other hand, offer no such exceptions. You can expect that the word processor you are currently using in-house will need to be upgraded within a year or so. This also applies to any other software you have installed. Luckily, Windows 2000 includes software publication as a core component of Group Policy, so upgrades should get easier and less time consuming.

Hardware is another story. There are vast numbers of processors being released, faster network components being brought to market, faster printers, better hard drives, more fault-tolerant servers—in other words, constant improvements are being made to the equipment we use on our networks. Keeping up is a losing battle. But we must keep up to remain competitive. Here, product life cycles are measured in days rather than months. A new computer is often outdated before you even open the box. As servers have become faster, more fault tolerant, and more reliable, IS experts are returning to the days of consolidated resources. Multiple servers are being migrated to one replacement server on a regular basis. Hardware upgrades should have a minimal impact on a well-designed network, but there will be times where the consolidation of services to a central computer will affect the availability of data and services.

Analyzing the Decision-Making Process

At some point in the design process, you will need someone to make a decision about some aspect of your proposal. This is true for both staff IS personnel and outside consultants. There is a theory in sales that basically says that you can't make a sale without talking to the decision-maker. This same theory holds true in network design—you'll never get a design approved unless you are talking to the decision-maker(s). This is the case with purchases of hardware and software as well.

Microsoft ✓ *Exam Objective*	**Analyze factors that influence company strategies.** ▪ Identify company priorities. ▪ Identify the projected growth and growth strategy. ▪ Identify relevant laws and regulations. ▪ Identify the company's tolerance for risk. ▪ Identify the total cost of operations.

We were recently involved with a company in which every proposal, no matter how small an issue, had to be presented to a committee. Each proposal had to include a business plan that outlined all of the alternatives available (and their advantages and disadvantages), a recommended course of action, at least one alternative course of action, a full estimate of total costs, and an ROI (return on investment) report that outlined the amount of time it would take for the proposal to pay for itself. The committee would listen to your proposal, accept your collateral information, and then discuss the options. At first we thought that this was the process for accepting input from outside consultants, but we later learned that *every* decision was made in this manner. Needless to say, we were frustrated from the outset of the job! Then we discovered that there was actually one person who said yes or no—the CFO. He listened to the input and suggested a course of action, and the committee almost always agreed to do things his way. Once we figured out the "secret," we were able to get decisions in a timelier manner. The point here is that, had we not looked beyond the committee (or our presentation), we would probably *still* be working on that project.

When Novell first came out with Novell Directory Services (NDS), there were certain limitations (which have since been corrected) that forced you to put together a good design *before* implementation. (We know this is a Microsoft study guide, but the theory of design is pretty much the same in both operating systems—bear with us.) We got involved in a project to design the NDS structure for a large health services company. We worked with the staff IS department to design a structure that would be stable, reliable, and easily extended to accept expected growth. We started off teaching the Net-Ware 4 courseware during the week and then "mentoring" them on the weekends to apply what they had learned to their own environment. Those weekends were a string of arguments. As a group, they were unable to agree on any standard design. Once we got done with our training/consulting contract, we left and they were supposed to finish the design and implement the migration. A few months later, we received a call from the director of the IS department, asking us to come in and create an NDS design for them. They had argued for months (and a couple of upgrades to NetWare 4), and the design they finally came up with was obsolete before they implemented it.

There are numerous factors that can influence the decision-making process within a company. Some are political, some are legal, and some are financial. Before you begin, you should analyze these factors to see what effect they will have on your final AD design. You wouldn't, for instance, suggest 50 new servers to a company that has a tight budget for the project or plan for 128-bit encryption for a company that has offices overseas.

Company Priorities

We in the IS industry tend to think that we are the center of the world (after all, everyone comes to us for answers), but the reality is that the migration or upgrade to Windows 2000 might be only one small project in the scheme of things. In any given company, at any given time, there are probably numerous projects in the works. We recently worked on the directory design team for a company that was dealing with the following issues simultaneously:

- Planning an upgrade to Windows 2000
- Finishing their ISO9000 compliancy testing
- Moving from a legacy e-mail package to Microsoft Exchange Server
- Setting up Internet access at every desk
- Designing an e-commerce Web site
- Checking for Y2K issues at every client computer

Our design project was definitely *not* at the top of the list. We had numerous problems gathering the information we needed to complete a good AD design—either personnel were not available, or that part of the network was undergoing changes so the information would not be valid in a couple of weeks, or some other issue would come up and the design team would be split up to put out IS fires. We had committed the cardinal sin of consultants: we believed that our project was the most important project going on, when in reality, internal politics made the e-mail upgrade the hot ticket.

Find out what is going on within the company and how important each project is in the scheme of things. Knowing that your design is considered a low-priority project can help you to plan deadlines and person-hours, and plan for changes of direction in the process. (There's nothing worse than getting halfway through a project only to have it canceled due to a lack of interest.)

Plans for Growth

We were recently involved in the design of a network for a company that was moving from one facility to another. We got to design the network from the wiring on up—not only was it fun, it was satisfying as well because the company accepted just about every suggestion we made. We set up the network, configured the workstations, and moved the 200 users to the new location. Only then did we find out that another business in the new building was planning to buy out the company and the move to the new facility was made to ease the transition. Now our network that was designed to easily support 200 users would have to support over a thousand users. Luckily, we had planned for a little growth, so all we had to do was move a few servers to reposition the services they provided. This *could*, however, have been a major problem had our design not been flexible. Always discuss the future of the company. Ask about mergers, acquisitions, and even if the company might be sold. Each of these factors can, and will, influence your AD structure.

Even the normal growth that occurs in a healthy company must not be taken for granted. Look at the past few years' revenue: Has the company's revenue grown each year? If so, does there appear to be a pattern? How many new employees has the company hired in the last few years, and again, is there a pattern? In a retail business, for instance, what happens when a new store is added to the company? What is the average number of new employees, what hardware and software is involved, what WAN links are added to the infrastructure? Is there a seasonal growth in business that should be taken into account? Progressive Education Services did some work for a couple of ski resorts at Tahoe. We were making changes during their slow season (summer) but had to plan for the additional overhead that would be added to the network once the ski season opened.

Companies often have a set of goals for growing their business—10-percent increase in sales, one new location each quarter, or even an additional five employees each month. Ask about growth goals and the strategies that exist to handle the additional network overhead. During your analysis of the management model and the business procedures, consider how these things would change given a 10-percent growth in staff.

Laws and Regulations

Throughout the world, there are laws and regulations that govern how business can be conducted. Some of these laws and regulations are so obscure that they are virtually unknown. We were working with a small company in Germany recently that drove this fact home. The company had a typical central management policy for all IT resources, including databases. We set them up so that all user information was managed from that central site. Only later did we find out about the German law that prohibits employee personal information from being managed from another state. In other words, we had set them up so that users were managed from the company's main location in Europe—located in Amsterdam—and that was illegal in Germany. The only way to get around the law was to have every employee sign a waiver allowing the administrative staff to manage personal information. The moral of this story is that you must be confortable with the local laws and regulations when creating a business solution.

This can be fairly easy if you always work in the same basic location—if for no other reason than repetition, you will soon know the regulations for your area. If you travel, though, this changes. We almost always bring in local consultants to look over physical aspects like cabling or electrical work. For the business side, we will either rely on the staff at the company or, once again, bring in a local consultant to look over our proposed design. Although this adds to the original bid, it saves time and money in the long run.

Risk Acceptance Level

In business, as in life, there are different tolerances for risk. We're the kind of guys who will jump out of airplanes or dive deep to meet a shark face-to-face, but we have friends who get nervous driving over the speed limit (not that we would ever do that!). There are some businesses that are willing to take big risks in the hope of big gains, just as there are businesses for which risk is a four-letter word. How much risk a company is willing to take will certainly have an impact on your design process. A low-risk company will be best served by a slow, methodical approach to the migration to Windows 2000 and Active Directory. You'll have to set up *every* contingency in a test lab before moving into a production environment. A high-risk company will be more willing to move Windows 2000 into its production environment and work out the bugs (oops—deal with the opportunities that present themselves) as they appear. We've found that the best approach is usually somewhere in the middle—put together a test lab, and practice, and then pick an area or department to act as the proving ground for your procedures.

From a design perspective, knowing the risk tolerance of a company helps in creating the project schedule (the lower the tolerance, the longer the project will take) and in budgeting (the lower the tolerance, the higher the cost). It can also help you to determine the level of fault tolerance that should be implemented. Windows 2000 Advanced Server, for instance, includes clustering capabilities that reduce downtime due to equipment failures. Or you might want to configure redundant WAN links between sites to ensure reliable communication.

Funding

In Bob's office, there is an old poster that hung in his father's transmission shop. It reads, "We can give you two out of three: Good, Fast, or Cheap!" Bob's dad used to call it his first law of business physics. Whenever we have a client that wants all three, we have to remind ourselves that not everyone has a background in "physics." The rule holds true for every aspect of business—including AD design. During your analysis of the business environment, you will have to find out which two the client is expecting. Not surprisingly, most clients want all three.

Budgeting a design project is tricky business: ask for too much and the project gets canceled (or in our case, some other consultant gets the job); ask for too little and your funding runs out before the project is finished. Microsoft's dream is that every AD design will provide a complete business solution for the client. The reality is that funding often determines how much of the dream you can provide. One of the skills that Microsoft expects you to demonstrate in the Design exams is the ability to prioritize tasks. Given a budget and a prioritized list of goals, you can then determine which goals can be met now, which should be deferred until later, and which are just not realistic given the current business situation. Funding will play a large role in making these decisions.

There are many costs involved in running a business. *Hard costs*—such as payroll, rent, insurance—are easy to budget for because they usually do not change over time. Given a list of hard costs, it is easy to budget for a month, a quarter, or even a year. There are other costs that are not so easy to budget for, sometimes referred to as soft costs. *Soft costs* include time lost due to server downtime, person-hours lost due to sick leave, and any other costs that are variable over time. Soft costs are much more difficult to budget for. When justifying the expense of an upgrade or migration to Windows 2000, you must include the savings in both hard costs and soft costs.

Earlier in this chapter, we stated that Microsoft is expecting MCSE candidates to show business skills as well as technical skills. Creating (and then justifying) a budget for a design project is one of those skills. Many of us (technologists) have never really taken the time to learn the process involved in budgeting. (Many of us have actually avoided this aspect of information services.) We don't know how many times we have heard someone say, "Can't do it, not in the budget." There are times when this is an accurate description, but more often than not, this is a statement made by someone who doesn't know how to justify costs to upper management.

Budget creation should start with an overall analysis of the company's finances. What are the total costs of running the business? What percentage of that amount is the IS budget? Have IS costs been increasing over the last few years? How about overall costs—does it cost more to keep the business running today than it did last year or the year before? Break down the overall cost of operations by department—which departments cost the most? In each department, break down the costs of business processes. Analyze the procedures involved in "doing business." What does it cost to produce one widget (or whatever product or service the company produces)? What does it cost to generate one invoice? What expenses are involved in maintaining the inventory database? Ask about the help desk—what is the average time to close each trouble call?

The goal of compiling this list of business expenses is to determine if a move to Windows 2000 can be economically justified. Spend some time thinking about each of the processes in the business model—exactly how is an invoice generated, and can the process be streamlined through the use of technology? Why does the company have such a large inventory? Would a better production control system provide better order-on-demand options? How often were the servers down last quarter, and what can be done to reduce the impact (or better yet, reduce downtime)? Look at every business cost to determine if a feature of AD can reduce it.

This philosophy of providing business solutions rather than technology is a paradigm shift in how Microsoft wants to present its products. Each of the Design tests will emphasize the skills necessary to analyze the business needs of a environment.

Summary

In many ways, this chapter was more about questions than answers. The real trick to AD design is in knowing which questions to ask. If you ask the right questions, you'll have gathered the information necessary to successfully design an AD structure. For your MCSE exam, knowing which questions to ask will help you focus on the relevant information and ignore the fluff. The case studies in the Microsoft tests are getting more and more complicated; you are often inundated with information, only some of which is relevant to the question. Asking yourself the questions we discussed in this chapter will help you determine the real business needs of the case study company.

When analyzing a business, always start with the basics. First determine the business model (departmental, project, product/service, or cost center) used to manage resources. Then look at each of the main business processes (information flow, communication flow, network services, product life cycles, the decision-making process, and funding) to determine its effect on your design project. The process of analysis has three goals:

- To determine the business needs of the company

- To determine how Windows 2000 and AD will help fulfill those needs

- To provide the background information necessary to make good decisions later in the design process

Notice that the second goal does not say "*if* Windows 2000 and AD" can help fulfill those needs. In real life, there might be situations where Windows 2000 is not the best solution. On your exam, however, it's a good bet that Windows 2000 will always be the appropriate answer!

The information gathered in your analysis of the physical and business environments will be used in the rest of the design process. Spending the time to gather all of the facts early will facilitate your decisions later—starting in the next chapter! From now on, each chapter will cover a more specific aspect of an AD design. In Chapter 4, we discuss the IT department—the current environment, the planned environment, and the impact of AD on the services it provides.

Key Terms

Before you take the exam, be sure you're familiar with the following terms:

business models

communication flow

cost center model

departmental model

hard costs

information flow

product/service-based model

project-based model

soft costs

Review Questions

1. A business model is _____ .

   A. The marketing plan for a product line

   B. A document used to apply for a business license

   C. A definition of the management philosophy of a company

   D. The wiring schematic of a network

2. The CEO of a company says, "Accounting has all of the figures you have asked for." Which business model do you suspect is used within the company?

   A. Departmental

   B. Project

   C. Product/service

   D. Cost center

3. The CEO says, "The group working on the new chewing gum flavor needs a color printer to make camera-ready art for the packaging." Which business model do you suspect is in use within this company?

   A. Departmental

   B. Project

   C. Product/service

   D. Cost center

4. The CIO says, "Last year, half of our IS budget was provided by the accounting department." Which business model do you suspect is in use within this company?

   A. Departmental

   B. Project

   C. Product/service

   D. Cost center

5. Which business model is least suited for a company with little or no internal IS staff?

   A. Departmental

   B. Project

   C. Product/service

   D. Cost center

6. Two companies, both of which have a readily recognizable brand name and a well-established Internet presence, decide to merge. Which of the following statements are true?

   A. Your best design is probably a multiple-tree AD structure combined into a single forest.

   B. Your best design is probably a single AD tree with multiple NT domains.

   C. You should immediately merge the two Web sites into one, using the registered domain name of the larger company.

   D. You should design two AD trees with no consideration for interaction.

7. Which of the following should be considered when planning for the physical location of your data sources?

   A. Available bandwidth

   B. Which users access the data

   C. The communication protocols in use on the network

   D. The configuration of the server that will host the data

8. When planning server placement, you should _____ .

   A. Place servers on the least trafficked network segments.

   B. Look at the services that the servers provide and place each server near the users who will access it.

   C. Place the servers near the employees who will manage them.

   D. Place the servers on the corporate backbone.

9. For a client that has a low tolerance for risk, which of the following statements are true?

    A. Migrate all servers to Windows 2000 immediately so as to limit the time involved.

    B. Plan a migration that is done in small steps so as to limit the effect of possible problems.

    C. Do not migrate to Windows 2000 until service pack 2 is available (most of the bugs are worked out).

    D. Do not discuss potential problems with management to avoid scaring them.

10. Company XYZ has analyzed its IT budget and discovered that over 80 percent of the budget is consumed managing the desktops of users—adding software, fixing user configuration mistakes, and implementing security. They estimate that they are losing thousands of dollars in business because desktop computers are unavailable while the user waits for an member of the IT staff to find the time to fix these issues. Which of the following upgrade/migration paths would best serve the needs of this company?

    A. Migrate all servers and workstations to Windows 2000 immediately so as to limit the time involved.

    B. Plan a migration that is done in small steps so as to limit the effect of possible problems.

    C. Do not migrate to Windows 2000 until service pack 2 is available (most of the bugs are worked out).

    D. Do not discuss potential problems with management to avoid scaring them.

(The answers to the questions begin on the next page.)

Answers to Review Questions

1. C. Business models define the relationships between groups within a company.

2. A. The CEO implies that there is a group of people whose job is handling the accounting needs for the company.

3. C. The CEO implies that resources should be given to a group working on a specific product.

4. D. This statement implies that IS "charged" or in some other way gathered funds from another internal department.

5. B. The basic structure of a project-based management model is dynamic. When projects reach completion, personnel and other resources are reassigned to other areas. This results in an AD structure that requires constant support.

6. A. Whenever a merge occurs between two companies, you need to analyze the impact of changes to their environment or their existing customer relationships. In this case, because both companies have readily recognizable brand names, you should avoid changes without good reasons.

7. A, B, D. When planning for the placement of data sources, you must consider the network traffic that will be generated during access and the proximity of the data to the users who will actually access it. You must also consider the overhead that access will place on the server hosting the data source.

8. B. Always place servers near the users who will access them.

9. B. Although some people might argue for answer C, the Microsoft solution is to plan for a slow migration so as to limit potential problems.

10. A. In this case, the costs of not acting quickly are greater than the costs of mistakes made in implementation. Once the company has moved to Windows 2000, you will be able to implement policies that limit the users' ability to make changes at their workstations.

Case Study: Stupendous Software

Take about 10 minutes to look over the information presented and then answer the questions at the end. In the testing room, you will have a limited amount of time; it is important that you learn to pick out the important information and ignore the "fluff."

Background

Stupendous Software produces a well-known manufacturing control software package that holds the largest market share in its class worldwide. The software is written in the United States, duplicated by a company overseas, and packaged by another company in the U.S. Given the technical nature of its product, one would assume that Stupendous Software is a hotbed for the latest products that the computer industry has to offer. Surprisingly, the opposite is true. Its internal network does not cover its entire facility, many employees do not have computers on their desk, and the applications they are using are, for the most part, out-of-date.

Problem Statement

Director of Marketing   "Basically, we sell one large application and a series of add-on components to provide additional functionality. Our main application is designed to control the flow of materials from inventory to production. Proper use of the product can eliminate the costs associated with overstocking but at the same time ensure that the production line is never stopped due to lack of parts. Most clients see a return on investment for the purchase of our product in under three years. We also sell a series of applications that can link our inventory control databases to purchasing, sales, and even payroll. The bottom line is that we can provide a complete turnkey manufacturing package for just about any type of manufacturing environment. On the flip side, though, there are other packages out there, so we can never rest on our laurels. Competition is tough, and losing a single client can have an domino effect that could kill us. The real key to our success is our support personnel—they handle customer support calls quickly and efficiently. We market the heck out of their services."

Director of Product Development "The hardest part of my job is ensuring that each component is written so that it integrates seamlessly into our main inventory control package. We have various areas of expertise represented within our programming staff—database development, accounting system development, human resources, every department of a traditional business. Our guys mostly work on a single package, so they often do not really know what the other components are capable of. Most of our communication between development groups is done through e-mail. We'd like to improve the functionality in that area to help us stay in touch. The word from upper management is pretty simple—nothing leaves our company unless it is as close to perfect as possible! As our product gets more sophisticated, we need to collaborate more and more to ensure interoperability between components."

CFO "Our business is really job control software, and we don't have a lot of internal expertise in the accounting side of software development. Last year, we partnered with Dollars R Us to bring in a high-end accounting package to our suite. The partnership has been so successful that our two businesses have become "sister companies"—they sit in on our developmental planning sessions and we sit in on theirs. I'd like to see better communication between the two companies; we've had a few issues about sales figures and development costs. Another problem I've got is bringing all of the accounting information together from each product team. We need better communication amongst ourselves so that we can get a better handle on our profitability."

CEO "This is a privately owned and managed company. I started the firm with $500 in my pocket, five years' experience working in the manufacturing realm, and some ideas. Now, seven years later, we're the biggest supplier in the business! We learned quite a few valuable lessons in those first years, two of which form the basis of our mission statement. First, never, *never* release software that isn't ready! And second, customer support is what separates successful software companies from the not so successful. When it comes to changing our IS system, we cannot afford a moment's downtime! Missing one sale, or one help-desk support call, is an unacceptable situation."

CIO "Our company has more technical employees by percentage than any other company I've ever worked for. Over 60 percent of our staff is dedicated to designing, writing, or supporting our software! Up to now, we've gotten by using local experts to support the network, but with the advent of the Internet and our sales pushing into the millions of dollars a year, I'm not sure how much longer we can go without increasing our IS staff. Right now, I've got myself and two other people to support our entire IS environment. That's why we brought you in—we don't have the time or experience to design a better system."

Questions

1. What business model best describes the internal management of Stupendous Software?

   A. Departmental

   B. Project

   C. Product/service

   D. Cost center

2. When creating the AD structure, which business model would you follow?

   A. Departmental

   B. Project

   C. Product/service

   D. Cost center

3. You have been asked to help update Stupendous Software's customer support infrastructure. Currently, support representatives simply e-mail each other when new issues arise, and each user stores all support messages in their inbox for future use. Which of the following options would you recommend to help them more efficiently store and search support information?

   A. An Internet support site to handle simple questions and provide software updates

   B. An Exchange public folder application that allows support reps to store and retrieve case information

   C. An MS SQL support database with a help desk front-end application

   D. Continuing with the e-mail–based support structure currently in place

4. Rank the following in order of importance.

Task	Task
	Create a closer tie with Dollars R Us.
	Streamline the process used to move new products from development to production.
	Ensure that the migration to Windows 2000 does not affect the business.
	Suggest technology that can improve communication between departments.

5. Listed below are some of the business solutions you may wish to implement for Stupendous Software. For each option, determine which type of software would be needed from the list of suggested software, and drop it in the appropriate section in the outline of business solutions.

Business Objective	Software Options
Create a corporate intranet.	MS Proxy Server
Enhance Internet services and management.	MS Outlook Remote Mail
Provide remote access to LAN resources.	MS FrontPage
Centralize access to customer and accounting information.	MS Visual Interdev
Enhance workflow and collaboration options.	Virtual Private Network
Maximize network uptime/ protecting data.	Backups, backups and more backups!!!
Increase integration with partners.	MS Exchange Public Folders

	RAS Services
	MS Exchange Chat Service
	Clustering technology
	MS Internet Information Server
	MS SQL Database Server
	Windows 2000 Trusts
	MS Exchange Calendaring
	Exchange Site Connectors
	Network Monitor
	MS Access as an SQL Client
	MS Exchange NNTP connector
	Uninterruptible Power Supply (UPS)
	PC Anywhere
	Server Mirroring
	RAID controller

CASE STUDY

CASE STUDY ANSWERS

Answers

1. C. Both the CFO and the director of product development give hints to a product-based business model. The director of product development says most of the employees work on one component, and the CFO says that the accounting information is tough to gather from the various development teams.

2. A. First eliminate the obvious—this is not a company in which the cost center model is used for management. There could be an argument for either the project or product model (mostly product because that seems to be the way management views the company), but neither of these would be acceptable in a company with such a small IS department. That leaves you with the departmental approach, even though it does not match the internal management philosophy of the company.

3. C. To make the data easily available, it is probably best to have the information stored in a database. Due to the statement of the CEO that uptime is critical, an Access database is probably not sufficient. Once this database is in place, using an Internet link to make it searchable by customers or leveraging Exchange public folders may also be extremely helpful, but neither is a full solution as a support database would be.

4. See table.

Task
Ensure that the migration to Windows 2000 does not affect the business.
Suggest technology that can improve communication between departments.
Create a closer tie with Dollars R Us.
Streamline the process used to move new products from development to production.

Listening to the comments made, it is apparent that downtime is unacceptable. A slow migration over time will be the best approach. Once that is done, you can begin to suggest technologies to address other issues, such as communication between departments and with Stupendous Software's sister company. Because they did not mention any problems with production processes, improvements to these aspects of the business should be a lower priority.

5. See table

Business Objective
Create a corporate intranet.
MS Internet Information Server
MS FrontPage
MS Visual Interdev
Enhance Internet services and management.
MS Proxy Server
Network Monitor
MS Exchange NNTP connector
Provide remote access to LAN resources.
RAS Services
PC Anywhere
MS Outlook Remote Mail
Centralize access to customer and accounting information.
MS SQL Database Server
MS Access as an SQL Client
Enhance workflow and collaboration options.
MS Exchange Public Folders
MS Exchange Calendaring
MS Exchange Chat Service

Maximize network uptime/protecting data.
RAID controller
Uninterruptible Power Supply (UPS)
Clustering technology
Server Mirroring
Backups, backups and more backups!!!
Increase integration with partners.
Windows 2000 Trusts
Exchange Site Connectors
Virtual Private Network

There are, of course, a number of other vendors out there making databases, e-mail software, and other software that you may prefer to those mentioned. That's fine in the real world, but for Microsoft certification, you should clear all non-Microsoft products from your cranium! Also, you may have placed some of these products in other locations (backup, for instance, could go in any of these areas).

Chapter

4

Analyzing the IT Environment

MICROSOFT OBJECTIVES COVERED IN THIS CHAPTER:

✓ **Analyze the structure of IT management. Considerations include type of administration, such as central or decentralized; funding model; outsourcing; decision-making process; and change-management process.**

✓ **Evaluate the company's existing and planned technical environment.**

- Analyze performance requirements.
- Analyze data and system access patterns.
- Analyze network roles and responsibilities.
- Analyze security considerations.

✓ **Analyze the impact of Active Directory on the existing and planned technical environment.**

- Assess existing systems and applications.
- Identify existing and planned upgrades and rollouts.
- Analyze technical support structure.
- Analyze existing and planned network and systems management.

In Chapters 2 and 3, we did a high-level analysis of the physical and business environments into which Windows 2000 and AD will be installed. Before we can begin to discuss the technical aspects of an AD implementation, we have one more environment to analyze—the IT department. Once again, we will stay at the overview level in our discussion. At this point in the design process, you are still gathering information to help you make wise decisions during later discussions. Some would argue that the IT department is just another business group and therefore should have been discussed in Chapter 3. We have two good reasons for isolating the IT department for analysis. First and foremost, given the nature of this text, Microsoft separates the information technology department in the exam objectives. As you can see in the list at the beginning of this chapter, there are a series of exam objectives focused on analyzing the technical environment of a company. Second, the IT department is not just a consumer of IT services, it also provides them. Because it is the IT department that will be supporting the final implementation of Windows 2000 and AD, it is important to have a firm grounding in the current and expected IT department.

In this chapter, we will begin with a discussion of the AD design considerations that are specific to the IT department. Once again, because it will manage the final Windows 2000 network, it is important to understand the specific management philosophy of the IT team. You'll want to understand the skill sets available, how funding is obtained (and maintained), what services are currently outsourced, and how decisions are made.

Once you have an understanding of the IT structure, you can move to a more specific analysis. We'll begin by discussing the current environment—what works, what doesn't work, and who does what within the department. We'll also consider any special needs that are mandated by the business, such as advanced security or specific services.

After you've analyzed the current environment, you can begin to make suggestions about implementation. We'll look at how the implementation of each technology you suggest will affect the current environment. If, for instance, it is decided to manage all applications as AD objects, we'll look at how this will change the current method of application management.

Administrative Considerations

Before you can begin the process of suggesting and implementing new technologies (or even business procedures), you must have an understanding of the department that will implement those suggestions—IT. How the IT (information technology) department is managed is critical to many of the issues we will be discussing in later chapters. Once again, this chapter's main focus is gathering information that will be used later in the design process.

We've had a few students get frustrated by the amount of time spent discussing "theory and fact finding." If you are beginning to wonder when the discussion of AD technology will begin, all we can say is that the facts you gather now will make your job immeasurably easier later. While Bob was working at Novell, he had a hand in the rollout of its NDS Design course. He found that, if adequate information was gathered prior to sitting down to design the directory structure, the final structure would not only be stable (and optimized), it would also be almost identical from student to student. In other words, adequate analysis will almost lead you by the nose to a good design.

Microsoft
Exam
Objective

Analyze the structure of IT management. Considerations include type of administration, such as central or decentralized; funding model; outsourcing; decision-making process; and change-management process.

Just as businesses have models for management (as discussed in Chapter 3), so too do departments. Because a departmental management philosophy is more granular (or to put that another way, more dependant upon the function of the department), there are no real cookie-cutter models that will fit every department. Each department will have its own management considerations. This first section describes the considerations that are relevant when discussing an IT department.

Central or Decentralized Management

There are two basic philosophies of IT management: central control and distributed control. In a shop using a central control management model, all IT resources are managed by a small group of people in a single location. In a decentralized model, resources are managed locally. There are advantages and disadvantages to both management techniques.

The management technique used by the IT department often mimics the overall philosophy of the company. In companies where the headquarters staff is in complete control of all facets of the business, the IT staff is more likely to use a central management model. Conversely, in companies where sites or departments are more autonomous, the IT staff is more likely to used decentralized management techniques.

Central Management

Centralized management mirrors the "glass room" philosophy of the mainframe era. All IT decisions and management come from a central location (hence the name of the model) by a small administrative staff. These IT professionals need to have a high level of expertise because they support all IT resources—from workstations to servers and everything in between. In larger environments, the workload is often distributed by expertise; WAN, server, workstation, applications—each component of the overall environment will have one or more individuals who specialize in it.

There are often less organizational units (OUs) in the AD tree because management need not be delegated to local staff. The directory administrators have complete control over the entire AD structure. Although this means that the administrator must have more experience and training, and therefore a higher salary, these costs are usually offset by a reduction in personnel and the number of people who need to be brought up to speed on Active Directory.

Because there is no local IT staff at each location, components of the environment must be as reliable as possible. Imagine a company with offices around the globe, as shown in Figure 4.1. This company is headquartered in New York City and has offices in Minneapolis, Tampa, London, Paris, and Frankfurt.

FIGURE 4.1 An international environment

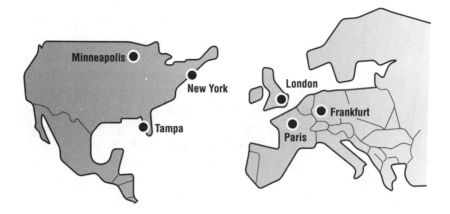

Assuming a central IT management philosophy, if a server goes down in Paris, someone from New York City must fly to France to effect repairs. Not only is this costly, it implies an unacceptable amount of downtime. This is probably the number-one problem with a centrally controlled IT environment in a large company: fixes generally take longer and cost more at remote facilities. Part of the drawback can be negated through your AD design—the more IT resources located near the IT staff, the less cost (and time) involved in repairs and maintenance. In most cases, the overall design of the network will be to place critical resources near the IT staff (rather than near the users who access them).

Automation is the key to avoiding the costs involved in long-range management. Most centrally controlled IT departments use tools to automate the distribution of applications, regular backups, and even the occasional server reboot. Remote management tools and scripted actions are used to accomplish the majority of IT functions. From an AD design perspective, this means that features like *Group Policy object (GPO) software publishing* will be used extensively.

The separation of the IT staff from the end users can also result in a slower support process. Often, any type of change, fix, or maintenance must be submitted to IT (often in triplicate) in the form of a request. The request will then be placed in a queue, awaiting completion. This sounds like a terrible system (from the users' perspective), but it is often extremely effective. Because many of the requests will originate in locations with no IT staff, most changes are made using remote management tools of one sort or another.

Given the distance between the IT staff and the users they support, most decisions are made after thorough analysis. A mistake *could* mean someone would have to travel to the remote site (not to mention the downtime or loss of productivity until the problem is fixed). In many ways, a centrally controlled IT department will be easier to migrate to Windows 2000—they are used to taking the time to design processes and procedures and are familiar with the concepts of many of the central management features.

Based upon the time it takes for actions to take place, centrally controlled IT departments are often considered more conservative than their decentralized colleagues. In reality, though, because of the need for cutting-edge management tools, central IT departments are often more up-to-date. They use the latest tools, master the processes of automation, and are always looking for new technologies to ease the maintenance of the network.

From an AD design perspective, the Active Directory structure of a centrally controlled IT environment is often simpler to design and maintain. Because a centrally controlled IT environment does not involve delegation of management roles, the tree often has fewer domains and organizational units. This simplicity is also reflected in the security strategy—fewer domains, fewer organizational units, fewer administrative staff, and a better-trained (or experienced) IT staff all add up to a simpler AD implementation.

For more information about security strategies, please see *MCSE: Windows 2000 Network Security Design Study Guide*, by Gary Govanus and Robert King (Sybex, 2000).

Decentralized Management

In stark contrast to a centralized management model, an environment in which *decentralized management* is used has administrative staff at most sites. These local administrators often have complete control over the resources at their locations. This management model creates a completely different type of environment for the AD design team. Look at the network of Katie's Dive Shops, shown in Figure 4.2. Here we have another company with multiple remote locations. It has stores in San Diego, Seattle, New Orleans, San Francisco, Chicago, Tampa, and Miami. Corporate headquarters is in Minneapolis, Minnesota.

FIGURE 4.2   Katie's Dive Shops

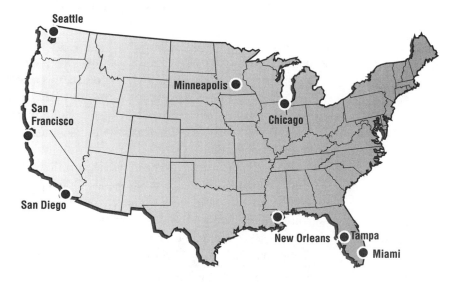

Each shop is a retail outlet, an equipment maintenance shop, and a PADI-approved training facility. Most shops also offer dive excursions, often working with local travel agencies to arrange package deals. Each shop is connected to a corporate network and has access to shared information from across the nation. (One of the trademarks of a Katie facility is that information about weather and water conditions for every location is posted in each store at the beginning of each day.) Students can take their classroom lessons at one shop, do their pool exercises at another, and finish with their open water dives at another. This flexibility has made Katie's Dive Shops a big success. Katie has taken great pains to ensure that someone with IT experience works at each shop (usually as the equipment maintenance and repair person). Her corporate IT staff trains these individuals on both the network and the specific retail store software packages that are used.

If a server goes down in one of the facilities, there is an IT professional available to fix the problem immediately. This is one of the hallmarks of a decentralized IT department—local maintenance of the IT resources. Rather than waiting for a headquarters staff member to fix any problems (either remotely or, worse yet, by coming to the site), problems are dealt with by a local staff member. The drawback to this is that the local person might not have the in-depth knowledge or experience necessary to deal with more complex issues. This is probably the biggest drawback to a decentralized management model. Based upon the smaller environment for which they are responsible, local staff members often do not have extensive experience or training to deal with more complex issues.

The overall AD structure is usually more complex in a decentralized environment. More divisions of responsibility exist, and to facilitate this, more organizational units are required. Of course, this also results in a more complex security strategy. *Delegation of responsibility must be done responsibly!* Care must be taken to avoid giving local administrators too much power in the AD structure. Although this is not necessarily a difficult task, it *does* take careful planning.

One of the biggest advantages of a decentralized environment is local support. When users express a need, the local IT representative can fulfill it quickly. There is usually no "Submit your request in triplicate (and we'll get around to it when we can)." Our experience has been that this responsiveness results in a much better relationship with end users. From a business perspective, the ability to respond to end-user needs on-site and in minimal time can be a great asset.

In general, the IT staff in a decentralized environment often has less training and is not as experienced "overall" than those in a centrally managed department. On the flip side, though, the local IT representative is often more knowledgeable about the components of their facility. Given the opportunity to work on-site, the IT person has a chance to learn each aspect of the local environment inside and out.

Decentralized environments are often viewed as less conservative than those that are classified as central. There is no greater motivation to "improvise and get the job done" than having an end user staring at you!

Funding

Funding is usually a touchy subject for IT departments. On the one hand, everyone knows the value of the services they provide, but on the other hand, many of those services are intangible and therefore hard to quantify. This is no more apparent than when trying to justify the expense of moving to a new operating system such as Windows 2000. Unfortunately, there is a catch-22 in funding: If everything is working well, no one wants to spend the money (if it works, don't fix it); if there are problems, no one will trust the judgment of the staff (fix what we have before we move to something new). The most important thing to remember about funding an IT department is that upper management (especially accountants) are looking for a *return on investment (ROI)*. Basically, the ROI describes the ways in which a change will reduce costs (or improve profits) and the length of time for these lower costs (or better profits) to outweigh the cost of the change. For example, let's say your company makes widgets. Under your current system, each widget costs $1.00 to produce. If you suggested a technology that costs $100.00 to implement but would reduce the cost of producing widgets to $.50, the ROI would be 200 widgets (200 × $.50 = $100.00). To be more accurate, your ROI would be the time it takes to produce 200 widgets.

The problem with the concept of ROI as it pertains to the costs of information technologies is that many IT benefits are intangible. If, for instance, you implement an online support system for customers that improves customer satisfaction (thereby increasing repeat business), there is no way to quantify that in dollars. Of course, you could go about justifying this example in another way: the better support system will probably reduce the amount of time it takes to close each incident. You could then quantify the dollar savings by calculating the amount of time spent on each call before and after the online support system was implemented and multiplying the time saved by the number of employees involved. The trick is to always justify your solutions with dollars (either saved or received).

We heard the worst example of this justification technique at a recent confer-
ence, but it does clearly explain the concept. Someone had calculated that
Windows 2000 Professional booted approximately twice as fast as Windows
NT 4 Workstation. Assuming an average boot time of 60 seconds, that means
an average savings of 30 seconds per day for each employee. That's 2.5 minutes each week, or 130 minutes (over two hours) each year *per employee*!
Given the average hourly wage of an employee and the cost of upgrading to
Windows 2000 Pro, you can give an accurate ROI. Of course, this example is
absurd. First, the time is in such small increments that it is not usable, and second, even if you ignore that fact, it would take years to achieve the ROI!

Various groups have done surveys that estimate the costs of upgrading to
Windows 2000. Rather than list a series of dollar amounts that would be
out-of-date by the time you read them, let us suggest that those surveys will
always be available on the World Wide Web. Perform an Internet search
with the keywords "Windows 2000," "cost," and "justify" and you should
find numerous Web sites with information. When planning your budget,
start with these figures and then adjust them to fit your environment. Your
area, for instance, might have much lower salaries than those used in the surveys (thus lowering expected costs), or you might find that your hardware
costs are lower than their estimates.

There are three costs to include in your budget: software, hardware, and
time. The software and hardware costs are easy enough to calculate; just use
the information gathered in the physical analysis. You should have a complete list of the hardware and software currently in your environment. In
your earlier studies for the MCSE, you were presented with minimum and
recommended hardware configurations. Compare what you have in place
with the recommendations to build a list of the purchases necessary.

More difficult to estimate is the amount of time that will be involved in
the process. Many a good consulting contract has ended up being a losing
proposition because of low estimates. Although there are no magic figures,
your estimate should include the following criteria:

Design time Remember that the time spent planning will decrease the
time spent implementing (hence the value of this manual)!

Travel time and costs In a larger environment, you might end up visit-
ing remote locations to perform upgrades or training.

Hardware purchases and configuration Hardware vendors always promise fast delivery, but add extra time to account for delays. Also add time to configure and test the hardware once it arrives.

Software purchases, installation, and configuration Perform a few installations and upgrades that simulate the processes you'll be doing in the field. Always add extra time here—nothing goes as smoothly in the field as it does in the lab!

Training time Both your IT staff and your end users will probably require some sort of training on the new operating system (and any new applications) that you install.

Support time This is one area that many IT professionals forget to budget for. No implementation ever goes exactly as planned! Set aside some time dedicated to user support after the upgrade.

We recently worked with a company that did an upgrade to Windows 2000. After the last computer was configured, the head of the department took a vacation—and was promptly called back to help fix a few problems. Advise your IT staff that vacations will be put off for a few weeks after the upgrade has been completed.

The bottom line with funding is to do your homework. Calculate the total cost of the upgrade as closely as possible. We always try to bounce our budgets off a few colleagues before we present them to management. They often find items that we have missed (or offer a suggestion to lower costs).

Once you've calculated your budget, be prepared to justify those costs. If you are a consultant, you will be asked some very tough questions: Why do you need that expensive server? Why does each workstation need 128MB of RAM? Why do we need to upgrade the line between Chicago and Detroit? You should be prepared with a logical explanation for the expense of every item on your budget. You should also be prepared for the ultimate question: Why should we upgrade to Windows 2000? Don't rely on the computer-geek answer, "Because it's the latest thing!" During your preparation for the MCSE exams, you have seen all of the features of Windows 2000 (not the least of which is AD). Look at the business environment and be prepared to list those features and the business solutions that they provide *in this specific environment.*

Exam Hint: The preceding paragraph describes a few of the case study questions you might see on the exam. Microsoft will present you with the solution and then a series of answers that justify that solution. You will have to pick the correct justification (not just the correct technology).

Outsourced Services

Over the last few years, more and more companies have started to outsource IT tasks. *Outsourcing* is hiring an outside firm to perform an IT task. Some outsourced functions are short term, such as hiring a consultant to lead the design process for your new AD structure. Other tasks that might be outsourced are ongoing, such as maintenance of a DNS server. In either case, processes that are outsourced will take careful consideration during your AD implementation. You will have to analyze each outsourced function and ask yourself these questions:

- Should it continue to be outsourced? Find out why the task was outsourced in the first place. If the situation has changed, determine if it would be better to bring the responsibility back in-house. If, for instance, the task was outsourced due to lack of experience, determine whether the skill has since been gained through experience or training. If the reason was costs, analyze the costs based upon Windows 2000 (as hard as it might be to believe, Windows 2000 makes many tasks much easier and cheaper than they were in Windows NT or some other legacy operating systems).

- Should it be taken over by internal staff? There are many tasks that were once secondary skills and are now critical to a Windows 2000–based network. It is often preferable to have critical tasks performed by your IT staff rather than an outside consultant. Look at each outsourced function to determine if it is mission critical. For each task that is critical to the IT environment, you will have to determine the benefits (and costs) of performing it in-house.

- Is it no longer needed? Many network services that were required in legacy networks are no longer required in a Windows 2000 environment. WINS, for instance, is not really required in a network in which all computers are running Windows 2000. (Be careful here, though; although Windows 2000–based computers might not need a particular service, be aware that you might have to continue to offer it to provide backward compatibility with older software.)

The biggest—and in our experience, most common—outsourcing decision will concern DNS. Because DNS has never been critical to Windows networking, and because DNS expertise is fairly rare, many companies have chosen to outsource the DNS service. Most Internet Service Providers (ISPs) offer DNS as a piece of their standard service package. We'll discuss the role of DNS in an AD environment in the next chapter. For now, though, you should already be aware of the critical nature of DNS in a Windows 2000 network. Windows 2000 Professional–based computers use DNS to "find" domain controllers. Without DNS, the logon service does not function. This leads to various design issues (discussed in more detail in the next chapter), such as whether clients should have to access an outside (rather than local) DNS server each time they log on to the network.

Another commonly outsourced service is the help desk. Many companies have an outside firm handle PC maintenance, software support, and server maintenance. If that is the case in your company, you will have to determine if your current vendor has the skills necessary to support a Windows 2000 network. If not, you will have to either find another source of support or move those services back into the realm of your IT department. If you decide to take over the help desk function, you will have to ensure that your help desk personnel have been given the opportunity to work with (or be trained on) Windows 2000.

Decision-Making Process

In Chapter 3, we discussed the decision-making process as it pertained to the entire company. Now that we are discussing an individual department, we must add a few new twists. The biggest change is that, in many companies, a decision made at the department level is not really a decision—it's a suggestion that will be kicked upstairs for further consideration. As consultants, we have actually been hired to provide technical and business justifications for a decision already made by the IT department. In other words, the technologists had already chosen a course of action but were unable to justify it in a manner that would be acceptable to upper management.

When presenting a suggestion for the use of technology, many of us (IT professionals) make the mistake of relying on the technical knowledge of our audience. We spend most of our careers presenting ideas to the departmental staff that is the easiest audience to sell on technology. Often, we are not even required to describe the benefits—our "techie" peers already know what it does, how it's implemented, and what the costs are. Although this may be sufficient within our department, we need to remember that at some point, an accountant is going to look over our suggestion. That accountant is going to want bottom-line justification for the costs involved.

The same rules that apply within the context of the company as a whole apply within the context of a department. Present technology with an eye toward reducing costs or increasing profits. Intangible benefits should be extra—do not rely upon them to completely justify the idea. Break down costs into small chunks—it's easier to get multiple small expenses past the accountants than it is to get one big one past them.

We know that this stuff sounds a little underhanded, but these are the tricks being taught at various business courses around the country. You've probably been told to always use pretty graphics and charts with lots of color when presenting to upper management. Although it sounds silly, these suggestions are based upon human nature—visually stimulating materials are more conducive to action (such as approving the funds). The same principle holds true when presenting costs—human nature is to avoid large expenditures!

Within the IT department, there are usually certain individuals who are considered responsible for a particular area of expertise. You might find, for instance, that one person is responsible for server maintenance, another for messaging systems, and yet another for wide area networking. We'll discuss the various IT roles later in this chapter. When presenting an idea for a new use of an existing technology or the implementation of something completely new, it is usually best to bounce the idea off of the person responsible for that area of the IT environment. That person, having both experience and a unique perspective, might point out flaws in your idea that would negate its value. On the other hand, because that person is the "expert," the department and company management probably values their opinion. Presenting your idea to them first, and garnering their support, can help you avoid the political battles that sometimes ensue over changes to the business procedures or processes.

The bottom line with decision-making within the IT department is that no decision should be made without consideration. Your job is to determine who does the considering, who presents the options to management, and in the end, who makes the choice. When it comes right down to it, you are "selling" technology to management. There's an old sales adage that says that the closer you are to the decision-maker, the closer you are to a sale. The same holds true when "selling" IT—knowing who makes (or helps to make) the final decisions will tell you who you need to focus on.

Current Change-Management Process

The *change-management* process defines how the IT department handles changes to the environment. If the company decides to upgrade from Microsoft Office 97 to Microsoft Office 2000, for instance, the change-management process would define how that upgrade is accomplished. To put things in focus, the upgrade or migration to Windows 2000 can be considered a change, and so the procedures used to accomplish this should be defined as part of the change-management strategy. Not all changes will be as major as the preceding two examples—a change can be as simple as upgrading the NIC driver on client computers or installing new printer drivers for a new printer. No matter how small the change, every company will have a change-management policy to perform the task.

Unfortunately, the change-management process used within a company is not always well defined. Upgrading drivers, for instance, is often the responsibility of non-IT personnel or local "gurus" recruited for the task. Even that, though, is a policy of sorts. Your job as part of the AD design team will be to document how changes are handled and then suggest alternatives that are more efficient or less costly. This is usually one of the most difficult of the early phases of the design process. In many companies, the change-management strategy is both undocumented and haphazard. For some reason, we, as an industry, seem to place more importance on the occasional task (like server installation or operating system upgrade) than we do the day-to-day administration that keeps our businesses running. One of the reasons for the success of Windows NT was that it popularized process automation. Although Microsoft didn't invent Dynamic Host Configuration Protocol (DHCP)— okay, maybe the protocol, although that's arguable, but not the process—NT made it a common component of business networks. NT also introduced the concept of printer server management of print drivers. (Before NT, you had to manually install print drivers on every workstation.) These first steps in the direction of a centrally controlled change-management process were the precursors of many of the new features of Windows 2000.

Change is a constant in the IT world: Buy a new printer and it comes with new print drivers. Buy a new NIC and it comes with new drivers. Have a problem with a piece of hardware—what's the first thing you do? Download the latest and greatest drivers. Every component of your network is a potential change-management client. Controlling the process of change is critical to a stable environment. Do it well, and your days are filled with spare time. Do it wrong, and you (or your peers) end up solving the same problems over and over again.

We know we're sounding a bit preachy here—change-management is one of our hot buttons! How many times have you worked for hours on a problem only to find out later (after you've found a fix) that one of your colleagues had fixed the same problem on another system "only last week"? We never want to hear, "So, how long did it take *you* to figure out that it was an out-of-date driver?" Proper documentation can eliminate the frustration (and long hours) of re-creating the wheel on every trouble call.

From a design perspective, your analysis of the change-management process should accomplish two tasks:

- It will provide you with a list of persons who are currently responsible for IT tasks.
- It will give you an idea of the current state of the environment.

The results of both tasks will be helpful during the planning and implementation of the Windows 2000 rollout.

Who Is Responsible?

Later in this chapter, we will discuss the concept of IT roles. During the early stages of the design process, you need to determine which persons should be assigned to each task. Starting with a list of current responsibilities will make the choices easier. It also helps you to build a list of current skill sets available and determine the amount of training that might be required before implementation. As we'll discuss later, one of the first goals of a design project is to build a design team with the correct mix of skills.

What Is the Current State of the Environment?

Documenting the standard procedures used to manage changes can help you determine the general condition of the network and its components. If, for instance, you ask what version of software is installed on the router and no one knows, you can begin to make assumptions about network components. One of the first rules of a design process is to make the current environment stable before introducing change. At this point in the design process, you should ensure that the latest drivers, fixes, and service packs are installed across your network.

Design Scenario: Carrie's Sleepy-Time Bedroom Furniture Outlets

During the analysis of the IT department of Carrie's Sleepy-Time Bedroom Furniture Outlets, you make the following notes:

CEO   "Sure, we're a nationwide chain, but because we sell factory seconds and overstocks, our margins are low. We need to improve the efficiency of our business to lower overall costs....Staffing has always been a problem for us—not many IT professionals want to work in the retail store, but we can't afford a dedicated computer person at each location...."

CIO   "We've just found the money to upgrade our links between the warehouses in each region and our corporate headquarters. It was lucky that [the CEO] read that article about lowering costs through better communication or it never would have happened....We've got three full-time IT employees here at headquarters and one support person at each regional warehouse. The regional guys are constantly on the road moving from store to store fixing problems....Now they want a Web site so that each store can order inventory over the Internet—we've barely got IP running right and they expect us to give Internet access to each store."

Regional IT Support Person   "You're lucky you caught me—I was just running over to the San Diego store to put out a fire. I installed a new NIC in one of their point-of-sale computers last week and it's been acting up. I was just out at the vendor's Web site looking for the latest drivers....I was replacing a printer last week and found a copy of Quake on the manager's box. Man, was he mad when I deleted it....I'm constantly running from store to store reinstalling software or reconfiguring stuff—our users are constantly messing up their environment...."

By this point, you're probably wondering why you accepted this project—your boss says the CEO of Carrie's is a friend of hers, so you'll have to at least look over the environment.

Which of the following IT management considerations would you consider to be the most important for this project?

1. Outsourcing

2. Funding

3. Decision-making process

4. Change-management process

Answer: B.   Although all of the answers are current issues for this company, the most pressing from an AD design perspective will probably be the issue of funding. Both the CEO and CIO mentioned costs during their interviews. Your proposal will have to heavily justify the costs involved through later savings if this project is to continue. (Given the tone of the interviews, I'd probably ask for payment up front too!)

Which feature or features of Windows 2000 will you use to lower support costs?

1. Dynamic DNS

2. Group Policy objects (GPOs)

3. Published applications

4. Remote Access Service (RAS)

Answer: B, C.   Given that the support personnel are constantly on the road going from store to store to fix problems, anything you can do to reduce those problems will save money. Using GPOs to lock down the users' environment and publishing applications from a central location will both reduce the amount of time spent in on-site fixes.

Analyze the Technical Environment

In the first section of this chapter, we discussed some of the considerations that need to be addressed during your analysis of the IT department. What we were *really* discussing were the types of things you would have to learn to be familiar with the business side of the IT department. You'll use those observations as you analyze the current (this section) and planned (the last section of this chapter) IT environments.

Microsoft ✓ *Exam* *Objective*	**Evaluate the company's existing and planned technical environment.** • Analyze performance requirements. • Analyze data and system access patterns. • Analyze network roles and responsibilities. • Analyze security considerations.

Analyzing System Access

In the Chapter 3, we discussed the importance of both information and communication flow within the company. At this point in the design process, you will use the information gathered earlier to help you analyze the efficiency of the current network infrastructure. Knowing who accesses what data and services and who talks to whom within the company gives you clues to the traffic produced on the network as well as the networks (from an infrastructure perspective) across which that traffic will travel.

Earlier in the design process, you gathered information about the physical infrastructure of the network. At this point, you'll begin to use the maps you created. For example, you might have produced a map similar to the one shown in Figure 4.3. This map shows the infrastructure of the network and the gross (as well as net) bandwidth of each connection and gives an overall reliability rating to each WAN link.

FIGURE 4.3 A typical network map

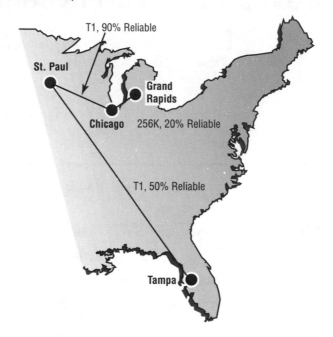

Combine the physical map with your spreadsheets of data and service access (created during your business analysis of the company), and you can begin to get a clear picture of where, and how much, traffic flows through the network. Your physical analysis already provides you with available bandwidth figures, but now you can correlate those figures with the business functions that generate the traffic. This type of analysis takes time, patience, and practice, but once you get the hang of it, it provides a fairly complete picture of the IT environment.

There are many methods to document the correlation between traffic and infrastructure. Our method is to first take the physical map and give each WAN link a unique identifier (that's a fancy way to say we number them), as shown in Figure 4.4.

The next step is to build a spreadsheet for each data source that shows which groups of users access it and where they are located, as shown in Tables 4.1 and 4.2. As you can see, we also include a general indication of the amount of access: H for heavy, M for medium, L for light, and N/A for no access.

FIGURE 4.4   Uniquely identified WAN links

TABLE 4.1   Inventory Data Access

	St. Paul	Tampa	Gr. Rapids	Chicago
Accountants	H	L	L	M
Sales	H	H	H	H
Production	H	N/A	N/A	H
Purchasing	H	N/A	N/A	M
Order Fulfillment	H	H	N/A	H
Upper Mgmt	L	L	N/A	L

TABLE 4.2 Sales Data Access

	St. Paul	Tampa	Gr. Rapids	Chicago
Accountants	L	H	L	L
Sales	M	H	M	M
Production	L	N/A	N/A	L
Purchasing	N/A	H	N/A	N/A
Order Fulfillment	H	H	N/A	H
Upper Mgmt	M	H	N/A	M

From this information, we can begin to plan for the placement of the data. For instance, from our examples, we can see that the inventory database will be accessed the most from users in St. Paul and the sales database will be accessed most from Tampa. Given this type of analysis, we can begin to make suggestions about where the data should be physically located.

The next step is to determine the amount of traffic that will be generated by remote data access across each WAN line. We build yet another spreadsheet that cross-references the WAN link identifier with the amount of traffic, as shown in Table 4.3. When looking at this table, remember that the inventory database was placed in St. Paul and the sales database was placed in Tampa. We take all of the access that will cross the link between two sites and average the lights, mediums, and heavies (access weightings) to come up with a final rating for how much traffic each site will place on each connection.

TABLE 4.3 WAN Traffic Analysis

Link	Traffic
1 (SP to T)	M
2 (SP to Chi)	H
3 (Chi to GR)	L

The weighting process becomes much more complex in a larger environment. For our simple exercise—with only one data source in St. Paul and another in Tampa and only three WAN links—all we had to do was look at who accesses the two databases. The Tampa users will produce a medium level of traffic on their link to St. Paul. The Chicago users access the inventory database heavily, and the Grand Rapids users won't place much of a load on the network in accessing either database. The tricky part of this analysis is to remember to include secondary traffic in your calculations. In our example, you would have to remember that *any* Grand Rapids traffic to St. Paul or Tampa would also travel on the link to Chicago.

Once you've mapped out the overhead placed on the network by user access, you can begin to formulate some design strategies. In our example, for instance, we already determined that the inventory database should be placed in St. Paul and the sales database should be placed in Tampa. We can also see that Chicago will generate a lot of traffic to St. Paul in accessing the inventory database. We should take careful note of the available bandwidth on that link—if it is approaching saturation, we might want to either upgrade the line or place a replica of the data on a Chicago server (limiting traffic to a nightly synchronization).

On top of the traffic generated by data access, your network must support the traffic generated by various services. Given a good analysis of the traffic on each link, you can now determine whether each site will need a domain controller to limit logon overhead on the line. You should also be able to consider the traffic generated by other network services such as DNS, WINS, PDC-BDC synchronization, and messaging systems (such as Exchange Server). Just keep adding traffic notes to your spreadsheet until you have a good idea of the types and amounts of *all* traffic that will cross each link.

Remember that at this point in our design project, we are still dealing with the original environment. The types of traffic on the wire will vary depending upon what operating system is currently in use.

Analyzing Security Needs

There's an old adage in network design that the three most important factors in a good design are reliability, security, and performance—in that order. Reliability is a touchy topic. We've already discussed the reliability of the network infrastructure (during the physical analysis of the network) and can assume that Windows 2000 itself will be more reliable than earlier Microsoft network operating systems (namely, Windows NT).

> The reliability of the hardware on your network is another story altogether. Buying high-quality components is the first step in providing a highly reliable network, but remember, every physical device *will* fail sooner or later! Although it's not mentioned directly in the test objectives, your next step in real life would be to determine which physical devices are mission critical. Perhaps you have a few servers that have to have 24-7 availability. You should rank the importance of each device on your network. For those devices that are deemed mission critical, you should take steps to ensure that they are fault tolerant.

Earlier, you gathered a list of network components, data sources, and network services. The next step in your design process is to determine the security needs of everything on your network *and* an overall security ranking for the environment. Some networks, such as Bob's home office network, need little to no security (heck, for quite some time, his Internet Web server had a blank password for the administrator account). Other networks, on the other hand, have a need for complex security schemes. Bob recently spent a little over a year teaching Windows NT networking courses to military personnel in Europe. Every class was filled with questions about Windows NT security (and, unfortunately, comparisons of Windows NT to other legacy operating systems). Those two environments—his home network and the networks on a military base—are the two extremes when it comes to network security. Most networks will fall somewhere in the middle.

Your list of resources and their security needs will be used to help design the AD tree *and* the overall implementation of Windows 2000. For more information about designing a security strategy, please see *MCSE: Windows 2000 Network Security Design Study Guide*, by Gary Govanus and Robert King.

Analyzing Performance Requirements

For the most part, today's networks are both reliable and secure when configured properly. This allows you the luxury to consider performance in your AD design. Performance is one of the trickier topics in any design discussion because *performance* is a relative term. What is considered great performance in one environment might be considered unacceptable in another.

During your interviews with key personnel, you should include questions that draw comments about the current state of the network. Surprisingly, these comments can often lead you to critical design decisions. If everyone complains about the network "being down," you should spend some time determining what is causing this condition. Is it faulty hardware? Unreliable WAN links? Operating system instabilities? Or are the downtimes due to faulty business processes?

There are many instances where people complain about the network when the real culprit is some other entity. Bob had one client, for instance, where the entire production department staff complained about the network being "down." What they really meant was that the sales order database, stored in a server at another site with a replica on the production plant server, wasn't always synchronizing completely overnight. This left the production department with no direction as to which product to manufacture, thus resulting in downtime. To the users, it seemed as if the network was to blame, when in reality, the database replication process was at fault.

The first step in analyzing performance needs is to ascertain expectations. In today's world, when many individuals have computers at home, it is not uncommon for users to have unrealistic performance expectations for the business network. Think about it—for under $1,000.00 it is possible to purchase a fairly high-end consumer computer. (We recently purchased a computer for our home lab that had an Intel 550MHz processor, 64MB of ram, a 13GB hard drive, a built-in 10/100 NIC, and a 16MB AGP graphics card for under $600.00 from a *major* vendor. Add $300.00 for a decent 17-inch monitor and modem and you've got a great home machine!) At home, the user sees blazing fast response; their games run well, Word loads in seconds, and their tax software runs without a hitch. Then they get to the office and expect the same performance from the SQL database that is supporting hundreds of users simultaneously.

Just recently, Bob was working at a company that had about 20 users that shared a T1 link to the Internet. The CEO complained about performance. He said that, even when he was the only one in the office on weekends, Internet performance was not acceptable. After their meeting, Bob sat down at a computer and accessed some graphic-intensive Web sites, and he was pleased with the Internet response times. He had the CEO come in and had him access a few of his favorite sites. To Bob, the performance looked fine; to the CEO, it was unacceptably slow. Bob started doing what he should have done in the first case, asking questions. When it was all said and done, he found out that the CEO had just had a cable modem installed in his house. He expected the same performance on a shared T1 line as he was getting from his cable modem at home.

The point here is that the analysis of performance needs is both a physical task *and* a social one. You need to determine what is acceptable in a given environment and then set your users' expectations to match. That is not to say that you *can't* improve performance, just that there are times when the costs involved in increasing performance outweigh the benefits.

Before you can set expectations, though, you need to determine the current performance conditions on each component of the network. This is a *big* task! You will need to master (or bring in someone who has mastered) tools to test the performance of many different types of hardware and software. You should always start with the basics and work up, so you begin your analysis at the workstation level. You can visit typical workstations throughout the company and talk to the users who utilize them. Have users access the tools they use in their everyday jobs—word processors, spreadsheets, shared databases, printers, everything! (This is a good time to start evaluating the users' perception of network performance.) Find out what works well and what doesn't. Find out if there is anything that doesn't work.

We recently worked on a network that supposedly had a fax server available for the users. Upon questioning, we found that no one had been able to make it work. The marketing department had found a work-around—they installed the fax components that come with Microsoft Outlook 2000 and were using that to do their faxes. Of course, this meant that they had to enter each contact twice: once in the company contact database and once in their personal contacts list in Outlook. Our solution was to move them to Exchange Server and create a shared contacts list. That way, they could continue using the fax solution they had found but wouldn't have to enter information twice.

The components you'll have to test include the following:

Workstations   Compare disk space, total memory, and operating system configuration against your software list and security needs analysis.

Servers   Use the tools included with Windows 2000 (Performance is a great place to start) to document the current level of performance (and any bottlenecks) on each existing server.

Routers, switches, and other network components   Just about every connectivity component on the market today comes with (or works with) some management software. Check for times of peak usage and check network performance at those times. Ensure that the actual throughput is not exceeding the thresholds of each component—in other words, try to find the bottlenecks on your network.

Software   Compare performance of workstation-based software on various hardware configurations. Determine the minimum hardware requirements to achieve acceptable performance. For server-based software (e-mail server, distributed database, etc.), determine the desired hardware to provide acceptable performance.

Wiring   Check LAN segments to determine if network utilization is too high (causing bottlenecks).

Training   Determine if users need training to increase their comfort level with the tools they use to perform their business tasks. We've found that properly managed training can often increase perceived performance dramatically.

There are two considerations to keep in mind during your analysis of performance. First, remember that perception is reality. Just because *you* believe that a component is performing at its optimum, unless your users also believe that, you have not done your job. Second, and probably most important, remember that sometimes good enough is good enough. There is always a point of diminishing returns on optimization. Once you reach this point, the cost of continuing to increase performance (by adding hardware or tweaking configuration) outweighs the benefits gained.

That last point is a lesson for life! We've had arguments with other network professionals about which is the most technically advanced operating system on the market. We usually irritate computer geeks by saying it doesn't matter. What does matter is which operating systems provide an acceptable level of reliability, security, and performance. Anything past acceptable is really unnecessary (and usually more costly). Theirs is the technical view; ours is the business reality view.

Design Scenario: Help Us Please! Inc.

You've been brought on to lead the AD design team for Help Us Please! Inc. The network has four physical sites:

- A factory in Ladysmith that manufactures widgets.

- The corporate headquarters in Minneapolis, which oversees all facets of the business, including all IT functions.

- A distribution center in Atlanta that acts as a warehouse and dispatcher for the company's East Coast customers.

- A distribution center in Billings that acts as a warehouse and dispatcher for the West Coast customers. This facility is also home to the corporate Web site. Two permanent IT employees who mange the Web site and any local technical issues are based here.

The network infrastructure consists of a 256K line between Atlanta and Minneapolis, a 56K link between Ladysmith and Atlanta, and a 56K link between Minneapolis and Billings. Both Billings and Atlanta are constantly in touch with the Ladysmith facility to check on inventory and shipping schedules. After analysis, you find that the link between Atlanta and Ladysmith is reaching saturation levels on a regular basis.

What is the first thing you would suggest to your client?

1. Replicate the inventory and scheduling database that is stored in Ladysmith to both Billings and Atlanta.

2. Implement GPOs to lock down the users' desktops for better control of the environment.

3. Upgrade the link between Atlanta and Ladysmith to a T1 line.

4. Add a link between Ladysmith and Billings.

Answer: D.   We know this isn't an "AD answer," but during the initial phases of the design process, you want to correct any problems to prevent them from affecting your final Windows 2000 environment. As it stands, all traffic between Billings and Ladysmith must first travel to Minneapolis, then Atlanta, and then finally to Ladysmith. Because these two facilities are in constant communication, a better design would be to have them connected directly.

IT Roles and Responsibilities

During your analysis of the physical infrastructure, the business environment, and the IT department, you will talk to many individuals. From a design perspective you can divide these people into three groups:

People with little or no technical knowledge   These individuals use a computer to accomplish their day-to-day work but have no IT skills (nor do they have the need for these skills).

Departmental gurus   These people are often used for departmental IT support. Usually, they either have a little knowledge about computers in general or have in-depth knowledge of one of the software packages used within the company. Every large organization has at least one of these people. They're the ones who always seems to know how to get your word processor to perform a certain function, or they know how to write macros for your spreadsheets, or maybe they just understand the relationship between the order entry system and the inventory database.

IT professionals   These are the true computer geeks of the company. They have knowledge and/or experience in key areas of the IT environment.

There are certain skill sets that are necessary to design, implement, and maintain any larger IT environment. Very few consultants (no matter what they might claim) have all of the skills necessary to do the job alone. From the first day of the design project, you should begin gathering the design team. The design team is made up of individuals with the *skills* necessary to design and implement an AD structure *within a given environment*. The makeup of the design team is critical to the overall design project. If the design team doesn't have the appropriate skills, the end design might not take all of the environmental variables into account. On the flip side, though, too many people on the team can make it more difficult to finalize the details. (It is especially important to avoid a situation where the team is divided along strict political boundaries; members can have strong opinions, but they need to be open-minded.) The best consultants we've ever known have all had the ability to interview key personnel and, from the information they gather, pull together a design team for a given project. That's not to say that all of the skills *have* to be found internally. Often your interviews with key personnel will highlight skill-set weaknesses. When you find that you are missing a necessary set of skills, you are faced with the choice of training internal staff or bringing in an outside expert.

You will need to determine what skills are necessary for your design project. Unfortunately, we can't give you a definitive list. The skills needed will vary depending upon the environment. There are, however, some general roles that usually need to be filled. We're going to present each role as a separate function, but you should be aware that multiple roles are often filled by a single individual (and occasionally, a single role will be split among multiple people). In general, your design team should have people to fill the following roles:

- IT management
- Windows 2000/AD expert
- Server support
- Workstation support
- Application support
- Printing support
- Wide area connection support
- Implementation testing
- Training support

The people fulfilling these roles will need a certain amount of expertise in order to provide valid information and suggestions to the team during the design process. Each person will probably also have their own priorities that might be at odds with the priorities of other team members. These differences are what create the dynamic environment necessary to create a stable AD structure. You will want to define each person's function within the design team, their priorities, and the level of technical knowledge necessary to fulfill their role in the design process.

IT Management

Any design project must have the support of upper management. It is usually the job of the IT manager to garner this support. The IT manager does not usually have a hands-on role in the design process or in the actual implementation. Instead, they are responsible for ensuring that the project stays on schedule and on budget. In many cases, the IT manager makes the decision to move to Windows 2000 and then leaves the actual implementation to the

IT staff. Given the limited role of IT managers in the actual "work" involved in a project, they need a specific set of skills:

- An ability to see the advantages of one technology over another without that vision being clouded by brand loyalty or technical prejudices.

- Project management experience. The design process in a large environment is a big project utilizing a large number of people, large budgets, and a lot of person-hours. The IT manager *must* be able to keep the team on track!

- Budgeting experience. The IT manager will be responsible for justifying to upper management the costs of the migration. The ability to create and justify a budget is mandatory.

- Presentation skills. The IT manager will often have to "sell" the proposed changes to upper management and to other departments.

Because the IT manager does not necessarily take a hands-on role in the design and implementation, this person does not usually need a heavy technical background. If necessary, the IT manger should attend a few "big picture" overviews of the Windows 2000 operating system. It is more important that the person filling this role have true management skills than it is for them to have technical skills.

Windows 2000/AD Expert

In many cases, the role of Windows 2000/AD expert will be filled by an outside consultant. No matter who takes on this role, there are certain skills that are necessary for a successful design. The Windows 2000/AD expert must understand the entire Windows 2000 operating system—both its strengths and its weaknesses. They must have experience installing and configuring all of the components involved in a Windows 2000 network—everything from DNS to AD, from DHCP to printer services, from user accounts to Group Policy. Their major responsibility will be to direct the design of the actual AD structure. As such, they will (at a minimum) need the following skills:

- An in-depth understanding of network directories and AD. Because they will lead the design of the AD structure, they must be familiar with how AD works and the various object classes that exist.

- An in-depth understanding of AD security.

- An understanding of the effect that AD will have on the network infrastructure. They must be proficient in the design of AD sites and site bridges and understand how network traffic is generated by AD.

- An understanding of the business needs of the company as a whole as well as the needs of each department.

This is the person who must know the most about AD and its function in the network. Because their area of responsibility will have an impact on all other aspects of the network, they must also be experienced in all other facets of the network. They will act as the center of the design team, ensuring that the overall recommendations will work together in a single AD structure. Our opinion is that this should be an experienced network professional with numerous network design projects under their belt. If you are relying upon internal staff, ensure that they receive adequate training—at least the full MCSE track to start. You might also consider training on specific aspects of your environment. This person should also have a background in business.

Server Support

The service support person should have experience working with the current servers on the system *and* knowledge of the idiosyncrasies of Windows 2000 Server. They will be responsible for the actual upgrade or migration of existing servers and will be aware of the services currently being offered to the network by server-based components of the environment (everything from DHCP to a server-based e-mail package). They will need the following skills:

- An understanding of the impact of each server on network traffic and the ability to document that impact

- An understanding of the upgrade/migration process

- In-depth knowledge of the server hardware currently in place as well as the hardware requirements for the new environment

- Working knowledge of Windows 2000 Server

This person will be responsible for determining whether the current hardware can support the move to Windows 2000 Server. If not, this person will also be responsible for determining the necessary physical changes mandated by the move. Their training and/or experience should at least be the equivalent of an MCSE. They should also have any vendor-specific hardware training available for the server hardware in use on the network.

Workstation Support

The workstation support person will be responsible for the configuration of all workstations on the network. Extensive hardware and operating system experience is mandatory. They will work hand in hand with just about every other member of the design team, so communication and documentation skills are also necessary. At a minimum, the workstation support person should possess the following skills:

- An in-depth understanding of the operating systems in use on the client computers

- Experience in maintaining the client software

- Working knowledge of PC architecture, with an emphasis on the specific hardware in the environment

- Working knowledge of the Group Policy objects in AD

- Experience automating the client upgrade process

This person is usually the jack-of-all-trades of the computer industry. They need to understand the local operating systems, hardware, and client software used at each computer on the network. Although an MCSE is not necessary in this role, this person needs to be an experienced IT professional. Vendor-specific training in operating systems and hardware will be a great benefit.

Application Support

The application support person is often the least respected member of the IT department—after all, they are *really* geeks, aren't they? The reality is that the application support specialist usually knows more about how to make computers "work" than the average network person. People are always fumbling around trying to get their word processor to format a sentence or their spreadsheet to calculate an average. The application person knows most of the capabilities of every piece of software in use on the system. They also usually know the best way to install each software package. Once you move to Windows 2000 and start using Group Policy objects to distribute applications, this person will take on a whole new importance in your department.

The application support person will be responsible for migrating all end-user applications to the new operating system. They'll need to know what updates, patches, and fixes are necessary; which software packages are not compatible with Windows 2000; and how applications will be accessed (locally or from the server).

Training for the application support person will consist of vendor-specific courses and seminars (on the software in use in the company). They should also have an understanding of AD because much of their function will be management of Group Policy objects. We would suggest that this person be at least an MCP and certified for any applications they will manage.

Printing Support

The same person who acts as the applications expert usually fills the printing support role. Printing is a critical piece of the network and has become a complex process. This person must understand the specific hardware in use and the printing components of a Windows 2000 network. In most cases, they will also need to understand third-party management software. If you are using printers that are directly connected to the network (the most common configuration anymore), they will also need to understand protocol-level addressing, print drivers, and network bandwidth issues. Because printing is so critical, we would suggest that this person be vendor-certified to support the brands of printers in your network. We would also suggest that they have Windows 2000 administrative training so that they can understand the concept of printing in an AD environment.

We've always lived under the law that two things are critical to our livelihood—the user interface (that's why we like Microsoft operating systems) and printing. These are the two IT components that most users see on a day-to-day basis. If they are satisfactory, then our users will be (in general) happy with the network.

Wide Area Connectivity Support

The most technical role to be filled on the design team is that of the connectivity expert. This person must understand routing, switching, protocols, and the cost structure of leased lines (as far as we're concerned, understanding all this is the hardest part). They will direct the team's efforts to connect all sites together—always with an eye on bandwidth control. They will determine which protocols are used on the network, which connectivity technologies will be implemented, and what routes will be available. They *must* understand all of the protocols in use, the hardware in use, and the wiring in place at each location. This person plays a central role in designing a stable network. (Notice that we didn't even mention AD in their skill set—they'll have to be competent in all network operating systems and networked applications in the environment.)

Training for a good wide area connectivity specialist includes vendor-specific certifications in both the network hardware in place and the operating systems in use on the network. At the very least, this person should be an MCSE, with a background in TCP/IP implementation. They'll also need to understand the various services (DNS, WINS, DHCP) in use on the network, at least from a bandwidth perspective.

Implementation Testing

The person in charge of implementation testing will work closely with all of the other members of the design team. The main responsibility of this role is to set up a test environment in which ideas, suggestions, and implementation techniques can be tested and perfected *before* they are attempted in the production environment. Our experience shows that overall costs of a major upgrade (such as the move to Windows 2000) can be reduced by 20 percent or so by performing adequate tests before implementation. Working out the bugs in your procedures prevents unnecessary downtime in the production systems. The most important skills that this person must have are the ability to document processes and an analytical mind-set to work through problems.

Although this person does not necessarily need to be an expert on any particular component of the IT environment (they can always ask the other team members for assistance), they should be familiar with a wide range of software and hardware. In the past, we have used promising college interns to fulfill this role. They get a few dollars for college and some needed field experience, and we save a few bucks in salary—it's a win-win situation.

Education Coordinator

The education coordinator must be involved in the employee interviews from day one. They must compile a list of skills necessary for each employee after the upgrade and then provide the necessary training to fulfill those needs (and often on a limited budget). Unless your company has a well-developed internal training department, our experience has shown that bringing in an outside training coordinator is usually the best bet. (Most training companies, such as Progressive Education Services—the company Bob works for—are willing to put together a complete training package for a reasonable price.) Because they usually have access to the latest courseware and a direct line to Microsoft education, this is usually the most effective way to provide training for your staff.

The Impact of AD on the Existing Network

In most cases, the migration to Windows 2000 and an Active Directory environment should provide more benefits than costs. That is not to say, however, that everything will continue to function as it did before the rollout of Windows 2000. Each and every component on your network might (and probably will) be affected by the upgrade. Before you begin the actual design of your AD structure, and certainly before you begin implementation, you need to assess the impact of the change and determine which processes or procedures will remain basically the same and which will need to be overhauled. No two migrations are exactly the same, but there are certain aspects of the IT environment that will warrant a close look:

- Applications

- Technical support processes

- System and network management

- The upgrade process and rollout procedures

- The network infrastructure

When considering each of these areas, keep your focus on what the environment looks like now and what you expect it to look like after the migration.

Microsoft ✓ *Exam* *Objective*

Analyze the impact of Active Directory on the existing and planned technical environment.

- Assess existing systems and applications.

- Identify existing and planned upgrades and rollouts.

- Analyze technical support structure.

- Analyze existing and planned network and systems management.

Applications

Out of all of the new or improved features that are available in Windows 2000 and Active Directory, those that pertain to application management might have the biggest overall impact on IT management techniques. By this time in your MCSE education, you should be quite familiar with the application management features of the Group Policy object (GPO) in AD. The ability to publish applications easily and efficiently, and the built-in ability of the GPO to correct common application problems such as the accidental deletion of files, could conceivably change the way network administrators look at end-user applications.

Earlier in your analysis of the environment, you built a list of the applications that are in use on the network and the users who access them. At this point in the design process, you need to take a closer look at that list. First, use the expertise of the application support person on the design team to document the current application management process. Then, document ways in which AD can change this process to make it easier and more efficient.

Once you've created a list of proposed management changes, you will need to present this list to the rest of the design team. Each member should look at the list and analyze the impact on their area of responsibility. The server support person, for instance, will probably want to think about the server storage required to hold application packages. The AD expert will want to consider the impact of GPOs on the overall AD structure. Even the training coordinator will want to include end-user training on the installation of published applications.

This process of proposing solutions and then having your proposals critiqued by the rest of the team should be a common procedure for the entire design process. We often develop tunnel vision when working on one aspect of the design and forget to consider the ramifications of our suggestions on the overall network. Having input from the rest of the team can bring those ramifications to light.

Technical Support Processes

No matter what Microsoft might say in its marketing material, Windows 2000 is a complex environment. Your technical support staff must be trained in the intricacies of the operating system *and* given an opportunity to work with the features before they are expected to support end users in a production environment. You should schedule a rollout of Windows 2000 Professional to all technical support personnel long before it is rolled out to the rest of the company. Technical training should also be high on the priority list for the support personnel.

Once again, you'll want to analyze the features of Windows 2000 and AD and compare those features to current support processes. If, for instance, your support personnel spend a lot of time at client computers (supporting those pesky end users), you might want to investigate remote control features or terminal server services. As always, present your ideas to the rest of the team before finalizing any decisions.

System and Network Management

The same story holds true here as for the earlier topics—analyze the current methods and philosophies used to manage the environment and document them. Then compare those processes with the features of Windows 2000 in order to propose changes. The biggest aspect of this topic is that you might want to consider the "why" of the management philosophy as well as the "how." If, for instance, certain functions have been outsourced due to a lack of expertise or inadequate staff, you might want to consider having those functions taken over by in-house staff. DNS comes to mind—because DNS is critical to the proper functioning of AD, it might be better to manage your DNS environment rather than outsource that task. You might also want to look at the centralized-versus-decentralized management philosophy question. If, for instance, a company uses a decentralized management philosophy (and hires outside consultants to handle management at remote sites) due to a lack of staff, you might want to consider the ease with which remote management of servers and workstations is accomplished in Windows 2000. As a matter of fact, many tasks are inherently easier in Windows 2000—this might free up some time for your staff to take on additional responsibilities.

 If you are going to lend this book to anyone in management, we suggest that you tear out this page (or at least scribble over the last paragraph). There's no use in letting them know you are going to have more free time after the upgrade is complete.

Summary

In earlier chapters, we showed you how to begin your analysis of a company by first looking at the physical infrastructure and then analyzing the business processes in use within the company. In this chapter, we took a close look at the department that will ultimately be responsible for the success or failure of the upgrade process. Because you are going to be counting on the IT staff to implement the AD structure that you design, it is imperative that you understand their motivations, what they are currently doing, and what they would like to be doing in the future.

We began by looking at the various management considerations in a typical IT department: centralized vs. decentralized management, outsourced services, the change-management process, funding, and even the decision-making processes within the department. Once you have a good feel for the department as a whole, you can then change gears and begin looking at the current environment that they support. How the system is currently used, what services it provides, and how those services are configured will help you design an AD structure that is more compliant with the business needs of the company. Finally, we discussed the process of proposing changes to improve the overall performance and efficiency of the IT environment.

Thus ends the analysis portion of the design process. At this point, in a real-life project, you have enough information (and support from your design team) to make the technical decisions that result in a well-designed and stable AD structure. The rest of this book will concentrate on more specific aspects of design, but we'll constantly be coming back to the information gathered during the analysis phase.

In the next chapter, we'll take an in-depth look at designing a DNS structure for a Windows 2000 environment. In many ways, this is the most important technical task in any design project. Because DNS is so important to Active Directory, it is safe to say that the AD Design exam will test your knowledge of DNS extensively. If you aren't comfortable with DNS, we suggest reading *MCSE: Windows 2000 Directory Services Administration Study Guide*, by Anil Desai (Sybex, 2000), to prepare you for the discussion about to take place!

Key Terms

Before you take the exam, be sure you're familiar with the following terms:

centralized management

change-management

decentralized management

Group Policy object (GPO)

outsourcing

return on investment (ROI)

software publishing

Review Questions

1. In a centrally managed IT environment, which of the following are true?

   A. The AD structure will generally have fewer OUs.

   B. The AD structure will generally have more OUs.

   C. The IT staff relies upon local personnel to support each site.

   D. Automation can be used to reduce IT management overhead.

2. In a decentralized IT environment, which of the following are true?

   A. The AD structure will generally have fewer OUs.

   B. The AD structure will generally have more OUs.

   C. IT responsibility is delegated to local staff members.

   D. The headquarters staff dictates all IT policies.

3. ROI refers to _____ .

   A. Repeat Over Interface messages

   B. Return on investment

   C. An aspect of DNS

   D. Router Oscillation Time

4. Change-management policies define which of the following?

   A. The process of hiring new departmental managers

   B. The processes used to maintain system components

   C. A text file used to automate the installation of Windows 2000 Server or Advanced Server

   D. A database used to track network utilization over time

5. Analyzing data access patterns will provide information that will be used in which of the following design decisions?

   A. Server placement

   B. AD site boundaries

   C. Data replication policies

   D. WAN design

6. How NIC drivers are updated on local machines is primarily part of which if the following IT considerations?

   A. Funding

   B. Centralized vs. decentralized management model

   C. Change-management

   D. Outsourced services

7. Which of the following features of Active Directory would best justify the move to Windows 2000 for a company that is having a hard time with users changing the configuration of their workstations?

   A. DDNS

   B. DHCP

   C. GPO

   D. AD site boundaries

8. Which of the following are goals of the analysis of the change-management process?

   A. Develop a list of persons who are currently responsible.

   B. Determine which workstations have the most recent print drivers.

   C. Get an overall feel for the current state of the environment.

   D. Determine the current methods used to maintain workstations.

9. You discover that the wide area link between two locations is currently running at 75 percent of its capacity. Which of the following are true?

   A. You need to determine what process is putting traffic on this line.

   B. This line is overutilized and you should not plan to add more traffic to it.

   C. You should immediately upgrade this line to a faster dedicated link.

   D. This number is fine. You should be able to run with a line at 100 percent of its potential.

10. What is the first step in the analysis of performance?

    A. Run a series of benchmark utilities to measure throughput.

    B. Compare the environment with the performance statistics you achieved on your last consulting job.

    C. Determine the expectations of the users.

    D. Create a baseline to use for comparison after you have optimized the environment.

Answers to Review Questions

1. Answer : A, D. In a centrally controlled IT environment, all IT decisions are made by a small group of individuals who are also responsible for implementation. Because there is less delegation of tasks, there are usually fewer OUs in the AD structure. To avoid repetitive management tasks, scripts and other automation techniques can be used.

2. B, C. An AD structure that contains more OUs also provides a more granular environment for delegation of management tasks.

3. B. One of the best ways to justify the expense of moving to a new operating system (such as Windows 2000) is to prove that the move will pay for itself over time. ROI refers to the amount of time this will take.

4. B. Change-management refers to the management of ongoing maintenance of IT resources.

5. A, B, C, D. Analyzing the traffic generated by system access can help in any decision that might impact the network infrastructure.

6. C. Change-management refers to any updates, fixes, or other changes made to components of the IT environment.

7. C. GPOs can be used to control a user's desktop and other aspects of the user environment.

8. A, C, D. During the analysis phase you are concerned with who and how, not specific instances.

9. A. Although this number *could* represent a problem, you will need to determine if this is a peak usage or if it is constant and what processes are placing this traffic on the wire. Without this knowledge, you cannot make any realistic assumptions about the line.

10. C. The first step when analyzing performance issues is to determine what level of performance is expected by the users of the system.

Case Study: Direct Mail Marketing, Inc.

Take about 10 minutes to look over the information presented and then answer the questions at the end. In the testing room, you will have a limited amount of time; it is important that you learn to pick out the important information and ignore the "fluff."

Background

Direct Mail Marketing has 200 offices spread throughout the United States. Its major product is a monthly mailing to every household in a given area. The mailing consists of coupons, special advertisements, and other marketing material relevant within the boundaries of the mailing. Approximately 75 percent of the marketing inserts are local in scope, while the other 25 percent represent coupons for national businesses. The company has recently started two new services: direct mailings for individual clients and Web-based coupons.

Physical Network

Connections   Seven main offices are directly connected to the corporate headquarters located in Chicago; all other offices connect to the closest of these seven. Physical connections vary from dedicated T1 lines to dial-up connections, depending upon the connection demands of the office and costs of local lines.

Network Traffic   There are seven major offices that produce over 70 percent of all network traffic: Chicago, Seattle, Los Angeles, Dallas, Tampa, Atlanta, and New York. The links to these major sites are approaching saturation.

Business Analysis

Server Placement   Each of the seven main offices contains servers that hold regional mailing lists. All satellite sites connect to these servers to download mailing information and to update the databases with new addresses or address corrections as well as demographic information purchased from local retailers.

CASE STUDY

Information Stores The amount of information being stored in each regional database is growing at alarming rates. With the advent of point-of-sales demographics, Direct Mail Marketing decided to include more demographic information. Its databases now store product choices made by individuals, potential salaries, even neighborhood analysis of demographic information to allow businesses to pinpoint potential customers.

Business Model The company is clearly managed through a departmental model. All of the traditional departments exist—sales, IT, marketing, purchasing, accounting, and so on.

IT Department Analysis

CIO "We've got an interesting culture here. We've developed several central IT groups within the headquarters staff that are responsible for setting standards and proposing new technology—a system admin group that sets standards for administrative tasks (such as creating user accounts or sharing data), an Internet group that oversees our Web presence, an infrastructure group that manages our WAN, and a DB group that designs and maintains our mailing and demographic databases. Each of our seven main offices also maintains its own IT staff, who are responsible for local resources and maintenance. They also support the satellite offices."

Manager System Admin Group "We've got over 5,000 users spread out over 200 physical locations. Our current NT domain structure is loosely based upon a multi-master model, but our recent growth has caused us no end of problems. We've ended up with too many domains and too many trusts. Managing standards across all of the sites, let alone enforcing them, has become a nightmare."

Manager Internet Group "We're a fairly new group within the IT department. In many ways, we should actually be our own department—Internet-based development has its own set of requirements that are often at odds with those of the overall IT goals. Security, for instance, is completely different for Web-based functions than it is for internal. First, security has got to be as foolproof as possible. We've begun selling access to demographic information over the Net—meaning that our bread-and-butter product is now exposed to every hacker out there."

Manager Infrastructure Group   "Since each of the seven main offices acts as a hub for numerous satellite offices, we've actually got a two-tier network: six medium-sized WANs connected through a national hub. Satellite sites very seldom talk to each other, but *every* site communicates with headquarters (and their local main office). Since we control the company backbone, we set standards for communication: which protocols are allowed, which firewall will be used (and how they are configured), and how much bandwidth is necessary for each site. Within each of the six 'sub-WANs,' though, we begin to lose control—I've gone out and found satellite sites with numerous protocols installed on every workstation. We can keep that traffic off the backbone, but we don't have a lot of control over the individual segments."

Manager DB Group   "Our worst enemy is bandwidth. It's amazing how much raw data is available for individual consumers. We decide which information should be added to our database and which should be discarded. Now that we're selling demographic information at both the satellite offices *and* across the Internet, our servers have begun to bog down. We used to have a few performance issues once a month (when we were creating the monthly mailings), but we could correct that by staggering our runs. Now, we never know when someone will run an advanced query, so we never know when our servers will be busy."

Manager Dallas Office IT Staff   "We support a complete regional mailing once per month as well as custom mailing requests. We are directly responsible for the databases being available in a timely manner, all system administration for our region, and physical support of over 40 sites. We accomplish this with six full-time staff members. The headquarters guys seem to think that they are in control, but at the same time they assume that my staff has the same levels of experience as they do. My guys are so busy putting out fires at the satellite sites that they don't have time for learning about new technologies."

Manager Satellite Site   "We rely on the Seattle office IT staff for all of our IT support. Those guys are great, but we sometimes have to wait for a problem to be resolved—downtime that we can't afford. Most of our problems are little things, like a user forgetting their password or deleting the wrong file, or not being able to get to a printer. It would be nice if I had someone local who could do that stuff."

Questions

1. Is the Direct Mail Marketing, Inc. IT department managed through a centralized or decentralized model?

    A. Centralized

    B. Decentralized

2. Given the staff available, which of the following design team roles would probably have to be brought in from outside the company?

    A. AD expert

    B. WAN expert

    C. Training coordinator

    D. Workstation support

3. Considering the structure of this company, where do you suppose Internet access points should be located?

    A. Only at the corporate headquarters in Chicago, with all other offices passing through a central Internet access point.

    B. At each main office (seven total access points), each of which has its own Internet service provider.

    C. Locally at each of the 200 offices, which will keep all WAN lines free of Internet traffic.

    D. Internet access should be restricted to dial-up modem access from the workstations of users who need Internet access.

4. Review the satellite site manager's lament that she experiences unnecessary delays because even simple problems must be taken care of by a member of the IT staff at a main office location. What is the best way to deal with this issue?

   A. Hire a part-time IT person at each location and make them the administrator of the satellite office.

   B. Hire a full-time IT person at each location and make them the administrator of the satellite office.

   C. Increase the size of the IT staff at the main office and improve the communication channels used by satellite offices to access support.

   D. Grant a local user (such as the manager or another a "computer literate" employee) limited administrative rights to deal with some small problems.

5. In what order would you perform the following tasks?

Task	Task
	Create an AD tree.
	Upgrade database servers and implement clustering technologies to provide load balancing and fault tolerance.
	Implement Group Policy objects to control the user environment.
	Upgrade the WAN links between the seven major sites to reduce potential bottlenecks.

6. The company has decided to go with the Internet design described in the answer to question 3 and open up limited Internet access to all users, allowing them to do research and send and receive Internet e-mail. The company wants to give employees relatively free access to Web information, but it also wants to monitor Internet usage and take precautions to protect network security. Assume that MS Exchange and TCP/IP are already in use on the network but are not connected to the Internet yet. Construct a high-level system that shows the steps that need to be taken to accomplish these goals.

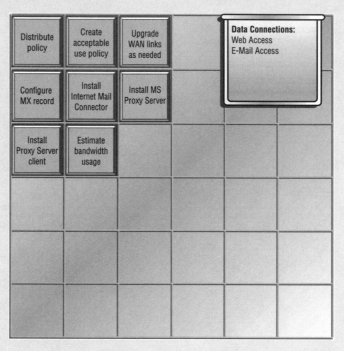

Answers

1. B. It sounds as though the headquarters IT staff would like to have control over setting standards for the company, but the local IT staff at each of the six main sites are responsible for the local resources.

2. C. The headquarters IT staff has groups who are responsible for connectivity and new technology. You should be able to pull from those groups for your design teams. The only skill that seems to be missing involves training—no one seems to be getting any!

3. A. As with most design questions, this is one that can be argued a number of ways. The fact that the company seems very interested in security, though, and has not mentioned cost factors, means that you probably are best off simply upgrading the WAN links to handle Internet traffic coming from the other offices, allowing the administrators to maintain a single point of access to the Web from the corporate headquarters. This greatly simplifies Internet traffic monitoring and filtering and is the most secure solution. It is also the most expensive option because greatly increasing WAN bandwidth doesn't come cheaply! Alternatively, answer B is also fine from a design standpoint. It is less expensive, but it is also more complex to design and less secure because you have more points of access, and therefore more points of vulnerability. Answers C and D are nightmare scenarios, especially in an environment where the IT staff is already stretched thin.

4. C. This all comes down to money. In a world where money was not an issue at all, the answer would be B. In a world where no additional funds are available, the answer is D. Somewhere between these is the option of adding staff (which are currently overworked and undertrained) to the main offices. Combined with reforming the support process to make the centralized IT staff more available, the addition of just a few additional IT staffers may make a substantial difference in problem response time both for the main office and for its satellites. Note that option A is of little value because part-time support is not likely to be on-site when problems occur and is therefore of little use in solving issues related to problem resolution time.

5. See table.

Task
Upgrade database servers and implement clustering technologies to provide load balancing and fault tolerance.
Upgrade the WAN links between the seven major sites to reduce potential bottlenecks.
Create an AD tree.
Implement Group Policy objects to control the user environment.

Remember the first rule of design—stabilize the current environment first! Protecting the company's databases (the source of its income) should be the first priority. Second, correct any bottlenecks that exist—adding Windows 2000 and AD could potentially add traffic to the network (of course, we *hope* it will reduce traffic, but you never take chances), so upgrading the lines is a critical step. After that is done, you can begin worrying about AD and its features (such as GPOs).

6.

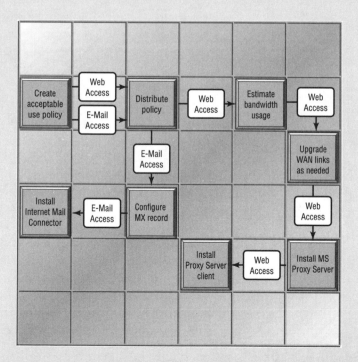

Note how, for each category of steps, planning steps are first, security steps are second, and implementation comes last.

Chapter

5

AD Naming Strategies

MICROSOFT OBJECTIVES COVERED IN THIS CHAPTER:

✓ **Design an Active Directory naming strategy.**

  ▪ Establish the scope of the Active Directory.

  ▪ Design the namespace.

  ▪ Plan DNS strategy.

✓ **Design the placement of DNS servers.**

  ▪ Considerations include performance, fault tolerance, functionality, and manageability.

  ▪ Plan for interoperability with the existing DNS.

Bob King offers these observations:

"Using a standard method to name and organize things is a part of everyone's daily life. If you were to look at my bookcases, you would find that the books are arranged in alphabetical order by author. Your Rolodex is probably alphabetized as well. My wife, Susan, keeps a separate address book for contractors we have used around the house (plumbers, lawn care, painters, etc.). In that book, the entries are alphabetized by type of service rather than the contractor's name. The list of how my life is organized goes on and on.

"We recently had to go out of town for a short while. We flew in my mother-in-law, June, to watch the place—feed the dog, water the plants, pick up the mail—all of the things that need to be done whether you're there or not. While we were gone, our dog, Kodiak, got sick. Because Susan had shown her mother where the various resources are kept, by the time we got home, June had taken Kodiak to his regular vet (nothing serious—it seems he got a few too many treats while we were away), had the carpets cleaned, and even ordered a bouquet of flowers to brighten up the kitchen for our return.

"By now, you're probably wondering what all this has to do with Active Directory. The point of this little look into my life is that June was able to accomplish these things because the resources we use in our daily lives follow an accepted set of naming standards. Let's look at a different scenario—one in which Susan isn't around to straighten out my messes.

"Before I got married, my filing system consisted of a bunch of shoe boxes with receipts, business cards, notes, and advertisements stuffed in without any planning. When I wanted to find out which plumber I had used that last time my sinks overflowed, I would either remember the company's name, look through the phone book to see if a name looked familiar, or dig through those shoe boxes. (Actually, I usually looked through my checkbook register for a check made out to a plumber!) If someone were watching my dog and needed to find his vet, he'd have ended up at some emergency veterinary clinic."

Which scenario would you rather have if *your* dog was sick? Before Bob got married, he might as well have discarded his records—they certainly weren't of any real use to him. Now think about your network. Which of these two scenarios would be closer to your organizational philosophy? If you need to schedule an update to an application on your desktop computers, do you know what version is on every machine (or have a mechanism for finding out)? If you need to schedule repairs on a printer, can you find the purchase date quickly? If you find a note on your desk that reads, " I've got a network problem. Bob King," can you find Bob's network information easily? When you hire a new employee, how long does it take to create and configure the account? For that new account, can they sit down and start working immediately or do you have to first figure out what permissions they need, then install their software, and then correct the mistakes you made?"

Each of these tasks can be made quite a bit easier by understanding the impact of naming in an Active Directory environment.

Naming can be a big topic in an Active Directory design process. We'll begin with a discussion of the importance of standardization, then we'll discuss Lightweight Directory Access Protocol (LDAP) and its naming structures (this information is mostly used to lay the groundwork for later chapters), and we'll finish with a discussion of DNS. The first half of this chapter will be useful for you as background, and in the second half, we'll concentrate on DNS naming strategies and designing DNS server placement.

Establishing the Scope of Your Active Directory Naming Standard

Microsoft *Exam* *Objective*	**Design an Active Directory naming strategy.**
	▪ Establish the scope of the Active Directory.

The first step in creating any naming standard guideline is to figure out exactly where your job begins and where it ends. Are you, for instance, going to include definitions for job titles, or is that standard defined by the human resources department? By eliminating those areas that are defined elsewhere in your company, you can find the starting point for this process.

Equally important is finding the end point of your naming standards. If, for example, you have registered the DNS domain name of Persistent-Image.com on the Internet, then your responsibility ends at that portion of the name that is defined by an outside agency (in this case, the naming structure of the Internet).

The process of finding the limits of your naming responsibilities is known as finding the scope of your Active Directory. It is the first step in designing any set of naming standards.

The Importance of Standard Names

A name uniquely identifies an object. No matter what operating system you are currently using, everything on your network has at least one name. Names are an extremely important component of your environment. Think about it—without a unique identifier, how would users print to a specific printer? Or how would your users find the server that contains their files? Or how would you find the Microsoft Web page?

In earlier networks, it was possible to take naming for granted. Duplicate names, for instance, were handled in a slipshod manner. Bob once worked for a company for two years with the account name Bob2. Luckily, he's never suffered from low self-esteem or he could have spent two years wondering if he would ever earn the title of Bob1. A few years ago, we were doing some research and discovered a list of the most popular names given to servers on business networks. The results surprised us. The first most popular "naming standard" was to use the names of various *Star Trek* characters. This was followed closely by the seven dwarfs in second place. When networks consisted of a couple of servers (up to seven in the latter case) and 20 or so users, administrators could get away with these types of names. Today, however, networks consist of hundreds of servers, thousands of users, and numerous other resources that require unique, distinctive, and user-friendly names.

Planning a Consistent Naming Standard for Objects

One of the first considerations when building an Active Directory structure is that of object naming. The design team should sit down and develop guidelines for naming everything from user accounts to printers to servers. This naming standard should then be applied to every object created in the AD tree. Surprisingly, this discussion is often one of the most heated of the entire design process. For some reason, people can get quite emotional about how objects are referenced.

When designing your naming standard, start with the basics. Begin by creating a standard method for naming user objects. There are many industry-standard methods in use, but you should come up with a standard that fits your company. Here are a few examples, and the outcome, for user Bob King:

- First Initial, full last name—BKing

- First name, last initial—BobK

- First initial, last initial, and some unique numeric identifier—BK1234 (Many companies will use the last four digits of the employee's company ID number or SSN.)

Our opinion is that the username should be easily identified with the user. When using a numeric or random component, this isn't the case. Also, be aware that using any component of a person's SSN can be potentially dangerous.

Once you've come up with a consistent standard, think about the possible exceptions to the rule. Your standard should define what should be done if two employees have the same name. If you had two users named Bob King, you might decide to include the middle initial or enough of the middle name to ensure uniqueness.

Remember that *no* standard can be made to handle every contingency. We've seen design teams bog down trying to come up with the "perfect" naming strategy. When designing a standard, design for the norm, plan for inconsistencies, and be ready to intervene when it doesn't work.

Complete this same process with every object class you will utilize in your tree. Printers, servers, applications, even organizations and organizational units will need unique names. Remember that your names will be used by end users, so they should be designed so that the name readily references the resources to *your* average user. We were once working as consultants on the directory design team for a company that had an office in Chicago. We had decided that all organizational units would have a three-character name and that the name would identify the object to end users. When we came to the name of the Chicago OU, the argument became quite heated—one group wanted CHI, another wanted ORD (the designator for O'Hare International), and yet another wanted CGO. The team deadlocked on this issue for over an hour. Remember, the names you choose are for your users' convenience—ensure that they make sense!

When we were deciding on a name for the Chicago OU, we finally got mad and called an end to the discussion. Everyone was instructed to go home that evening, look over their last six months' e-mail, and count the number of times Chicago had been referenced with each abbreviation. CHI won by a landslide.

In Chapter 11, we'll detail the more commonly used object classes and provide a "cookie-cutter" naming standard that you can customize to your environment. Consistency is the key when designing your naming standard. Consistent names facilitate many aspects of Active Directory use and management.

Planning a Consistent Usage Standard for Properties

If you have gotten far enough into your MCSE studies to be studying for the Design test, you should be quite comfortable with the various classes of objects and their properties. The user class, for instance, contains properties such as login name, first name, last name, telephone number, and even application associations and group membership. From a network administration perspective, the use of most of this data is apparent—login name is used to identify the user, group membership is a list of the security groups of which a user is a member, and so on. Some of the information stored in the Active Directory database, however, is not really "network" related. Strictly speaking, the title property is not used by any of the default processes of Windows 2000. (For the purists, you *could* write a script that uses this information, such as to assign permissions based upon title, but by default, it has no real network purpose.)

If you are not comfortable with the basic format of the Active Directory database, we suggest that you read *MCSE: Windows 2000 Directory Services Administration Study Guide* (Sybex, 2000) by Anil Desai.

After you have created an object naming standard, the next step is to take a closer look at each of the object classes to standardize property use. Active Directory might be a critical piece of the overall Microsoft network environment, but at its heart, it is only a database. If you're going to store data, you might as well spend the time to ensure that you can use that data once it has been entered. Once again, begin with the basics. You've defined your naming standard for user objects. Now look at each of the properties available for the user class and decide if the data will be mandatory, optional, or not used. Table 5.1 gives a few examples for a user object.

TABLE 5.1 User Properties Standards

Property	Use*	Format	Description
Login name	M	First initial, Last name	User's account name.
Telephone number	M	###-###-#### X####	Telephone number and extension.
Title	O	Use only titles approved by human resources.	HR will approve all titles. Perhaps a script can be written that will check the value entered against a preapproved list.
Managed by	R		Reserved for future use.

* M=Mandatory, O=Optional, R=Reserved

There are many more properties for a user object. When defining standards for properties, you should create a list that includes all of them. Remember that the Active Directory is extensible, so the list may vary depending upon what changes you have made to your schema. You can find a complete list of objects and their properties in the Windows 2000 online help system. Perform this task with every class of object that you will utilize in your environment!

A list of standards for properties is a great tool for consultants. Once you have come up with the list of objects and their associated properties, your "default lists" can be used as a cookie-cutter design tool from client to client.

One more time, let us emphasize: Consistency is key! Remember, two of the goals of AD are to make the data it stores accessible and to make it usable. If you enter information in a haphazard manner, your database will not live up to either of these goals. Let's say that you decide to enter a title for each user. In Table 5.1, we suggest that you use the list of company titles that might be defined by the HR department. This will help to make the information useful later. On the flip side, letting anything get entered will negate some of the benefits of a central database. If, for instance, your administrator in Chicago enters "Manager" and your administrator in London enters "Mgr," you will not be able to perform an effective search for all managers in your company. If you tried using "Man*" as your search criteria, you wouldn't find any managers in London. You could use "M*", but that would also return all mail-room clerks—hardly the list for which you were looking.

Active Directory Names

Windows 2000 Active Directory follows two industry-standard methods of naming objects within the tree:

Lightweight Directory Access Protocol (LDAP)   The industry standard method of accessing, locating, and manipulating data held in directory databases

Domain Name System (DNS)   The standard service used by TCP/IP environments to resolve host names into IP addresses

These two naming standards are used in completely different ways. LDAP names are used by Active Directory internally to find objects. You might, for instance, submit a query that asks for all users whose first name attribute begins with the letter *S*. Whatever software you were using to access the directory would convert your request into the appropriate format, and AD would use the LDAP names of the objects to perform your search. As such, end users will not need to understand much of the LDAP naming standards in place in your environment (their software should hide most of this from them).

DNS, on the other hand, is used to locate physical resources. The basic function of DNS has not changed—DNS has always been a name resolution service that resolves Fully Qualified Domain Names (FDQNs) into IP addresses. There are a few "nontraditional" aspects of Microsoft DNS, such as dynamic updates and SRV records, but in general, the functionality is the same.

Even these nontraditional aspects of Microsoft DNS are not exclusive to Microsoft. Each of the new DNS technologies used in Windows 2000 is defined by industry-standard Requests for Comments (RFCs).

A strong background in DNS is a prerequisite for AD design. If you are not comfortable with the mechanics, implementation, and maintenance of DNS in its traditional format, we suggest reading *TCP/IP Jumpstart* (Sybex, 2000) by Andrew G. Blank or, for more advanced readers, Mark Minasi's *Mastering Windows 2000 Server* (Sybex, 2000).

Lightweight Directory Access Protocol (LDAP)

Many administrators can spout a definition of what LDAP does—often just by repeating the name back to you, such as, "It's a protocol used to access a network directory." If pressed for more information, these individuals will give you the same example used in every trade magazine article ever written: "Suppose you wanted to write a company phone book that would retrieve its data from the name and telephone properties of the directory database. LDAP would be the mechanism used to gather the information." Although these answers are technically correct, they in no way touch upon the importance of LDAP to both the acceptance of directories in the business world and the impact they will have on the way business is done in most companies. To truly understand the impact of LDAP on your AD design, you need to have an understanding of what LDAP is capable of. For this, you'll need a little history lesson.

DAP and LDAP

Two industry-standard protocols are available for use in accessing directories:

- Directory Access Protocol (DAP)
- Lightweight Directory Access Protocol (LDAP)

Directory Access Protocol (DAP) was defined as a part of the X.500 specification. *Lightweight Directory Access Protocol (LDAP)*, on the other hand, was defined independently of X.500 as a method for accessing both X.500 and non-X.500 directories. Each has its strengths and weaknesses, but LDAP has become the preferred method of access because of its less-proprietary nature and lower overhead on the client. LDAP clients with the proper permissions can search, add, delete, and modify objects and attributes within a directory. LDAP functionality consists of 16 calls, used for directory management.

To be totally honest, any discussion of the X.500 standards with regard to directories is going to be a history lesson. The *X.500 recommendations* placed too much overhead on the client side of the directory access equation. Client software used to access any X.500 directory needs to know the schema of that directory. This results in client software that is proprietary to a particular directory implementation. X.500 is significant because it laid the groundwork for a consistent, industry-standard directory structure. All of the big players in the directory market—Novell, Netscape, and Microsoft—follow the hierarchical structure laid out by the X.500 committee, but none of them bought into the "standard."

With the release of LDAP v3, the LDAP specifications expanded to include a complete directory structure (rather than just a protocol to be used to access a directory). The result is that LDAP has become the de facto industry-standard directory architecture. Novell, Netscape, and even Microsoft have all bought into LDAP v3 (albeit with varying amounts of compliance). Because DAP is integral to an X.500 environment, but not to an LDAP environment (such as Active Directory), we'll let you research that on your own. For our purposes—passing the exam!—it's enough to talk just about the limitations of DAP and how LDAP overcomes those limitations.

Limitations of DAP

Although DAP is the access protocol defined within the X.500 specifications, it is not the access method that is getting the most press. That honor goes to the Lightweight Directory Access Protocol (LDAP), a protocol that is *not* defined within the X.500 recommendations. LDAP was developed in direct response to the major weaknesses of DAP:

- Using DAP-based software places a tremendous amount of overhead on the client computer. Many client machines, especially PCs or Macintosh computers, lack the resources necessary to support any DAP services.

- DAP was designed specifically to communicate with X.500 directories. This means that many vendor-specific products will not be accessible if you're using DAP-enabled software.

These two limitations of the DAP protocol have hindered the implementation of X.500 directories on production systems. Although the X.500 specifications are a great model, they are limited by the fact that they *are* only a model. Most commercial products are X.500 compatible but do not conform 100 percent to the model set forth by the standard. In effect, this lack of a multivendor access protocol has made X.500 directories an interesting theory but not a real-world solution. Combine this with the fact that, even if you take a chance and implement an X.500 directory, many of your client computers will lack the necessary horsepower to access the database—and you end up with a great idea whose time has not yet arrived!

LDAP was developed to overcome these limitations. Rather than becoming part of the X.500 recommendations, LDAP has been developed through a series of RFCs. This ensures that the protocol is developed as an open standard, available to anyone wishing to develop a directory-based product.

How LDAP Differs from DAP

The major difference between DAP and LDAP is that LDAP is not a client-based service. Yes, clients will use LDAP-enabled client software to communicate with a directory server, but they will communicate with an LDAP service on a server instead of directly with the Directory Service Agent (DSA) of the network directory. The LDAP service will interpret a client request and pass it along to the DSA.

Microsoft has built LDAP functionality directly into the core of Active Directory service. LDAP naming, and LDAP connection solutions, are used to find, read, and manage objects within the directory database. As such, understanding LDAP is critical to getting your mind around Active Directory and passing the exam.

In effect, this means that a vendor can build into its directory software an LDAP service that can accept standard LDAP requests and convert them into whatever format is necessary for the vendor's product. It also means that one client software package will be able to access information from the directories of multiple vendors.

Cross-vendor support is not the only benefit of an LDAP implementation. The overhead has been moved from the client to whatever server is supporting the LDAP service. This allows users with limited resources access to the information within the directory. Don't be surprised to see palmtop computers with the capability to access a directory remotely through the use of an LDAP solution.

Directory-Enabled Applications

Actually, the reduction in client-side resource use opens up a slew of possibilities for directory-based applications. One of the more basic uses might be the set-top box for a cable company. The cable company could easily configure a directory-based application that would provide current schedules or authenticate users to view special programming, as shown in Figure 5.1. For example, this would allow the cable company to demand authentication for a viewer to watch shows intended for mature audiences. The user account could store the birth dates of everyone in your household. When you chose a program to watch, the cable's directory server could compare your age against the age requirements of the program.

FIGURE 5.1 LDAP cable set-top implementation

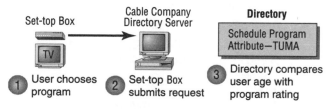

Why stop at the obvious—how about a directory-enabled refrigerator? Imagine a refrigerator that could scan the bar codes on the products it held and build a shopping list for you. Using LDAP, that list could then be sent to a directory at your market, and your weekly groceries could be waiting for you when you arrived at the store. Such a refrigerator would be quite intrusive, but the possibility is interesting!

These types of directory-enabled applications are available only because of the low demands that LDAP places on the client device. LDAP can be used by just about any device that can hold a microprocessor.

LDAP Functionality

Although the methods of their implementations differ, LDAP is really nothing more than a subset of the functions available in DAP. The development of LDAP centered around five design considerations to reduce the load on the client device:

- Implementing only a subset of the functions provided by DAP

- Offloading the complex operations necessary to locate resources in a distributed environment

- Simplifying the encoding of attribute types and values

- Using ordinary strings to represent data

- Using standard communication protocols (such as TCP) instead of complex, function-specific protocols

LDAP defines four actions:

Compare   Works just like the DAP Compare function. The client can compare object attributes for a match to given criteria.

Search   Works just like the DAP Search capability. The client can search all or some of the directory for objects that have attributes matching a given set of values. LDAP also uses the Search function to emulate the DAP Read and List functions. (Basically, the "search" is conducted using predefined search conditions.)

Abandon   Works just like the DAP Abandon function. The client can use this request to inform the LDAP service that it no longer needs to continue the query.

LDAP also defines functions that can be used to modify the database:

Modify   This is the equivalent of the DAP Modify request. LDAP simplifies the language involved by supporting three operations:

- Add values

- Delete values

- Replace values

Add   This request is used to add a new entry to the database.

Delete   This function allows the deletion of an entry from the database.

Modify RDN   This function requests that the name of an object be changed.

LDAP has sufficient functionality to satisfy most user or administrative needs. LDAP is probably going to be the access protocol of choice for most directories on the market.

From a design perspective, it is extremely important for you to understand the functionality that LDAP provides. If, for instance, your design requires remote administration of the AD structure, you must know how to use an LDAP-compliant utility to modify the content of the directory.

These two facets of LDAP (less client overhead and multivendor support) have made it the rising star of the directory industry. Most, if not all, directories on the market include an LDAP service as part of the basic package. Using LDAP-enabled software, a client could easily pull information from an AD server, as well as from most other directory services available.

It's also important to understand the functionality of LDAP because LDAP is going to be your key to interconnectivity—both to foreign systems such as Novell Directory Services and to various other Microsoft applications, such as Exchange Server.

What Does LDAP Have to Do with AD?

Although the X.500 specifications are supposed to guide developers in their efforts to create a network directory, in reality, the recommendations are too vague to completely define a commercially viable product. This means that most "X.500-compliant" directories are, in reality, proprietary databases. These proprietary databases would be unable to communicate or share data without some mechanism that can bridge the gap between compliance and compatibility, hence the development of LDAP. As discussed earlier, LDAP defines a series of basic functions that might need to be performed on *any* directory database. A vendor just needs to write a small server-based component that can take these LDAP requests for service and convert them into whatever format is appropriate for their own directory product. LDAP can also be used for server-to-server communication. In Chapter 9, we'll discuss Active Directory connectors that are add-on components that allow AD to communicate with other directory services. You might, for instance, want to mix a Novell NDS and Microsoft AD solution for your business. Using LDAP, these two products have a common protocol for accessing and modifying each other's information. Microsoft has gone so far as to make LDAP the default protocol used to connect to and mange an Active Directory database.

LDAP can be seen as the TCP/IP of the directory age. One of the driving reasons for the development of TCP/IP was to allow dissimilar systems to communicate using a common protocol. LDAP can be used for the same basic purpose.

LDAP Names

As we mentioned earlier, each object within the directory structure must have a unique name. There are four different types of names that can be used to reference an object within AD:

- Relative distinguished names (RDNs)
- Distinguished names
- Canonical names
- User principal names

Relative Distinguished Names

The *relative distinguished name* of any object is that portion of its name that uniquely identifies it in the container within which it resides. In other words, if you create within the education container a user whose object is named

Katie, and if the education container is in turn within the KingTech.com tree, as shown in Figure 5.2, the relative distinguished name of the object is CN=KATIE. Another way to look at this is to see the relative name as that portion of the distinguished name (described in the next section) that is an attribute of the object itself.

FIGURE 5.2 A relative distinguished name

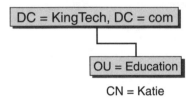

CN = Katie

If you have taken any of the Novell CNE courses, you will have been taught a different definition for *relative name*. The definition used here is not only the Microsoft definition, it is also the definition used in the LDAP specifications. In this case, Microsoft is more "industry standard" than Novell.

Distinguished Names

The *distinguished name* of any object is the relative name of the object plus the names of the containers that make up the path to that object. The object CN=Carrie in Figure 5.3, for instance, has a distinguished name of CN=Carrie, OU=Education, DC=KingTech, DC=com.

The *DC* in the distinguished name is the abbreviation for domain component. It refers to the DNS domain name within the AD tree. These components act as the point of logical connection between DNS and AD.

FIGURE 5.3 A distinguished name

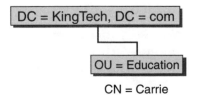

CN = Carrie

DN: CN = Carrie, OU = Education, DC = KingTech, DC = Com

Notice that the distinguished name of the object identifies the nature of each container in the path.

Canonical Names

Canonical names are created in the same fashion as distinguished names— only the notation is different. In our earlier example, CN=Carrie's canonical name would be written as KingTech.com/education/Carrie. The major difference is that here we work from the top down in the directory hierarchy to create the name rather than from the bottom up.

User Principal Names

LDAP relative and distinguished names are long and difficult to remember. Rather than force users to use these inconvenient names for identification, Active Directory also assigns each security principal a more user-friendly name known as the *user principal name*. A *security principal* is any object that can be assigned permissions within the directory structure, namely users, groups, and computers. The user principal name is the object's relative name combined with the name of the domain tree in which it exists. Using our sample tree for KingTech.com, shown in Figure 5.4, user Susan's principal name would be Susan@KingTech.com.

FIGURE 5.4   A user principal name

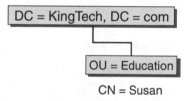

User principal names are designed to avoid some of the complexity that is inherent in a hierarchical design. If a company has a deep OU structure, as shown in Figure 5.5, a user's distinguished name might end up being too long to be convenient. User Tom, for instance, has a distinguished name of CN=Tom, OU=education, OU=Glendive, OU=Montana, DC=wildlands, DC=com. Forcing Tom to use such a long name to log in to the network would be inhumane at best. The user principal name of Tom@wildlands.com is much easier for Tom to remember.

FIGURE 5.5 A deep OU structure

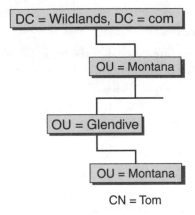

DN: CN = Tom, OU = Education, OU = Glendive, OU = Montana, DC = Wildlands, DC = com

UP = Tom@Wildlands.com

The Technical Side of Naming

Now that you are aware of the various forms of names that are used in AD, we can expand our discussion to the behind-the-scenes procedures that are implemented when objects are created. Microsoft has added numerous components to the AD environment to ensure that naming requirements are met.

Domains in AD

You should already be aware that NT domains still exist in Windows 2000. Microsoft likes to gloss this over, but the fact remains that certain limitations are inherent in this continued use of old technology. The first major aspect of domains is that, although Microsoft has added an X.500-compatible structure for management purposes, these containers are not really a part of the domain structure. In other words, OUs do not really "exist" within the domain itself. A working definition of a domain could still be "a logical grouping of computers and users managed through a central database." The format of this database has changed a little, but certain aspects have, unfortunately, stayed in place. The first of these limitations is that computers and usernames within a domain must be unique. Take a look at Figure 5.6. Within this hierarchical structure, we have two users whose common name (CN) is BKing.

FIGURE 5.6 KingTech AD structure

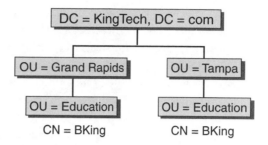

The distinguished names of these user objects are indeed unique: CN=BKing, OU=Education, OU=**Grand Rapids**, DC=KingTech, DC=Com and CN=BKing, OU=Education, OU=**Tampa**, DC=KingTech, DC=Com (the difference between the names appears in bold). Because the names are unique, one might assume that this is acceptable. The reality is that this would depend upon the domain structure that had been implemented within this database. Look at the two domain structures shown in Figure 5.7.

FIGURE 5.7 Two possible domain structures

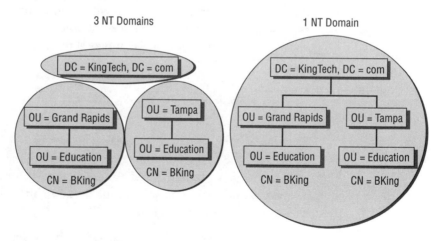

In the design on the left, the two BKing accounts are in different domains; in the design on the right, the two accounts exist in the same NT domain. Because domains still act as if they were a flat database, the design on the right is invalid—computer and usernames must be unique across the domain within which they exist.

Domain and Tree Security Identifiers

As you should be aware, most updates and changes to the AD directory can take place on any directory server in your tree. An environment in which this can take place is known as a multi-master environment. A *multi-master environment* is one in which all replicas are equal; that is, changes can be made on any copy and then replicated to all other copies. There are, however, certain functions for which a multi-master environment is not feasible. Changes to the schema, for instance, should be made at one, and only one, server and then replicated from there. Microsoft was aware of this fact, so AD has certain functions that are handled as single-master procedures. In other words, one server is responsible for the action (such as changing the schema) and for passing the results to all other servers. To control this, certain servers are designated as operations masters. An *operations master* is the only server that can perform a specific task. Some operations master roles are domain based and others are responsible for an activity for the entire AD forest.

If you are making comparisons to Novell NetWare, you might be inclined to brag about the fact that there are no single-master actions in NDS. Although this is technically true, even Novell will recommend that changes to the schema be done at only one server at a time and that those changes be allowed to replicate before any complex activity within the directory database is attempted.

When considering your naming strategy, you must be aware of two operations master roles:

Domain naming master (DNM)   This server is responsible for generating a unique *security identifier (SID)* for each domain that joins the forest. There can only be one DNM server in each AD forest. From a design perspective, this server *must* be available when any domain is created in or added to your environment.

Relative ID master (RIM)   The RIM server is responsible for generating a sequence of relative IDs for each domain controller in a domain. By using a single server to generate the relative IDs (10,000 at a time) that will be applied to all security principals created within the domain, the system ensures that the SIDs for each object will be unique. There is a RIM for each domain within your forest.

When a security principal is created, the domain controller in which the action takes place adds the domain SID (created by the domain naming master) and one of the relative IDs in the sequence it received from the relative ID master to create a unique SID for the new object. Because each domain controller is given a sequence of relative IDs, it is not critical that the RIM be available as each object is created. It is, however, important that the RIM functions be processed on a server that is reliable. It is conceivable that a server will use the last of the IDs granted by the RIM and need to request more. If the RIM is not available at that time, no new security principals can be created (at that server).

Notice that we said it is not critical that the RIM be available for the creation of security principals under normal circumstances. For this reason, placement of the RIM server is not a big consideration when designing your physical network.

Okay—back to AD design. Most of the LDAP naming that we've discussed so far will be of more use during the design of your OU hierarchy within the AD structure. Because this is the "naming" chapter, though, we thought it appropriate to place it here. The only real "rules" for LDAP naming that you should remember is that object CNs (relative names) must be unique within a single OU and that usernames and computer names must be unique within an NT domain. Otherwise, just follow the common-sense guidelines we sketched in "The Importance of Standard Names" earlier in this chapter.

AD and DNS

Years ago, long before Microsoft (let alone any Windows products), groups were working on solutions to the networking problems they faced at the time. Most of those problems revolved around communication. Computer systems designed by different vendors were unable to communicate, WAN links were crude and undependable, and "off-the-shelf" solutions didn't exist, so everyone wrote their own software. Somewhere along the line, someone had the great idea that it would be nice to be able to share information between dissimilar systems by using a shared backbone of "high-speed" connections. This was the birth of the Internet.

A communication protocol was needed that would act as a standard method for communication (replacing or augmenting the proprietary protocols in use by each vendor). Into this void came TCP/IP—the protocol of choice for today's networks. TCP/IP was specifically designed to act as the communication protocol used between *any* devices on a network—no matter what the vendor. TCP/IP is often referred to as a protocol, when in reality it should be referred to as a suite of protocols and services. One of those services is DNS. The main function of DNS is to hide the complexity of TCP/IP addressing from end users. TCP/IP and the DNS service are both critical components of AD design. Active Directory uses DNS to find the IP addresses of servers and services on your network. Therefore, without TCP/IP and DNS, Active Directory will not function.

Scared yet? You should be! A working knowledge of TCP/IP is a prerequisite for the Active Directory Design exam. If you need to brush up on your TCP/IP skills, we recommend *TCP/IP Jumpstart* (Sybex, 2000) by Andrew G. Blank. A few of our consultant friends are expecting a lot of work correcting the mistakes made by those administrators who implement Windows 2000 and Active Directory without a good understanding of TCP/IP and its related services (such as DNS).

What Is DNS?

The basic function of *Domain Name System (DNS)* is to resolve user-friendly domain names into IP addresses. When a client enters a Fully Qualified Domain Name (FQDN), the DNS server is queried for the IP address of the corresponding server. DNS is the tool most commonly used to find resources on large IP networks such as the Internet. Although DNS has been working as the main name-resolution service on the Internet for quite some time, it does have a few weaknesses. For our discussion, we'll look first at how DNS is structured, then at a few of its weak points.

Why DNS?

Before the Internet was created, there existed a network known as the ARPAnet. This network tied together a few university and Department of Defense (DOD) sites so that they could share research material. (This is a bit simplistic, but it will suffice for our discussion.) Because of its ties to the DOD, this network is sometimes referred to as DARPAnet.

For an overview of Internet history from the perspective of network security, see *Mastering Network Security* (Sybex, 1998) by Chris Brenton.

Because the network was small, each computer on the Net had a small text file, known as a *hosts file*, that listed a user-friendly name for each host (computer) and its IP address. When another host was added to a site, the hosts file on each computer that might need to communicate with the new computer was updated with its address.

As an example, suppose that two networks were tied to the ARPAnet—KingTech and PS Consulting. Each of these networks has five hosts that must be accessed across the network. The hosts file for each client device must include a "friendly name" and the IP address of all 10 hosts. A sample hosts file is shown in Table 5.2.

TABLE 5.2 Sample Hosts File

IP Address	Host
131.107.2.100	Localhost1
131.107.2.101	Localhost2
131.107.2.102	Localhost3
131.107.2.103	Localhost4
131.107.3.100	Remotehost1
131.107.3.101	Remotehost2
131.107.3.102	Remotehost3
131.107.3.103	Remotehost4
131.107.3.104	Remotehost5

Each computer needing to access hosts on these two networks needs a hosts file with the IP address of all of the hosts it might access. So keeping these "simple" text files up-to-date could require quite a bit of management.

What Are DNS Domains?

DNS was created to alleviate some of this management overhead. Basically, DNS is this text file (the hosts file) broken into logical units known as *domains* and distributed across multiple computers known as DNS *servers*. The logical domains are organized in a hierarchical structure, much like the DOS file system. There is a very specific format, known as the *namespace* of the DNS system, for the names used in a DNS system. The concept of a namespace will be very important in understanding how AD is accessed by clients, so let's redefine the term to ensure that we are all in agreement:

> A *namespace* is a set of rules governing how objects (DNS records in this case) are formatted within a directory.

On the Internet, domain names are registered with a central consortium to ensure that they are unique and that their format follows the namespace rules set forth for the Internet. This consortium, known as InterNIC (short for Internet Network Information Center), controls the last section, or "upper level," of domain names and has created a specific set for use on the Internet. Domain names on the Internet will end with one of the following, based on the purpose of the domain:

.edu	Educational institutions
.com	Commercial organizations
.org	Nonprofit organizations
.net	Networks
.gov	Nonmilitary government organizations
.mil	Military government organizations
.num	Telephone numbers
.arpa	Reverse DNS
.xx	Two-letter country codes (such as .ca for Canada)

Actually, this list is not really complete. Most of us are used to typing in domain names like www.royal-tech.com, and we are taught that this is the resource's complete name. In this case, www represents the host (our Web server), and royal-tech.com is the domain. In reality, the full name of any domain ends in a period. The period represents the root of the domain namespace, much like DOS paths should really start with C:\ but are rarely typed that way.

When a domain name is registered, InterNIC (or one of the other companies that now provide this service) will determine if the requesting agency has chosen the appropriate upper-level domain. If so, and if the name is not already in use, InterNIC will reserve the name for the requesting party and add a record to DNS for the new domain.

The following steps show how a DNS request is translated into an IP address during a typical query:

1. The client requests a resource; for our example, let's assume it's the Web page www.royal-tech.com. One of the configuration parameters for IP clients is the IP address of a DNS server. The client software will query this server for the IP address of the corresponding resource.

2. The DNS server will process the query, first checking to see if information for the royal-tech.com domain is included. If not, it will check a local cache. The local cache contains the IP addresses of resources that have recently been resolved to IP addresses. If the IP address for www.royal-tech.com is in the cache, the server will return this information to the client.

The DNS cache is a physical file that holds the IP addresses that the DNS server has resolved; if someone accesses a site once, they might want to do so again. Caching the IP addresses speeds up response time because the DNS server will not have to query any other servers for the information the second time. Because the Internet is a dynamic environment, these cached entries are given a Time To Live (TTL) so that they will be re-resolved every so often. In the Microsoft implementation of DNS, the default TTL for cached entries is 60 minutes.

3. If the information is not available locally, the DNS server will forward the query to a root server. Each DNS server on the Internet contains a *public cache* file that holds the IP addresses of the root servers for each top-level domain tree (.com, .edu, .org, and so on).

4. The root DNS server will search its database for the record of a DNS server registered for the .com domain. If such a record exists, it will return the IP address to the local DNS server.

5. The local DNS server will then query the .com DNS server for the IP address of a resource named royal-tech. If such a record exists, the remote DNS server will return the IP address to the local DNS server.

6. The local DNS server will query the royal-tech.com DNS server for the IP address of a host named www. If such a record exists, the remote DNS server will return the IP address of the www server to the local DNS server.

7. The local DNS server will return the IP address to the client. The client will then begin the process of connecting to the royal-tech.com Web server. This process is depicted in Figure 5.8.

FIGURE 5.8 A typical Internet DNS query

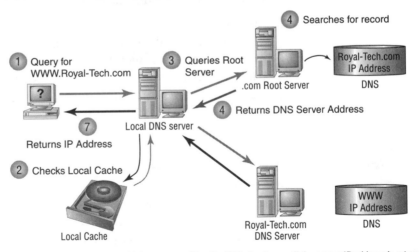

Steps 5, 6, and 7 result in local DNS servers walking the DNS structure until the proper IP address is returned.

The DNS Structure

The example in Figure 5.8 demonstrates both the distributed nature and the hierarchical design of DNS. Each DNS server contains records for resources only in the domains for which it is responsible. If the DNS server receives a request for information that it does not contain, it will pass that request up or down the structure until the appropriate DNS server is found.

You could see DNS as a DOS-like structure—a series of directories (or domains) organized in a treelike format, as shown in Figure 5.9.

FIGURE 5.9   The DNS hierarchical structure

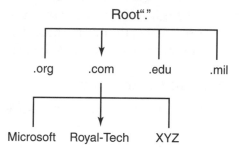

The hierarchy of domains within the DNS structure allows the database to be broken into smaller sections, which can in turn be distributed across multiple servers. This reduces the hardware required at any given server, as well as the network bandwidth required to support queries.

Imagine a system that was *not* broken into smaller pieces. First, the database would be huge (a record for *every* resource on the Internet). Few companies would be able to afford the kind of equipment that would be required: large hard drives, tons of memory, and multiprocessor servers would be mandatory. With fewer DNS servers available, each would have to handle more queries from clients. This would result in more network traffic, which would in turn require more bandwidth on the link to the Internet. Without the capability to distribute the workload across multiple servers, DNS would probably not work for name resolution on large IP networks.

This capability to break the database into logical pieces and distribute those pieces across servers is critical to any network directory that hopes to serve in medium or larger environments. As you'll see in a bit, Active Directory takes this a step further.

DNS Records

Due to the various services that can be listed in a traditional DNS database, the format of each record can get quite complex, but the bottom line is that DNS is a series of text files containing IP addresses for hosts in an IP-based network. These text files must be created and maintained manually (once again, in a traditional DNS implementation; we'll discuss the AD implementation in a few pages), a task that can consume a lot of time in a large environment. If a company is forced to change its IP addressing scheme, the DNS records for each resource must be updated in DNS. If a resource is added (another mail or Web server, for instance), a record must be added to the DNS database.

The manual nature of DNS management is both a blessing and a curse. On one hand, the simplicity of a text file offers advantages in a mixed environment. On the other hand, a database that does not offer any automation will require a lot of person-hours in a large environment.

DNS Fault Tolerance

To provide fault tolerance, DNS defines two types of DNS servers:

- Primary servers

- Secondary servers

Primary DNS servers copy the domain information they contain to secondary servers on a regular basis. Clients can be configured with the IP address of multiple DNS servers. If the client attempts to contact a DNS server and receives no response, it will proceed to the next DNS server in its list. This ensures that clients will continue to function normally even if the network loses a DNS server to some catastrophe, as shown in Figure 5.10.

FIGURE 5.10 Primary and secondary DNS servers

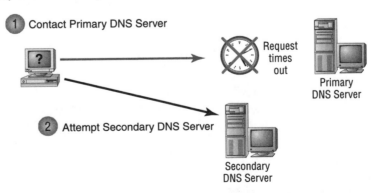

Although the primary/secondary arrangement of servers provides a level of redundancy, it is configured in a limited manner known as a *single-master environment*. All changes to the DNS database *must* occur at the primary (or *master*) DNS server and be propagated to the *secondary DNS server*. If the master DNS server should fail, no changes can be made to the database until one of the secondary servers has been promoted to the status of master.

DNS in Short

The Domain Name System is a database used to resolve host names into IP addresses. The namespace it defines follows a set of rules that is the industry standard. The database can be broken into smaller pieces (domains) and distributed across multiple servers. The service provides a mechanism for combining these separate files into a logical whole. Using a series of primary and secondary servers, the service adds a limited amount of fault tolerance to the database by replicating domain information to multiple servers.

All in all, DNS is a success. It has fulfilled its purpose in a large environment (the Internet) for quite some time. You might be wondering, "If DNS is so great, why don't we use it as our network directory instead of implementing Active Directory services?" The answer to this question revolves around functionality. DNS was designed for a specific purpose: resolving a host name into an IP address. DNS handles its intended function very well—so well, in fact, that AD incorporates DNS into its own design—but DNS could not handle the extra functions that would be placed upon it in an expanded role. DNS is based on a series of text files that are seen as a flat-file database. Adding additional functionality (holding the configuration information for a router, for instance) would stretch the limits of such technology.

DNS in an Active Directory Environment

Microsoft Windows 2000 uses DNS as the major means of resolving user-friendly names, such as FileServer1 or ColorPrinter, into the IP address of resources. If there is one aspect of AD design that is most critical to a stable environment, it is DNS implementation.

When you deploy Microsoft DNS services in an AD environment, you have two choices:

- Use traditional, text-based zone files.

- Integrate the zone information with Active Directory.

Not surprisingly, Microsoft suggests the latter option! When you integrate DNS with AD, all zone information is stored in the AD database—a distributed, replicated, fault-tolerant database—which is then stored on all of the AD servers within your organization.

Exam Hint: Due to its importance to Active Directory, DNS design and implementation is tested heavily throughout the entire MCSE exam suite. By the time you are ready to take the AD Design exam, you should know DNS inside and out.

AD can store one or more *DNS zones*. All domain controllers can then receive dynamic DNS information sent from other Windows 2000 computers. Each Active Directory server can also act as a fully functional DNS authority, updating the DNS information stored on all of your AD servers.

In other words, once DNS has been integrated with AD, every AD server acts as a primary DNS server for all zones. In fact, *all* zones stored by AD must be primary—if you need to implement old-fashioned secondary zones (perhaps in a mixed DNS environment), you will have to stick with the old-fashioned text-file-based DNS.

Exam Hint: If you are presented with a scenario that describes a DNS implementation that must use secondary DNS zones, you must use traditional text-based DNS.

In addition to integration with Active Directory, the Microsoft implementation of DNS provides the following functionality:

SRV resource records   *SRV resource records* are a new type of record (defined in RFC 2052) that identifies the location of a service rather than a device.

Dynamic update   Microsoft DNS is more properly called DDNS: *Dynamic* Domain Name System. It is capable of allowing hosts to dynamically register their names with the zone, thereby reducing administrative overhead.

Secure dynamic update   Windows 2000 Server security is used to authenticate hosts that attempt to dynamically register themselves within the zone.

Incremental zone transfer   With *incremental zone transfer*, only changed data is replicated to other AD servers.

Interoperability with DHCP   A server running DHCP services can register host names on behalf of its clients. This allows non-DDNS clients to dynamically register with the zone.

Active Directory uses DNS to locate domains and domain controllers during the logon process. This is made possible by the inclusion of SRV-type records in the DNS database. Each Windows 2000 domain controller dynamically registers an SRV record in the zone. This record represents the domain Netlogon service on that server. When a client attempts to log on, it will query its DNS server for the address of a domain controller. The bottom line here is that, even if you are not going to use DNS for anything else, you will have to install and configure it for the logon process to work properly. Let us stress this one more time—DNS is critical to an AD environment!

The process of installing and configuring DNS is covered in *MCSE: Windows 2000 Network Administration Study Guide* (Sybex, 2000).

Dynamic DNS (DDNS)

One of the biggest weaknesses of traditional DNS configurations is that the text file must be manually updated. Every time a host is added to your environment, you must create a DNS record for it. With DDNS, Windows 2000–based computers can automatically add their name to DNS as they initialize and remove themselves when they are shut down.

AD Integration with DNS

As discussed earlier, previous versions of DNS were based on text files. For Windows 2000, the DNS service has been integrated into Active Directory. This integration results in two major changes in DNS deployment:

- DNS is required for locating Windows 2000 domain controllers. The Netlogon service uses the DNS database to register the domain controllers on your network. DNS is then used by clients when requesting a list of domain controllers during the logon process.

Exam Hint: This means that the Netlogon service relies on DNS to find a domain controller—remember this fact!

- The DNS database is stored within the Active Directory database. This allows you to take advantage of several AD features to improve the performance, reliability, and fault tolerance of DNS.

Microsoft strongly advises using an AD-integrated DNS system on all Windows 2000 networks. Doing so will provide many benefits:

- Multi-master replication

- Enhanced security

- Automatic replication and synchronization with new domain controllers as they are added to the domain

- Replication that is faster and more efficient

Let's examine each of these advantages in more detail.

Multi-Master Replication

In a traditional DNS implementation, DNS updates use a single-master model in which a single authoritative DNS server is designated as the source of all updates for the zone. This represents a single point of failure. If this server is not available, update requests cannot be processed. You would think that secondary copies of a zone stored on another server could take over this functionality, but the reality is that, if the master copy becomes unavailable for a specific (it varies with vendor) amount of time, all secondary DNS servers for the zone consider themselves "out-of-date" and also stop providing name resolution services to clients.

In an AD-integrated environment, a multi-master update model is used for DNS changes. Because the DNS database is stored within the AD database (which is replicated to all domain controllers), the zone information can be updated by the DNS service running on any domain controller in the Windows 2000 network. In this case, all Windows 2000 Active Directory servers that have DNS services installed act as the primary source and can accept client requests for changes and replicate (through AD) those changes to all other DNS servers. It also means that, in the event of a DNS sever going down, all other AD DNS servers can continue to service client DNS queries.

Enhanced Security

Once the DNS database is moved into the AD database, its information can be protected using all of the security tools available for any other data in the AD database. The DNS data is stored in a dnsZone object container (named after the DNS domain that it represents), which has an access control list (ACL). This ACL can be used to control which users or computers can make changes to the DNS data. This is known as a *secure update environment* and is the default configuration for AD-integrated DNS environments. This prevents unauthorized servers from adding their information to your environment.

Automatic Replication and Synchronization with New Domain Controllers

Directory-integrated zones are stored on all domain controllers, so replication and synchronization is not an additional resource on the servers. In other words, there is no additional overhead placed on a domain controller to facilitate zone transfers. Using a built-in replication process reduces administrative overhead (you don't have to configure a second replication service).

This has the added benefit that less time must be spent planning for replication. As you configure AD replication, you are also planning DNS replication.

Replication Is Faster and More Efficient

In traditional DNS replication (the single-master model), all updates involved the transfer of the complete zone file, so if one record was added or changed, the entire file had to be replicated. With AD-integrated DNS, DNS updates are handled in the same manner most other changes to the database are handled—on a per-property basis. If you change the IP address of a particular host, only the changed information will be replicated.

Designing a Zone Structure for DNS

DNS is critical to the functioning of an Active Directory network. As such, a good DNS design can greatly improve the performance of your network and reduce the impact of DNS on the network. In reality, coming up with a good DNS zone design is not difficult if you follow a few guidelines and understand a few of the basics of DNS.

Microsoft ✓ **Exam Objective**

Design the placement of DNS servers.

- Considerations include performance, fault tolerance, functionality, and manageability.

- Plan for interoperability with the existing DNS

The Difference between a Zone and a Domain

A zone starts out as a file that contains the information for a single DNS domain name, such as KingTech.com. Think of the zone as the physical storage of the data and the domain as the logical organization of that data. This concept is easier to see than it is to explain. Assume that you are installing and configuring DNS services for the KingTech domain. When you create the first zone, your environment will look like that shown in Figure 5.11.

FIGURE 5.11   A single-domain DNS structure

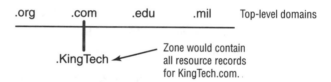

All of the resource records for the KingTech.com domain are stored within a single zone. In a traditional DNS implementation, this would be a single text file. In an AD-integrated design, these records would be stored in a single dnsZone object container (named KingTech.com).

If the environment required a subdomain named education.KingTech.com, you would have the choice of adding the subdomain to the original zone, as shown in Figure 5.12, or creating a new zone (usually on another server) for the education.KingTech.com domain, as shown in Figure 5.13. In a traditional DNS implementation, the resource records for the education subdomain would be stored in a separate text file. In an AD-integrated implementation, a new dnsZone object container would be created.

FIGURE 5.12   The domain and subdomain in the same zone

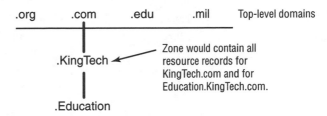

FIGURE 5.13   A multidomain, multizone configuration

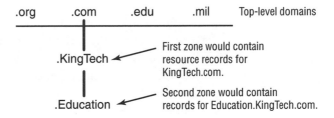

Zone Planning Guidelines

There are only two hard-and-fast rules when it comes to planning your DNS zone structure:

- There can be no more than 65,553 resource records within a single zone.

- Do not place more than 1,000 zones on a single DNS server.

Staying within these two guidelines should be easy for all but the largest of companies. After you have ensured that you have not exceeded the maximum limits for a DNS server, the rest of your planning will be a bit more subjective.

The first step to take when deciding upon zone boundaries is to analyze the traffic patterns on your network (if you are designing a new network, this will take a bit of experience). DNS is designed to limit the amount of broadcast traffic placed on networks, but it does create some traffic that must be taken into account during planning.

To review DNS traffic, you can use the DNS server statistics or DNS performance counters provided with System Monitor.

DNS generates two types of traffic:

- Server-to-server traffic caused by zone transfers and by interaction with other services on the network (such as performing a WINS lookup)

- Client-to-server traffic generated by both dynamic updates and DNS queries

In general, this traffic is negligible, but it can have a negative effect on slow WAN links or links that are saturated with other types of traffic (low available bandwidth). This issue will be more important if you are using a mixture of DNS implementations because some DNS services do not support incremental zone transfers. In other words, in many older DNS products, the entire zone must be transferred each time there is a change.

Microsoft AD-integrated DNS will, however, produce more traffic than earlier versions of DNS. Because clients can dynamically add themselves to the DNS zone, each time a computer comes online (or offline), a change will be made to the DNS database. This change (the new record or the deletion of the record) will have to be replicated to all DNS servers in the zone.

Design Scenario: Creating DNS Domains and Subdomains

Company XYZ had a total of 5,100 computers, each of which is configured to dynamically register itself with DNS. Those computers are distributed across four physical sites. Tampa has 3,000 computers, Grand Rapids has 1,500, Reno has 500, and Clearwater has just 100.

The company's network consists of a hub design with the Tampa office as the hub. There is a 256K link to Reno, a dial-up connection to Grand Rapids, and a 56K dedicated line to Clearwater. During the analysis of network traffic, the following information was discovered:

- In the Tampa office, computers authenticate to the network an average of five times each business day (forcing a new dynamic write to the DNS database).

- Both Grand Rapids and Reno average three authentications each day.

- The link between Grand Rapids and Tampa is a dial-on-demand line.

- The link between Tampa and Reno is saturated on a regular basis.

- The line between Clearwater and Tampa has plenty of available bandwidth.

Based upon this information, how many DNS domains and subdomains would you create?

Looking at this scenario, you should notice two facts: First, you really want to limit additional traffic on both links; the 256K line is already running at capacity, and the company has to pay connection charges each time the dial-up line is initialized. For this reason, you'll want to configure at least three zones: Tampa/Clearwater, Grand Rapids, and Reno. This will keep zone transfers to a minimum over the Tampa-Reno and Tampa-Grand Rapids links. Because the line to Clearwater has plenty of available bandwidth, you could leave it as a part of the Tampa zone.

Choosing and Placing DNS Servers on Your Network

Once you have finished planning your DNS zone structure, you must move to planning for DNS server placement. There are two issues to consider:

- Server placement

- Server capacity

Server Placement

The exam objective for this section asks you to consider performance, fault tolerance, functionality, and manageability when considering the placement of DNS servers. Most of these considerations will revolve around the WAN links in the environment.

Exam Hint: Remember that DNS is critical to the Netlogon service. It will always be better to have too many DNS servers than not enough.

Performance

During your analysis of DNS traffic on your network, you should have developed a good feel for the impact DNS will have on your infrastructure. Planning server placement will be a subjective decision based upon this "feel." Consider the effects of DNS query traffic and compare those effects with those of zone transfer traffic. For example, if you have two physical sites connected through a WAN link, you will have to determine whether you should place a DNS server on each side of the link or whether one central server will suffice. It is easy to trace the traffic generated by both processes and determine which will have a bigger impact on performance (zone transfer or DNS client query). Unfortunately, we can't give you a hard-and-fast rule about which will have the bigger impact—which function will generate more traffic is based upon too many variables.

Fault Tolerance

You must consider the effect of the WAN link going down. In such a situation, will your users still be able to log on to local resources? Remember that DNS is used by the Netlogon service to locate domain controllers. Without DNS, clients will not be able to log on to the network. The bottom line here is that a DNS server on both sides of most WAN links is the safest design.

Functionality

Here you will need to make a more subjective decision. Consider the distribution of computers across your various physical networks. As with most services, it is best to place DNS servers as close as possible to the users who will access them. If you plan on one DNS server and your office has a backbone wiring scheme, place that server on the backbone. If you can limit the number of DNS queries that cross routers, do so. Analyze the traffic patterns and place DNS servers on subnets that will generate the most DNS traffic.

Manageability

Like functionality, this is a more subjective consideration. If your company uses a distributed management model (you have site administrators), you should consider placing DNS services on local servers. If, however, you follow a centralized management model, keep the DNS servers on centrally controlled servers. Consider staffing—do you have a local person who is capable of managing the DNS service?

Exam Hint: For most of these types of questions (where should I place this or that?), Microsoft has a history of describing the management philosophy during the scenario setup. For the Design tests, this is critical information!

Server Capacity Planning

Because each DNS server loads its configured zones into memory at initialization, you will usually see the biggest performance boost from adding RAM to your server (rather than upgrading the processor or buying faster hard drives). The amount of RAM needed in any server is based upon many variables:

- How many services does the server provide to the network?

- How many clients does the server support?

- Is the server used for file and print services?

- How many DNS queries will the DNS server need to service simultaneously?

Because RAM recommendations are notoriously inaccurate, we'll stick with just the RAM necessary to implement DNS (you'll have to deal with the other variables yourself). In a typical environment, DNS consumption is as follows:

- Approximately 4MB of RAM for the service itself (without any configured zones)

- Approximately 100 bytes of server memory for each resource record within each zone configured on the server

For example, if a server was configured with one zone that contained 1,000 resource records, that DNS service would need the following:

4MB for the DNS service

100KB for the zone (100 bytes × 1,000 records)

4.1MB of RAM

Naming for Both AD and DNS

The mix of DNS and Active Directory names can be a bit confusing within a Windows 2000 forest. When you add domains to an AD structure, they are arranged in a hierarchical structure, as shown in Figure 5.14.

FIGURE 5.14 A hierarchical relationship of domains

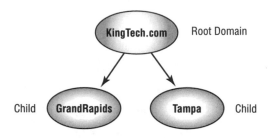

> **Microsoft**
> **Exam**
> **Objective**
>
> **Design an Active Directory naming strategy.**
> - Design the namespace.
> - Plan DNS strategy.

The first domain created in Active Directory is known as the *root domain*. The root domain begins the namespace that is defined with the tree. Only one name can be given to the root domain, and Microsoft recommends that, if you plan to connect to the Internet, the domain name be the same as the domain name you have registered on the Internet. In our case, for example, our root domain was named Royal-Tech.com because this is the domain that we have registered on the Internet. You cannot change the name of the root domain without removing AD (thus destroying your tree) and creating a new tree. For this reason, it is critical that you take time to plan your structure.

Our opinion is that you should register a domain name on the Internet, even if you plan no Internet presence, and use this name for your root domain. That way, if you later change your mind about joining the Internet, you won't have to re-create your forest, but this opinion can vary from company to company due to security considerations.

Each domain added to the structure will derive its DNS name from the domains above it in the AD domain structure. In Figure 5.15, we have added the DNS name for each domain in our tree to the example environment.

FIGURE 5.15   DNS names for NT domains

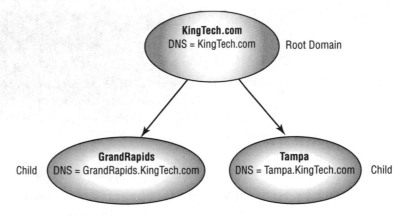

Naming Guidelines

When naming your Windows 2000 domains, you should keep the following guidelines in mind:

- The Active Directory root domain must be unique within any DNS hierarchy with which it will interact. This means that, if you are connected to the Internet, you should register a domain name and use it as the name of your root domain.

- If you are not connected, or not planning to connect, to the Internet, you are free to use just about any names you chose. If, however, you plan to have an Internet presence, you must conform to the Internet naming standards. For more information on DNS standards, see RFCs 1034, 1035, 1039, and 2052. Microsoft is recommending that you use a naming standard that has been set aside for this purpose—end your DNS domain with the extension .local. For example, if King Technologies, LLC did not plan on developing an Internet presence, we would name the first domain KingTech.local.

- Domain names should be meaningful to end users, stable (not subject to change), and chosen with an eye toward expansion. (Using long but meaningful names might seem like a good idea, but as you add domains to your structure, the overall DNS names can become unwieldy.)

DNS Strategies

When you're deciding upon a DNS naming strategy for your environment, four main options exist:

- Use your registered DNS domain name as the name of the AD root domain. This allows you to use the same DNS name for your internal and external networks. It is also the method recommended in most Microsoft publications.

- Use a subdomain of your registered name as the name of your AD root domain. We might, for instance, use a DNS zone for Royal-Tech.com that holds resource records for our public hosts (Web server, e-mail server, etc.) and use GrandRapids.Royal-Tech.com as the name of our root domain.

- Use a different DNS name for your AD structure and a registered name for your Internet presence. This maintains complete separation of your public and private resources.

- Use the same name for both your internal and external DNS system, but separate the two systems with a firewall and manually maintain the appropriate records in each DNS server.

We'll discuss each of these options in turn.

Using Your Registered DNS Name

This is usually the easiest strategy because most companies will already have a working DNS system that uses the registered name. The only real drawback to this strategy is that you must ensure that your DNS implementation supports SRV records. SRV (service) records identify the location of a service; most importantly to the AD tree, SRV records are used to identify domain controllers. If you are currently using a DNS system that does not recognize SRV records, you will need to either upgrade it or install at least one Windows 2000 DNS server.

Current implementations of Bind DNS services that are version 4.9.6 or greater support SRV records. If you decide to stick with a non–Windows 2000 DNS solution, you must ensure that your DNS system meets at least this version of Bind compatibility. You will probably also want to ensure that your DNS system supports the following:

- Dynamic updates
- DNS change notification
- Negative caching
- Incremental updates

For this to be the case, you must be using a Bind DNS system that meets version 8.*x* or greater. Currently, Microsoft is suggesting version 8.2.1 or better.

For the die-hards, you can read more about these capabilities in RFCs 2136 (dynamic updates), 1996 (DNS change notification), 2308 (negative caching), and 1995 (incremental updates). Just be warned—we've always found the RFCs to be the perfect cure for insomnia.

Using a Subdomain of Your Registered Domain

In this case, you have a registered domain name but want to keep your internal resource records in a different zone. You will configure AD and DNS with the subdomain name and use another DNS zone to look further into the overall DNS structure. For example, in Figure 5.16, Royal-Tech.com is registered on the Internet, but we decided to go with GR.Royal-Tech.com as the name for our root domain. Our ISP handles queries for Royal-Tech.com, and our internal servers just need to worry about internal records (GR.Royal-Tech.com).

FIGURE 5.16   Using a subdomain as the root domain

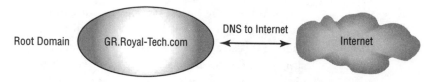

Root Domain — GR.Royal-Tech.com — DNS to Internet — Internet

This DNS configuration allows you to continue to use your existing DNS servers without upgrading or updating them. It also allows for a complete separation of AD data in the DNS structure. On the flip side, though, your AD DNS names are longer because the names actually start at the third level (rather than the second), and you will need a working DNS server that the root domain can use for queries outside of the local domain structure.

Exam Hint: This solution is handy for small to medium-size companies that already have an outside service handling their DNS functions.

Using Different Names for Internal and External DNS Systems

This deployment completely separates your internal DNS from the outside world. This arrangement should be used if you do not have a registered DNS name, never foresee connecting to the Internet, or want to clearly differentiate external from internal resources. The biggest problem with this arrangement is that, if you change your mind and want to connect to the Internet, you will need to completely reinstall your AD forest.

Using the Same Name on Internal and External DNS Systems

This is the most difficult scenario to manage because it requires manual manipulation of the DNS database on the external DNS server, but it is also the most secure environment due to the complete separation of internal and external DNS services. As shown in Figure 5.17, this model has two DNS servers—one for external use and one, on the other side of a firewall, for internal use. The external DNS server only has those resource records that should be made available to the public (this DNS server will have to be managed manually).

FIGURE 5.17   Same name—two DNS systems

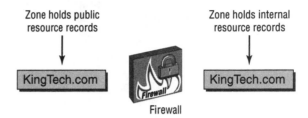

Zone holds public
resource records

Zone holds internal
resource records

KingTech.com

KingTech.com

Firewall

So How Do I Decide?

We've discussed some of the variables in planning your DNS naming strategy, but so far, we really haven't given you much direction. Unfortunately, most of these decisions will be made based upon business needs. Our examination in Chapter 3 of the physical, logical, and business models for the company should help you make your choices.

Exam Hint: Most of the DNS design questions will be found in case studies. When answering case studies, always remember that Microsoft's new philosophy is that the business needs, not the technology, should drive the design. The only time that technology should drive your design is when that technology can provide a more efficient business solution. Review the business goals of the case study when making your decisions!

With that said, Figures 5.18 and 5.19 provide design flowcharts to use when your company either has or does not have an existing DNS solution.

FIGURE 5.18 A DNS design flowchart for existing DNS solution

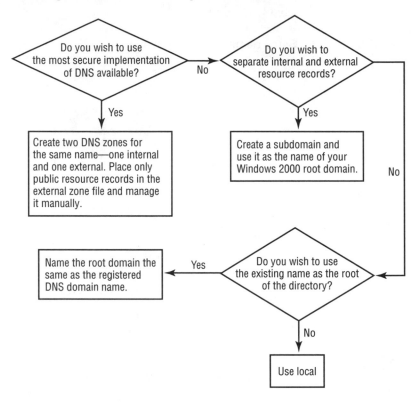

FIGURE 5.19 DNS design flowchart—no existing DNS solution

Create a subdomain for the newly registered DNS name.

Summary

This chapter covers the first step in designing a successful Active Directory environment—setting naming standards and configuring DNS. Because DNS is critical to Active Directory, Microsoft will test your knowledge of DNS quite heavily. If you are not comfortable with TCP/IP and DNS, we suggest that you pick up a copy of *TCP/IP Jumpstart* (Sybex, 2000) by Andrew G. Blank.

Although this has been a fairly long chapter, the good news is that, when properly planned, a good naming standard and a good implementation of DNS goes a long way toward creating a stable AD environment. Remember the following key items:

- Standardized names are critical to a directory that is easy to use and manage.

- LDAP names are used for internal searches.

- Microsoft DNS services provide some new capabilities to your DNS solution (dynamic updates, incremental updates, and AD integration).

- Active Directory and DNS names meet at the NT root domain. Your strategy for naming the root domain should revolve around the business needs of your client or company.

Now that you know how domains will be named, and how those names are used by DNS, we can move to planning a domain structure. In Chapter 6, we will discuss designing a domain structure for an Active Directory environment.

Key Terms

Before you take the exam, be sure you're familiar with the following terms:

canonical names

Directory Access Protocol (DAP)

distinguished name

DNS zones

Domain Name System (DNS)

incremental zone transfer

Lightweight Directory Access Protocol (LDAP)

multi-master environment

primary DNS servers

relative distinguished name

secondary DNS server

security identifier (SID)

single-master environment

SRV resource records

user principal name

X.500 recommendations

Review Questions

1. Choose all of the following that are true about LDAP.

   A. It is a protocol used to access the information in the directory.

   B. LDAP services run on the directory sever.

   C. LDAP client-side applications must be written for the directory that they are going to access.

   D. LDAP client-side applications can access information in any LDAP-compliant directory.

2. Which of the following actions can be accomplished using LDAP?

   A. Reading the AD database

   B. Creating new objects within the AD database

   C. Modifying existing objects within the AD database

   D. Manually starting a replication between two AD servers

3. Which of the following best defines "relative distinguished name"?

   A. The portion of an object's distinguished name that is not a part of your current context

   B. The portion of an object's distinguished name that is an attribute of the object itself

   C. An object's location in the directory structure relative to the root of the tree

   D. An object's location in the directory relative to the closest AD server object

4. Which of the following would be a properly formatted distinguished object name?

   A. CN=Bking\OU=education\O=kingtech.com

   B. CN=Bking, OU=education, DC=Kingtech, DC=com

   C. DC=com, DC=Kingtech, OU=education, CN=Bking

   D. Bking@Kingtech.com

5. Select all that are true. User principal names _____ .

  A. Are the user's relative distinguished name added to the DNS domain of their AD tree

  B. Are designed to be more user friendly than distinguished or canonical names

  C. Can be duplicated with the domain because the DN is actually used to find the user

  D. Are only used when an AD-enabled e-mail service has been installed

6. The main function of the domain naming master server is to _____ .

  A. Ensure that a set of rules are followed when objects are named within the tree

  B. Generate a unique SID for each domain that joins a forest

  C. Approve the name of each new security principal added to the forest

  D. Be configured to allow duplicate names in a distributed environment

7. The main function of the relative ID master server is to _____ .

  A. Work with the security subsystem to authenticate users

  B. Generate the public/private key pair used in the authentication process

  C. Generate for each AD server a series of SIDs that it can use when creating objects

  D. Generate the relative distinguished name for new user objects

8. Within Microsoft's implementation of DNS, an incremental zone transfer is _____ .

 A. An update of all DNS servers in which the entire zone is transmitted in 64K segments

 B. An update of a DNS server in which transmission is controlled using the GTSP (Global Timing Sequence Protocol)

 C. An update of a DNS server in which only the changed data is replicated

 D. The process of moving DNS services from one server to another

9. Which of the following is the primary reason that DNS is required in an AD environment?

 A. The Active Directory database is stored within the traditional DNS database.

 B. AD uses the DNS zone transfer protocol during replication.

 C. Netlogon uses DNS to find domain controllers.

 D. DNS is *not* required in an AD environment.

10. In a Windows 2000 DNS server, each zone can have a maximum of _____ records.

 A. 1 million

 B. 1,024

 C. 65,553

 D. There is no theoretical limit.

11. A Windows 2000 DNS server should not be configured with more than _____ zones.

 A. 100

 B. 1,000

 C. 1 million

 D. There is no limit.

12. Which two of the following are reasons that DAP was replaced by LDAP?

    A. DAP was a proprietary protocol created by Novell, and its use required licensing.

    B. DAP placed too much overhead on the client computers used to access the directory.

    C. DAP packets are not passed by many of the routers currently on the market.

    D. DAP can not communicate with non-X.500-compliant directories.

13. The user account Ggovanus is located within the Education OU, which is within the Persistent-Image.com domain of an Active Directory structure. Which of the following is the relative distinguished name of this object?

    A. CN=Ggovanus.OU=Education.O=Persistent-Image

    B. CN=Ggovanus

    C. CN=Ggovanus, OU=Education, DC=Persistent-Image, DC=com

    D. Ggovanus@Persistent-Image.com

14. An implementation of DNS in which an ACL is used to control which users or computers can make changes to the DNS data is known as _
    _____ .

    A. An authenticated environment

    B. A secure update environment

    C. An ACL-based update environment

    D. A Kerberos-initiated environment

15. Which of the following are benefits of using an Active Directory–integrated DNS configuration?

    A. Single-master environments are simpler to administer.

    B. Multi-master environments are more fault tolerant.

    C. Enhanced security.

    D. More efficient replication.

Answers to Review Questions

1. A, B, D. LDAP defines a standard method for accessing the information stored in any compliant directory. The LDAP client application passes a request to the LDAP service running on the directory server. The LDAP service formats the request for the specific directory for which it was written.

2. A, B, C . LDAP was designed to allow full administration of an LDAP-compliant directory.

3. B. The relative distinguished name is the name you give the object when you create it. It is an attribute of the object itself rather than a part of the path to the object.

4. B. DNs identify the object by using its relative distinguished name and each of the containers to the top of the tree. Each component is separated with a comma.

5. A, B. The UPN is the relative name plus the DNS domain name of the object, such as Bking@Royal-Tech.com. No usernames can be duplicated within either a DNS or NT domain.

6. B. The domain naming master server generates a unique SID for each domain that is added to the AD forest. This domain SID is a part of the unique SID generated for every object.

7. C. The RIM controls all SIDs used to identify objects within an NT domain. This prevents duplicate SIDs from being assigned to objects.

8. C. One advantage of Microsoft DNS is that the entire zone file does not have to be replicated each time the content of the DNS database changes.

9. C. The Windows 2000 Netlogon service uses DNS to find domain controllers during the logon process.

10. C. Each zone with a Windows 2000 DNS zone can contain about 65,000 entries.

11. B. Although placing more is possible, the additional overhead on the server would degrade server performance.

12. B, D. LDAP was developed in direct response to the major weaknesses of DAP: (1) Using DAP-based software places a tremendous amount of overhead on the client computer. Many client machines, especially PCs or Macintosh computers, lack the resources necessary to support any DAP services, and (2) DAP was designed specifically to communicate with X.500 directories. This means that many vendor-specific products will not be accessible if you're using DAP-enabled software.

13. B. The relative distinguished name of any object is that portion of its name that uniquely identifies it in the container within which it resides.

14. B. An ACL can be used to control which users or computers can make changes to the DNS data. This is known as a *secure update environment* and is the default configuration for AD-integrated DNS environments. This prevents unauthorized servers from adding their information to your environment.

15. B, C, D. Multi-master replication allows changes to be made to any copy of the data, thereby eliminating the single point of failure in a single-master design. Updates are controlled by AD security, and because AD replicates only changes (rather than the entire database), replication is more efficient.

Case Study: Memory Makers, LLC

Take about 10 minutes to look over the information presented and then answer the questions at the end. In the testing room, you will have a limited amount of time—it is important that you learn to pick out the important information and ignore the "fluff."

Background

Overview   A company in Grand Rapids Michigan—Memory Makers, LLC—has asked you to look over its current IS situation and plan a move into Internet e-commerce. Memory Makers sells collectible toys, everything from Easy-Bake ovens to G. I. Joes. Its inventory changes on a daily basis, and much of its business is made up of customer requests for particular items.

CEO   "With the baby boomers getting older, we are assured that our volume of sales should continue to grow! While we're never going to be major employer (by gross numbers) in Grand Rapids, we expect our contribution to this community to grow with our business."

CFO   "Our facilities here in Grand Rapids should be sufficient to handle our expected growth in sales for the foreseeable future."

Current System

Overview   Memory Makers is currently using a peer-to-peer network of Windows 95/98 desktop computers. A database of inventory is stored on the receptionist's desktop machine, which is a Pentium-class computer with 64MB of RAM and plenty of disk space. No security has been placed on the database, no backups are being made, and no business process is in place to keep the database up-to-date. There is no IS staff on-site and no plans to hire anyone.

CEO   "We know that we need to move into the twenty-first century, and we have set aside funding for it. What we don't have is internal expertise—we deal in toys! That's where you come in—you tell us what would be the best solution."

CASE STUDY

CIO   "After compiling a business plan, we see the advantages of moving to some form of e-commerce. We looked at the numbers, though, and decided that our best bet is to outsource our technical support (instead of hiring internal staff). Our major concerns are to keep future costs under control and to be able to use off-the-shelf applications for which training is available."

Current Issues

Internet Presence   Like every other business in the world, Memory Makers wants to ride the wave of e-commerce. It has registered a domain (Memory-Makers.com) and has a simple Web page being hosted by a local ISP. It would like to expand this side of its business to include sales of current inventory and Internet requests for special items.

Business Procedures   It also has a few problems with the business procedures that are currently in place. The inventory database is always a week or more out-of-date, there is no security in place, and there is no central control of the IS environment.

Example Problem   A perfect example of the types of problems the company is facing is the complete loss of its inventory database, which happened last week (and which prompted the call to your company). The receptionist was out for the day, so one of the employees sat down at her computer to turn it on so that the shared resources on it would be available. During the day, her computer ran out of disk space (the sales staff was printing a series of huge graphics through the printer the machine shares to the network). In an attempt to clear the "out of disk" errors, someone started deleting files—and inadvertently deleted the Access database containing all inventory information.

Goals

Memory Makers would like to first create a secure environment in which mistakes like the loss of the inventory database are less likely to happen. Once this has been accomplished, it would like to create an effective Web presence. The first goal is to create a self-sufficient environment because Memory Makers has no IS staff on-site. You will be its sole support system.

Security

Overview   Before any other action is taken, the CEO wants the precious inventory data safe and secure. He wants only a few people to be able to make changes, while allowing everyone else to view the information. If possible, he would like the database to be up-to-date so that the sales associates know what is currently in stock.

Sales Manager   "My staff doesn't always know what we have in inventory. We lose a lot of sales saying that we don't have something that has just been added to our inventory."

Purchasing Manager   "We'd like to know what the sales staff is getting requests for. That would help us when we are looking for items."

Fault Tolerance

Because the entire business revolves around what is in stock, the inventory database has to achieve an almost 100-percent availability rating.

Maintenance

The company has decided to outsource the entire implementation and maintenance of its environment to your company. No on-site IS staff will be available. Your recommendations will decide the future of Memory Makers' network.

Performance

Once the e-commerce site is in place, sales are expected to triple overnight. You will have to design a system that can handle the overhead of a busy Web-based business.

Funding

As the baby boomers get older, the market for collectible toys from the '60s and '70s has grown by leaps and bounds. Memory Makers was able to find some venture capital that it is using to fund this expansion into the e-commerce arena. Funding should not be an issue, but as with all other consulting jobs, dollar accountability is critical to a continued relationship with the client.

Questions

1. Which of the following would be valid justifications for your choice of Windows 2000?

   A. Because Microsoft leads the industry, your best bet is usually to go with its flagship product.

   B. Windows 2000 is based upon Windows NT—a solution that has been in the market long enough to prove itself reliable, secure, and stable.

   C. Windows 2000 integrates well with other products that Memory Makers is going to have to implement, such as Internet Information Server, Exchange Server, and SQL Server.

   D. The advanced security built in to Windows 2000 will ensure that any data is protected.

2. Given the nature of this exam, we are going to assume that you recommend a Windows 2000 network solution. How many domains would you create?

   A. 1

   B. 2

   C. 3

   D. One for each department

3. Which of the following ADS/DNS implementation models would you recommend?

   A. Use Memory-Makers.com as the name of the ADS root domain so that the DNS namespace is the same for both the internal and external networks.

   B. Use a subdomain of Memory-Makers.com (such as HQ.Memory-Makers.com) as the name of the root domain.

   C. Use a different DNS name for the ADS structure and a registered name for the Internet presence.

   D. Use Memory Makers' registered name for the name of the root domain, but keep a separate DNS server outside a firewall to service external requests.

CASE STUDY

4. Which of the following would be your first action on behalf of this client?

   A. Purchase a server and a copy of Windows 2000 and get the client up and running as soon as possible.

   B. Purchase a backup unit and software and implement a backup and restore procedure.

   C. Create a SQL database to hold the company's inventory database and implement a business procedure to ensure that inventory and sales information is entered in a timely manner.

   D. Train an on-site staff member in the basics of network administration.

5. From a business-needs perspective, reorder the following tasks in the order in which they should be performed.

Task	Task
	Design an inventory database.
	Purchase backup equipment and software and implement a backup strategy.
	Upgrade all clients to Windows 2000.
	Register a domain name with InterNIC.
	Design and implement a Web site.

6. Memory Makers has decided to upgrade to SQL Server 7 due to its desire to have a more dependable and efficient database system. Once the SQL server is installed, though, a number of additional tasks will still need to be completed. Listed below are some of these steps that need to be taken to ensure that Memory Makers' data is properly secured and backed up. Connect each of these steps as part of either the backup or security plan.

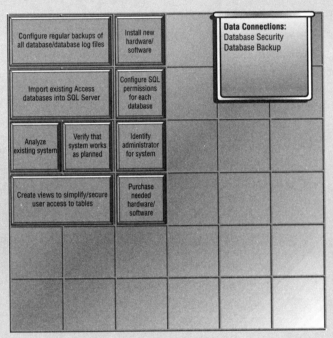

7. Which of the following are valid concerns for Memory Makers?

   A. Replacing its current ISP

   B. Supporting multiple currencies

   C. Getting legal advice regarding international trade laws

   D. Assessing available bandwidth to its Web server.

Answers

1. A, B, C, D. This is one of those marketing questions that Microsoft always throws into its tests. The point here is that you not only have to know how to implement technology, you also have to know how to justify it.

2. A. A Windows 2000 domain can contain 1 million objects, more than enough for the given scenario. A single-domain environment is easier to implement, maintain, and troubleshoot than a multidomain solution.

3. A. Microsoft recommends that the root domain be named the same as your registered domain name in most cases (answer A). In reality, though, we would chose answer B because Memory Makers has no on-site IS staff. It might be better to let a third party manage its external DNS service and just have internal resources listed in its local ADS database. This is a touchy issue, though—because you will be providing *all* of the support for the system, if you have the expertise necessary to support DNS, you might want to keep control. In this case, answer A would be more correct. This is one of those cases in which the supporting information doesn't really give you enough information to fully answer the question. In this situation, it is better to go with the Microsoft-suggested solution.

4. B. Before anything else, secure the current environment! Doctors take an oath that basically says their first rule is to "do no harm." Consultants should have to take the same oath!

5. See table.

Task
Register a domain name with InterNIC.
Purchase backup equipment and software and implement a backup strategy.
Design an inventory database.
Design and implement a Web site.
Upgrade all clients to Windows 2000.

Surprised? Registering a domain name takes a few minutes, and the number of distinct (and catchy) names is decreasing every minute. Take care of that right away! Then solve the immediate problem—get the current environment stable! Part of the company's current business needs is a workable, scalable, and stable inventory database. Because this is an immediate business need *and* will be of use during your Web site design, it makes sense to do it early. Once the business is stable, move into a new venue—e-commerce. As for upgrading the clients, in reality, Windows 95 or 98 might suffice for quite some time.

6.

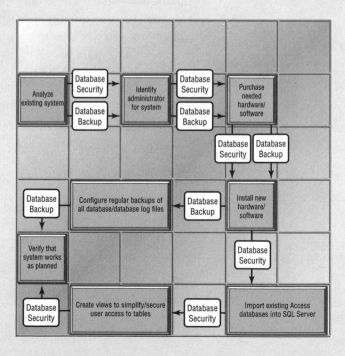

As always, a number of things go into making a new design work. With SQL Server, you have the advantage that security is by default very tight, and you can import first and create accounts later, or vice versa. Configuring security before allowing users in is crucial, however! Planning what you need to back up helps you decide what hardware you need to buy and install. This is followed by incorporating the tape drive into the backup process and making sure that backup is done regularly, properly, and successfully!

7. A, B, C, D. Opening a site that will do business on the Web requires companies to think about international trade issues, as well as the potential increase in network traffic.

Planning a Domain and OU Structure

MICROSOFT EXAM OBJECTIVES COVERED IN THIS CHAPTER:

✓ **Design an Active Directory forest and domain structure.**

- Design a forest and schema structure.
- Design a domain structure.
- Analyze and optimize trust relationships.

✓ **Design and plan the structure of organizational units (OU). Considerations include administration control, existing resource domains, administrative policy, and geographic and company structure.**

- Develop an OU delegation plan.
- Plan Group Policy object management.
- Plan policy management for client computers.

We'll bet you're wondering if we're ever going to talk about Active Directory design in this Active Directory book—so far we've spent pages talking about the research that goes into a design project, discussed the importance of naming standards, and even helped you decide how you'll use DNS in your new environment, but we haven't said word one about the AD structure. The sheer number of pages you've had to wade through before we begin to spotlight Microsoft's premier technology should tell you that these Design exams are a whole new ball game! (They should also drive home the fact that the preinstallation phase of a design project is just as important, if not more so, than the implementation phase.)

Finally, here in Chapter 6, we're going to look at Active Directory and its treelike structure. At this point in a real-life design project, you have enough information at your fingertips—the analysis of the physical network, the analysis of the business environment, the analysis of the IT department, a set of standards to use when naming objects, and even the name of the first domain—to begin the process of designing the AD tree. Of course, even this stage is still only a pen-and-paper exercise. But at least it's actual AD work as opposed to research.

In this chapter, we'll start by defining a few of the common components in an AD environment—most of the first few pages should be review, but you might need to fill a few gaps in your knowledge set with information you'll need when you start to make design decisions. After we've laid the groundwork, we'll begin our discussion of tree design. First we'll look at domains in an AD design, paying special attention to trust relationships. We know that Microsoft downplays the importance of trust relationships in its marketing material, but trusts still play a critical role in Microsoft networking. After helping you decide on the number and boundaries of the domains within your network, we'll move on to the creation of organizational units, paying close attention to three specific design issues: upgrading an environment from Windows NT, designing to facilitate the delegation of authority, and designing with an eye toward Group Policy.

OUs vs. Domains

In just about every article we've read about Windows 2000 and Active Directory, the authors seem to want to ignore NT domains and concentrate on the OU structure. That's understandable because OUs are new and exciting (for some of us anyway) and domains have been around for quite some time (and have garnered a fairly bad reputation). The reality, though, is that NT domains are a critical piece of the AD environment—and more important to network administrators, a critical piece of the AD design. As you'll see later, domains are physical in nature and OUs are logical. They both have their place in your design, but knowing which to use (OU or domain) is key to a stable design.

What Is a Domain?

You might recall the definition of a *domain* from earlier versions of NT: a logical grouping of computers and users managed through a central security accounts database. According to this definition, a domain could be thought of both logically and physically:

- Logically, it was an organizational grouping of resources allowing central management of those resources.

- Physically, it was a database containing information about those resources.

Combining the logical with the physical gave you a management or security boundary; administrators for a domain could manage all resources in that domain by default.

The definition of a domain has not changed in a Windows 2000 environment. The only real change is that we now have to work this definition into a bigger picture—that of the entire network. In earlier versions of NT, domains were tied together by establishing trust relationships between them. In Windows 2000 Advanced Server, trusts still exist, but they are established by default and function quite differently than before.

In Windows 2000 Advanced Server, domains act as the building blocks for an AD tree structure. The first domain created becomes the *root domain*. The root domain acts as the top of the structure and determines the beginning of the AD *namespace*. The name of this domain must match the top level of your desired namespace. After the first domain is created, each subsequent domain is added to the tree somewhere beneath it. In other words, additional domains are always children (although not necessarily children of the root domain), whereas the root domain has no parent. This concept is illustrated in Figures 6.1 and 6.2.

FIGURE 6.1 The root domain

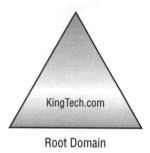

Root Domain

In Figure 6.1, the first domain for the company King Technologies has been named KingTech.com. As the first domain added to the tree, it becomes the root domain. All subsequent domains will follow the naming pattern of <something>.KingTech.com, as shown in Figure 6.2.

FIGURE 6.2 Subsequent domains

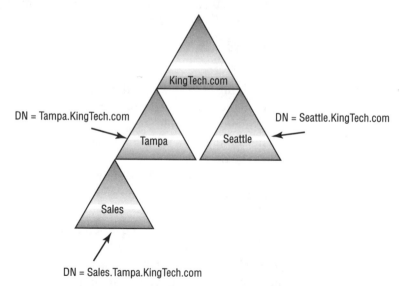

Figure 6.2 demonstrates the principle of *hierarchical naming*. Each subsequent domain adds the names of all domains above it to create a distinguished name.

DNS Domains and NT Domains

In Chapter 5, we discussed DNS (Domain Name System) domains. A DNS domain represents a piece of the overall DNS namespace. DNS is a service used to find resources: A process submits a host name and DNS attempts to find a record that matches. If a match is found, DNS returns the appropriate IP address to the requestor. As such, we could define a DNS domain as *a bounded portion of a DNS namespace used to find IP host information.*

In this chapter, we will discuss NT domains, concentrating on how they relate to Active Directory. For our purposes, we can define an NT domain as *a bounded area of an AD namespace used to organize network resources.*

Comparing the two definitions, we can make two generalizations:

- DNS domains are for finding resources.

- AD domains are for organizing resources.

We know that everyone says that the Active Directory database is used to "find" resources, so let us clarify. Although AD holds information about resources on the network, it uses DNS to find and resolve distinguished names into IP addresses. In other words, AD and DNS work together to return connection information to users or to other processes that request such information, as you can see in Figure 6.3.

FIGURE 6.3   AD and DNS work together to provide services.

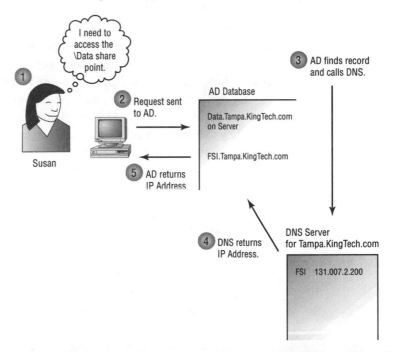

In Figure 6.3, Susan uses the AD database to find a share point. Here is what happens:

1. Susan browses the directory and clicks the \Data resource.

2. The client software sends a request to an AD server.

3. The AD server searches the directory database for the resource record. In the record, it finds the DNS name of the server on which the share point is located. AD queries DNS for the IP address of the appropriate server.

4. DNS searches its database for the record for server FS1.Tampa.KingTech .com. Once it finds this record, DNS returns the IP address to AD.

5. AD returns the IP address of server FS1.Tampa.KingTech.com to the client.

At this point, the client software can establish a connection with the server using the appropriate TCP/IP technologies.

DNS is a critical piece of the AD puzzle. Without DNS, AD cannot resolve user requests into IP addresses of resources.

Partitioning the Database

In large environments, the AD directory database can become quite large. As you saw earlier, the X.500 recommendations specify a method of breaking the database into smaller pieces, known as *partitions*, and distributing them across multiple servers. The X.500 recommendations also include a methodology for replicating changes to multiple copies of the same partition.

For the Active Directory database, domains act as the boundaries of partitions. In other words, each domain represents a partition of the overall directory database, as shown in Figure 6.4.

FIGURE 6.4 Each domain is a partition of the AD database.

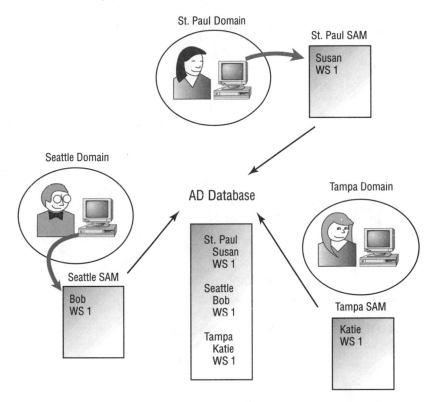

Breaking the database into smaller pieces places less overhead on each Active Directory server. It also grants the administrator more control over the amount and route of traffic generated by the database replication process. Consider the environment depicted in Figure 6.5. Because there is only one domain defined, each AD server holds records for every resource in the enterprise. If a new printer is installed in Seattle, information about that printer will have to be updated on every AD server in the entire company. The same holds true for *every* change made to the database. If user Katie in Tampa changes her password, that change will have to be replicated to every AD server across the entire network. Although this design is functional, it is probably not the best design possible for the network.

FIGURE 6.5 Company XYZ domain structure

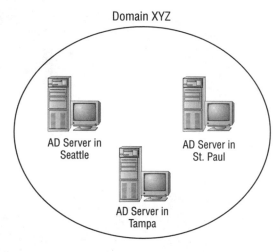

The King Technologies Company has come up with a much better design, as you can see in Figure 6.6.

FIGURE 6.6 King Technologies domain structure

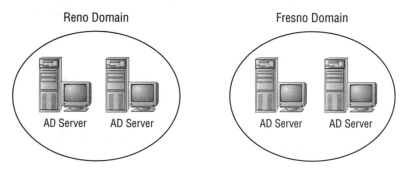

In this design, each server contains records only for objects that are in its own geographic area. Notice that this design has two benefits:

- It limits the amount of traffic generated between the two locations.

- It ensures that no server is overburdened by holding records that are of no real value to its purpose.

We'll look at various design strategies in more detail later in this chapter.

What Is an OU?

Domains act as administrative boundaries: it is easy to give one administrator control over all resources within a domain. In many cases, though, using domains as the boundary for administrative privileges does not offer enough granularity of management. Administrators would often like to be able to limit an assistant's power to a particular group of users or a particular geographic area. For these needs, AD includes the *organizational unit* (OU) object class. OUs form logical administrative units that can be used to delegate administrative privileges within a domain. Rather than add another domain to an existing structure, it is often more advantageous to just create another OU to organize objects.

Organizational units can contain the following types of objects:

- Users
- Computers
- Groups
- Printers
- Applications
- Security policies
- File shares
- Other OUs

Remember that the AD schema is extensible, so the list of types of objects that OUs can contain might change if you change the schema of your tree.

There is only one type of object that an OU cannot contain, and that is any object from another domain.

Easier Access, Easier Management

You could define an OU as a container object designed to allow organization of a domain's resources. An OU is used in much the same way a subdirectory in a file system is used. There is an old adage about creating subdirectories in DOS:

There are only two reasons to create a subdirectory: to ease access or to ease management.

You might, for instance, create the DOS structure shown in Figure 6.7. Most of us would find this type of layout comfortable (and familiar). If you take the time to analyze why this structure works so well, you'll find that all subdirectories were created for one of two reasons: management and access.

FIGURE 6.7 Typical file structure

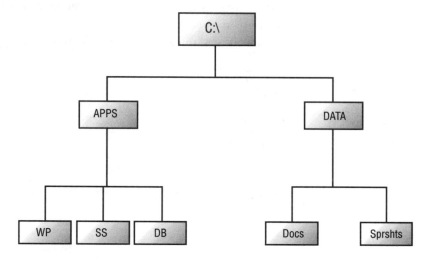

Here are two examples of how directories help ease access and management:

APPS   Naming a directory APPS lets a user know exactly where to find applications, making access easier. It also lets an administrator know where to place any applications stored in the file system, making management easier.

DATA   Again, the name helps both access and management. Placing both the APPS and DATA directories directly off the root of the drive makes navigation easier for users. Separating the data from the applications also simplifies setting up backup programs (you can back up everything under DATA rather than all .doc files in \APPS\WP and all .xls files in \APPS\SS, and so on).

The same reasoning applies to every directory in the file structure shown in Figure 6.7. This philosophy also works when designing the structure of your AD tree. OUs should reflect the business structure of your company. Do not create containers for political reasons or just for the sake of structure.

The bottom line is, if you can't justify a container for either management or user convenience, then you probably don't need that OU.

How Do I Decide—New Domain or New OU?

This is a tough section—there are really three different answers to this question—the real-life answer, the Microsoft marketing answer, and the exam answer. We know that the major focus of this book is to prepare you for the MCSE exam, but we wouldn't feel comfortable if we didn't address all three answers.

The Microsoft Marketing Answer

Because the AD can theoretically contain millions of object records, the Microsoft marketing answer seems to be that one domain will be enough for most environments. Planning your site boundaries and site connectors carefully should allow you to control the replication of AD changes (and the various other types of communication—often referred to as chatter) between servers within the domain. This is a great answer in theory, but the reality is that, past a certain size (and this varies based upon the number of changes to the database and the type of objects created), the hardware required to support the "one large database" is cost prohibitive. To be fair, there is another theory that suggests that the budget allocated to any department will increase as the company increases—only slower. Put another way, in a company with 100 users, the budget will be large enough to support 100 users; in a company with a 100,000 users, the budget will be quite a bit larger. ("Only slower" represents the fact that business growth usually occurs before the budget growth does, so we always seem to spend a good percentage of our careers working under dollar constraints.)

The Real-Life Answer

In reality, we spend most of our design efforts trying to control network traffic over our WAN links. Although sites and site connectors allow you a certain amount of control over the traffic between servers, changes do have to be replicated. The amount of traffic between domains is much smaller than the amount of traffic generated between servers within a single domain.

The Exam Answer

The MCSE exam will contain questions that are worded so that you will have to make this choice—OU or domain. There are standard justifications for creating one or the other.

Here are some of the reasons to create an OU rather than a new domain:

- To delegate administrative control, giving an individual the ability to add, delete, or modify objects in a limited portion of the tree.

- To ease management by grouping like objects. You might, for instance, create a container to hold users with similar security requirements.

- To control the visibility of objects.

- To make administration more straightforward, assigning permissions once to the OU rather than multiple times for each object.

- To make administration easier by limiting the number of objects in a single container. Even though the limit on the number of objects within a single container is large (well over a million), no one wants to page through a huge list every time they need to manage one object.

- To control policy application. We'll discuss changes to the system policy process later, but for now, just be aware that policies can be set at the OU level.

- To be used as a holding container for other OUs. This would be the same as the APPS directory in the DOS example earlier. The APPS directory does not really hold any files; it just acts as an organizer for other directories.

- To replace NT 4 domains. In earlier versions of NT, delegation of administration was achieved by creating multiple domains.

Reasons to create a new domain rather than an OU are listed here:

- When there is a need for decentralized management of users or resources where administrators do not want to share control of a domain

- When you want to make delegation easier in cases of diverse environments, such as a network in which different languages are spoken

- If unique domain-level security policies are mandated

- When you want to control directory replication traffic (for instance, across a WAN link with limited bandwidth)

- When you are upgrading from an earlier version of NT that was configured as a multidomain environment

- When you are preparing for future changes to the company

- If the default trust relationships do not meet your needs

Exam Hint: Know these exam reasons inside and out! Most of this exam will revolve around the actual design issues that you will face, based upon a series of case studies. One of the choices will be creating a multidomain environment—you'll need to know when it is appropriate.

What Is a Forest?

Domains and organizational units combine to form the Active Directory tree. Domains act as the physical divisions, or partitions, of the overall database, and organizational units form logical groupings of resources within each domain. As we discussed earlier, this structure defines the namespace for the environment. In other words, every object within the AD tree has certain aspects in common with every other object. In the structure shown in Figure 6.8, for instance, every security principal object within the tree has a user principal name that ends in KingTech.com.

FIGURE 6.8 KingTech.com AD tree

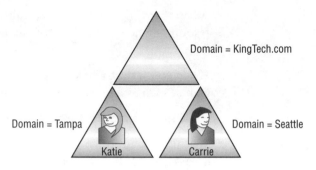

Domain = KingTech.com

Domain = Tampa

Katie

Domain = Seattle

Carrie

User principal names =
Katie@KingTech.com
Carrie@KingTech.com

Not only do the user principal names all end the same, all of the other types of names have a common format as well. The two users shown in Figure 6.8 both have distinguished names that end in DC=KingTech.DC=com. The user principal name is really what interests us at this point, though. Although it might not be apparent from the simple structure of the King Technologies tree, there is an inherent weakness in this single namespace design. Suppose that King Technologies were an internationally recognized brand name. Being popular has certain advantages, one of which is that it is conceivable that some other large company, let's call them MicroSofts, might want to merge with King Technologies to capitalize upon its success. (By the way, King Technologies is open to this type of arrangement—we could use the money!) What we end up with is two Internet-registered domain names, both of which have brand appeal. In a single namespace environment, we would have to choose between the two names—would our e-mail addresses end in MicroSofts.com or KingTech.com? Remember, the user principal names all end in the name of the root domain. Not an easy choice, is it?

For these types of situations, or for any situation where a single namespace will not fulfill the business needs of a company, you can create an AD forest. A *forest* is two or more separate AD trees joined together by trust relationships. (We'll review the principals of trust relationships later in this chapter.) Setting aside security issues—you'll have to read the other Sybex study guide that we wrote, *MCSE: Windows 2000 Network Security Design*

Study Guide, by Gary Govanus and Robert King (Sybex, 2000) for that discussion—this allows the sharing of resources and even administrative tasks between the two AD databases. Conceptually, the multiple trees become one big environment, but an environment that contains multiple namespaces, as shown in Figure 6.9.

FIGURE 6.9 An AD Forest

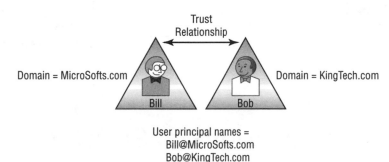

This concept can also come in handy for any situation in which your company has a close relationship with another company. This might sound cold, but in business, we've always believed that the best way to make money was on someone else's effort—often called the OPE (Other People's Effort) principle. At its most basic, this translates into passing as much of the effort involved in doing business as possible to an outside entity. As an example, let's look at the Great Style Shirt Company. Great Style makes great shirts (hence the name), but it doesn't make buttons. Anytime the company designs a shirt that needs buttons, it contracts with an outside company to provide the button stock necessary for its production facility. In business, Great Style is in the power position over the button company because Great Style is the "customer" in the relationship. In a traditional environment, Great Style would have to call the button company every so often to order buttons—the right amount, color, and style for whatever shirt is being produced at the time. This means that, in a traditional environment, the "work" of keeping track of button needs is handled by Great Style.

Now let's move to an AD world. If both companies are using Windows 2000 (and AD) as their network operating system, the two companies could create a trust between the two trees, thus easing the process of sharing information. Great Style could then demand (we told you this might sound a little cold) that the button company access its production database and send just the right number of buttons each week. Notice that now the "work" of controlling inventory has been moved from Great Style to the outside vendor.

The Great Style Shirt Company example is probably a bit extreme, but it does describe the power of Windows 2000 and AD. AD is flexible enough to handle any business configuration that you might need to implement.

Exam Hint: The decision to create a forest should be fairly straightforward on the MCSE exam. In most cases, a forest is created in an environment in which two distinct namespaces need to exist—the one thing that a single AD tree cannot do!

Designing a Domain Structure

At this point in your design project, you are ready to begin the process of building the structure of your AD tree. You have gathered all of the information necessary, analyzed the network traffic, and created your naming standards. Using the resources you now have at hand, it is time to sit down and put together your tree.

Microsoft Exam Objective

Design an Active Directory forest and domain structure.

- Design a forest and schema structure.

- Design a domain structure.

- Analyze and optimize trust relationships.

During our discussion of DNS in Chapter 5, we have already determined the name of the root domain. The root domain forms the top of the AD tree and the base of the namespace. If the root domain is named KingTech.com and it has two child domains, Tampa and Orlando, beneath it, as shown in Figure 6.10, the names of those child domains are Tampa.KingTech.com and Orlando.KingTech.com.

FIGURE 6.10   The domain structure for King Technologies

Earlier in this chapter, we included a list of reasons for creating a new domain as opposed to using an OU to organize the objects within your AD structure. Although that list is a good starting point, designing your domain structure (especially for larger or more complex environments) will require that you have a more in-depth understanding of the mechanisms of the Active Directory service.

Schema Considerations for Design

The concepts of AD forests are fairly straightforward, but there are certain conditions that must be met during their creation. First, all domain control-lers must share a common database structure, or *schema*. This means that any extensions made to the AD database in one tree must also be made to all other trees within the forest. Say, for instance, you add an application (such as Microsoft Exchange Server 2000) that extends the AD schema. You will have to add those extensions to all other trees within the forest structure. This is easy to do if your company controls all of the trees, but it does com-plicate matters in a situation (such as the Great Style example) where auton-omous groups manage the trees.

The trees within the forest must also share a common *global catalog* (GC). The global catalog for the forest will be that of the first domain created in the first tree (sometimes referred to as the *forest root domain*).

Global Catalog Servers

A *global catalog server* is an AD server that holds a partial replica of the entire forest. This replica holds a limited amount of information about every object within the forest, usually properties that are necessary for network functionality or properties that are frequently asked for.

The list of properties will be different for each class of object. User objects, for instance, will need to store certain information for network functions—a great example is their Universal Group Membership list. During the logon process, the user's object is checked to retrieve this list. AD will then confirm the user's membership with each universal group by using information stored in the global catalog. Once membership has been confirmed, the security IDs for each group can be added to the user's security token. The global catalog might also contain various properties that might be frequently searched upon—telephone numbers, for example. On the other hand, the global catalog will probably store less information about printer objects because fewer of their properties will be needed on a regular basis.

By default, the global catalog will be created on the first domain controller installed in the AD forest. The service itself has two major functions. First, it is critical to the logon process. When a user logs on to the network, a security token is created for them. This token includes information about the groups of which they are a member. If a global catalog server is not available during the logon process, the user will not be able to log on to the network—instead, they will be limited to logging on to the local computer.

Members of the Domain Admins group can log on to the network without accessing the global catalog. If this wasn't the case, a malfunctioning global catalog server could conceivably prevent an administrator from logging on to fix the problem.

The second function of the global catalog is to facilitate searches of the Active Directory database. If you perform a search for, let's say, the phone number property of a user in another domain, your request could be answered by the global catalog server rather than a domain controller from the target domain. To put it more simply, searches can take place on servers that are more local to the user, thereby reducing network traffic and decreasing the time it takes to receive results.

The search capabilities of global catalog servers bring us to an important design issue. By default, only one global catalog server is created, but the system can support an unlimited number of them. To reap the benefits of the global catalog, you must think about how many you would like and place them appropriately. It is best to have a global catalog server at each physical location—otherwise, your search will cross your WAN links, thereby eliminating the benefits of the service. This design also prevents the situation in which users are unable to log on to the network because a WAN line has gone down.

On the flip side, though, too many global catalog servers can increase network traffic. Remember that the catalog contains an incomplete copy of every object in your forest. Let's say that user Joe changes his phone number; this change would have to be replicated to every global catalog server in your environment.

The amount of network traffic that would be generated during replication explains why the global catalog does not contain every property of every object. The traffic generated to keep complete replicas up-to-date would probably exceed the bandwidth available on most networks.

Windows 2000 creates the first global catalog server for you and determines which properties of each object class it will store. In most cases, this default list of stored properties will be sufficient. There might be situations, though, where you want to add a property to the list that the global catalog stores. You can control the attributes of each object class stored in the partial partition of the global catalog by using the Active Directory Sites and Services tools.

Single-Master Functions

We've discussed the difference between single-master and multiple-master environments. In short, single-master environments use a single instance of a database to accept and then replicate changes. Multiple-master environments allow changes to any replica of the database. Each replica has the capability to update all other replicas with changed data. Most of the changes made to the Active Directory database are handled in a multiple-master manner. The change will occur at any local AD server, and that server will synchronize those changes with the rest of the AD servers in the domain (and the global catalog server, if necessary).

There are, however, certain operations that, by the nature of what they do, need to be handled in a single-master manner. For these operations, one server is designated as the *operations master*. All updates or changes occur at the operations master, and this server is responsible for synchronizing the changes to all other servers. Because these responsibilities can be moved from server to server (as best fits your network), Microsoft used to refer to them as Flexible Single Master Operations (FSMOs). You might still run across that term in some of the documentation.

Do not let the word *flexible* confuse you—this is mostly a marketing word. These operations are truly "single-master." They are "flexible" only in the fact that you can determine which server will perform them.

Some of these single-master operations are forestwide tasks. In other words, one server performs the task for your entire AD forest. Other operations are performed by one server in each domain. In either case, only one server performs the operation, so it is important that you take these tasks into account when planning server functionality (and disaster recovery). By default, the first domain controller installed in your forest or in each domain, as appropriate, is assigned the role of operations master for each function.

Forestwide Operations

There are two forestwide operations master roles:

- Schema master

- Domain naming master

Once again, it's important to remember that only one server in the entire forest performs these tasks. You must ensure that this server is reliable and has enough horsepower to perform them. You should also place it in a physical location where any outside links are fairly reliable. If these servers or the links to them are unavailable, certain administrative functions will not be accessible.

The *schema master* controls the structure of the AD database. Any updates or modifications made to the database structure must be made on this server first. It will then replicate these changes to the rest of the AD servers in your forest. This ensures that all AD servers are "speaking the same language." There should never be a case in which one server knows about a new object class or property but another server does not.

The *domain naming master* is responsible for adding or removing domains from the forest. It ensures that each domain is given a unique name when added to the forest and that any reference to a removed domain is cleaned up.

Domainwide Operations

There are three domainwide operations master roles:

- Relative ID (RID) master
- Primary domain controller (PDC) emulator
- Infrastructure master

Once again, only one server in each domain performs each of these tasks. These servers will need to be both powerful enough to handle the extra workload and reliable enough to be available when necessary.

The *relative ID master* controls the creation of security IDs for new objects created in the domain. Each object has a security ID that is made up of a domain identifier (the same for every object in the domain) and a unique relative ID that differentiates the object from any other in the domain. To ensure that these IDs are unique, only one server in each domain generates them.

The *primary domain controller (PDC) emulator master* has the capability to act as a PDC for non–Windows 2000 clients and NT 4 (and earlier) BDCs. This allows for a mixed environment of Windows 2000 and earlier NT version servers on the same network. Even in a Windows 2000–only AD environment, though, the PDC emulator performs an important function. When a user changes their password, whichever domain controller accepts the change will first pass the change to the PDC emulator operations master. This server then uses a high-priority function to replicate this change to all of the other domain controllers in the domain.

Each domain controller in a domain knows which server is acting as the PDC emulator. If a user tries to log on to the network but provides an incorrect password, the domain controller will first query the PDC emulator to ensure that it has the latest password for the user before denying the request to log on. This prevents a denial of service in the event that a user attempts to use their new password before it has had a chance to be replicated to all of the domain controllers in the domain.

The *infrastructure master* is responsible for updating group-to-user references when group members are renamed or relocated. It updates the group object so that it knows the new name or location of its members.

The Effects of Trusts on Design

By this time in your quest for the MCSE, you should be quite familiar with the concepts of *trusts* between domains. If you worked extensively with NT 4, it is easy to forget the difference between the two operating systems (NT and Windows 2000) and thus get confused about the effects of trusts within your structure. To review, it is important to remember that trusts are *transitive* in nature—in other words, if A trusts B and B trusts C, then A trusts C (this is much easier to remember if you've ever taken a logic class), as shown in Figure 6.11.

FIGURE 6.11 Transitive nature of trusts

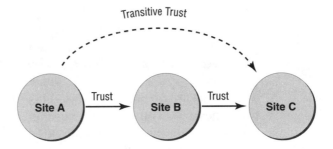

When a domain is added to an AD tree, a two-way trust between the new domain and its parent domain in the structure is automatically created. Because we have a hierarchical structure and transitive trusts, this results in an environment where all domains (within a tree) trust all other domains within that same tree, as shown in Figure 6.12.

FIGURE 6.12 Automatically configured trusts

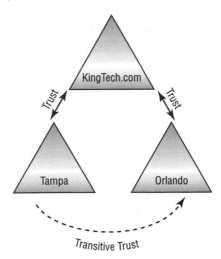

The same rule applies when a tree is added to a forest. A two-way trust relationship will automatically be created between the root domains of each tree, as shown in Figure 6.13. Once again, due to the transitive nature of trusts and the hierarchical nature of AD, this results in an environment where all domains within the forest trust all other domains in the forest.

FIGURE 6.13   Trusts between trees within a forest

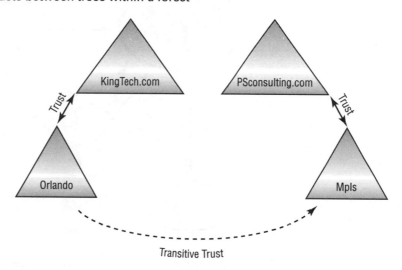

The bottom line for most AD design projects is that we never have to worry about creating trust relationships so that users from one domain can be granted access to resources in another. (This also eliminates one of the biggest headaches from Windows NT networks—trust management in large environments!) Although the default trusts will be adequate for almost all situations, be aware that you can override the defaults by managing trusts manually.

There are two exceptions to the default trust relationships of which you should be aware. First, any trusts between Windows 2000 domains and Windows NT domains must be created and managed manually. In a large network, this by itself might be enough incentive to upgrade all of your NT servers to Windows 2000 as quickly as possible. Second, when a Windows NT domain is upgraded to Windows 2000, all existing trust relationships remain as they were before the upgrade occurred. This last exception warrants more discussion because it could easily have an impact on the functionality of your final AD implementation.

As an example, take a look at the Windows NT domain and trust configuration shown in Figure 6.14. This domain design was known as a multimaster domain model in Windows NT and was quite common.

FIGURE 6.14 A multi-master domain model for Windows NT

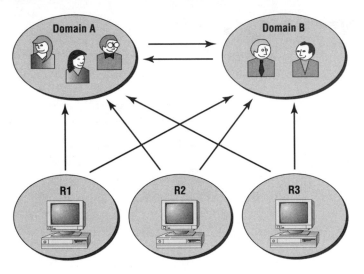

In the multi-master design, user accounts were created in the master domains (domains A and B in this example), and physical resources were created in resource domains (domains R1, R2, and R3 in this example). This design allowed for central control of user accounts but still allowed local control of physical resources such as servers, printers, or workstations. In a typical Windows 2000 environment, the resource domains are unnecessary—you can use OUs to grant or deny management capabilities to resources. (During the upgrade, the three resource domains would be rolled into whatever domain structure had been designed for the AD tree.) If that final domain structure were as shown in Figure 6.15, the "exception" to the rules would work in our favor.

FIGURE 6.15 A multi-master model after an upgrade

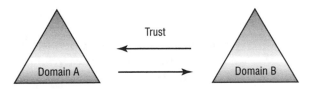

Because the trust relationships that were in place before the upgrade are preserved, the end result is basically the same result we'd get if we had created two new domains (rather than upgrading existing ones). There is still a two-way trust between domain A and domain B—exactly what we would want in most environments.

There might be times, however, when what we call a "rogue" domain exists in a Windows NT environment. By rogue domain, we mean a domain that does not fit into the strict definitions of the various domain models commonly used in Windows NT domain designs. (For more information about the traditional domain structures used in Windows NT see *Mastering Active Directory,* by Robert King [Sybex, 2000]) You might, for instance, find a domain that includes both user account information and resource records and is managed from a central location. This would result in a domain structure such as that shown in Figure 6.16.

FIGURE 6.16   A rogue Windows NT domain

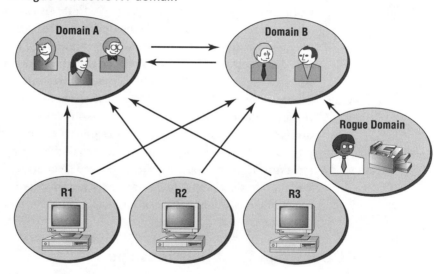

The one-way trust between domain B and the rogue domain would allow central management of the resources in the rogue domain, but it does not allow users from the rogue domain to be granted permissions in any other domain in the environment. After an upgrade to Windows 2000, the structure might look something like that shown in Figure 6.17.

FIGURE 6.17 A rogue domain after an upgrade to Windows 2000

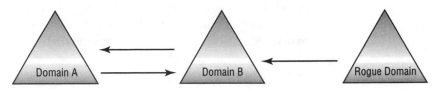

Notice that there is still only a one-way trust between domain B and the rogue domain. This results in an environment where users from the rogue domain *still* cannot be granted permissions to resources in the rest of the tree. This is not *necessarily* bad, but it certainly does not match the default configuration for an AD tree.

Analyzing Trust Relationships

Before you begin the process of designing your domain structure, you will want to analyze any existing trusts. We find this easier if we draw them out (the end results look much like the figures we're using in this chapter). Once we have a map of the trust relationships that exist before the upgrade, we will determine which domains will be rolled into other domains in the final AD structure. This will usually include any resource domains in the Windows NT network and any domains that include both user accounts and resource records. We agree with Microsoft's minimalist philosophy toward domains in that we usually try to design structures with as few domains as possible. This allows us to draw another domain map that represents the structure after the upgrade. Then we need to analyze the trust structure as it will manifest itself by default—any existing trusts will stay the same, and any new domain we create will automatically generate a two-way trust to its parent domain.

Optimizing Trust Relationships

Once we've got a picture of what the trust structure will look like after the upgrade, we can then plan for any changes we will need to make to optimize the environment. You will want to pay close attention to any resource domains that were not rolled into a master domain and any rogue domains that existed before the upgrade. You'll also want to ensure that two-way trusts are appropriate for your environment. You might, for instance, have a political situation where one domain should not be accessible from any others. (We tend to rely on other pieces of security to solve these issues so that we don't have to add trusts to the list of ongoing management tasks.)

The bottom line with trusts is that, in most cases, the default configuration in which each child domain has a two-way trust with its parent and the root domains of every tree have a two-way trust to the root domain of every other tree seems to be adequate for almost every situation.

Design Scenario: International Coffee, Inc.

International Coffee, Inc. has recently purchased two competing companies and has hired you to build a unified Windows 2000 network. After the merge, International Coffee is the largest supplier of coffee in the world. The first merged company was Small-Time Java, a regional supplier of coffee beans to the European market, and MegaBucks, a coffeehouse franchise that purchases more coffee than any other company in the Untied States.

CEO "The goal of the two purchases was quite simple—first, we wanted to get our name into the European market—our demographic research shows that Europeans drink more coffee per person than people in any other region of the world. Although Small-Time Java was not a big player in that market (brand recognition was almost zero), it did have a complete distribution network in place. We can now begin selling our coffee through that network. Our second goal was to take advantage of the MegaBucks name—it has franchise facilities in just about every major U.S. market. It was also our biggest customer for custom coffee blends—we have decided to move our coffee into the European market by franchising MegaBucks stores throughout Europe."

CIO "Before the recent mergers, our network was almost, but not quite, large enough to qualify as an enterprise environment. We have sites throughout the U.S. and Central and South America. Now that the merger has been finalized, our new environment is definitely one of the larger networks out there! We now tie into a large number of distribution centers, have too many retail outlets to count, and have to develop connectivity to our new European offices. All three preexisting networks were based upon Microsoft NT 4—and all three were designed following the single-master model."

CFO "Our goals are simple—increase the market penetration of the International Coffee brand name and grow the image of MegaBucks from a U.S. firm to an international player."

Based upon this information, what suggestions could you make concerning the domain and AD structures for International Coffee, Inc.?

The first question you should ask yourself is, "Do we have one consistent namespace, or are we dealing with multiple namespaces?" In this case, we can safely say that Small-Time Coffee is going to be completely merged into the corporate identity of International Coffee—the only reason it was purchased was to acquire its distribution channel in Europe. MegaBucks, on the other hand, has a well-established identity, one that International Coffee wants to grow. It is safe to say that MegaBucks will probably continue to be a well-known brand name even after the merger is complete. In this case, we would suggest that the company build two separate trees (one for International Coffee and another for MegaBucks) and join them in a forest configuration.

At a minimum, how many domains will exist in the final forest?

Although we don't have enough technical data to make a definitive statement, it is safe to assume that al least two domains will be needed (a root domain for each tree). After that, we would have to analyze the network traffic and estimate the AD replication traffic to determine if more domains are needed.

Designing an Organizational Unit Structure

Organizational units provide structure within a domain. This structure is hierarchical in nature, just like the structure built by adding domains together. Each OU acts as a subdirectory to help administrators organize the various resources described within the directory. The structure must be meaningful to users and administrators alike for it to be of any value to the network. A structure designed without people in mind can do more harm than good, as demonstrated in Figure 6.18.

FIGURE 6.18   A bad OU structure

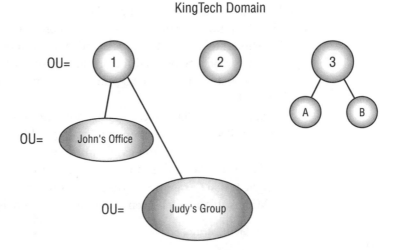

There are a couple of problems inherent in this design:

- Many of the OU names are not user friendly. A name of 1 might mean something to the administrator who created it, but it will probably mean nothing to the system's users.

- Naming containers after people *might* make things easier for a while, but as soon as there is a change in personnel or business structure, all such containers will need to be renamed.

Microsoft
✔ **Exam**
Objective

Design and plan the structure of organizational units (OU). Considerations include administration control, existing resource domains, administrative policy, and geographic and company structure.

- Develop an OU delegation plan.

- Plan Group Policy object management.

- Plan policy management for client computers.

What Makes a Good OU Model?

There are various *models* of good OU structures. A model defines categories of OUs and the relationships between them. The model you create for your tree should follow the business practices of your company. More than in any other form of network, a directory-based network demands that administrators understand the business practices and workflow of their company before designing the system.

Creating an OU model can be a difficult task—especially on your first attempt. Because a good design makes your life (and the lives of your users) easier in the long run, you would like to come up with a good, stable design the first time! With this in mind, some "cookie-cutter" models have been designed to act as guides during the planning stage of your own design.

Microsoft suggests seven different basic models for OU structures:

- Geographic

- Object based

- Cost center

- Project based

- Division or business unit

- Administration

- Hybrid or mixed

In the sections that follow, we will take a look at the advantages and disadvantages of each design model.

Geographic Model

In a geographic model, OUs are structured by geographic location, as shown in Figure 6.19. The KingTech Corporation has created a first level of OUs to represent continents and a second level to represent countries. This type of configuration is helpful if each country has its own administrator; you can easily grant administrative privileges to a local user account.

FIGURE 6.19 A geographic model

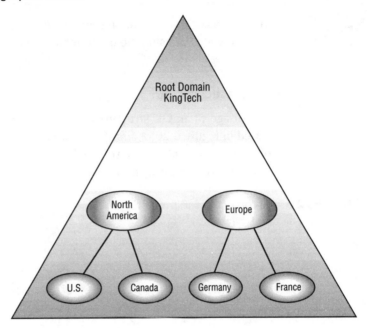

A geographic model offers a number of advantages:

- OUs will be fairly stable. Most companies sometimes reorganize internal resources, but the locations of their offices are usually stable.

- Corporate headquarters can easily dictate domainwide policies.

- It is easy to determine where resources are physically located.

- A geographic naming standard is easy for both users and administrators to understand.

A geographic model also has some disadvantages:

- This design does not mirror the business practices of KingTech in any way.

- The entire structure is one large partition (single domain). This means that *all* changes to all objects must be replicated to all AD servers worldwide.

In most cases, the replication traffic on the wide area links will outweigh any of the benefits of using the geographic model.

Object-Based Model

The design of an OU structure can also be based on object types, as illustrated in Figure 6.20. A first-level container would be created for each class of object that exists in the tree. Below this first level, a geographic layout might make administration easier.

FIGURE 6.20 An object-based model

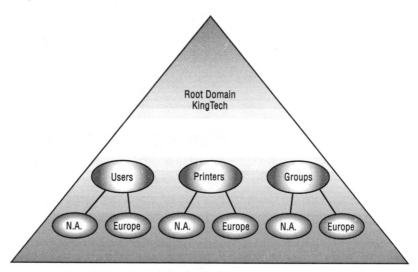

Here are some advantages of the object-based model:

- Resource administration is easier because each OU represents a specific class of object.

- Permissions are based upon OUs. It's easy to create OU-wide permissions, such as "All users should be able to use all printers."

- Administration can easily be delegated by resource type. For example, you can create a printer administrator who has permissions to add, delete, and modify all printers in the enterprise.

- A company reorganization should have little effect on the design. The same resources (with the possible exception of users) should exist no matter how the company is organized.

- Distinguished names are consistent for all objects in a class.

- It resembles the DNS structure, so it may lessen the learning curve for some administrators.

Disadvantages of the object-based model include the following:

- It is harder to define OU-based policies because all users are in the same containers.

- This flat structure will have to be created in each domain.

- There are too many top-level OUs. This can make navigating the administrative tools more difficult.

- If the schema is extended to accept new object types, new OUs will have to be created.

We've been working with directory-based networking for quite some time and we've never liked the object-based design. It offers the administrator little opportunity for customizing the environment to meet a particular business need. We might, for instance, have a printer that should be visible to only a particular group of users. Although this goal is possible with the object-based model, accomplishing it is more work than it might be in other models.

Cost Center Model

A company may decide that the OUs within its AD tree should reflect its cost centers, as shown in Figure 6.21. This model might be used in a company where budgetary concerns outweigh other considerations. A nonprofit organization, for example, might have separately defined divisions, each of which is responsible for its own management and cost controls.

FIGURE 6.21 A cost center model

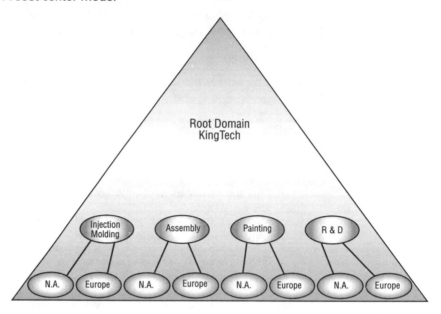

The cost center model has one main advantage: Each division or business group manages its own resources.

This model also has some disadvantages:

- Users might not be grouped together in a way that reflects their resource usage. A color printer, for instance, might belong to one department but might also be used by other departments as needed.

- Delegation of administrative privileges can be confusing.

The cost center design does not really take full advantage of the power of Active Directory. Most companies have departments, and each department might have its own budget, but there is usually some overlap of resources.

Project-Based Model

Some companies might prefer an OU structure that is based on current project teams. A manufacturing firm, for instance, might want to create an OU for each resource group in a shop floor manufacturing process. The project-based model is shown in Figure 6.22.

FIGURE 6.22   A project-based model

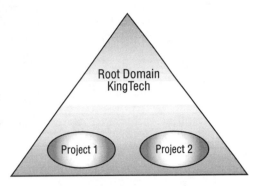

For certain environments, the project-based model offers some definite advantages:

- This model works well in an environment where resources and costs must be tracked.

- Because each project group is a separate OU, security between groups is easy to maintain.

Project-based design also has a couple of disadvantages:

- Projects often have a finite lifetime, so many OUs will have to be deleted and the resources redistributed.

- If projects change frequently, this type of structure will require a lot of maintenance.

We've found that a project-based structure will work for smaller companies with a limited product line. As a company grows (along with the number of active projects), the workload of maintaining a project-based design gets out of hand.

Division or Business Unit Model

The OU structure can also reflect a well-known business structure if such a structure exists. A typical well-known structure would be the various departments within a law enforcement agency. You can see an example in Figure 6.23.

FIGURE 6.23 A division or business unit model

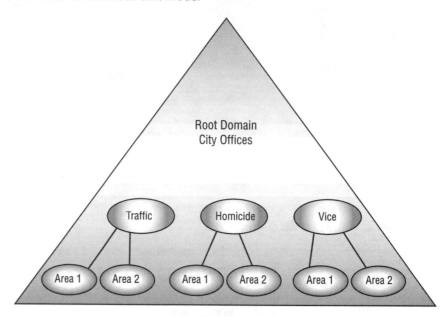

Here are some advantages of the division or business unit model:

- This structure is very user friendly because it is based upon a structure with which users are already familiar.

- For the same reason, it is easy to locate resources.

And here is a disadvantage: Although the structure is based on a well-known environment, there is always the chance that the business divisions will change. Any such change would force a redesign of the OU structure.

The division or business unit model works well in environments that are defined in a very rigid fashion, such as police departments and government offices.

Administration Model

One of the more frequently used models is a structure based upon common administrative groupings within a company, as shown in Figure 6.24. This model works well because it is based upon the actual business structure of the particular company.

FIGURE 6.24 An administration model

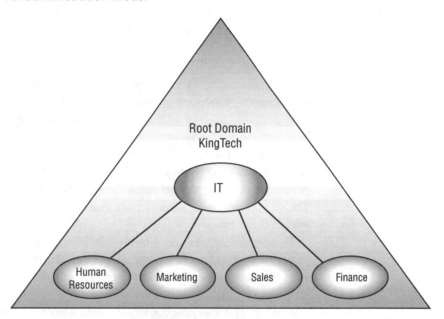

The administration model offers these advantages:

- This model is designed from the perspective of the network administrator and makes the administrator's job easier.

- Because most companies are departmental—from both a physical and a logical perspective—this model fits most enterprises.

It also has these disadvantages:

- This model is division oriented, so all resources from a single division or department will be grouped under a single OU. This might be confusing for users.

- In companies where many resources are shared between departments, this model might not reflect the business model of the company.

This is one of the more commonly implemented OU models. It works reasonably well for most companies.

Probably the biggest advantage of the administration model is that in most companies this design matches the organizational chart. In other words, the design has already been created—all the network administrator has to do is implement it!

The administration model also matches the way many NT 4 networks were created. First, one department would install an NT server, creating its own domain and user accounts. Later, another department would see the benefits enjoyed by the first department and would in turn install its own NT server. In the process, this department would create its own domain and Security Accounts Manager (SAM) database. Next, the two departments would see the potential benefits of sharing resources and would create trusts. The end result is a network already modeled on the administrative groupings within the company.

During the upgrade to Windows 2000 Server, the administrator has the option of redesigning the structure, but because the users are already familiar with the "departmental" concept of multiple domains, it makes sense to keep the structure as it is. This results in less confusion for end users, less retraining, and less productivity lost due to confusion.

Hybrid or Mixed Model

Most companies will settle on a hybrid structure that combines two or more of the standard models.

Remember that a structure will be more stable and need fewer adjustments if it accurately reflects the business structure of your company. The standard models are often too rigid to do this.

A typical hybrid structure is shown in Figure 6.25.

FIGURE 6.25 A hybrid model

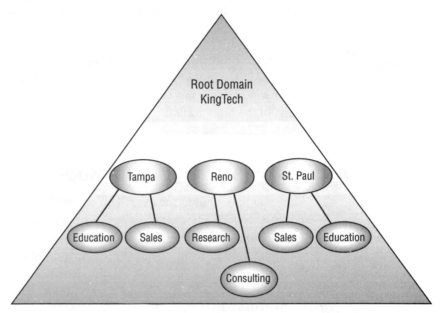

Advantages of a hybrid model follow:

- The structure can be customized to closely match the way in which business is conducted by the company.

- Employees are usually comfortable with the design because it reflects the way they actually work.

This model does have one disadvantage: It requires a greater understanding of the company for which it is intended than the other models do. For this reason, many outside consultants will avoid hybrid models.

Because of its flexibility, the hybrid model is probably the best overall design. It does, however, require more planning before implementation than the other models. Administrators of a hybrid model AD will have to create a set of rules governing when, why, and where new containers will be created. Here are some questions to ask yourself during this process:

- Which resources are departmental?

- Which resources are regional?

- Which resources are dedicated to a specific project?

Once you have answered these questions, you can start designing a structure that closely mirrors the way in which your business is structured.

The biggest problem with the hybrid model is that most businesses are dynamic. In other words, the way they do business changes as the market changes. Such changes could result in a design that no longer meets the needs of the organization.

Other Aspects of Planning an OU Model

After you have chosen the overall structure that you will use for your OU model, there are a few other things to consider before you start implementation. Most of the following topics are administrative concerns. Proper planning of these details will make administering your network easier down the line.

Name Standards

The names you give to OUs are used internally within the domain and can be seen when searching for particular objects. As such, it is important that the names you choose are meaningful *both* to your users and to your administrators.

OU names are not part of the DNS namespace. Users do not use DNS services to "find" an OU. This makes sense because OUs are not physical resources—they are logical structures used to organize the objects in your database.

OUs are identified by a distinguished name—also known as a *canonical name*—that describes their location in the hierarchical structure. Basically, this is the X.500 name for the object in the tree. An OU named Tampa that is located in the KingTech container would be known as Tampa.KingTech. These names are used most often for administrative tasks.

OU Ownership

Each OU in the structure has an object that acts as its owner. The owner of an OU can do the following:

- Add, delete, and update objects within the container

- Decide whether permissions should be inherited from the parent container

- Control permissions to the container

- Decide whether permissions should be propagated to child containers

 By default, the user who creates an OU is its owner.

Delegating Administration of OUs

One of the most important features of Active Directory (and one of the most marketed features) is its management flexibility. You can expect to see a few questions on the MCSE exam that require you to analyze an environment with a focus on delegation of management tasks. During the design of your OU structure, you will want to consider the management philosophy of the IT department—if they use a decentralized management model, you will want to create an OU structure with containers for each area of management responsibility. (Note that, depending upon other factors, this can also be accomplished through the creation of multiple domains.) If, for instance, a company has local administrators for each site, you will want to ensure that your structure includes containers for each site so that the proper permissions can be assigned.

For every OU in a domain, there is a set of permissions that grant or deny Read and Write access to the OU. This allows for a delegation of administrative privileges down to the lowest level of your structure. Any permissions assigned at the OU level pertain to all objects within that OU. There are various levels of authority you might want to delegate to other administrators:

Changing container properties   Administrators can change OU-wide properties, such as OU policies and other attributes.

Creating, deleting, and changing child objects   These objects can be users, groups, printers, and so on.

Updating attributes for a specific class of object   Perhaps your help desk personnel should be allowed to change *only* users' passwords (but not any other attributes of a user account).

Creating new users or groups   You can limit the class of objects that an administrator has the permission to create.

Managing a small subgroup of objects within the tree   You might want an administrator to manage only objects in a particular office.

Planning for Group Policy Object Management

As you should already be aware, *Group Policy objects (GPOs)* are used to control the environment of users and/or computers within your network. To put it mildly, there are many configuration options available within the GPO structure. Luckily, the topic of this book does not demand that we list them all (for more information about the capabilities and configuration of GPOs, see *MCSE: Windows 2000 Directory Services Study Guide,* by Anil Desai [Sybex, 2000]). Our focus is on creating a domain and OU structure that facilitates the use of GPOs as a management tool. For this, there are a few basic concepts with which you must be comfortable.

Where Are GPOs Assigned?

You can create GPOs that will affect users and computers at the site, domain, or organizational unit level within the AD structure. In other words, you can create a set of rules for user or workstation environments that will affect objects (those users and computers) within a given site, within a specific domain, or within an organizational unit. From a design perspective, this allows you to create a single GPO that will be applied to an entire domain or create different GPOs for each OU within the domain. A third option is to create a GPO for each site defined within your AD structure. During the design of your domain and organizational unit structures, you will have to determine which of the three options (or which combination of the three options) will best fit the business needs of your company or client. To do this, you will use (once again) the information gathered about the company and IT management philosophies.

You might, for instance, be working with a company in which all users are presented with a common interface to the network. In such an environment, you could create a single GPO for each domain and it would be applied to all users within that domain. On the other hand, you might be working with a company where a person's interface is dependent upon their job function (accountants only get to change their screen saver, whereas the engineers can change actual display settings). In this type of environment, you might want to create OUs for each different level of control so that GPOs could be created appropriately.

How Are GPOs Implemented?

If you decide to go with multiple types of GPOs—site, domain, and/or organizational unit—you will need to consider how those GPOs will be assigned to the users or computers. Remember that GPOs are executed in a specific order—first the site GPO is executed, then the domain GPO, and finally the OU GPO—and that the effects are cumulative. In other words, the configurations defined within the site GPO can be overwritten by those of the domain GPO, which in turn can be overwritten by the settings in the OU GPO.

Being the flexible operating system that it is, Windows 2000 and Active Directory allow you to control the inheritance of GPO settings. You can define a domain that cannot be overwritten by OU GPOs, or you can create an OU GPO that stops the execution of site and domain GPOs. No matter what technique you finally decide to use, your AD structure will have to reflect your desired outcome. If you want GPOs that are different for each department, you will need to create departmental sites, domains, or OUs.

Design Scenario: Company ABC

Company ABC has hired you to lead a project team that will plan and implement the upgrade from Windows NT 4 to Windows 2000. During your analysis, you gather the following facts:

- There are six physical sites located throughout the U.S.

- Available bandwidth between the sites is adequate for any type of AD design that you might implement.

- The company has approximately 2,000 users across its entire network.

- The company management philosophy is departmental.

- The IT management philosophy is decentralized.

The following notes were gathered during the interviews with key employees:

CIO "We've got good IT personnel at every facility. They can handle anything that we throw at them, from large database design and management to Web site design and implementation."

Local IT staff   "We are responsible for all of the resources within our facility. I don't really like the idea of some 'central IT group' dictating what I should do within the bounds of my site. We are more than willing to follow a general set of standards for IT tasks, such as user naming or e-mail use, but in many ways, our needs are different than the needs of any other office in the company. For instance, we manage the corporate Web site. This adds a whole new dimension to Internet connectivity that other sites don't have to deal with. And that works both ways. Joe in Houston, for instance, has most of the company's market research staff at his site. They all need unlimited access to the Internet, whereas our users don't even know what the Internet looks like. I like the idea that the corporate IT staff lets us pretty much do as we please—as long as information can flow as needed!"

Based upon this information, how many domains would you suggest for ABC?

Given adequate bandwidth and a relatively small number of users (relative to the capabilities of AD), we would suggest one domain, using sites to control AD replication traffic.

Within the domain, what OU model would you use?

Because each physical location is responsible for its own resources, the company will need a design that allows easy delegation of IT permissions to staff for each site. We would suggest a geographic model for this company. If more granularity is required for management, we would use a hybrid model—with geographic OUs that contain departmental OUs.

Summary

At this point in a real-life design project, you will have a fairly complete picture of what the final version of your AD structure will look like. The next steps would really revolve around testing your design against a few other incidental considerations (those considerations actually make up the rest of this book). For instance, the next step would be analyzing your design for efficiency—getting a handle on AD replication, designing site boundaries, and planning the placement of the operations masters within your network.

Although the structure is not yet finished, it could certainly be considered a "beta design"—really all that's left is to ensure that each piece works the way you had planned.

To get to this point, you used the information gathered during your analysis of the network infrastructure and business needs to create both an overall domain structure and a organizational unit structure that will fulfill the needs of your company/client.

In the next chapter, you'll begin to optimize your design for efficiency on the network—reducing, or at least directing, the traffic generated by AD on your network infrastructure.

Key Terms

Before you take the exam, be sure you're familiar with the following terms:

domain

domain naming master

forest

global catalog server

Group Policy objects (GPOs)

hierarchical naming

infrastructure master

namespace

operations master

organizational unit

partitions

primary domain controller (PDC) emulator master

relative ID master

root domain

schema

schema master

transitive

Review Questions

1. The first domain created within an AD tree is known as the
   _____ .

   A. Master domain

   B. Root domain

   C. First domain

   D. Binding domain

2. _____ is used to organize resources, and _____ is used to find resources.

   A. DHCP, WINS

   B. DNS, AD

   C. AD, AD

   D. AD, DNS

3. A partition is _____ .

   A. One attribute of an object

   B. A section of the overall AD database, also known as a domain

   C. A clustered-server domain controller group

   D. A section of a Group Policy object

4. Which of the following are reasons to create an OU rather than a domain?

   A. To ease delegation of management responsibilities

   B. To ease management by grouping like objects

   C. To control the visibility of objects

   D. To control directory replication traffic

5. Which of the following are reasons to create a new domain rather than an OU?

A. When administrators are adamant in their desire to control specific areas of a structure

B. To make delegation easier in diverse environments

C. To control directory replication traffic

D. When the default trust relationships do not meet your needs

6. What are the requirements when two AD trees are combined to create a forest?

A. They must have a common schema.

B. They must share a common global catalog server.

C. A two-way trust is established between the root domains of each tree.

D. They must share a common namespace.

7. Of the following operations master roles, which are forestwide roles?

A. Schema master

B. Relative ID master

C. Infrastructure master

D. Domain naming master

8. If domain 1 trusts domain 2 and domain 2 trusts domain 3, which statement is true?

A. There is no relationship of any sort between domain 1 and domain 3.

B. Domain 3 trusts domain 1.

C. Domain 1 trusts domain 3.

D. You do not have enough information to determine the trust relationship between domains 1 and 3.

9. Which of the following are true statements?

   A. When a new domain is added to the AD tree, a two-way trust is automatically created between it and its parent domain.

   B. When an existing Windows NT domain is upgraded to Windows 2000, all existing trusts remain as they were before the upgrade.

   C. When an existing Windows NT domain is upgraded to Windows 2000, all existing trusts are eliminated and the Windows 2000 default trust relationships are established.

   D. All trust relationships must be created manually.

10. Group policies are executed in which order?

   A. Domain, site, OU

   B. Site, domain, OU

   C. OU, site, domain

   D. Domain, OU, site

(The answers to the questions begin on the next page.)

Answers to Review Questions

1. B. The first domain created within an AD tree is known as the root domain. Because all user principal names are in the form of *<username>@ <root domain name>*, it is critical that this domain be planned carefully.

2. D. AD is used to organize resource records within a database. Users query the AD database to obtain information (such as the IP address) about a resource. DNS is used to resolve that IP address into a hardware address so that communication can occur.

3. B. Each domain represents a piece of the overall AD database, which is stored on domain controllers. Domains are tied together by trusts, which create one logical database out of the pieces. The process of breaking a database into pieces is known as partitioning and each piece is known as a partition.

4. A, B, C. Directory replication traffic is based upon domain membership of Windows 2000 servers. OUs are logical objects, not physical, so they do not affect network traffic in any way.

5. A, B, C, D. In most cases, the creation of a new domain will be in response to a physical aspect of the network (to control replication traffic or to facilitate management in a multilanguage network). Occasionally, though, a domain will be created for a political reason, such as complete separation of administrative responsibilities.

6. A, B, C. One of the reasons to create a forest is to facilitate communication and administration in environments where separate namespaces must be maintained, so answer D is incorrect.

7. A, D. Only two roles are forestwide roles: schema master and domain naming master.

8. C. Remember that trusts are transitive. Also be aware of the wording here—in this particular case, the trusts are all described as one-way trusts, so you cannot assume that domain 3 trusts domain 1.

9. A, B. Answer A is the default trust relationship for *new* domains, and B is that of *upgraded* domains.

10. B. This is critical information when planning for GPOs because each GPO can override the settings of any preceding GPOs.

Case Study: Memory Makers, LLC

In Chapter 5, you took a first look at Memory Makers, LLC of Grand Rapids. After looking over the information, you decided that a Windows 2000 solution made sense for its business. So far, you have made the following recommendations to them: Memory Makers will have only one DNS domain with no subdomains; the root NT domain will be named the same as the registered DNS name—Memory-Makers.com; certain problem areas within the IT environment will be fixed before the upgrade takes place (instituting a backup process and securing the inventory database were critical!).

Background

Overview   A company in Grand Rapids, Michigan—Memory Makers, LLC—has asked you to look over its current IS situation and plan a move into Internet e-commerce. Memory Makers sells collectable toys—everything from Easy-Bake ovens to G. I. Joes. Its inventory changes on a daily basis, and much of its business is made up of customer requests for a particular item. When interviewed, the CEO and CFO had a consistent view of the future.

CEO   "With the baby boomers getting older, we are assured that our volume of sales should continue to grow! While we're never going to be a major employer (by gross numbers) in Grand Rapids, we expect our contribution to this community to grow with our business."

CFO   "Our facilities here in Grand Rapids should be sufficient to handle our expected growth in sales for the foreseeable future."

Current System

Overview   Memory Makers is currently using a peer-to-peer network of Windows 95/98 desktop computers. A database of inventory is stored on the receptionist's desktop machine, a Pentium-class computer with 64MB of RAM and plenty of disk space. No security has been placed on the database, no backups are being made, and no business process is in place to keep the database up-to-date. There is no IS staff on-site and no plans to hire anyone.

CEO "We know that we need to move into the twenty-first century, and we have set aside funding for it. What we don't have is internal expertise—we deal in toys! That's where you come in—you tell us what would be the best solution."

CFO "After compiling a business plan, we see the advantages of moving to some form of e-commerce. We looked at the numbers, though, and decided that our best bet is to outsource our technical support (instead of hiring internal staff). Our major concerns are to keep future costs under control and to be able to use off-the-shelf applications for which training is available."

CIO "I'm not really much of a computer guy—I'm just the person who everyone turns to when the computers don't work. I managed to get the Windows 95 network running and share a few printers, but that's about the extent of my experience. We've got about 50 users spread over 4 departments: purchasing, sales, management, and shipping and receiving. The people in purchasing need the most help; they spend most of their time searching Internet auctions for good deals. The sales staff doesn't even have a computer on every desk yet; they print out current inventory reports every hour and pass them around. Management uses Excel to make the usual management-type spreadsheets. Oh yeah, and they have a golf game that they play on a regular basis. Shipping and receiving uses their computers to track shipments. It's really not that complex now, but we expect to grow and we want to be ready."

Current issues

Like every other business in the world, Memory Makers wants to ride the wave of e-commerce. It has a registered a domain (Memory-Makers.com) and a simple Web page being hosted by a local ISP. The company would like to expand this side of its business to include sales of current inventory and Internet requests for special items.

Goals

Memory Makers would like to first create a secure environment in which mistakes like the loss of the inventory database are less likely to happen. Once this has been accomplished, they would like to create an effective Web presence.

Considerations in Design

Overview   The first goal is to create a self-sufficient environment because Memory Makers has no IS staff on-site. You will be its sole support system. Various issues will have to be considered.

Security   Once the e-commerce server is up and running, the site will be open to the Internet. You will have to take special precautions to protect against intrusions.

Fault Tolerance   Because the entire business revolves around what is in stock, the inventory database has to achieve an almost 100-percent availability rating.

Maintenance   Memory Makers has decided to outsource the entire implementation and maintenance of its environment to your company. No on-site IS staff will be available. Your recommendations will decide the future of its network.

Performance   Once the e-commerce site is in place, sales are expected to triple overnight. You will have to design a system that can handle the overhead of a busy Web-based business.

Funding   As the baby boomers get older, the market for collectable toys from the 1960s and 1970s has grown by leaps and bounds. Memory Makers was able to find some venture capital that it is using to fund this expansion into the e-commerce arena. Funding should not be an issue, but like all other consulting jobs, dollar-accountability is critical to a continued relationship with the client.

Questions

1. How many AD trees and NT domains would you suggest for this environment?

   A. One tree, four domains (one for each main department)

   B. One tree, one domain

   C. Two trees (one for the company and another for the e-commerce environment), and two domains (one for each tree)

   D. One tree, two domains (one for the company resources and another for the e-commerce environment)

2. Which OU model would you recommend?

   A. Geographic

   B. Cost center

   C. Project-based

   D. Departmental

3. What would you name the root domain of this AD structure?

   A. Toys.com

   B. MM.com

   C. Memory-Makers

   D. Memory-Makers.com

4. Management is concerned about the amount of time employees are spending browsing the Internet. What is the best way to keep personal Internet usage at reasonable levels, even while allowing users to use the Web for research and other business-related tasks?

A. Deny all users access from their desktops and have a single kiosk station from which users can do research.

B. Configure a firewall to block out all commercial sites, as well as other common sites such as Yahoo!, CNN and USA TODAY.

C. Craft a policy on acceptable Internet usage and set up logging to track user access. Make it clear to users that their browsing will be monitored and define clear penalties for improper use.

D. Leave the Internet open to all users. Eventually they will tire of it, and the problem will go away.

5. You have been asked to provide Memory Makers with a recommendation as to what steps it will need to take to upgrade its Web site. Memory Makers has a number of different goals for the new Web site. For each goal, select the tasks that will need to be completed from the list shown. Assume that the ISP will continue to host and manage the site but that Memory Makers will be responsible for the site's content.

Goals	Tasks
E-commerce	Configure secure site access.
Content update	Train Webmaster.
Inventory control	Identify a process for ensuring quality control.
Customer support	Allow data entry workers access to the database to make changes and fill orders.
	Identify or hire a Webmaster.
	Outsource help desk support.
	Install FrontPage 2000 on client machines.
	Purchase SSL certificate.
	Create Internet-accessible database solution

Answers

1. B. This environment is small and simple—make the AD structure match!

2. D. The only hint you've had of the division of labor within the company has been discussion of four departments: purchasing, sales, management, and shipping and receiving.

3. D. The easiest, and usually best, solution is to name the topmost domain the same as the registered DNS domain for the company.

4. C. This is not a question that has a "right" or "wrong" answer, but option C has the advantage of allowing users to go wherever they may need while adding the threat of monitoring to keep them from abusing the privilege.

5. See table.

Goals
E-commerce
Purchase SSL certificate.
Configure secure site access.
Content update
Install FrontPage 2000 on client machines.
Identify or hire a Webmaster.
Train Webmaster.
Inventory control
Create Internet-accessible database solution.
Allow data entry workers access to the database to make changes and fill orders.
Customer support
Outsource help desk support.
Identify a process for ensuring quality control.

There are a number of ways to upgrade a Web site, of course, but these are some of the basic steps. Note that, due to the lack of an IT staff, many of the tasks may need to be outsourced, including the development of the site itself.

Chapter 7

Planning an Efficient AD Design

MICROSOFT EXAM OBJECTIVES COVERED IN THIS CHAPTER:

✓ **Design an Active Directory site topology.**

  ▪ Design a replication strategy.

  ▪ Define site boundaries.

✓ **Design the placement of operations masters.**

  ▪ Considerations include performance, fault tolerance, functionality, and manageability.

✓ **Design the placement of global catalog servers.**

  ▪ Considerations include performance, fault tolerance, functionality, and manageability.

✓ **Design the placement of domain controllers.**

  ▪ Considerations include performance, fault tolerance, functionality, and manageability.

AD design is, in many ways, a balancing act. You have to weigh convenience for users against cost of services. Up to this point, we've concentrated on providing a true business solution, but we've ignored one of the biggest business considerations—costs. There are many costs involved in the installation, configuration, and maintenance of a network, but until recently, the industry has concentrated on the immediate costs of installation and paid little attention to ongoing costs.

Microsoft has embraced the concept of *total cost of ownership (TCO)*. TCO reflects more than just buying a couple of PCs and some software; it includes the cost of support, updates, upgrades, connecting those PCs, supporting the network—every cent spent to acquire, configure, and maintain your IT environment. Most of the experts agree that the ongoing costs far outweigh the initial purchase price of hardware and software.

One of the more expensive ongoing costs of a network is bandwidth. In a single-site environment, bandwidth is cheap—lay some cable and you own the world! As soon as you move to the world of WANs, however, costs start to skyrocket. Controlling the traffic placed on wide area links is one of the most important aspects of network design.

Although you cannot eliminate all of the traffic on your networks (after all, networks exist to move data), you can design your networks to eliminate unnecessary traffic and control what's left. That's what this chapter is all about—eliminating as much of the AD traffic as possible and taking control of what's left.

We'll start off by looking at the reasons for AD traffic and how AD performs the replication process. This information is not directly related to any of the exam objectives, but a firm understanding will help you to assimilate the replication information that *is* pertinent to the test! After this overview, we'll move to a discussion of network traffic and server load analysis. The first step in any optimization process is to get a good picture of the current situation and to provide a good estimate of the impact of any changes. After we show you how to look at the current situation and measure the impact that AD traffic will place on it, our discussion will move to specific design issues—in particular, the placement of servers within the environment.

Understanding Replication

Each Windows 2000 domain has at least one server that acts as a domain controller. Unlike in earlier versions of NT, each domain controller is involved in managing changes and updates to the database. Earlier versions of NT were configured in a *single-master environment*. The primary domain controller (PDC) maintained and managed the master copy of the domain database and was in charge of replicating changes to the backup domain controllers (BDCs) of its domain. In a single-master environment, the master (in this case, the PDC) is a single point of failure. If for some reason the PDC is unavailable, no changes can be made to the database.

In Windows 2000 Server, each domain controller holds a complete copy of the AD directory for its own domain. In this respect, it is much like earlier versions. The difference, however, is that each Windows 2000 domain controller can accept and make changes to the database and then replicate those changes to other domain controllers. An environment like this, where multiple computers are responsible for managing changes, is known as a *multimaster environment*. A multi-master environment offers numerous advantages over the old single-master configuration. Here are some of those advantages:

- There is no single point of failure. Because every domain controller can accept changes to the database, there is no domain controller that is critical to the process.

- Domain controllers that can accept changes to the database can be distributed throughout the physical network. This allows administrators to make changes on a local computer and let a background process (replication) ensure that those changes are updated on all other domain controllers in a timely and efficient manner.

Replication vs. Synchronization

The first important concept to understand when looking at AD updates is the difference between replication and synchronization. These two terms are often used interchangeably in the industry. Microsoft has a specific definition for each.

Replication

Directory *replication* is the process that takes place when one Windows 2000 domain controller updates another with changes to the AD database. Replication relies on a homogeneous environment: All domain controllers involved must be Windows 2000 servers and have identical schemas, and there must be a high level of trust between the servers involved.

Synchronization

Directory *synchronization* occurs between dissimilar implementations of a directory service. For example, because both Active Directory services and Novell Directory Services follow an industry-standard method of access, it is possible for each environment to update the other with information from its own database. You might, for instance, want to create users in the Novell directory but manage them from within the Active Directory environment.

In such a case, an agent, known as a *security principal*, would perform the synchronization, importing or exporting objects and changes from one directory to the other. Microsoft supplies security principals that can synchronize data between the following:

- Windows 2000 Server AD and Novell Directory Services (NDS). This agent allows you to create and manage Novell accounts in Microsoft AD. You can create an object in AD and the agent will push that object to NDS.

- An agent that allows synchronization between the AD database and a Microsoft Exchange Server directory.

Because Windows 2000 Server AD is fully LDAP compliant, it is conceivable that other environments will be added to this list in the future. For now, though, only these two are available.

 We'll discuss synchronization between AD and other directories in Chapter 9, "Planning for Active Directory Connectors." For now, we'll concentrate on the replication process.

Knowledge Consistency Checker (KCC)

Because we can assume that there will be occasional changes to the Active Directory, and knowing that each partition of the database can be replicated across multiple domain controllers, it is safe to assume that network traffic will be generated by AD. We'll discuss the types of traffic in an upcoming section, but for now we need to introduce the service that guides this traffic—the *Knowledge Consistency Checker (KCC)*. The KCC is a process that runs automatically and is responsible for generating the replication topology between domain controllers.

Types of Replication

There are two basic types of replication in a Windows 2000 Server environment:

- *Intrasite replication* occurs between domain controllers within a site.

- *Intersite replication* occurs between domain controllers in different sites.

When planning your site structure and replication strategy, it is important to understand the methods used for each type of replication traffic.

Intrasite Replication

As defined earlier, intrasite replication involves domain controllers from the same site. These computers use *remote procedure calls (RPCs)* to perform the replication process.

The KCC generates a *ring topology* for replication among the domain controllers within the site, as shown in Figure 7.1. This ring topology defines the path through which changes will flow within the domain. Any changes will follow the ring until all domain controllers have received them.

Creating a ring topology ensures that there are two paths that changes can follow from one domain controller to another (either direction on the ring).

FIGURE 7.1 A ring topology for replication

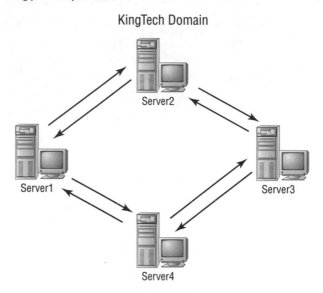

The KCC will also configure the ring so that there are no more than three hops between any two domain controllers within the domain. On occasion, this will call for the creation of multiple rings within a single domain, as you can see in Figure 7.2.

FIGURE 7.2 The three-hop rule of intrasite replication

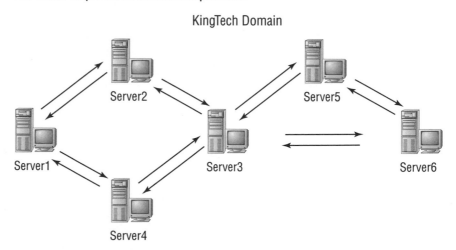

There is no "master" KCC server within a site. Each domain controller runs the KCC service to generate the intrasite topology for the site in which it resides. Assuming that all of the domain controllers are able to communicate and that there are no other problems within the domain structure, each domain controller should arrive at the same topology as every other domain controller. After this analysis, the KCC will create the appropriate AD connection objects on the local server. In this way, each of the domain controllers is included in the overall replication process. The KCC periodically analyzes the replication topology within a site to ensure efficiency. If a domain controller has been added or removed, the KCC will reconfigure the ring for optimum efficiency.

Intersite Replication

The replication topology between sites is created in a completely different manner. First, within each site certain domain controllers need to be assigned the role of *bridgehead server*. Bridgehead servers are responsible for the physical act of transferring replication traffic between sites.

The KCC on one domain controller in each site is given the task of reviewing the intersite topology and creating connection objects for incoming traffic on all bridgehead servers within the site. To put that another way, the KCC on each bridgehead server does *not* create the connection objects for the local server—this task is off-loaded to another server within the site (which does not even have to be a bridgehead server itself). This server is known as the *InterSite Topology Generator (ISTG)*. The first AD server to boot within a site will assume the role of ISTG—there is no election and there are no criteria for accepting this responsibility. The same server will hold this role until it becomes unavailable for a specific amount of time (the default is 60 minutes and can be changed through a Registry edit), known as the KCC site generator renewal interval. The ISTG writes a new value to one of its properties (the KCC site generator renewal interval) every 30 minutes. Because this is seen as changed information, it is replicated to every other domain controller within the site. All domain controllers within the site monitor this attribute to ensure that the ISTG is available. In the event that a new ISTG needs to be established, each domain controller looks at the list of domain controllers within its site, using the globally unique identifier (GUID) value to determine which servers should take over the role.

All in all, the information about the KCC is of academic interest but of little use during the design process. All you can influence is how often the role is advertised—you have no control over which domain controller accepts the responsibility.

Behind the Scenes of Replication

Understanding the process of replication can give you the skills necessary to optimize that traffic and design your AD environment to minimize its impact on the network. Later in this chapter, you'll learn about a few tools you can use to analyze replication traffic, but to use these tools effectively, you must have an understanding of the processes that produce this traffic. In the next few sections, we'll discuss the process of replication from an academic perspective, and then we'll use our new insights during our analysis.

Update Sequence Numbers

When a change is made to the database stored on a domain controller—either through a user action or through replication from another domain controller—the domain controller assigns the change an *update sequence number (USN)*. Each domain controller keeps its own USNs and increments the value for each change that occurs.

With respect to a single domain controller, you can think of the USN as a change counter. Each domain controller will have different values for changes that occur on its copy of the directory database. These values are not synchronized between domain controllers within a domain.

When the domain controller writes the change to the database, it also writes the USN of the change to that property. This is seen as a single transaction and will succeed or fail as a whole. In other words, AD will protect against a change being applied to the database without a corresponding USN also being recorded. This is an important feature because USNs are used to determine which changes need to be replicated to other domain controllers. This process is depicted in Figure 7.3.

FIGURE 7.3   Applying a change to the database

Object—Bob

Property	USN	Value
Telephone number	6	555-1000

If the value of the telephone number property for user Bob needs to be changed, the domain controller will check its current value for the database USN. Let's say the last USN applied to a change was 3. When the system writes Bob's new telephone number to the database, it will increment the USN and write *both* the changed data and the USN to Bob's object. The system USN will also be incremented to reflect this new value (so that the next change to the database will receive a higher USN).

Multiple USNs

There are a couple of new concepts to keep in mind here. First, notice that the domain controller is keeping track of the highest USN value that it has assigned to a change. (Microsoft doesn't really have a name for this value, but we're going to call it the DCUSN for *Domain Controller USN.*) This allows the domain controller to increment the value for each change, ensuring that no duplicate USNs exist and that each USN is larger than the one before it. Second, each property of every object really stores two values: the actual data (like Bob's telephone number) and the USN assigned to the value the last time the attribute was changed.

 Reread that preceding paragraph! Its two main concepts—a domain controller USN value that represents the highest USN assigned and the fact that *every* property stores the USN assigned at the time of change—are crucial to understanding how replication works.

The Process of Replication

Now we can discuss the process of replicating Bob's new telephone number to all domain controllers within the domain. Each domain controller stores the DCUSN from all other domain controllers at the last time of replication, as shown in Figure 7.4.

FIGURE 7.4 DCUSN tables

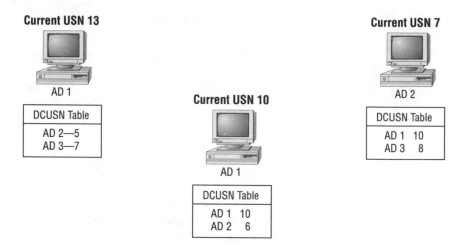

During the replication process, each domain controller sends its current DCUSN value to all of the other domain controllers in the domain. These servers compare this current value to the value that they have stored in their DCUSN table. If the current value is higher than the stored value, changes need to be replicated.

Look back at Figure 7.4. During replication, domain controller AD 2 will send its current DCUSN, which is 7, to both domain controllers AD 1 and AD 3. The last time that replication occurred with AD 1, the USN for AD 2 was 5. Because the current value is 7, AD 1 will request changes 6 and 7 from AD 2. AD 2 will search its database for the properties with these USN values and replicate them to AD 1, as shown in Figure 7.5.

FIGURE 7.5 Replication of specific changes

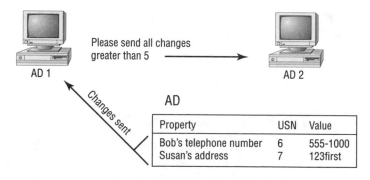

Benefits of Using USNs

Using USN values to determine which changes to replicate eliminates the need for precise time stamps for changes (and for time to be synchronized among the domain controllers). Time stamps are also assigned to each change, however, for tie-breaking purposes. These time stamps decide which change should be implemented if a specific attribute was changed on two or more domain controllers during the replication interval. In that event, the change with the latest time stamp is placed in the database; any other changes are discarded.

Using USNs also simplifies the recovery process after a failure. When a domain controller comes back online after a recovery, it just needs to ask all of the other domain controllers for all changes with USN values higher than the last value stored in its DCUSN table. This is true even if the replication process is temporarily interrupted (a wide area link goes down, for instance). When communication is reestablished, the domain controller will request all changes with USNs greater than the last change applied to the database.

Propagation Dampening

As you saw earlier in this chapter, the KCC creates the replication topology for intrasite replication. The KCC creates a loop topology so that domain controllers have multiple paths for sending and receiving updates, as shown in Figure 7.6.

FIGURE 7.6 Replication topology

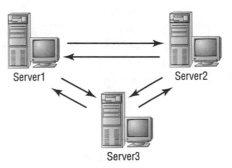

Although a loop topology increases fault tolerance and can increase performance, it can also result in a domain controller receiving the same update from two different domain controllers. To prevent this, Active Directory uses a *propagation dampening* scheme. Propagation dampening is the process of preventing unnecessary replication of directory changes.

Up-to-Date Vectors

USNs can be used to determine which changes have been replicated from another domain controller, but they do nothing to prevent changes from being replicated from multiple sources. This is why, in addition to USNs, Windows 2000 domain controllers also store *up-to-date vectors*. An up-to-date vector identifies the source of the originating write to a property. The *originating write* to any property identifies the source domain controller for the change. If a user changes their password, for instance, and that change is made to the copy of the directory stored on Server1, on Server1 the change would be considered an originating write; the change made there is directly related to some action performed by a user. In contrast, a *nonoriginating write* would be a change that was received through the replication process. Another way to look at this is to consider the server where the change originates as the source of the originating writes.

As an example, let's look at the process of updating a change in an environment with three domain controllers: Server1, Server2, and Server3. If a user changes their password at Server1, the server updates the value in the database and assigns that change the next incremental value for its USN. What is actually stored in the directory will contain this:

```
Password, Server1, USN-7
```

The USN value will follow the rules outlined earlier.

When this change is replicated to Server2, Server2 writes the change and increments its own USN. The actual record in the directory database remains the same as it was at Server1:

```
Password, Server1, USN-7
```

Server1 has also replicated this change to Server3. Server3 stores the same information, including the up-to-date vector information. When Server2 begins the replication process with Server3, Server3 will send its current USN value *and* all of its up-to-date vectors. Server2 compares the up-to-date vectors received from Server3 to its own. Server3 will not send any changes that have already been replicated to Server2.

Measuring the Traffic

Unfortunately, there are no magic numbers to use when trying to determine the amount of network traffic that AD will generate in a given environment. Each network will be different—different types of changes will be made to the database, different management styles will generate traffic in different patterns, and each wide area network will have different amounts of available bandwidth. The job of the design team is to estimate the amount of traffic that will be generated (based upon their intimate knowledge of the physical and business models in use by the company) and plan accordingly.

Tools for Measuring Traffic

When you have a firm grasp on the types of traffic that will be generated, you must find ways to measure that traffic. Luckily, Windows 2000 Server includes utilities that can be used to measure and analyze network traffic and the impact of services upon a server:

- Performance
- Network Monitor
- Replication Monitor

Performance

The Performance tool (this name doesn't sound complete; the same tool used to be called Performance Monitor in Microsoft NT, but the menus and documentation are quite specific and consistent in its naming) is the best utility for determining the overhead being place on a server by a given process. The secret to using the Performance tool is to determine which statistics are relevant to your needs. You should already be familiar with the basic functions and configuration of the Performance utility, so we can concentrate upon those objects and counters that might be of interest during your analysis of AD traffic. Performance includes an object that is specific to directory service statistics—NTDS (NT, as in Windows NT, Directory Service). The NTDS object includes numerous counters, as shown in Figure 7.7.

FIGURE 7.7 NTDS counters

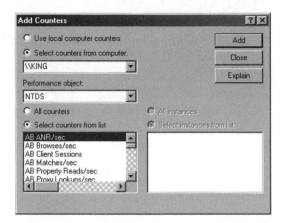

Each of the counters can provide information that will be useful during the design process. We don't need to look at each of the counters in detail at this point—what we need to do is concentrate on those counters that will indicate network traffic (either directly or by providing a service across the network).

The Address Book is a convenient applet that acts as a contacts manager, allowing you to store information about people of interest. The NTDS statistics listed here measure the overhead of using the Address Book to locate information from within the AD database:

AB ANR/Sec The rate at which Address Book clients perform Ambiguous Name Resolution operations

AB Browses/Sec The rate at which Address Book clients perform browse operations

AB Client Sessions The number of connected Address Book client sessions

AB matches/sec The rate at which Address Book clients perform find operations

AB Property reads The rate at which Address Book clients perform property read operations

AB Proxy lookups/sec The rate at which proxy clients perform search operations

AB searches/sec The rate at which Address Book clients perform key search operations

The next few counters (any of the DRA counters) can be used to quantify the amount of traffic that is generated by the replication process. For many of these counters, the name explains the information it provides; for those that don't, we have supplied an explanation:

- DRA Inbound Bytes Compressed (Between Sites, after compression) since boot

- DRA Inbound Bytes Compressed (Between Sites, after compression)/sec

- DRA Inbound Bytes Compressed (Between Sites, before compression) since boot

- DRA Inbound Bytes Compressed (Between Sites, before compression)/sec

- DRA Inbound Bytes Not Compressed (Within Site) Since Boot

- DRA Inbound Bytes Not Compressed (Within Site)/sec

- DRA Inbound Bytes Total Since Boot

- DRA Inbound Bytes Total/sec

- DRA Inbound Full Sync Objects Remaining (The number of complete objects that need to be replicated to finish the process)

- DRA Inbound Object Updates Remaining in Packet (The number of partial updates remaining in the replication process)

- DRA Inbound Objects Applied/sec

- DRA Inbound Objects Filtered/sec

- DRA Inbound Objects/sec

 There is a list of the same counters for outbound Address Book traffic as well.

There are also a large number of counters available for tracking the number of reads, writes, and searches of the directory database. Although this information is a great start, Performance includes many other counters and objects that will be of value during your design project. Remember that you need to analyze the entire network, not just the impact of AD. You have to ensure that the additional traffic generated by AD will not adversely affect existing network performance. Here are a few of the objects that you should track:

Redirector   This object offers counters that measure the overall outgoing traffic on a server.

Server   This object contains counters that measure the amount of traffic coming into a server from the network.

TCP   This object is made up of counters for various aspects of TCP communication.

There will be an object available for each protocol you have installed. You will have to look at each of them to determine which protocols are generating the most overhead on your server.

Browser   This object has counters that are relevant to the Browser service. The Browser service generates a tremendous amount of traffic on the network.

DHCP Server   The counters for this object provide information about the overhead being generated by providing DHCP services.

DNS   Because DNS is a critical part of any AD environment, tracking its overhead is important to making good AD design decisions.

Memory   As always, memory is a big factor in determining if additional services (such as AD) can be placed on a server.

If you are not comfortable with the objects and counters available in the Performance tool (or if you're not experienced in using Performance to gather information), we suggest reading *MCSE: Windows 2000 Directory Services Administration Study Guide*, by Anil Desai (Sybex, 2000). Knowledge of Performance is assumed in the Design test, and you might be asked to analyze sample information. All in all, the counters provided in the Performance utility can provide the kind of information that is critical for making good design decisions—if you know how to use it. Therein lies the trick! Information is useless without a basis for comparison. We'll discuss a common method of analysis after our discussion of the utilities available.

Network Monitor

The Performance tool is one of the best utilities available for analyzing the burden placed on a server by a given service. It is *not*, however, the best tool for capturing and analyzing network traffic. For this task you will need a packet analysis tool. Luckily, Microsoft Windows 2000 Server includes such a tool—Network Monitor. Although a complete discussion of protocol analysis is beyond the scope of this manual, you will need to understand the basics of Network Monitor for the Design exam.

Protocol analysis is one of those skills that is found in only the best of the beanie-wearing computer geeks! Most of us will never reach the level of knowledge necessary to fully analyze a network trace. That is not to say, however, that we cannot learn to recognize traffic patterns and troubleshoot basic network issues. If you would like an in-depth discussion of protocol analysis, we suggest reading *Introduction to Network Analysis*, by Laura A. Chappell (available at podbooks.com).

The opening screen of Network Monitor, shown in Figure 7.8, contains four areas of interest. Each provides a different type of information. (We've labeled the four areas in the figure to make it easier to see which is which.)

FIGURE 7.8   Network Monitor main window

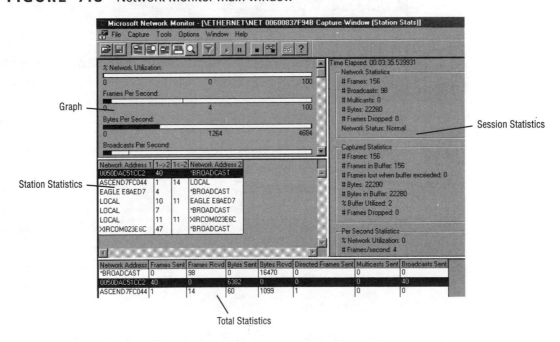

Graph Provides a graphical representation of current network activity

Session Statistics Provides statistics about individual sessions on the network

Station Statistics Provides detailed information about the traffic generated by each station on the network

Total Statistics Provides information about the packets that have been captured in this Network Monitor session

Once you have captured the appropriate network traffic (more on this later), you can then analyze its content. True protocol analysis involves opening up individual packets and analyzing their content—an action that requires extensive knowledge of networking and protocols. Luckily for us, this is not usually required for the level of analysis needed to fit our needs. (We say luckily because packet-level analysis is dry and boring—if you think we're putting you to sleep *now*, imagine if we were to discuss something even more boring!) For our purposes, we just need an overview of the amount of traffic generated by specific network services. Opening the captured data, often referred to as a network trace, will result in a view that is similar to that shown in Figure 7.9.

FIGURE 7.9 A network trace

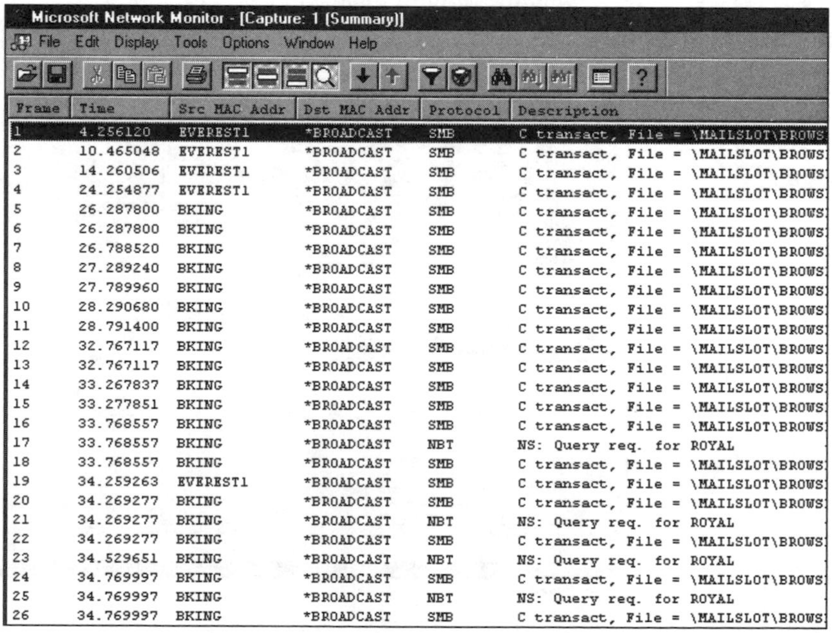

The network trace displayed in Figure 7.9 was gathered in a time period of less than five minutes, but it still contains almost 1,800 packets! Looking at all of that information at once can be a bit overwhelming. If can also be frustrating if you are trying to concentrate on a specific type of traffic. To reduce confusion, you can filter the results so that you are presented with only relevant information. In Figure 7.10, for instance, we are presented with only the ARP traffic on our network. Limiting the display in this way allows you to focus in on specific aspects of your network.

The information gathered through the use of Network Monitor can be of great value when you are making AD (or general network) design decisions. It provides you with a detailed view of what is happening on your network and gives you the opportunity to see "firsthand" what effect the addition of a service (such as AD) has on the wire.

FIGURE 7.10 A filtered trace

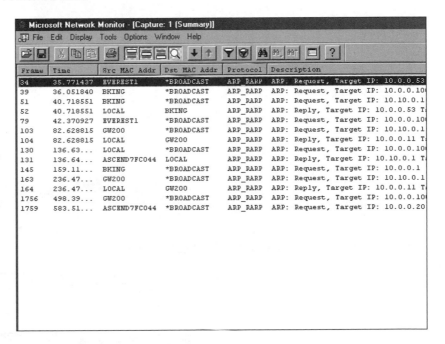

Replication Monitor

The Replication Monitor utility is installed with the group of tools found in the Support directory on the Windows 2000 Server CD-ROM. This tools allows you to monitor the status of the AD replication process (hence the name) as well as force replication within any given site, tree, forest, or domain. The main screen, shown in Figure 7.11, displays the current synchronization status along with the current USN values for the AD database.

You can also use Replication Monitor to force an immediate replication between domain controllers and to check the AD database for errors, as shown in Figure 7.12.

FIGURE 7.11 Replication Monitor

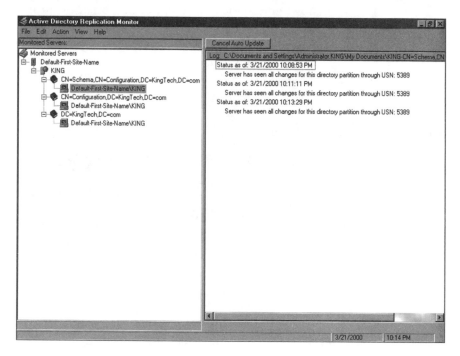

FIGURE 7.12 Actions available in Replication Monitor

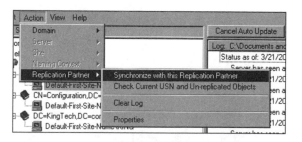

Replication Monitor provides AD-specific information that can be useful during your design project. You can, for instance, make some changes to your AD database, configure Network Monitor to capture traffic, and then use Replication Monitor to force an immediate update, thus generating the traffic you want to capture.

Method of Comparison

Using Performance as a design tool requires a little planning. Follow the three-step analysis model:

1. Isolate

2. Re-create

3. Extrapolate

First, create a lab environment in which you can control the traffic on a given network segment. This usually means isolating at least a server and a workstation on a single wire. Second, re-create the traffic you want to measure; make specific changes to the database (based upon your earlier analysis of the environment, you should be able to estimate the types of changes that will be made). Measure the impact of each type of change on both the server upon which the change was made and a server that receives those changes during the replication process. Given a baseline for a single occurrence of a specific change, you can extrapolate the effects of multiple occurrences.

You'll use these tools later in designing your AD site boundaries.

AD Sites

AD sites are used to organize well-connected computers within a network to optimize the use of available bandwidth. The definition of *well-connected computers* varies from textbook to textbook, but for our purposes, we'll define it as computers that are connected over highly reliable, fast connections with adequate bandwidth. Now you can see why the definition varies—terms like *high reliability*, *fast*, and *adequate* are subjective in nature. Unfortunately, this is the best definition available. We'll define high reliability as links that have no history of connection problems, are as fast as LAN speeds (10Mbps or better), and have bandwidth that is adequate enough to handle your estimate of the AD traffic that will be generated (using the tools described earlier and your knowledge of the business, you should be able to provide a fairly accurate estimate of network traffic). In general, well-connected computers are usually those that are connected by LAN technologies as opposed to WAN technology.

Computers that are connected by links that do not match our three criteria (reliable, fast, available bandwidth) should not be organized into the same AD site. In an environment with numerous or frequent changes to the AD database, the traffic generated by the replication process can be excessive, thereby saturating slower WAN links. Proper design of the AD site boundaries can help you control the AD traffic and optimize your Windows 2000 environment. Here are a few of the types of traffic that sites can optimize:

Workstation logon traffic   When a user logs on to the network, Windows 2000 computers search for domain controllers in the same site as the workstation.

Replication traffic   When changes are made to the AD database, they must be replicated to all domain controllers for the domain where the changes occurred. Site boundaries can be used to control when and how those changes are replicated between domain controllers in different sites.

Distributed File System (DFS)   If a file is located on multiple servers, the user will be directed to a server within their own site.

File Replication Service (FRS)   FRS replicates the contents of the SysVol directory and uses site boundaries to determine its replication topology.

Site-aware applications   Third-party application vendors can easily use the site boundaries to provide a fault-tolerant environment for their applications. You might, for instance, install an application in multiple locations and let AD direct users to the closest available copy (using site boundaries as the guide).

Site Boundary Design Considerations

Planning for replication and other types of traffic requires you to balance three major considerations: performance, efficiency, and costs. Each of these will play a role in the final design decisions that you make.

Performance

For our discussion of AD sites, we are referring to performance strictly in terms of AD replication. The best performance would be a situation in which changes are immediately replicated to all domain controllers in a domain. As an example, if User TomS in Figure 7.13 has a connection to server FS1 and changes his password, that change would have to be replicated to all of the other domain controllers within the Montana domain (FS2 and FS3). In a perfect world, this update would be immediate. In reality, though, there will a certain delay to the actual replication of the change. This delay is known as replication latency. *Replication latency* is the time it takes for all domain controllers within a domain to be informed of a change to the AD database. The smaller the latency, the better the performance.

FIGURE 7.13   Replication latency

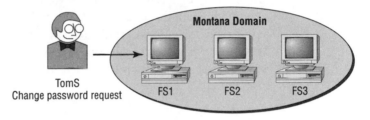

Efficiency

At odds with performance is replication efficiency. In a real-world implementation, it is usually not efficient to replicate a single change. It is usually more efficient to batch multiple changes into a single transfer of data. If an administrator is creating multiple user accounts, for instance, it would be more efficient to update the other controllers with multiple accounts rather than opening a connection and replicating each change as it is made. For more information on the costs of connecting computers using IP see *TCP/IP: 24seven*, by Gary Govanus (Sybex, 1999).

Costs

For the replication process, the cost of replication is measured in bandwidth used to accomplish the transfer. Within a LAN, these costs are negligible (in most cases), but across wide area connections, the costs can be substantial.

We've stressed this point numerous times (and that should be taken as an exam hint!)—wide area connectivity is one of the most expensive components of any network. Controlling the traffic across these expensive links should be a prime design objective.

Your goal as an AD design engineer is to balance these three considerations. You are looking for a site structure that provides the most efficient and least costly replication while also minimizing replication latency. For intrasite replication, you would expect to see a low latency to ensure that users within a site are always using recent information in the database. Efficiency is maintained by batching the changes for replication. Within a site, changes will be replicated within five minutes. The originating server (the server where the change occurred) will notify its replication partners within the site of the changes and they will request an update when convenient. Replication between sites in another story: Intersite replication assumes that there is limited bandwidth available for the transfer. The process starts with a compression of the data about to be replicated, usually to about 10 percent of its original size. This optimizes the use of whatever bandwidth is available. To further optimize intersite replication, you can schedule when replication will occur between sites (of course, this can result in a higher replication latency).

Planning Domain Controller Placement

Before planning the site boundaries for an environment, you should plan the placement of domain controllers. The bottom line here is usually performance from the users' perspective. Domain controllers must be placed so as to respond to user requests in a timely manner. This is, of course, a subjective decision. *Timely* will be defined differently in each environment. Your earlier analysis of the business will help in making these decisions.

Microsoft
Exam
Objective

Design the placement of domain controllers.

- Considerations include performance, fault tolerance, functionality, and manageability.

In most cases, you will want to place a domain controller at each location that contains users. This prevents users from having to cross a slow WAN link to log on to the network. There might be times when you will not want to place a domain controller at a given location. If, for instance, a location has a small amount of users and plenty of available bandwidth on its wide area link, you might decide not to spend the money to place a server in it.

Design Scenario: The International Widget Company

The International Widget Company (IWC) has hired you to design its new Windows 2000 Active Directory structure. You have analyzed the physical and business environments and found the following:

- The company has four main sites connected by T1 lines in a hub structure. The corporate headquarters, located in Los Angeles, acts as the hub of the network infrastructure. Tokyo, New York, London, and Frankfurt all connect by T1 lines that have adequate bandwidth.

- Each of the four main sites is connected to 10–15 smaller locations. Most of the locations have 256K links to their closest main office.

- There are four locations—Urawa, San Diego, Bristol, and Baumholder—which contain less than 20 users and are connected by ISDN lines to the closest main location. The employees in these offices are the phone sales staff for IWC.

You have decided to go with a single-domain structure. IWC has fewer than 7,000 employees and little plans for growth or acquisitions.

Plan the domain controller placement for International Widget Company.

First, this is an artificial scenario. You haven't really been given enough information to completely design the placement of domain controllers. To do that, you would need to know the number of users at each site, how they use the network, and the estimated amounts of traffic that will be generated by AD, the logon traffic, DNS requests, and any other services that the network might provide. On the exam, if you see a scenario that is not really complete, your first task is to dig a little deeper into the content to determine what aspect of AD design the question is "testing." In this case, the only real information you have been given is that you have four sites with very few users who probably won't utilize the network much. Based upon this, your answer should be that you would place at least one domain controller in each site *except* the four small locations. Here you can assume that their use of the ISDN lines is limited so there should be plenty of available bandwidth for logon traffic.

Planning Site Boundaries

Site boundaries are defined by the IP subnetting structure of the network. *Sites* define the physical structure of the network by organizing subnets into physical groups that match our criteria for well-connected computers. If, for instance, your network consists of a location in Tampa that contains three subnets and another in Detroit that contains one subnet, you might define two AD sites—one that contains the three subnets in Tampa and another that contains the subnet in Detroit. Because sites define physical boundaries, a site may contain domain controllers from more than one NT domain.

Microsoft ✓ ***Exam*** ***Objective***	**Design an Active Directory site topology.** • Design a replication strategy. • Define site boundaries.

When planning site boundaries, you should consider the estimated amount of traffic that will be generated between servers. Although the data *is* compressed when sent between sites, the compression does not occur until the amount of data exceeds 50,000 bytes. In some cases, the estimated "bursts" of traffic will be less than this amount—in such cases, there may be no reason to create a separate site because no real traffic reduction would take place. Of course, you might want to schedule the replication traffic on the line, in which case a site would be appropriate.

Site Links

The connection between sites is known as a *site link*. A site link is usually a representation of the wide area connection between two locations, although it can also represent a backbone that connects multiple locations. An example of each situation is shown in Figure 7.14.

FIGURE 7.14 Site links

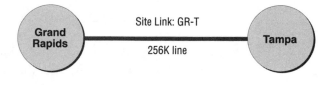

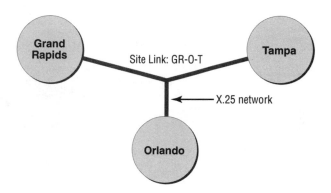

Each site link is made up of four components:

Transport   The actual technology used to transfer data, such as a T1 link or 256K line.

Member sites   Those sites connected by the site link.

Cost   A value assigned to the connection and used to determine the path of replication in the event that two or more paths are available. Assigning costs to site links allows you to build a fault-tolerant replication topology.

Schedule   The times that replication will occur.

Schedules

Site links are used to connect physical locations for the purposes of replication. To control the impact of replication traffic on wide area links, you have the option to schedule when replication can occur. Based upon your traffic analysis of each link, you should be able to determine whether a fixed schedule is needed and, if so, at what times each link has enough available bandwidth to handle the additional traffic. Obviously, you would want to schedule replication traffic for periods in which there is little traffic on the link.

When you apply a schedule to a site link, you are determining when replication can travel across the link. In environments where traffic crosses multiple site links, it is possible to set up schedules in which replication cannot function. In Figure 7.15, for instance, we have a large single-domain environment that spans multiple locations. To improve logon performance, a domain controller has been placed in each facility. Because of the limited bandwidth available to some locations, schedules have been set up for the site links.

FIGURE 7.15   Site links in a large environment

The site link S1-S2 has been scheduled to allow replication between 8:00 PM and 11:00 PM. Site link S2-S3 has been set up for replication between midnight and 2:00 AM. Given that there is *never* a time when traffic can move completely across the environment from site S1 to site S3, replication will never occur between those two sites. When designing your replication schedules, you must always consider the entire path that traffic must follow to complete the process.

Other Control Mechanisms

Using schedules is only one of the ways available to control replication traffic on site links. You can also assign costs to each site link to control the path that the traffic will follow. In Figure 7.16, for example, the company has two main locations and six remote locations. Each remote location connects to a main office with a 256K line. Most of the remote locations also have dial-up connections to other remote locations.

FIGURE 7.16   Assigning costs to site links

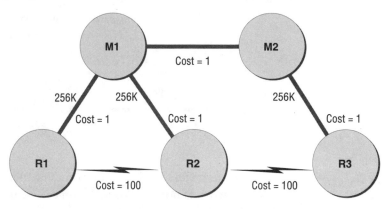

By assigning a high cost to the dial-up links between remote sites, you can ensure that replication traffic will use the 256K lines to the main offices—lines that should (hopefully) be more reliable and have more available bandwidth. The cost of replication is the sum of the costs for all site links involved. Moving from site R1 to site R2 over the dial-up connection would have a cost of 100. The same replication process would only have a cost of 2 if the path was R1-M1 and M1-R2.

You can also control the amount of traffic placed on a line by setting the number of minutes between replication attempts on site links. By default, replication will occur every 15 minutes. Increasing this interval will not result in less overall traffic, but it will cut down on the frequency of the traffic—perhaps lessening congestion. (Remember, though, that this *will* increase replication latency.)

Site Link Bridges

Site links are considered transitive in nature—that is, if three sites are connected by site links, as shown in Figure 7.17, a replication path exists between all of the sites. (Site 1 can replicate with site 3 by using the two site links.)

FIGURE 7.17 The transitive nature of site links

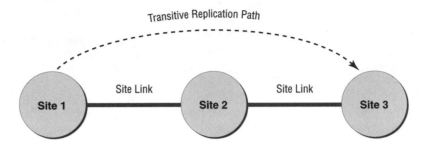

This system works well in a fully routed IP network. In the event that your entire network is not fully routed, you can turn off the transitive nature of site links and configure all replication paths manually. There will be few real-world implementations in which this ability is of value, but you will need to understand it for the MCSE exam. Once the transitive nature of site links has been disabled, you will have to configure *site link bridges* between sites that are not physically connected. In the example shown in Figure 7.18, for instance, there are site links between Grand Rapids and Tampa, Tampa and Orlando, and Orlando and Jacksonville.

FIGURE 7.18 Site link bridges

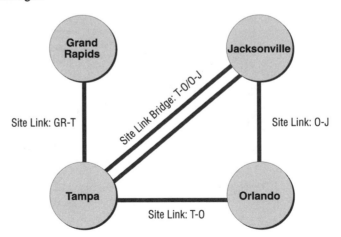

Because the site links are no longer transitive, a site link bridge has been created between Tampa and Jacksonville. This bridge uses the T-O and O-J site links as its replication path. Notice that, in the example, there is still no replication between Grand Rapids and Orlando or Jacksonville. That would involved creating two more site link bridges, as shown in Figure 7.19.

FIGURE 7.19 Multiple site link bridges

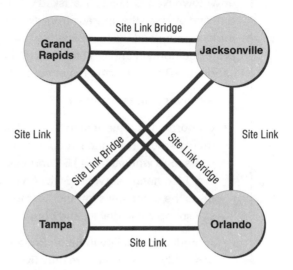

As you can see, site link bridges can quickly become confusing. Most experts agree that site link bridges should only be used where absolutely necessary.

Replication Transports

The replication process uses two different methods of communication—remote procedure calls (RPCs) over TCP/IP and Simple Mail Transfer Protocol (SMTP). RPCs will be used if a direct connection with the replication partner can be achieved. SMTP messages, on the other hand, are used when a connection cannot be established with the replication partner. The replication process will send its data in the form of simple mail messages, utilizing the SMTP capability to store and forward messages as recipients become available. SMTP is an ideal mechanism in an unreliable environment. There is a drawback, though—because the data is sent in mail format, it is encapsulated within an SMTP packet. This encapsulation can add 80 to 100 percent more traffic than RPCs.

Design Scenario: The Exciting New Product Company

The Exciting New Product Company (ENPC), headquartered in beautiful downtown New Orleans, has asked you to design its Active Directory structure and oversee the upgrade from Windows NT 4. You have performed the infrastructure and business analysis, designed a namespace, and have a projected domain and OU structure. Now you are thinking about the replication of AD changes and the effect of AD traffic on its network.

In its network infrastructure, ENPC has four locations:

- Corporate headquarters in New Orleans. This facility houses the entire management staff and IT department for ENPC. There are over 200 users (and workstations,) 5 Windows NT 4 servers (2 file and print servers, 1 Exchange server, 1 SQL server, and an IIS Web server that supports the company's intranet), a modem pool so that traveling salespeople can dial in, and physical links to the other three sites.

- A production facility in Baton Rouge, where the company does light assembly work. There are only five networked PCs in this location. These PCs are used to access the SQL database to help determine production schedules. This office uses an ISDN dial-on-demand connection each night to download a replica of the SQL database to a local server.

- A shipping and receiving facility on the outskirts of New Orleans. This facility has a 256K leased line connecting ENPC's 25 networked PCs to headquarters.

- A large purchasing department located in Atlanta. This location has over 200 users, 3 file and print servers, and a large, heavily accessed IIS Web server that maintains the company's Internet Web site. They are connected to the Internet by a T1 connection. They connect to headquarters over a virtual private network (VPN) on the Internet.

Describe the replication topology that you would suggest for ENPC.

Because the company's network infrastructure follows a classic hub design, the replication topology should follow suit. A site link to each location is appropriate.

> Are there any special circumstances that might make you plan for AD replication traffic control?
>
> The production facility downloads the database at night, and (given the current state of the telephone industry) you can assume it is long distance from a suburb to downtown New Orleans, so you should limit the AD traffic to after business hours (lowering the ongoing connectivity costs by dialing during a time when calls are less expensive). There are only five PCs in this facility and no real reason for real-time connectivity.

Planning Operations Master Server Placement within Sites

As we have discussed in earlier chapters, there are certain functions that are limited to specific servers within an AD forest or domain. The placement of these servers is critical to good performance. Luckily, the "rules" of placement are straightforward, but you will need to know them both for real-life implementations and the MCSE examination.

Microsoft ✓ *Exam Objective*	**Design the placement of operations masters.** • Considerations include performance, fault tolerance, functionality, and manageability.

Schema Master

There is only one schema master server per forest. By default, it is the first server placed in the Active Directory environment. In most cases, this server should be in the [root] domain of the AD tree and must be available anytime you need to make modifications to the AD schema. Although this server is not critical for normal operations of Active Directory, there will be times when it must be available (during any schema modifications). The placement of this server is not a critical design factor, although keeping it close to the central IT staff might be a good idea because they will probably be in charge of all schema modifications. There is only one schema master server per enterprise.

Domain Naming Master

Like the schema master, the domain master computer is used during a specific function—adding a new domain to the AD forest. By default, the domain master is the first AD server added to the environment. The domain master server ensures that no duplicate domain names are created within the forest. Although this job is critical, it is not necessary to the day-to-day functions of the network. There is only one domain master server per enterprise.

Primary Domain Controller Emulator

The PDC emulator replaces a Windows NT 4 primary domain controller to allow for mixed environments of Windows 2000 and Windows NT 4. It is also necessary in networks that are made up completely of Windows 2000 computers. When a user changes their password, it is sent to the PDC emulator first. Whenever a user is denied access to the network due to an incorrect password, the authenticating servers will query the PDC emulator before denying the request. From a design perspective, this means that the PDC emulator must be a dependable computer that is centrally located to ensure access at all times (you never know when a user will decide to change their password). There is one PDC emulator for each domain in the enterprise.

Relative Identifier Master

Each object within the AD database is assigned a unique identifier known as its security identifier (SID). The SID is a combination of a unique domain identifier (created by the domain naming master during the creation of the domain) and a relative ID (RID) that is unique within the domain. To ensure that the RIDs are unique, one AD server in each domain assumes the role of relative identifier. The relative ID assigns to each domain controller within the domain a pool of values that are used as the RID for any objects created. If a domain controller uses all of the RIDs assigned to it, it will contact the relative identifier master for another pool. Once again, this role is not critical to the day-to-day functions of the network. Once the original pools have been assigned, the relative identifier master can go offline with no real effect on the network. It must, however, be available when a domain controller exhausts its supply of RIDs or that domain controller will be unable to create new AD objects. There is one relative identifier master per domain.

Infrastructure Master

The infrastructure master for a domain is responsible for maintaining the cross-references between domains when an object is renamed. Put another way, if you rename an object within the AD database, the infrastructure master will ensure that the new name (and any changes to the SID) are replicated throughout the forest. Due to a quirk in AD, a global catalog server *should not* be assigned the role of infrastructure master. If this happens, the change will not be replicated across domain boundaries. Once again, there are no day-to-day functions that will be affected by the temporary loss of this server. At worst, if the infrastructure master is offline, updates will be delayed until it is brought online again. There is one infrastructure master for each domain within the forest.

Of all of the "master" servers, only the PDC emulator provides a service that requires it to be online and available most of the time. From a design perspective, each of the master roles should be assigned to computers that are reliable and able to handle the workload of the additional task.

Global Catalog Servers

Global catalog servers (GCSs) hold partial replicas of every object within the AD forest. GCSs are used to perform out-of-domain searches of the AD database. If, for instance, you try to access a printer that is defined in a domain other than the one in which you are currently working, the GCS will provide you with the address of that printer. In a simpler search, you might be trying to find the e-mail address of a user in another domain. The GCS would be queried for this information. A little-known, and little-advertised, fact is that a GCS is queried every time a user logs on to the network. In other words, access to a GCS is critical for network functionality.

We learned that little tidbit at Microsoft Technology Week 2000 in New Orleans. When the presenter dropped that bombshell, the crowd got quiet. Everyone was thinking of the number of Windows 2000 servers that they would need to deploy to ensure local access to a GCS!

Microsoft
✓ *Exam*
Objective

Design the placement of global catalog servers.

- Considerations include performance, fault tolerance, functionality, and manageability.

Microsoft has, in various documents, stated that it is not mandatory to have a GCS at each location. Because a user *could* access a GCS across a WAN link during the login process, this is technically true, but you should consider the ramifications of such a design carefully. If the WAN is congested, the logon process will take too long. If the WAN link is down, a user will not be able to log on to the network (even to access local resources).

Design Scenario: Operations Master Server Placement for Exciting New Product Company

The Exciting New Product Company (ENPC), headquartered in beautiful downtown New Orleans, has asked you to design its Active Directory structure and oversee the upgrade from Windows NT 4. You have performed the infrastructure and business analysis, designed a namespace, and have a projected domain and OU structure. Now you are thinking about the replication of AD changes and the effect of AD traffic on ENPC's network.

For its network infrastructure, ENPC has four locations:

- Corporate headquarters in New Orleans. This facility houses the entire management staff and IT department for ENPC. There are over 200 users (and workstations), 5 Windows NT 4 servers (2 file and print servers, 1 Exchange server, 1 SQL server, and an IIS Web server that supports the company's intranet), a modem pool so that traveling salespeople can dial in, and physical links to the other three sites.

- A production facility in Baton Rouge, where the company does light assembly work. There are only five networked PCs in this location. These PCs are used to access the SQL database to help determine production schedules. This office uses an ISDN dial-on-demand connection each night to download a replica of the SQL database to a local server.

- A shipping and receiving facility on the outskirts of New Orleans. This facility has a 256K leased line connecting ENPC's 25 networked PCs to headquarters.

- A large purchasing department located in Atlanta. This location has over 200 users, three file and print servers, and a large, heavily accessed IIS Web server that maintains the company's Internet Web site. They are connected to the Internet by a T1 connection. They connect to headquarters over a virtual private network (VPN) on the Internet.

How many domains would you create for this environment?

Based upon the fact that there are relatively few users and a fairly simple wide area network, one domain should be sufficient.

Where would you place the following servers: schema master, domain naming master, primary domain controller emulator, relative identifier master, infrastructure master, global catalog server(s)?

Schema master   Because the IT staff is centrally located, place the schema master in the headquarters office.

Domain naming master   One domain means one domain naming master. Once again, the central location of the IT staff suggests the headquarters office.

Primary domain controller emulator   The infrastructure is based upon a hub design. The PDC emulator is used as the final authority for denials based upon faulty passwords, so putting this server in the headquarters is your best choice.

Relative identifier master   The hub design of the network also leads you to put this server in the headquarters facility.

Infrastructure master   In a single-domain environment, the infrastructure master can be anywhere. The headquarters building is probably the safest bet because the IT staff is located there.

Global catalog server(s)   Because each location has a server *and* the global catalog is accessed during the logon process, place a catalog server at each location.

Summary

In this chapter, we discussed the various design considerations involved in planning for an efficient Active Directory environment. The first design task was to analyze both the existing and predicted traffic on the network and load on the servers. We discussed three main tools to accomplish this: Performance, Network Monitor, and Replication Monitor. Using the three-steps process—isolate, re-create, and extrapolate—you should now be able to predict the effects of AD on your existing infrastructure.

Based upon the information gained in the traffic and server-load analysis, we then moved to a discussion of site links and the ability to regulate or control the effects of AD replication traffic on specific network segments. Using site link costs and scheduling and limiting the frequency of replication, you can take control of the AD replication process.

Last, we discussed the issues involved in the placement of various types of servers within the network. These servers—schema master, domain naming master, primary domain controller emulator, relative identifier master, infrastructure master, and global catalog server—provide services that are necessary to the health of AD and should be placed carefully.

In the next chapter, we will begin our discussion of desktop management using the tools included in Windows 2000 Server. This topic is of great importance to the future direction of Microsoft networking and is heavily tested.

Key Terms

Before you take the exam, be sure you're familiar with the following terms:

bridgehead server

replication latency

intersite replication

security principal

InterSite Topology Generator (ISTG)

single-master environment

intrasite replication

site link

Knowledge Consistency Checker (KCC)

site link bridges

multi-master environment

synchronization

originating write

total cost of ownership (TCO)

propagation dampening

update sequence number (USN)

replication

well-connected computers

Review Questions

1. Which of the following best describes a multi-master environment?

   A. Multiple changes are sent from the servers.

   B. All servers can accept changes and replicate those changes to other servers.

   C. It is a distributed management business model.

   D. Two or more management consoles are run at a server simultaneously.

2. The process of one domain controller updating the copy of the domain database stored on another domain controller is known as _____ _____ .

   A. Synchronization

   B. Replication

   C. Distributed File Copy

   D. Subnet updating

3. The process of importing or exporting directory information between dissimilar directory systems (AD and NDS, for example) is known as _____ .

   A. Synchronization

   B. Replication

   C. Distributed File Copy

   D. Subnet updating

4. The service that is responsible for generating the replication topology is called the _____ .

   A. RepGen

   B. Traffic Control Process

   C. Synchronization Consistency Checker

   D. Knowledge Consistency Checker

5. The function of the InterSite Topology Generator (ISTG) is to _____ .

   A. Generate reports on AD network traffic

   B. Create the AD connection objects between sites

   C. Automatically configure routers with static routes to optimize AD network traffic

   D. Perform the authentication between domains necessary for inter-site replication

6. Propagation dampening is used to _____ .

   A. Prevent unnecessary replication of directory changes

   B. Analyze the number of domain controllers and propagate another one automatically to ensure fault tolerance

   C. Reduce the impact of AD network traffic on a particular segment by increasing the time between packets

   D. Reduce hard disk use by only committing changes that have been confirmed from multiple sources

7. In what order would you perform the following tasks.

   A. Re-create

   B. Isolate

   C. Extrapolate

8. Well-connected computers are _____ . (Choose three.)

   A. Connected by reliable lines

   B. Connected by fast lines

   C. Connected by lines with adequate available bandwidth

   D. Hardwired into the network

9. The amount of time that it takes for a change to be replicated to another domain controller in known as _____ .

   A. The delta factor

   B. Replication latency

   C. Synthetic time

   D. Wire lag

10. Intersite replication traffic will be compressed when what amount of traffic is involved?

   A. 10,000 bytes or more.

   B. 25,000 bytes or more.

   C. 50,000 bytes or more.

   D. It is always compressed.

Answers to Review Questions

1. B. In a multi-master environment, all replicas are peers and can accept changes and replicate those changes throughout the domain. This is the exact opposite of a Windows NT 4 domain structure, which is a single-master environment (one main copy of the accounts database, stored on the PDC, accepts all changes and replicates them to other domain controllers).

2. B. Replication keeps the copies of the domain database current with each other.

3. A. Synchronization refers to exchanging information with a non–Active Directory database.

4. D. The KCC is a process that runs automatically and is responsible for generating the replication topology between domain controllers.

5. B. The ISTG automatically creates the AD connection objects necessary to create the replication topology designed by the Knowledge Consistency Checker (KCC).

6. A. The replication process uses originating write values to ensure that changes are not replicated back to the server upon which they originated.

7. B, A, C. When measuring the impact of any network traffic, you should first isolate that traffic from the rest of the network so that your measurements are not influenced by outside factors, next re-create the traffic and capture/analyze it, and then extrapolate the traffic generated by a single occurrence to an estimated amount generated within a given environment.

8. A, B, C. All domain controllers within a single site should be well connected.

9. B. It takes time for a change to be replicated to every domain controller in a domain.

10. C. After a certain size, the overhead of compression and decompression is offset by the savings in traffic on the wire.

Case Study: University of the Mind

Take about 10 minutes to look over the information presented and then answer the questions at the end. In the testing room you will have a limited amount of time—it is important that you learn to pick out the important information and ignore the "fluff."

Background

You've been hired to design and implement the University of the Mind (U of M) network. The U of M consists of a main campus located in Chicago and two auxiliary campuses located in Rolling Meadows and Milwaukee. It has recently been given a federal grant to improve its current IT environment. If this project is a success, there could be a lot of work improving and upgrading various universities around the country.

Current System

General Information   Currently, the U of M is using a mix of Novell NetWare, various flavors of Unix, and a few Microsoft Windows NT 4 servers to provide a diverse set of services to the faculty and students. Because there is no central IT department, each educational department has installed and maintained its own computer resources. Unfortunately, this approach has led to no communication between departments and inefficient use of resources.

Dean of U of M   "I keep reading about how networks can streamline workflow, cut down on redundant management, and reduce overall costs of business. With our grant money, we have the opportunity to accomplish all of these things *and* provide a better educational environment for our students."

Head of the Computer Education Department   "We have no central IT staff—each department manages its own resources. Here in the computer department, we concentrate on teaching programming skills, so we don't have a lot of expertise in the networking arena. It's actually kind of funny in a way—we've got a great infrastructure since our 'educational status' provides us with free connectivity. We've got a T1 link to the Rolling Meadows campus, a microwave connection between our two buildings here in Chicago, and a 256K line to Milwaukee—all of which are free and all of which are basically unused. We've even got direct connections to the Internet—only a couple hops off the backbone, but we take little advantage of those assets."

Environment

Chicago   The Chicago campus is made up of 2 buildings, each with 22 floors. The buildings are connected by a 10Mbps microwave system. Although the buildings are wired, each department manages the assets on its own floors. At this time, there are somewhere between 15 and 20 servers in each building—made up of everything from NetWare 3.11 to old versions of Unix. There are a few Windows NT 4 servers as well.

Rolling Meadows   The Rolling Meadows campus is a 10-acre facility with numerous small buildings dedicated to various aspects of agricultural studies. It has a T1 connection to the Chicago campus, but no service actually uses the bandwidth. Because the campus has a dedicated link to the Internet, all messaging systems use the Internet as their medium of message transfer.

Milwaukee   The Milwaukee campus consists of three floors of a large building in downtown Milwaukee. Because it offers business classes, it has a large number of workstations and a few Windows NT 4 servers, but no real network services (other than file and print) are currently offered. Your research shows that the 256K link to the Chicago campus is basically unused.

Current Issues

Dean   "We have two basic problems at this time and quite a few little irritations that we would like to correct. First, and most important, at this time we have no real transfer of information between our three campuses. Course scheduling, attendance records, grade records, and even departmental budgets are all dealt with locally. This results in administrative concerns that could eventually endanger our educational accreditation. Second, we are currently losing potential students because we cannot offer them the types of services that other schools our size are offering—Internet access in their dorm rooms, a campus intranet, electronic registration for classes, and a host of other computer-related services. That's exactly why we received our grant money—to bring us up-to-date and make us more competitive."

Head of the Biology Department   "We've got classrooms in both buildings here in Chicago. I don't know much about computers, but I know that we should be using our resources to provide better opportunities to our students. Heck, on a really snowy day, we sometimes even lose the connection between the two buildings—that's not right, is it? [The computer guys] always blame it on the microwave relay, but maybe we could fix that?"

Security

Educational records must be kept confidential. The dean would like to see two separate IT environments—one for the use of students and another to be used only for administrative functions.

Questions

1. How many domains would you create for the U of M Windows 2000 network?

   A. One

   B. Three: Chicago, Milwaukee, and Rolling Meadows

   C. Four: one for each building in Chicago, Milwaukee, Rolling Meadows

   D. Two: Chicago/Rolling Meadows, Milwaukee

2. How would you suggest that the school ensure the security of administrative resources?

   A. Create two AD trees and tie them together in an AD forest.

   B. Create two domains, one for student resources and one for administrative resources.

   C. Create two OUs, student and administrative. Delegate authority to each as appropriate.

   D. Add new lines to each building to create completely separate physical networks.

3. How many sites would you define for this environment?

   A. One

   B. Two

   C. Three

   D. Four

4. What is the minimum number of domain controllers needed for this environment?

   A. One

   B. Two

   C. Three

   D. Four

5. In which order would you perform the following?

Task	Task
	Upgrade or replace the microwave relay between the two buildings in the Chicago campus.
	Bring together the IT experts from each department to form the nucleus of a systemwide IT group.
	Implement a campus intranet.
	Consolidate administrative functions to a central location.

6. The University of the Mind would like to centralize its data storage and also wants to allow all of its campuses to have access to student and scheduling data locally. Use the centralized data connector to specify which options should be used to secure and consolodate data storage and the shared data connector to specify which elements you need to incorporate to allow for data distribution to remote sites.

Set up Access database to replicate data amongst themselves.	Create Access database at remote locations.		**Data Connections:** Centralized Data Shared Data
Configure each remote site as subscriber to Chicago publications.	Plan and apply appropriate permission to all databases.		
Plan strategy for data replication using SQL Server.	Install SQL Server at remote locations.		
Configure Chicago server as publisher/distributor of student/administrative data.	Install SQL Server at Chicago campus.		
Design, create, or import all existing databases into new system.	Regularly back up all databases.		
Plan strategy for data replication using Access.	Create Access database at Chicago campus.		

Answers

1. **A.** This environment is small enough to warrant a single-domain design.

2. **C.** Creating multiple trees would add unnecessary administrative overhead. Using the benefits of Active Directory, you can place resources in separate OUs and use AD security to manage access.

3. **C.** Even though the school has plenty of available bandwidth, planning for future growth is advised. Defining each physical location as an AD site allows the best control over the amount of replication traffic using the wide area links.

4. **C.** Because you are going to define three AD sites, you will need a minimum of three domain controllers (one for each site).

5. See table.

Task
Bring together the IT experts from each department to form the nucleus of a systemwide IT group.
Consolidate administrative functions to a central location.
Implement a campus intranet.
Upgrade or replace the microwave relay between the two buildings in in the Chicago campus.

Before doing anything else, you must build a project team to help make decisions! Once that is accomplished, you can then start to concentrate on the business needs of the environment. For U of M, the primary concern is to take control of the administrative functions, followed by building a list of IT services that can be offered to students. Upgrading the infrastructure would be low on the list of priorities.

6.

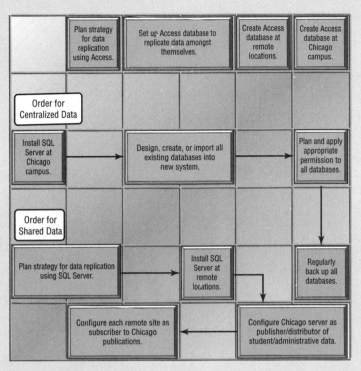

The first goal, of course, is to get a full and immediate backup of the system. Once this has been done, you can continue on with creating a policy for backing up the central databases regularly. Replication will be accomplished by bringing all data to be replicated into SQL server, because full replication can only be accomplished with SQL. Also, Access is not efficient, stable, or secure enough to use it in a distributed environment.

Chapter

8

Planning for Desktop Management

MICROSOFT EXAM OBJECTIVES COVERED IN THIS CHAPTER:

✓ **Analyze the business requirements for client computer desktop management.**

- Analyze end-user work needs.
- Identify technical support needs for end-users.
- Establish the required client computer environment.

In NT 4, you could create system policies (using the System Policy Editor) to configure user and computer settings stored in the Windows NT Registry. System policies could be used to control the user environment and user actions, as well as to enforce system configuration settings for computers running Windows NT Workstation, Windows NT Server, and Windows 95. Basically, though, system policies in earlier versions of NT are really just Registry settings that define the behavior of operating system components.

Windows 2000 Server introduces a whole new level of central control over user environments. The Group Policy Editor, a new utility for Windows 2000 Server, extends the functionality of the System Policy Editor and enhances administrators' abilities to configure user and computer settings by fully leveraging the Active Directory database.

In this chapter, we'll discuss the components of AD Group Policy objects, the areas that they can influence, how they are executed, and how to secure them. Based upon that discussion, we can then discuss the creation of a desktop-management policy.

What Is Desktop Management?

It's funny how the IT industry seems to go in cycles. In the days of the "big iron," or mainframes, there was no such thing as a personal computer. Each station was just a dumb terminal that connected to, and used the power of, a large, centrally controlled and managed mainframe computer system. From an administrative perspective, those environments didn't really even have a workstation component—there was little to manage at the terminal because all the processing occurred at the central computer. "Workstation management" (although the phrase didn't really exist at the time) was at best a physical function—it entailed the skills and techniques necessary to ensure that the dumb terminals were connected to and communicating with the central system. The user's interface was created, managed, and run from the central system. There were no concerns over screen savers, color schemes, wallpaper, or any of the other user interface components that are common today. Users had no input into the look and feel of their computer interface—all of those components were created by a group of programmers who were (in most cases) insulated from the day-to-day work of the average user. This really wasn't a big deal, though, because most of the terminals could display only text (usually green text on a black background).

As PCs entered the business environment, we saw a switch from central control to a distributed model. Users were given a certain amount of control over their environment—they were allowed to pick out color schemes, increase the size of the text, and even add custom components such as screen savers and wallpaper. The business world embraced the idea of *personal* computers (notice the emphasis on personal!). Management was euphoric over the perceived cost savings—a few PCs certainly cost a *lot* less than a mainframe, and users felt empowered by the freedom they were given to create a personal workplace (virtual though it is) that fit their needs.

All good things come to an end—and so did our days of wild abandon with the PC. Somewhere along the way, someone started to look into the total costs involved in supporting a PC-based environment. Sure, PCs at a couple of thousand dollars were cheaper than mainframes, but business costs don't stop at acquisition. Business costs include the maintenance, upkeep, and replacement of components, and over time, management started to notice that those costs were getting out of control. Numerous cost analyses were run, and the bottom line was that PCs were a lot more expensive than originally thought.

Costs of Support

Putting a definitive dollar figure on the total costs involved in supporting a network can be a tough job. Many of the costs are easy to quantify:

- Initial cost of equipment
- Initial cost of software
- IT staff salaries

Other costs *can* be quantified, but they're harder to budget for because they are not consistent:

- Software upgrades

- Hardware upgrades

- Hardware maintenance

- Software installations

- Training costs

- Help desk costs

Then there are the costs that are even less tangible, and therefore even more difficult to quantify:

- Loss productivity due to inefficient software, failed workstations, down servers, down WAN lines

- Training/retraining employees

- User error

- Lost revenue due to customers' inability to access support

The process of estimating costs becomes even more difficult when you realize that many costs change over time. When you upgrade to Windows 2000, for instance, you can expect that training and help desk costs will increase for the first few weeks or months (depending upon how good your design is) and then (hopefully) drop down to less than they were before the upgrade as users and administrators become more familiar with the environment.

As you can see, the costs associated with supporting a complex network are themselves complex. Part of your job during the design process is to quantify costs that are static, estimate costs that are variable, and minimize associated intangible costs. All in all, this might be one of the most difficult phases of a design project.

One of the areas in which we hope to reduce costs is workstation management. The process of keeping a workstation up and running is one of the larger costs in most IT budgets. Hardware and software costs are actually minimal in the overall budget for maintaining workstations—and they are fairly static. You can easily estimate the costs of replacing broken components, upgrading hardware, and purchasing software. Harder to estimate are those intangible costs associated with the PC—lost productivity and IT support costs.

One of the basic precepts of support is that software cannot fix hardware. There's not much we can do to reduce the hardware-related costs of PC maintenance (except through proper purchasing practices). What we *can* control are the costs of PC configuration by limiting the amount of time we actually spend at each workstation and by limiting the control users have over their PC environment.

We in the IT industry walk a fine line here—if we limit users too much, we inhibit creativity, but if we allow too much freedom, support costs soar. One of the topics missing in Microsoft's discussion of change management is training. Users who are given a little training are less likely to make mistakes that mandate IT intervention.

Group Policies Overview

Group policies are used to define user or computer settings for an entire group of users or computers at one time. The settings that you configure are stored in a *Group Policy object (GPO)*, which is then associated with Active Directory objects such as sites, domains, or organizational units. Many different aspects of the network, desktop, and software configuration environments can be managed through group policies.

What Are GPOs?

The following list describes, in general terms, the different types of policies that can be created (and enforced) using Windows 2000 Server's Group Policy Editor:

Application deployment policies   These policies affect the applications that users access on the network. They are used to automate the installation of software in one of two ways:

> **Application assignment**   The group policy installs or upgrades applications automatically or provides users with a shortcut that they cannot delete.
>
> **Application publication**   The group policy advertises applications in the directory. The applications then appear in the Add/Remove Programs list found in Control Panel. This gives users the ability to install and remove programs using a process with which they are already familiar.

File deployment policies   These policies allow the administrator to place files in special folders on the user's computer, such as the `Desktop` or `My Documents` folders. For example, an employee telephone directory could be placed in the `My Documents` folder each time a user logs on to the network.

Script policies   These policies allow an administrator to specify scripts that should run at specific times, such as logon/logoff or system start-up/ shutdown.

Software policies   These policies work much like system policies did in earlier versions of NT. Administrators can use them to globally configure most of the settings in user profiles, such as Desktop settings, Start menu options, and applications.

Security policies   These policies are some of the more important ones that you will configure. Using security policies, an administrator can restrict user access to files and folders, configure how many failed login attempts will lock an account, and control user rights (such as which users are able to log on locally at domain servers).

As you can see from this list, you can make policies do more than you could in earlier versions of Windows NT. Most of this additional functionality comes from the integration of policies with Active Directory services.

In effect, the Group Policy objects for each container define their own folder structure, which works like a namespace. These structures are tied to one of the three places at which a GPO can exist in the Active Directory tree: site, domain, or organizational unit. Their placement will determine which users or computers will be affected by the settings in the GPO. The first rule to remember with policies in Windows 2000 is that they can be applied only to users or computers—they will have no effect upon other classes of objects in the AD tree.

At the root of the GPO structure are two nodes, Computer Configuration and User Configuration (also known as *GPO nodes*), as shown in Figure 8.1.

As the names imply, each of these subnodes contains parameters that can be configured based upon either the computer that is attaching to the network (Computer Configuration) or the user who is logging in to the network (User Configuration).

FIGURE 8.1 The root of the GPO structure

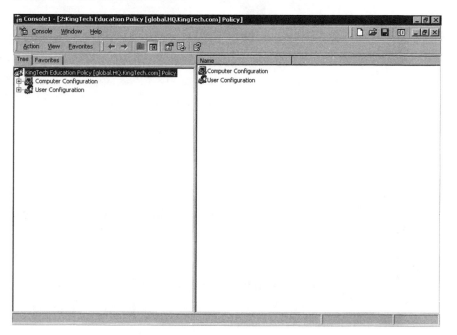

Computer Configuration

The following tasks are among the options available within the Computer Configuration settings area:

- Create policies that specify operating system behavior and the appearance of the desktop

- Assign applications

- Assign settings

- Set file deployment options

- Specify security settings

- Specify computer start-up and shutdown scripts

Computer-related policies are applied when the operating system initializes.

User Configuration

Among the options available within the User Configuration settings area are parameters that can be used to perform the following:

- Create policies that determine operating system behavior, Desktop settings, application settings, and assigned and published applications
- Set file-deployment options
- Set security options
- Assign user logon and logoff scripts

User Configuration policy options are applied when a user logs on to the computer.

Using Computer and User Configuration

The bottom-line difference between the Computer Configuration settings and the User Configuration settings is when they are applied. For Computer Configuration options, the policy is applied as the operating system boots. This means that the configuration options set in the Computer Configuration area will affect *any* user who logs on at the specified computer. User Configuration policies, on the other hand, are applied *after* the operating system has initialized and *only* to specified users or groups based upon a fairly complex series of rules that we'll discuss later.

For example, if you were trying to lock down user Bob, you would use a policy created within the User Configuration area. If, however, you were trying to lock down a particular computer, you would create a policy within the Computer Configuration area.

At first glance, the ability to apply a policy to a particular computer might not appear to be too useful. If your company has a computer located in a public area, however, these options can be very beneficial. Imagine a computer in a public library. It could have a policy set up so that all temp files are deleted at shutdown—or better yet, at logoff. This would delete any private e-mail or Internet browser temporary files that had been copied to the local machine. Using Computer Configuration settings would clean up the computer's environment *and* secure files against undesired access at the same time!

Each of these nodes—Computer Configuration and User Configuration—acts as the root of a GPO structure. Within each you will find a series of folders and subfolders. Each of these nodes contains configurable options for a specific area of your environment.

Although group policies are managed through AD-based tools, the actual policies are still specific files, just like in NT 4. These files are located in a structure called the *group policy template* in the system volumes, called SysVol, folder of the domain controllers in the \Policies subfolder. As an object in the directory, each policy you create has a unique SID. Within the \Policies subfolder, you will find a series of subfolders, as shown in Figure 8.2. Each subfolder is named with the SID of the GPO that it contains. As you can see in the right side of the figure, within each GPO folder are two folders, MACHINE and USER, and a file, GPT. The GPT file contains a version number that is used to determine if the policy has been changed since the last time it was applied to a user or computer. The version number is used to prevent processing a policy when it is not necessary.

FIGURE 8.2 Policies folders

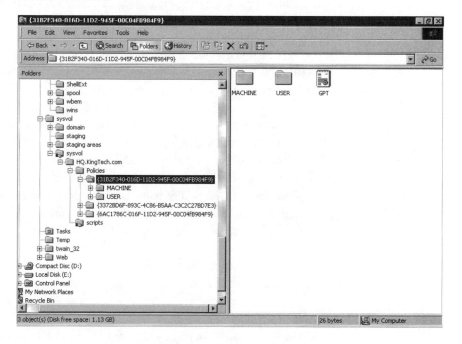

Software Settings

The Software Settings node of the GPO is the same for both the user and computer policies. This node allows you to manage the installation and maintenance of software for a user or computer. Applications can be managed in one of two different modes: assigned or published.

Assigned Mode

Assigned mode is used when you want everyone using the policy to have an application on their computer. Suppose, for instance, that you want everyone in the education department at KingTech to have Microsoft PowerPoint on their computers. Your first step would be to create a *package*. A *software package* contains all of the files necessary to install an application along with a description of all system changes needed (Registry changes, file locations, etc.). Many applications now include a premade package when you purchase them (or have a package available for download on their Web site). If the application does not have a package, one must be created. There are many third-party products on the market that can accomplish this task. Place the application package in some shared folder available to the network.

Once you have your package, adding it to a policy is a straightforward procedure. First, decide if you wish to assign the application based upon user identity or if you wish this application to be available on all computers within a site, container, or organizational unit. The answer to this question will determine whether you should work in the Computer Configuration node or the User Configuration node of the policy.

You will then have to choose how this application should be distributed. Your choices are to *assign* or to *publish* the application.

When an application is assigned, the policy will advertise it to the user the next time they log in (or to a computer the next time it initializes). When an application is advertised, it is not actually installed on the computer. Only enough information is installed to make its shortcut appear on the Start menu and to create the appropriate file associations.

The first time a user tries to run an application by using the icon on their Start menu or attempting to open an associated file type, the application will be installed on their computer. The user can delete an *assigned application*, but because it is advertised, the icon and associations will be re-created the next time they log on.

Using the software installation mechanism of group policies can greatly ease administration of the applications in use by your users. In our education center in Grand Rapids, Michigan, we use Windows 2000 and group policies to control the computers in our classrooms. We've created packages for each of the applications that we teach. We then assign them to whichever user accounts our students will use to access our network. Each night, we can put a new clean image down on our classroom computers (avoiding the hassle of cleaning up student work manually and greatly reducing our risk for virus infection), and when a student logs in the next day, all of the applications they need are available. The best part for us is that we don't have to worry about setting up specific machines for specific classes. We use the same clean image on all of the computers; who logs in at a computer will determine which applications are made available.

If your users move from computer to computer, you can reap the same benefits. Administrators no longer have to worry about installing applications on computers—that task will happen automatically when a user tries to use the tools they need. Because Microsoft has created a standard format for software packages, many applications (not just those from Microsoft) can be installed using this method. (You can also create your own packages for software that does not ship with a premade package.)

Published Mode

Another option available is to publish the application package. When you use *published applications*, nothing is installed automatically on the client computer. Instead, the application is added to the list of available programs in the Add/Remove Programs applet in Control Panel. This allows users to install the application on their own if they so desire. They do so by using a familiar interface—the Add/Remove Programs applet. They also do not have to have the disks (floppies or CD-ROM) at their computer—all of the files needed to install the application are part of the package.

From a design perspective, you will need to decide which software should be installed and what method (assigned or published) will be implemented. Because software distribution can also be used to maintain and upgrade installed software, you will also want to use the information you gathered earlier to build an application management plan for your environment.

Policy Inheritance

Having looked at a few of the options available, the next step is to determine how and why policies are applied to users, groups, and computers. We'll look at how policies are applied by default and then we'll look at how those defaults can be changed.

First, let us stress this one last time:

- User policies are obtained when a *user* logs on to the network.

- Computer policies are obtained when a computer boots.

Exam Hint: No other classes of objects receive policies—just users and computers.

The Order in Which Policies Are Applied

As we discussed earlier, policies can be associated with various objects in the Active Directory structure—domains, sites, and organizational units. There is also a local policy that is stored on and managed at the local client computer. Because you have the option to place policies at various points in your hierarchy, the first question that should come to mind is, "Which policy or policies will apply to which users and computers?" In a perfect world, the answer to this question would be short and sweet. Unfortunately, a simple answer would probably also imply a simple solution, and a simple solution would not meet the needs of today's complex networks. The truth of the matter is that most of the rest of this chapter will revolve around answering that "simple" question.

Default Order of Application

The default order in which group policies are applied is as follows:

1. The local policy, if one exists.

2. Policies assigned to the AD site object, in an order specified by the administrator.

3. Policies assigned to the domain, in an order specified by the administrator.

4. Policies assigned to organizational units, starting at the top of the AD tree and working from parent to child OU until the context of the object (user or computer) has been reached. Once again, if an OU has more than one policy, they will be applied in an order set by the administrator.

This order can be influenced in numerous ways, but the default behavior is that the policies are applied in the order listed above. Each policy that is processed will override those settings made in policies applied earlier in the process. In other words, if a parameter is set to "true" in the local policy, the site policy could change it to "false," the domain policy could change it back to "true," and then various OU policies could change it back and forth so many times that it could be hard to determine what the settings will be once the process is done! The point here is that the implementation of group policies takes some prior planning to avoid these kinds of issues.

The general philosophy is that the policies should be designed so that the least restrictive are applied first. You should plan your policy strategy so that the policies are more restrictive as they work through the order. This means several things:

- Local policies should be the least restrictive. In most companies, local policies won't be used at all so that all policy management can occur within the Active Directory database.

- Site policies should be extremely generic. Perhaps you have decided that no computer should display the last logged-in username in the Log onto Windows dialog box. This type of overall configuration is best done in the policy that will affect the most users, such as the policy assigned to the site.

- Domain policies should contain configurations that are specific to the needs of the users and computers defined within the domain. This sounds obvious, but it is possible for a single site to contain resources from multiple domains. This option allows you to be a little more specific as to who or what will be affected by a policy. Here you might want to configure the DNS suffix that all computers within the domain will use when dynamically updating DNS.

- Organizational unit policies should contain configuration parameters that apply to a branch of your AD tree. Perhaps no users in the Sales OU (and those OUs under it in the tree) should be allowed to run programs other than those that are company approved. Here you could configure the policy with the list of approved programs.

You can use this cascading effect to reduce the number of places in which you have to manage certain parameters—sweeping parameters only have to be configured once (in the site or domain policy) rather than in each OU policy.

Placing Policy Objects

Look at the AD organizational unit structure shown in Figure 8.3. In our example, we have an education OU that contains a Michigan OU, which in turn contains OUs for each of the levels of schools that we support. This seems like a workable design—resources from each type of school can be placed within a container that represents their type (K–6, middle school, or high school). Under each container (K-6, Middle Schools, and High Schools), we might have containers for each individual school—but we'll leave that level of containers out to avoid confusing the issue.

FIGURE 8.3   The education department

Within this type of structure, certain aspects of our users' environment will be similar. All of our students, for instance, should be able to use Internet Explorer. Other items of control, though, will differ based upon age group—first-graders should probably have a different Home Page setting than high school students. This is where the cascading nature of group policies comes in handy.

Our first step will be to determine which type of policy files we wish to use—local, site, domain, or organizational. The process of assigning a policy to a site is the same as for assigning them to a domain or OU. In real life, we would sit down with the teachers and administrators and ask for input: What types of controls do they desire, and how sweeping should those decisions be? After our research we might come up with a list that looks something like this.

- All students:

  - Advertise basic programs to all computers—word processing, spreadsheet, and database.

  - Run a script that checks for viruses each time a user logs on.

  - Do not allow printers to be published to AD.

  - Limit access to the display options in Control Panel.

- Based upon grade:

  - Add appropriate URLs to the Favorites list in Internet Explorer.

  - Assign specific applications.

  - Redirect all data, Desktop settings, and other personal information to network locations.

In a real-world scenario, the list would probably cover pages, but for our purposes, this should be sufficient. As you can see, there are certain policies that should apply to all students and others that should be applied only to specific groups of students.

The second step in our process will be to determine which policies should be applied to computers and which to users. Some of the parameters will be available to only one or the other, but some can be configured in either manner. The next step is to determine the type of policy to use—local, site, domain, or organizational unit. Because our environment is a single domain and a single site, we could use either a site or a domain policy as our most generic. Given our single-branch scenario, we could even use a higher-level OU as our least-restrictive policy—but this would be rare in a true business.

If planned carefully, the default order of cascading group policies can work fairly well. The problem is that it is often necessary to have a policy apply to one group of users but not another, even if those users exist in the same organizational unit. At other times, you might want to allow one container within your AD structure to set its own policy without having to worry about it being overwritten by a policy in a lower container. The opposite is also true—there might be a time when you want a lower-level policy to be the *only* policy applied to the users in an organizational unit.

Based upon what we've discussed so far, these cases would require very careful planning of both the placement of policies *and* the AD organizational units themselves. Luckily, Microsoft has provided us with three methods for taking control of which policies will be applied in any given situation:

- Filtering policies by security group membership

- Blocking policy inheritance

- Preventing a policy from being overwritten by policies above it in the AD tree

By understanding the default mechanisms involved in *policy inheritance* and the various methods available to override those defaults, an administrator can use group policies to take complete control over their network.

Filtering Policies through Group Membership

Each GPO created has its own set of properties as an object in the AD structure. These properties refer to the *object*—not to the parameters that the GPO passes to the user or computer to which the policy itself is applied. To see these properties, right-click the GPO in the Microsoft Management Console (MMC) and choose Properties, as shown in Figure 8.4.

FIGURE 8.4 Accessing the properties of a GPO

The properties dialog box of a GPO can be used to gather information about the policy, manage the policy, determine where the policy will be applied, and manage who will use the policy.

Active Directory GPO Security

Like any other object in the AD database, GPOs have access control lists (ACLs). The ACL lists those objects that have been granted permissions to the object itself. GPOs have a unique permission—look at the bottom of the permissions list in Figure 8.5 and you will see the Apply Group Policy permission.

FIGURE 8.5 Security tab of the GPO properties dialog box

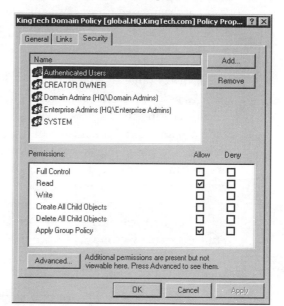

The permissions shown in Figure 8.5 are the default permissions granted when a Group Policy object is created. Table 8.1 lists these default permissions.

TABLE 8.1 Default Permissions to a GPO

User or Group	Permissions
Authenticated Users	Read, Apply Group Policy
Creator Owner	None
Domain Admins	Read, Write, Create All Child Objects, Delete All Child Objects
Enterprise Admins	Read, Write, Create All Child Objects, Delete All Child Objects
System	Read, Write, Create All Child Objects, Delete All Child Objects

The important assignment for our discussion here is the assignment made to all authenticated users. Basically, this assignment is what creates the default rules. Any user who logs in to the network and whose user object exists in this domain (because this is a domain policy) will have the policy applied to them.

As an example, let's return to the KingTech education department. The policies we've discussed so far have all revolved around the needs of the students—limiting their ability to change configurations or adding tools that they will need to their desktops and applications. The problem with the default GPO assignments is that this policy will also be applied to the teachers and administrative staff at KingTech (because they too will be authenticated users in this domain). To correct this, we could create a security group—perhaps named Students—and change the default permissions to this GPO. Remove the Authenticated Users group from the list and add the Students security group, as shown in Figure 8.6.

FIGURE 8.6   Using security groups to limit GPOs

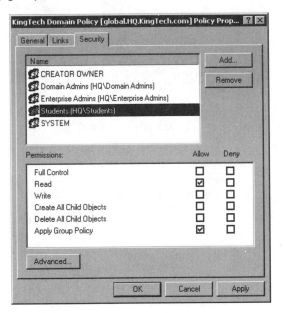

Make sure to give the Students group both the Read permission and the Apply Group Policy permission. Without the Read permission, they would be unable to read the various parameters set in the policy itself.

Blocking Policy Inheritance

At any site, domain, or organizational unit, Block Policy Inheritance can be set to block the inheritance of group policies. Because this setting is made directly to the site, domain, or OU instead of to a particular GPO, it will block *all* policies from reaching the designated area. In effect, you are creating an autonomous branch of your structure that will not inherit policies from above itself in the tree.

To block the inheritance of group policies, access the properties of the site, domain, or OU where you wish the block to begin. To do this, highlight it in the MMC, right-click, and choose Properties. You will be presented with the object's properties dialog box. On the Group Policy tab, shown in Figure 8.7, you will find an option to block policy inheritance. Select this option, and inheritance will be blocked.

FIGURE 8.7   Blocking inheritance

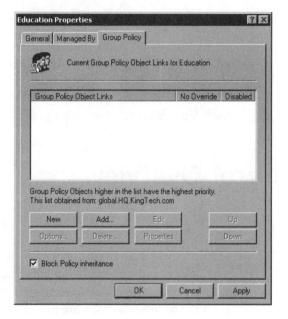

Mandating a Policy

There will be times when you want to block inheritance as we just discussed, but there will be other times when you want to ensure that a higher-level policy setting is not overwritten by a policy later in the policy list. To prevent a policy from being overwritten, access the properties of the container in which you wish to protect the policy. On the Group Policy tab, click the Options button. You will be presented with the dialog box shown in Figure 8.8.

FIGURE 8.8 The Policy Options dialog box

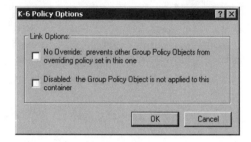

Here you can either select the No Override option or disable the policy in this container.

As you can see, group polices can greatly ease the administrative overhead of workstation management. GPOs are a component of a larger management tool known as Intellimirror. Intellimirror is a big piece of the overall change management philosophy for Microsoft—so you can bet it will be included in the MCSE exams!

Intellimirror Overview

Intellimirror is a set of management technologies built in to Microsoft Windows 2000 that are designed to increase the availability of services and reduce the overall costs of supporting users of Windows-based operating systems. Once configured, Intellimirror configurations enable users' data, software, and operating system settings to follow them wherever they might need them—whether they are on- or offline. Intellimirror provides three major areas of control:

- User data management, which consists of the files, documents, and other information that users access.

- User settings management, which allows for the customization of the operating system and applications of the user's computer environment. You can, for instance, mandate language settings, custom dictionaries, desktop layout, and other user preferences.

- Software Installation and Management allows the management of the installation, configuration, repair, and removal of applications and their patches and upgrades.

Although most of the functions that make up Intellimirror can be implemented through AD group policies, AD is not a necessity. From the perspective of AD design, *Intellimirror* is more a marketing term than a technology. All of the functionality of Intellimirror is included in the AD group policy structure. You will, however, need to be aware of a few particulars about Intellimirror for your exam. In this short section, we'll discuss a few of the salient differences in how Microsoft presents GPOs versus how they present Intellimirror.

Once of the best features of Intellimirror is the fact that it can be configured on stand-alone (non-networked) computers and that certain aspects can be configured so that they are available on or off the network.

User Data Management

Managing the vast amounts of data that exist in a large environment can be a daunting task. Designing an environment where that data is always available—given network outages, server downtime, and roaming users—has been almost impossible. Intellimirror provides the tools to ensure data availability under any circumstances. These services can be set up manually or on a per-user basis, or they can be configured through the use of group policies.

One of the key services that Intellimirror can provide is the ability to redirect data folders (such as the My Documents folder) to a network location. This provides all of the benefits that are inherent in a server-based storage environment—central backups, accessibility from other computers, and security. Of course, *just* moving the data to a server would leave the user at the mercy of the network—if the server (or some other component of the network) fails, the user will not be able to access their data.

To combat this single point of failure, redirected folders can be configured so that the data is synchronized back to a copy stored on the local computer. When folders are configured in this way, each time a user saves a file to the folder, the save is performed both to the network location *and* to the local drive. This configuration guarantees that data will be accessible at all times—even when the network is unavailable. If the network is unavailable, the user can work with the local copy of the data. When the network eventually becomes available, resynchronization with the network copy will occur (without user intervention). In the event that both copies (the local and the network versions) have changes, the synchronization manager will give the user the choice of saving both copies or synchronizing against one or the other.

User Settings Management

There are no capabilities in Intellimirror that we have not already covered in our GPO discussion. This area allows you to manage the end users' environment—Desktop settings, color scheme, and so on.

Software Installation and Management

This component of Intellimirror is basically just the software distribution that we discussed with GPOs—with one additional twist, software repair. If a user tries to open an application that is managed through Intellimirror and that attempt fails due to missing or corrupted files, Intellimirror will manage the replacement of those files automatically.

Design Scenario: Using GPOs and Intellimirror

Your company has a series of issues with the current implementation of AD. This system was designed by an outside consultant who made sure the basic domain and OU structure was sound but did not take the time to properly analyze your business needs before implementation. After using Windows 2000 for six months, your upper-management team is starting to ask when the reduced administrative costs and more reliable environment will become apparent. You are given the task of solving certain key issues that remain:

- Your company has an internal department of transitory employees who move from department to department filling in as needed. No matter where they are working, these employees need access to their own personal directories and any software that they are familiar with.

- Your sales staff is complaining that their quotes for clients are not available when they are away from the office. The former administrator set up a dial-in solution to alleviate this issue, but the number of calls has increased to the point where performance has suffered.

- The human resources department is complaining that it takes an average of six working days before a new hire is fully set up with a computer and software. Your research shows that the hardware is usually available within two days of the request but that account and computer setup takes the additional time.

- Your sales staff uses a series of computers located on the sales floor to perform demonstrations and to allow clients to browse through the online sales information. Customers are then allowed to create an order form online using a preconfigured Excel spreadsheet. These computers are in a public place and need to be protected against customer mistakes that corrupt the interface and applications installed on them. Your research shows that 3 out of the 10 computers need some sort of IT support (either putting the desktop back to the company default or reinstalling corrupted applications) each week.

For each issue, describe which components of Windows 2000 will allow you to correct the problem.

Because this chapter discusses GPOs and Intellimirror, you can assume that those technologies will be the answer in each case. You will, however, need to explain which function of the GPO or Intellimirror environment will be used.

Use an AD group policy to define the various environmental configurations that these transitory users will need. This will ensure that their environment is consistent no matter which computer they work from. Also, redirect their data folders to the network so that they will be available from anywhere on the network.

The dial-up solution *might* be viable, but there will be times when a salesperson does not have access to a phone line at a client site. A better solution would be to configure the Intellimirror folder redirection feature to ensure that a copy of the data is on the network (to provide for central backup and management). Then implement the synchronization of that data to a local folder on the salespersons' laptops. This ensures that the data is available even when they have no access to the network.

First, you might suggest that hot-spare computers be kept in inventory to reduce the time between need and availability. This will remove the average two-day wait for equipment (and also provide emergency equipment to replace any failed hardware without delay). Next, use the software publication features of group policies to distribute software to specific groups of users. When a new employee is hired, add them to the appropriate AD groups and their software needs will be met automatically.

Use an AD group policy to lock down the user interface of these public computers so that customers cannot change them. Also, use Intellimirror to provide software protection in the event of user error (Intellimirror will rebuild the application if a file has become corrupted or deleted).

Creating a Desktop-Management Policy

Knowing the change management capabilities available in Windows 2000 is only the beginning of the design process. Now we must discuss the actual implementation of these technologies to provide for business needs. From a design perspective, this means designing a desktop-management policy that will be used across the board to manage workstations within the environment.

Microsoft ✓ *Exam* *Objective*

Analyze the business requirements for client computer desktop management.

- Analyze end-user work needs.
- Identify technical support needs for end-users.
- Establish the required client computer environment.

Overview

Centrally managing any component of a complex environment requires an intimate knowledge of the particulars of that component. If, for instance, you wish to manage the traffic generated on your network, you will have to understand the types of traffic, analyze existing traffic, and estimate any additional traffic that will be generated due to changes to the environment (this is a great review of earlier chapters!). The same applies to desktop management. Up to this point in the chapter, we've been looking at the technologies available to manage the users' workstations. Now we need to move to the next step—analyzing the current environment.

Assessing the Existing Environment

The first step in designing a desktop-management policy is to gather information about the current state of your environment. You'll need to look at what hardware you have, what applications are in use, and the needs of your users. Much of the information you will need will have been gathered earlier in the design process—now you will need to look at that information with an eye toward desktop management.

Hardware

You will want to look over the hardware used within your environment to ensure that you do not specify configuration options that would conflict with the capabilities of computers on your network. You do not want, for instance, to mandate a particular display setting on computers that do not have hardware that is compatible with that setting.

Applications

Your next step to is to analyze the use of applications within your network. Earlier in the design process, you built a list of all software in use on your network and who uses it. You can use this list to determine which software should be published to which users or computers.

User Needs

You will also have to look at the needs of your users. You might, for instance, want to mandate a particular video display setting for most users within your company. You will have to determine if any of your users have a business need that is at odds with this policy. A user in the marketing department, for instance, might need a higher resolution for working with graphics files.

Looking to the Future

At this point, you will also want to think about the future of your network environment and the business that it supports. If you have an application that is constantly being upgraded, patched, or altered in some way, you might want to ensure that it is managed from a central location (through Intellimirror) to reduce the administrative overhead of managing it.

Available Resources

You will also want to look at the IT resources that are available and how they are currently deployed. If your company has a limited number of IT professionals on staff, you will be more likely to configure central management of the desktop environment. A general rule of thumb is that there are two types of environments in which a desktop-management policy is most likely to be implemented:

A highly managed network   In an environment where users are given little freedom, you are likely to use GPOs to control their workstation environment. GPOs allow you to take complete control over the look and feel of their desktop as well as to limit the types of actions that users can take.

A network with a large number of computers and users relative to the size of the IT department   IT departments that are "understaffed" are more likely to limit the effect of user actions than companies with large IT departments are. Limiting user actions also limits the types of mistakes they can make, thereby limiting the amount of IT support they will need.

Design Considerations for a Desktop-Management Policy

There are four main goals for the use of GPOs within an IT environment:

- Enforce common security standards
- Enforce user and computer configurations
- Simplify the process of configuring computers
- Simplify software management

Enforce Common Security Standards

In many companies, the network has developed over time—first one department put up a server, and then another, and another, until the entire company was networked. The next step in the evolution of networks was to tie these separate environments together into a single system. The end result of this effort was the development of complex network operating systems such as Windows 2000.

As the networks become more complex and they begin to provide mission-critical services, it is imperative that a set of security standards be put in place to protect against user mistakes or unwanted access. Enforcing such standards on a user-by-user or computer-by-computer basis is cumbersome and time-consuming at best. At worst, such granular activity leads to mistakes in security configuration. Those mistakes can be exploited by unscrupulous or inept users accessing confidential information or making unwelcome changes to the environment. Using GPOs to enforce security can help to reduce these risks.

Enforce User and Computer Configurations

Even though our users are becoming more and more computer literate, we still spend more time fixing user mistakes than we do improving the functionality of our networks. Most of these user mistakes could be avoided through the application of AD group policies that are configured to mandate the user preferences and limit a user's ability to make changes.

Simplify the Process of Configuring Computers

This is almost a corollary to the preceding goal—when a new computer is set up for a user, someone must spend time installing the proper software, setting up the default user preferences, and doing all of the other tasks that must be done before a user sits down to use the computer. Group policies can be used to perform this configuration as the user logs on to the network.

Software Management

One of the most exciting capabilities of Intellimirror is that it gives you the ability to distribute and manage applications remotely. Anything that can be done to reduce the amount of time spent managing a single desktop will reduce overall IT costs and free up IT staff for other duties.

Specific Configuration Considerations

Microsoft suggests some specific GPO configurations to use in a given situation. These suggestions are valid in both your real-world system *and* in the exam room.

Optimizing GPOs for Slow Links

The hierarchical nature of the GPO structure within Active Directory lends itself to optimization of processing over slow links. You have the option of disabling processing of most of the nodes within the hierarchy. Disabling a node prevents its settings from being downloaded to the client computer. In general, you should always disable any nodes in which you have not made configuration changes.

Exam Hint: Disable GPO nodes in which everything is left at its default setting. This reduces the amount of traffic that must be sent to the client computer.

There is a tool named GPResult.exe that comes with the Windows 2000 Server Resource Kit. This command-line utility displays the group policy settings in effect on a computer and the user logged on to the computer.

You can also configure certain nodes to not download when a slow link is detected. This allows the nodes to be implemented when a normal connection is made but reduces the amount of information that must be transferred when a slow link is used. This option is usually associated with dial-in connectivity. Table 8.2 lists various types of GPO settings, whether they are implemented over slow links by default, and whether this can be changed.

TABLE 8.2 Optimizing GPO Performance Over a Slow Link

Type of Setting	Downloaded by Default?	Can Be Configured?
Security settings	Yes	No

TABLE 8.2 Optimizing GPO Performance Over a Slow Link *(continued)*

Type of Setting	Downloaded by Default?	Can Be Configured?
Administrative templates	Yes	No
Software installation and maintenance	No	Yes
Logon/logoff and start-up/shutdown scripts	No	Yes
Folder redirection	No	Yes

The GPO Refresh Rate

By default, group policies are refreshed every 90 minutes, give or take 30 minutes to randomize the process (this helps to avoid a situation in which all computers are refreshing simultaneously). During a refresh, the entire GPO file is downloaded to the client computer—whether changes have occurred or not. Lengthening this interval can reduce the impact of GPO traffic on your network.

Summary

In this chapter, we have discussed the options available with Windows 2000 for managing the desktop environment. Microsoft has placed a lot of emphasis upon Intellimirror and Group Policy objects in both its marketing and MCSE programs. As such, you will need to be quite familiar with the concepts of desktop management.

In many ways, this chapter is not very true to the subject (AD design). In a real-life design project, very little time would be spent designing AD to support desktop management. Really, the only things you would consider would be creating container objects to group users with like needs together.

You will also have to think about where group policies will be applied—at the domain, OU, or site level. The big consideration here is to be able to determine which users and computers will be impacted by a given GPO.

In the next chapter, we will discuss the concept of AD connectors. An AD connector is used to "connect" the Active Directory environment to another directory service database such as that found in Exchange Server or Novell NetWare. To be truthful, this is mostly a nonissue as we write this book (there just aren't a lot of connectors available). It is, however, critical to Microsoft's goal of being the directory service that acts as the central database for network control in a mixed environment.

Key Terms

Before you take the exam, be sure you're familiar with the following terms:

assigned application

GPO nodes

Group Policy object (GPO)

policy inheritance

published applications

software package

Review Questions

1. Which of the following types of GPO would you implement to ensure that a virus software was run each time a user logs on to the network?

    A. Application deployment

    B. File deployment

    C. Script

    D. Software

    E. Security

2. Which of the following GPO types would you implement to control the Start menu options for a user?

    A. Application deployment

    B. File deployment

    C. Script

    D. Software

    E. Security

3. Which of the following GPO types would you implement to control which users can log on at domain controllers?

    A. Application deployment

    B. File deployment

    C. Script

    D. Software

    E. Security

4. Which of the following types of group policies would you implement to ensure that users have an updated copy of your employee phone book installed on their laptop each time they log on to the network?

   A. Application deployment

   B. File deployment

   C. Script

   D. Software

   E. Security

5. Which type of group policy would you implement if you wanted users to have the option to install an application on their computer?

   A. Application deployment

   B. File deployment

   C. Script

   D. Software

   E. Security

6. In which order do the following policies get applied?

   A. Policies assigned to organizational units, starting at the top of the AD tree and working from parent to child OU until the context of the object (user or computer) has been reached. Once again, if an OU has more than one policy, they will be applied in an order set by the administrator.

   B. The local policy, if one exists.

   C. Policies assigned to the domain, in an order specified by the administrator.

   D. Policies assigned to the AD site object, in an order specified by the administrator.

7. Which of the following define areas to which GPOs can be assigned?

   A. Domain

   B. Domain controller

   C. Site

   D. Organizational unit

8. Which three of the following are methods used to control which policies will be applied in a given situation?

   A. Filtering by group membership

   B. Blocking inheritance

   C. Editing the GPO Registry to delete ACL memberships

   D. Preventing policies from being overwritten by polices above it in the AD tree.

9. Which of the following lists the default permissions granted to the creator/owner of a GPO?

   A. None

   B. Read, Apply Group Policy

   C. Read, Write, Create All Child Objects, Delete All Child Objects

   D. Read, Write, Create All Child Objects

10. By default, authenticated users have which of the following permissions to any GPO that applies to them?

   A. None

   B. Read, Apply Group Policy

   C. Read, Write, Create All Child Objects, Delete All Child Objects

   D. Read, Write, Create All Child Objects

Answers to Review Questions

1. C. Script policies allow you to run a script such as logon/logoff or system start-up/shutdown at specific times.

2. D. Software policies are used to globally configure most of the settings in users' profiles.

3. E. Using security policies, an administrator can restrict user access to files and folders, configure how many failed login attempts will lock an account, and control user rights (such as the ability to log on at domain controllers).

4. B . File deployment policies allow the administrator to place files in special folders on the user's computer, such as the `Desktop` or `My Documents` folders.

5. A. Application deployment policies are used to automate the installation of software.

6. B, D, C, A. Knowing this order of execution will be *very* important on your exam!

7. A, C, D. Policies can be assigned at three levels—domain, site, and OU.

8. A, B, D. Filtering by group memberships, blocking inheritance, and preventing policies from being overwritten allow the administrative staff to control where and when policies will be applied.

9. A. The creator/owner of a GPO has no special permissions to that object.

10. B. By default, authenticated users have the minimum permissions necessary to execute a GPO.

Case Study: King Technologies

Take about 10 minutes to look over the information presented and then answer the questions at the end. In the testing room you will have a limited amount of time—it is important that you learn to pick out the important information and ignore the "fluff."

Background

King Technologies has offices in Orlando, Tampa, Minneapolis, and Grand Rapids. Its Windows 2000 network is a single-domain environment with a regional OU design. There have been four OUs created within the KingTech .com domain, one for each physical location. All user accounts are located within the regional organizational units.

Environment

Each office has approximately 200 users, from various departments. The entire sales department is located within the Orlando office. Although the IT department, which is based in Tampa, follows a centralized management model, there are IT staff members at each location to handle local issues and support.

Goals

Public Access   Because a few of their computers are located in public facilities, a strict password and account lockout policy should be implemented with *no* exceptions.

User Permissions   No users should be able to change network settings or edit the Registry on workstations.

Applications   The company has standardized on Office 2000 as its application suite, including using Outlook to access e-mail on an Exchange Server. The entire company uses a customized application for order processing, but only members of the sales, accounting, and production departments should use it.

Hardware   The sales force uses laptops and needs access to departmental and personal data when out of the office. IT personnel should have the ability to completely manage *all* workstations. The production facility in Tampa has 10 PCs that are used to access the production schedule. These computers should *only* be able to run this one application.

Questions

1. Which of the following policies should be implemented through a group policy that is associated with the KingTech.com domain?

   A. Password policy.

   B. Account lockout policy.

   C. Assign Microsoft Office to appropriate users.

   D. Limit computers that can access the production schedule.

2. You have implemented a policy to limit the applications that can run at 10 computers in the production department. At which point in the AD structure would you associate this GPO?

   A. Domainwide computer-based policy

   B. Domainwide user-based policy

   C. Computer-based policy associated with the Tampa OU

   D. User-based policy associated with the Tampa OU

3. You have implemented policies at the domain level that control password, account lockout, and access to the Registry for all users. You have also implemented a policy at the Tampa OU that limits the applications that can run on 10 computers in production. When an administrator logs on to the network at one of those computers, they are unable to make changes to its environment. Which of the following would be the best fix for this problem?

   A. Instead of creating a computer-based policy for those computers, create a user-based policy that limits the users who sit at them.

   B. Create a group policy for administrators that allows full access and change the priority so that it is the first policy to be executed.

   C. Create a group policy for administrators that allows full access and change the priority so that it is the last policy to be executed.

   D. Instead of using policies, configure Windows 2000 permissions to limit who can access the production schedule.

4. You are asked to advise King Technologies on a password policy. They want to maintain a "strict password and account lockout" policy. Which policy might you suggest?

   A. Passwords with a minimum of 12 characters and account lockout after 3 failed attempts

   B. Passwords with a minimum of 12 characters and account lockout after 1 failed attempt

   C. Passwords with a minimum of 8 characters and account lockout after 3 failed attempts

   D. Passwords with a minimum of 8 characters and account lockout after 1 failed attempt

5. When an IT staff member logs in at a production machine in Tampa, in which order will the GPOs will be processed by default?

Task	Task
	GP_Order_Proc
	GP_Admin
	GP_Production
	GP_All

6. As part of your recommendation for King Technologies, you have been asked to review and reform its user support system. Review the case study with a focus on how the IT staff is organized and then reorder the tasks below so they reflect the flow of user support incidents through the system.

Support Path	Tasks
	Central IT staff contacts local IT staff
	Problem resolved
	End user reports problem
	Support incident initiated by central IT staff
	Local staff closes support incident
	Problem investigated by local IT staff

Answers

1. A, B, C. Look through the list of goals in the case study to find those settings that are universal in nature—they should be applied domainwide.

2. C. The best technique would be to create a computer-based policy associated with the Tampa OU (because production is located in Tampa). Use GPO security to limit its effect to only those computers that need to be controlled.

3. C. Remember that the each policy has the ability to overwrite the configuration settings put in place by earlier policies.

4. C. Any of these will work, and in fact we are choosing the least secure option in this case. The key distinction here is between "strict" and "draconian." Passwords longer than eight characters or with a single-failure lockout are a recipe for user frustration and extra administrative headaches. Passwords scribbled on Post-it notes around the office or users who stop logging out altogether are a good indication that your security policy is cranked a bit too high!

5. See table.

Task
GP_All
GP_Order_Proc
GP_Admin
GP_Production

The order is local, site, domain, then OU. There are no local or site policies, so the domain policies will execute first.

6. See table.

Support Path	Tasks
End user reports problem	Central IT staff contacts local IT staff
Support incident initiated by central IT staff	Problem resolved
Central IT staff contacts local IT staff	End user reports problem
Problem investigated by local IT staff	Support incident initiated by central IT staff
Problem resolved	Local staff closes support incident
Local staff closes support incident	Problem investigated by local IT staff

The key here is that it is far easier to keep track of common problems and solutions if you use the centralized structure of the IT staff. Tampa should receive all support e-mails or calls and can then assign a ticket to a technician in one of the remote sites. This allows the central IT staff to suggest solutions for problems that have occurred previously at other sites and also allows them to verify that support issues are being resolved.

Chapter

9

Planning for Active Directory Connectors

MICROSOFT EXAM OBJECTIVE COVERED IN THIS CHAPTER:

✓ Plan for the coexistence of Active Directory and other directory services.

Throughout your studies for the MCSE examinations, you have been hearing about how Windows 2000 networking and Active Directory are based upon "open standards" and "industry-standard protocols." By now you should know LDAP, X.500, DNS, and even WINS, inside and out! But until now, probably no one has talked about how the use of industry-standard components is going to make managing a heterogeneous environment easier.

In this chapter, we are finally going to discuss how AD can be configured to talk to, share information with, and even manage other directory services that you might have implemented in your environment. This is accomplished by installing and configuring a software component called an AD connector. For this exam objective topic, we've got some good news and some bad news. The good news is that this appears to be a very low-priority objective on the MCSE test. (That's not to say that you *won't* see a question about connectors—just that it appears that there are not a lot of questions on them.) The bad news is that, at the time that this manual is being written, there is only one viable connector to use in our discussion—the connector to the Exchange Server 5.5 directory service database.

We'll begin this chapter with a brief overview of what connectors do, their structure, and a few of the configuration options that should be common to all connectors (when they are released). After laying that foundation, we'll move to a discussion of the Exchange Server 5.5 connector—mostly as an example of how connectors will affect your overall Active Directory design.

As we write this, Microsoft has included on TechNet Plus a beta version of a connector for NDS, named MSDSS for NetWare. It is also available through the Microsoft Certified Solution Provider (MCSP) program. Because our focus here is on how connectors will affect your AD design, we feel that we can avoid the whole "beta issue" and still cover the concepts in enough detail for our purposes by concentrating on the Exchange Server connector.

What Are AD Connectors?

An *AD connector* is a software component that allows synchronization between dissimilar directory services. *Directory synchronization* is a process that keeps the information in two separate directories synchronized; that is, changes made to information in one directory will be propagated automatically to the other. You should remember that one of the most important features that Microsoft is marketing about Windows 2000 and Active Directory is the concept of a single point of management for all network resources. If you have an environment in which multiple directories exist, you could conceivably have multiple points of management for a single resource. As an example, look at Figure 9.1.

FIGURE 9.1 Multiple directories

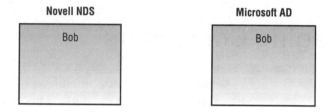

In this example, user Bob has accounts in both the Novell and Microsoft environments. Without some method of synchronization, Bob's two accounts would have to be managed separately—if Bob were to leave the company, for instance, his information would have to be deleted in both locations. Even management of less-critical changes would require multiple administrative steps. For example, if Bob were to change his telephone number, someone would have to make the change in both directories to keep the information current.

Adding an AD connector to this example, as shown in Figure 9.2, would alleviate the redundant management tasks. Bob's account information could be changed in the AD database and the changes would be propagated to NDS.

FIGURE 9.2 Adding an AD connector

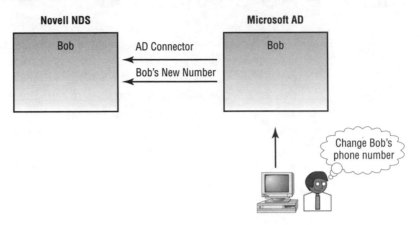

Managing Connectors

Just about every network directory on the market today, including Microsoft Active Directory, is based upon the X.500 recommendations. Most are also capable of using LDAP as a method of connecting to, searching, and managing the content of their directory database. Even though almost all vendors tout their compliance with industry standards, they don't mention that there is a lot of room for interpretation within those standards. AD connectors manage the communication between diverse directories, using the proper syntax and form to allow translation of requests from one directory to another.

When installing and configuring an AD connector, there will be certain tasks that are common no matter which vendor's directory the connector is designed to communicate with. Many of these configuration options will have a bearing on your overall AD design—if for no other reason than they produce overhead on the network that will compete for bandwidth with other AD processes.

Connector Agreements

Installing an AD connector adds a service to a Windows 2000 server. This service becomes a component of the AD subsystem. Once this software has been installed, you must build a relationship between AD and the target environment. A *connection agreement* defines this relationship. The connection agreement holds the communication configuration between the two environments. These configuration options can include the following:

- The directory (or directories) involved

- The names of servers to be contacted for synchronization

- The object classes to be included in the synchronization process

- The direction in which synchronization should occur

- Any scheduling information for the synchronization process

- How deleted objects will be dealt with

- A list of attributes to be synchronized (and a description of how attributes map to each other)

- A method of creating new objects

- Authentication methods

- A list of which containers will be involved in synchronization and how they map between the directories

Only one instance of a particular AD connector can be installed per Windows 2000 server—but that connector can have multiple agreements defined. You might, for instance, install an NDS connector on a server but create connection agreements to multiple NDS trees, as shown in Figure 9.3.

FIGURE 9.3   Multiple agreements for a single connector

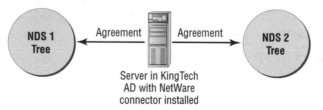

A few of the configuration options for AD connectors merit a more detailed discussion because these options can have a large impact on your overall AD design.

Configuring Bridgehead Servers

Bridgehead servers receive and forward the changes between the directories. As such, your bridgehead servers should have adequate resources to handle the additional overhead if they are performing this function. Because each connector will place a different amount of overhead on a server and the amount of information to be sent will differ from system to system (based upon the number of changes made to the directories involved), there are no hard and fast "numbers" that can be used as a basis for comparison. (We'll actually look at the overhead placed upon a server acting as a bridgehead for an Exchange Server connector later in this chapter. You can use that information as a guide when planning for your own needs.) There are, however, certain conditions that you will have to consider when choosing which servers will act as the bridgeheads for any environment:

- The bridgehead server should have adequate resources (CPU and memory) to support the overhead of handling synchronization traffic.

- It should be well connected to the network. In general, the bridgehead servers should be highly available—usually this means placing them on your backbone or in the center of the physical environment.

- If at all possible, the bridgehead server should also act as a global catalog server. If this is not possible, then the bridgehead server should at least be on the same network segment as a global catalog server. (During the creation of a new object in AD, the connector contacts a global catalog server to ensure that an object with the same name does not already exist.)

Exam Hint: That last bullet item is a big design consideration!!!

Source and Destination Containers

AD connectors use the X.500 directory structure (containers within containers, which hold leaf objects) as the basis for synchronization. When objects are updated between directories, the process occurs between containers in the directories. In other words, if a new user object is created in the Tampa container in one directory, the synchronization process will attempt to create that user in the Tampa container of the target directory.

In the case of the Exchange Server connector, for instance, if a recipients container of the same name does not exist in the target directory, it will be created during the synchronization process. For instance, suppose you have a recipients container named Persistent Image in your Exchange directory. If you were synchronizing mailboxes from it with an AD environment and a container with the same name did not exist in AD, it would automatically be created.

You have the option of configuring which containers will be polled for changes, to which container the changes should be written, and what types of objects should be synchronized.

Synchronizing Deletions

By default, an object that is deleted in one directory is not automatically deleted in any other directories to which a connector has been configured. Instead, a file that lists the objects that have been deleted is created on the server running the AD connector. This prevents accidental deletion of objects that need to be removed from only one directory or the other. This might come in handy if, for instance, you had configured a connector to your NDS directory to allow management of both environments during the migration process to Microsoft Active Directory. In this case, as you deleted objects in the Novell directory, you would not want those objects to be deleted in Active Directory.

You have the option, though, to configure your connector so that deletions are indeed synchronized across the connector. If you have installed the Exchange Server connector, for instance, and you delete a user object in Active Directory, you would probably want the corresponding mailbox to be automatically deleted from the Exchange directory.

Monitoring Connectors

There are two very useful tools available to monitor your AD connectors to ensure that they are working correctly and to analyze their impact on the AD connector server, the bridgehead server, and the network:

- Custom Performance objects and counters

- Connector logging

One of the hardest things about writing this book has been staying on target—it's very difficult to discuss technology at the design level without discussing the mechanics of that technology. This MCSE exam is *not* based upon your ability to actually perform any physical tasks—rather, it is testing your ability to design an efficient Active Directory environment given a description of the business environment in which it will be implemented. This little section about monitoring AD connectors comes very close to crossing the line between a discussion of design issues and a tutorial on implementation. With that said, because this information does not appear to have been included in any of the Microsoft Official Windows 2000 curricula, we believe that it needs to be introduced here. So even though it may not be information you'll need to pass the Design exam, it *will* be used in your test lab during any actual implementations you might be involved with. Testing the overhead placed upon servers being utilized as bridgeheads, for instance, will be helpful in determining the placement of that role within your network.

Performance Objects and Counters

Installing an AD connector on a Windows 2000 server will add a series of new objects and counters within the Performance utility. These new counters will allow you to monitor the additional resources used by the connector processes. Of course, you also have the traditional objects available—processor, memory, disk, network, and all of the others. Create a baseline *before* implementing the connector and then compare the counter values after the installation with the values from your baseline.

For more information about using Performance or creating a baseline, please see *MCSE: Windows 2000 Directory Services Administration Study Guide*, by Anil Desai (Sybex, 2000).

Connector Logging

An Active Directory connector logs events to the application log within the Event Viewer. These events are divided into five different classifications:

Replication   Events that occurred during the replication process.

Account Management   Events that occurred during an attempt to write or delete an object during replication.

Attribute Mapping   Events that occurred while attributes were mapped between Active Directory and the other directory database. (We'll discuss mapping a little later in this chapter.)

Service Controller   Events that occurred when the connector services were started or stopped.

LDAP Operations   Events that occurred while the directory was being accessed. (LDAP is the protocol used by the connector to communicate between the two directories.)

The Exchange Server 5.5 Connector

The only real connector available at this time is the connector for Microsoft Exchange Server 5.5. We'll use this connector as an example of how connectors will affect your overall Active Directory design, to show you some of the considerations that you will need to take into account during the configuration of a connector, and to present some connector design examples for different types of environments.

Planning a connector strategy can be a full-blown design project in and of itself. Microsoft actually suggests that, for the Exchange connector, you create a completely separate design team whose sole responsibility will be creating an operational plan that describes your strategy for connecting Microsoft Active Directory with your Microsoft Exchange Server organization.

If it's this complex when connecting two Microsoft directories, imagine what it will be like when you try to connect directories from multiple vendors!

An Overview of the Exchange Server Connector

Like any other AD connector, the Exchange connector is designed to allow synchronization between two different directories—in this case, Active Directory and the Exchange Server directory. In the long run, this connector is used to manage both AD and Exchange objects in a single step, as shown in Figure 9.4.

FIGURE 9.4 A single point administration

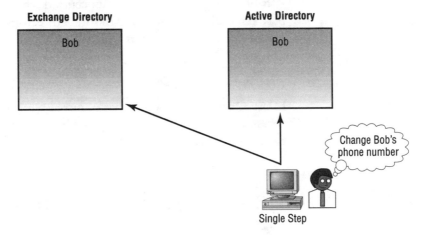

You can configure this connector for one-way or two-way synchronization. You might, for instance, want all changes to be made through Active Directory, so you would configure the connector so that changes are only propagated from AD to Exchange and not from Exchange to AD—this would be an example of one-way synchronization. Two-way synchronization would allow changes made in either environment to be synchronized to the other.

For this connector, there are two special uses that might have a big impact on the implementation phase of your design project:

- The Exchange connector can be used to populate a new Active Directory database with information from an existing Exchange directory.

If, for instance, you are already using Exchange Server and have recipients created for all of your users, you can configure the connector and let the connector create AD user objects for each Exchange account.

- The Exchange connector can be used as middleware to populate your AD database with objects from any other foreign system that you can synchronize with Exchange, as shown in Figure 9.5. To do this, you configure an Exchange connector to the foreign system (such as Lotus Notes or Novell GroupWise) and let the synchronization occur so that the Exchange directory is populated with the accounts from the foreign system. Then configure the AD-to-Exchange connector and let it populate your AD database with objects corresponding to the Exchange accounts. In this way, you can use what we call "pass-through" synchronization to populate your AD database with objects from most other directories.

FIGURE 9.5 Pass-through synchronization

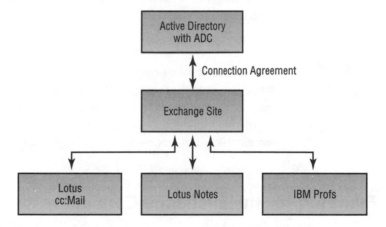

 We've used the latter technique a few times and it can save you a lot of time and effort. We've gone so far as to put up a temporary Exchange server and connect it to a client's current e-mail package. Let the accounts synchronize and then use an Exchange connector to bring those accounts into Active Directory. You can then uninstall the Exchange connector and bring down your temporary Exchange server—after the user accounts have been created for you!

The key features of the Exchange connector are as follows:

Bidirectional synchronization   When configured, this allows you to make changes in either directory and have those changes synchronized to the other.

Selective attribute synchronization   You can specify which attributes of Active Directory and Exchange objects should be synchronized through the connector.

Change synchronization   Only those objects that are changed will be processed by the synchronization software (as opposed to all objects whether they are changed or not).

Attribute-level changes   Only those attributes that have changed are replicated across the connector. If you change Bob's telephone number, *only* his telephone number will cross the link. This seems like common sense, but you would be surprised at the number of directory synchronization products that actually do a complete copy of the entire object if any changes are made.

This last bullet item brings to mind one of the biggest advantages of managing your directories through AD. Active Directory allows you to design a more granular management model than the Exchange directory allows. In AD, you can give an individual permissions to a particular attribute (as opposed to the container-level management delegation available in Exchange).

Planning for the Exchange Connector

Planning for AD connectors should be considered a subproject of your overall design process. Although connectors can have an impact on your overall AD design, in many ways, planning for connectors requires its own design process.

Microsoft
Exam
Objective

Plan for the coexistence of Active Directory and other directory services.

Microsoft has suggested the following process be used when planning for directory synchronization:

- Form the deployment planning team. It is important that the AD design team be represented on this team, but in most cases, the majority of its members will be from your Exchange support staff. Whoever is on this team *must* have knowledge of both Exchange and Active Directory.

- Examine your domain structure and Exchange site topology. Because the Exchange site topology does not always match the business structure of the company, you will have to analyze where the two structures differ.

- Determine your management strategy. Decide where the objects will be managed—always from one of the other directories or always from a single directory.

- Decide which object classes and attributes will be synchronized.

- Create your connection agreement plan.

- Test your connection agreements in a lab or other controlled environment.

- Determine the schedule for synchronization.

- Develop (and implement) a backup and restore strategy.

A few of these steps need a more detailed discussion.

Form the Deployment Planning Team

No other component of your overall AD design project has as many codependencies as the implementation of an AD connector. Your team must contain members from IT management, the Active Directory administration staff, the schema management staff, and the network services group. Each of these people will have knowledge and skills that will contribute to the overall connection implementation strategy.

During the initial installation of the Active Directory connector (ADC), there will be changes made to the AD schema. For this reason, someone on the connector implementation team must be a member of the Schema Admins group—at least during the installation of the first ADC.

Examine Your Domain Structure and Exchange Site Topology

You will need to gather information about your Exchange sites—how they are managed (and by whom), which accounts exist in which recipients containers, and the objects that will need to be synchronized. If your AD users exist in multiple Windows 2000 domains, you will have to build a list of where each mailbox recipient's AD account is located. The easiest scenario (as we'll see in a bit) is when all mailboxes for an AD domain reside in the same Exchange site. If this is not the case, you will have to configure multiple connection agreements from each Exchange site that has mailboxes to the appropriate Windows 2000 domains. This is probably the biggest hassle in setting up this connector—and in some cases, it can take almost as long as the full AD design process.

At this point you should begin to plan the placement of your bridgehead servers. Remember that the bridgehead servers must have enough available resources to handle the additional overhead of supporting synchronization traffic, be well connected and highly available to the network, and either be global catalog servers or be physically located near one (preferably on the same network segment).

Although there are no definitive numbers that can be applied to the overhead of hosting the ADC, acting as a bridgehead *will* have an impact on overall performance of a server. Microsoft has released the following guidelines to give you a starting point when planning for the ADC.

On a Pentium-class (200MHz) server with 128MB of RAM, adding the ADC should add an average of 8 to 24 percent to the CPU usage. For domain controllers that might be contacted during the synchronization process, expect 6 to 66 percent more CPU utilization, and at the Exchange Server 5.5 bridgehead, expect an additional 0 to 91 percent CPU utilization. These numbers are not written in stone (and there is a wide range of possible increases), but they can be used as a starting point when determining which servers should accept each role. You should, of course, test this in a lab environment before implementing it in a production environment.

As a comparison, those same functions on a more powerful computer—Pentium II (450MHz) with 256MB of RAM—are as follows:

- On the server running the ADC, 1 to 12 percent higher CPU utilization

- On the domain controller contacted during the synchronization process, 0 to 30 percent more CPU utilization

- On the connecting Exchange Server 5.5 bridgehead, 20 to 36 percent more CPU utilization

For a large environment in which you expect a large amount of synchronization traffic, you might even want to dedicate servers to these tasks.

One general rule of thumb—place the server hosting the ADC on the same subnet as the Exchange server and the bridgehead servers if at all possible. If not, try to avoid synchronization across slow or heavily burdened WAN links.

Determine Your Management Strategy

You have the option of controlling the direction in which information is synchronized. You can manage all objects through the Exchange Server Administrator program or manage all objects through Active Directory and its tools. After wracking our brains and reading hundreds of pages of Microsoft documentation, we can think of many reasons why you would want to manage your entire environment through Active Directory, but we can't think of a single reason why you would want to limit yourself to managing objects through the Exchange Server 5.5 directory. Nevertheless, you will need to know that the option is available should you desire to set yourself up this way.

The biggest reason to manage all of your objects through Active Directory is its ability to delegate administrative tasks down to the attribute level of individual objects. You can, for instance, grant an individual the ability to change their password *without* granting any other permissions. On the Exchange Server side, however, you are forced to grant permission at the container level; those permissions then pertain to all objects within the container.

The most common practice is to keep the ability to manage objects from both directories and let those changes synchronize in both directions. This allows your Exchange administrators to continue their current functions without much additional training, but it also allows your AD administrators to set up complete accounts (as in complete with e-mail mailboxes).

Decide Which Object Classes and Attributes Will Be Synchronized

One of the biggest decisions you will have to make when configuring the Exchange Server connector will be to determine which objects and attributes will be synchronized from directory to directory. You might not want, for instance, your Exchange custom recipients (placeholders that contain the e-mail address of a foreign mailbox and appear in the global address book for convenience) to be synchronized to your AD database—this would effectively create AD contact objects for nonemployees. You might, however, want your AD distribution groups to be synchronized to your Exchange directory, thus automatically creating e-mail distribution lists out of AD objects. These decisions will have to be considered carefully; as you synchronize more types of objects, you potentially add more network traffic to the process.

When deciding which objects will be synchronized, you should have two primary goals:

- Only synchronize objects that have a purpose in both environments. In other words, if you are not going to use AD distribution objects within your AD structure, do not include AD or Exchange distribution list objects in the synchronization process.

- Make sure the objects end up in containers that make finding them (the objects) easy for both your users and your administrators.

Microsoft recommends that you accomplish the second goal by mirroring your Exchange OU and AD OU structures. You might, for instance, create the following recipients container within your Exchange sites:

- Custom Recipients

- Mailboxes

- Distribution Lists

In your Active Directory OU structure, you would then create the following containers:

- Contacts

- Users

- Groups

This organization ensures consistency across both environments.

We are not all that impressed with the implementation Microsoft suggested. First of all, because the Exchange directory is not as adaptable as the AD structure, you will end up limiting your options for your Active Directory design. Second, and probably more relevant, mailboxes cannot be moved from one recipients container to another in Exchange Server 5.5. The end result is that this plan *might* work if you are implementing both directories at the same time, but it is probably not going to work if your Exchange organization exists before you design and implement Active Directory.

There are three ways to configure the synchronization between AD and Exchange in Microsoft's recommended implementation:

- The easiest way
- The most complex way
- The middle ground

The Easiest Way

If all of the mail recipients within a single Exchange site exist within a single Windows 2000 domain, you have the option of using the simplest connector configuration. In this case, on the Exchange Server side, you configure the Exchange site as both the source and the target of the synchronization process. At the same time, configure the Windows 2000 domain as both the source and target for the other end of the connector. In effect, this means that all objects within the Exchange recipients hierarchy will be synchronized to the Windows 2000 database and all security principals within the Windows 2000 domain will be synchronized to the Exchange Server site.

The secret to this configuration is to move all of the Exchange Server objects to one container within the Active Directory OU structure. After these objects have been synchronized, you can move them to other OUs and AD will track them for future synchronization.

The Most Complex Way

Create three connection agreements that map each of the Exchange containers to the matching AD OUs. Configure one agreement in which the Exchange Custom Recipients container maps to the AD Contacts OU (resulting in all objects from each container synchronizing to corresponding objects in the other). Configure a second agreement that maps the Mailboxes container in

Exchange to the Users OU in Active Directory, and finally, configure a third agreement that maps the Exchange Distribution Lists container to the AD Groups OU. This configuration is shown in Figure 9.6.

FIGURE 9.6 Three separate connection agreements

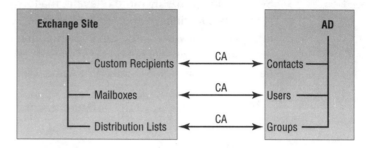

CA = Connection Agreement

The Middle Ground

Instead of configuring three separate connection agreements as suggested in the preceding example, you could configure one connection agreement that maps between the parent containers in both environments, as shown in Figure 9.7.

FIGURE 9.7 A single connection agreement

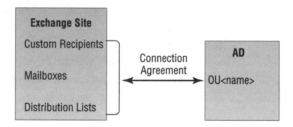

In this configuration, the first time you synchronize the directories, the AD connector will automatically create within the AD structure containers that mirror those in the Exchange hierarchy.

Active Directory Connector Object, Attribute, and Schema Mapping

Once the AD connector has been installed, an ADC policy object is created with Active Directory. This policy object contains a default mapping of objects and attributes between the Exchange Server directory and Active Directory. These *mappings* define which object classes within AD are functionally the same as object classes with the Exchange Server schema. It is possible to change the default lists, but most environments will not require this action. You should, however, be aware of the default mappings.

In general, the user, group, and contact objects within Active Directory are synchronized with objects in the Exchange directory. The following four tables list how attributes within these AD object classes map to attributes within the Exchange environment.

Table 9.1 lists the attributes that are common to all three synchronized classes and how they map to the Exchange schema.

TABLE 9.1 Common Attributes

Windows 2000 Attribute	Exchange Attribute
description	Admin-description
autoReply	AutoReply
businessRoles	Business-Roles
co	Co
company	company
delivContLength	Deliv-Cont-Length
department	department
displayName	Cn
displayNamePrintable	name
distinguishedName	distinguishedName

TABLE 9.1 Common Attributes *(continued)*

Windows 2000 Attribute	Exchange Attribute
dnQualifier	dnQualifier
employeeID	employeeNumber
extensionAttribute1	Extension-Attribute-1
extensionAttribute2	Extension-Attribute-2
extensionAttribute3	Extension-Attribute-3
extensionAttribute4	Extension-Attribute-4
extensionAttribute5	Extension-Attribute-5
extensionAttribute6	Extension-Attribute-6
extensionAttribute7	Extension-Attribute-7
extensionAttribute8	Extension-Attribute-8
extensionAttribute9	Extension-Attribute-9
extensionAttribute10	Extension-Attribute-10
extensionAttribute11	Extension-Attribute-11
extensionAttribute12	Extension-Attribute-12
extensionAttribute13	Extension-Attribute-13
extensionAttribute14	Extension-Attribute-14
extensionAttribute15	Extension-Attribute-15
facsimileTelephoneNumber	facsimileTelephoneNumber
generationQualifier	generationQualifier
homephone	homephone
homePostalAddress	homePostalAddress

TABLE 9.1 Common Attributes *(continued)*

Windows 2000 Attribute	Exchange Attribute
houseIdentifier	HouseIdentifier
info	Info
initials	initials
l	L
Language	Language
mail	Mail
mailnickname	Uid
mobile	mobile
otherTelephone	Telephone-Office2
otherHomePhone	Telephone-Home2
telephoneAssistant	telephone-Assistant
pager	pager
personalPager	personalPager
personalTitle	personalTitle
physicalDeliveryOfficeName	physicalDeliveryOfficeName
postalCode	postalCode
secretary	secretary
sn	Sn
st	St
street	street
streetAddress	postalAddress

TABLE 9.1 Common Attributes *(continued)*

Windows 2000 Attribute	Exchange Attribute
telephoneNumber	telephoneNumber
telexNumber	telexNumber
teletexTerminalIdentifier	teletexTerminalIdentifier
textEncodedORAddress	textEncodedORAddress
title	Title
userCertificate	userCertificate
userCert	user-Cert
userSMIMECertificate	userSMIMECertificate
url	url
x121Address	x121Address
autoReplyMessage	conferenceInformation
importedFrom	Imported-From

Table 9.2 lists the default mapping of an AD user object to an Exchange mailbox.

TABLE 9.2 User-to-Mailbox Mappings

Windows 2000 User Object Attribute	Exchange Mailbox Object Attribute
givenName	givenName
manager	manager
altRecipient	Alt-Recipient
publicDelegates	public-Delegates

TABLE 9.2 User-to-Mailbox Mappings *(continued)*

Windows 2000 User Object Attribute	Exchange Mailbox Object Attribute
mdbUseDefaults	mdb-use-defaults
mdbOverQuotaLimit	MDB-Over-Quota-Limit
mdbStorageQuota	MDB-Storage-Quota
submissionContLength	submission-cont-length
mDBOverHardQuotaLimit	DXA-task
protocolSettings	protocol-Settings
mapiRecipient	mapi-recipient
msExchHomeServerName	home-MDB
msExchHomeServerName	home-MTA
deliverAndRedirect	deliver-and-redirect
garbageCollPeriod	garbage-coll-period
securityProtocol	security-Protocol
deletedItemFlags	DXA-Flags
objectSID	Assoc-NT-Account
authOrig	Auth-Orig
unauthOrig	Unauth-Orig
dLMemSubmitPerms	DL-Mem-Submit-Perms
dLMemRejectPerms	DL-Mem-Reject-Perms
folderPathname	Folder-Pathname

Table 9.3 lists the default mappings for an AD contact object to an Exchange Server Custom recipient.

TABLE 9.3 Contact-to-Custom Recipient Mappings

Windows 2000 Contact Object	Exchange Custom Recipient Object
givenName	givenName
Manager	Manager
targetAddress	target-Address
protocolSettings	protocol-Settings
mapiRecipient	mapi-Recipient
AuthOrig	Auth-Orig
UnauthOrig	Unauth-Orig
dlMemSubmitPerms	dl-Mem-Submit-Perms
dlMemRejectPerms	dl-Mem-Reject-Perms

Table 9.4 lists the default mappings for an AD group object to an Exchange Distribution List object.

TABLE 9.4 Group-to-Distribution List Mappings

Windows 2000 Group Object	Exchange Distribution List Object
member	member
msExchExpansionServerName	home-MTA
managedby	owner
oOFReplyToOriginator	OOF-Reply-To-Originator
reportToOriginator	Report-To-Originator

TABLE 9.4 Group-to-Distribution List Mappings *(continued)*

Windows 2000 Group Object	Exchange Distribution List Object
reportToOwner	Report-To-Owner
hideDLMembership	Hide-DL-Membership
authOrig	Auth-Orig
unauthOrig	Unauth-Orig
dLMemSubmitPerms	DL-Mem-Submit-Perms
dLMemRejectPerms	DL-Mem-Reject-Perms

Some attributes do not synchronize through the connector by default:

- Windows 2000 attributes
  - All individual account information, such as Account Logging and Account Password
  - Profile information
  - Routing and Remote Access dial-up permissions
  - Access control lists (ACLs)
- Exchange attributes
  - Advance Security Settings
  - Access control lists (ACLs)
  - Home information Store

Determine the Schedule for Synchronization

You can set up individual connection agreements to synchronize at specific times throughout the day. You will have to use the infrastructure information you gathered earlier in your AD design project to determine what times would work the best in your particular environment. You will also have to determine what level of synchronicity is acceptable to your company. The two directories can best be described as "loosely synchronized." That basically means that, at any given point in time, changed information from one directory might not have been synchronized to the other. You will have to determine how up-to-date the information must be based upon the business needs of the company. In some cases, changes made in one directory must be made in the other very quickly; in other cases, there is an acceptable amount of delay. Microsoft makes two suggestions that you should keep in mind during your test:

- If you expect large numbers of changes, you should configure multiple agreements that synchronize at different times.

- If it is acceptable, you should configure your agreements so that synchronization occurs at night.

Microsoft-Defined Solutions

Microsoft defines four different model environments that you should follow when planning your AD connector implementation. From a design perspective, one of these "cookie-cutter" solutions will work in every environment that you can imagine. From an exam perspective, you should be able to identify these environments and describe the proposed AD connector solution.

Model 1: A Single Windows 2000 Domain and a Single Exchange Server Site

Basically, this is the simple solution we discussed earlier. In general, smaller companies with a single physical facility and under 5,000 users will use this connector strategy. Figure 9.8 depicts a Model 1 environment.

FIGURE 9.8 A Model 1 environment

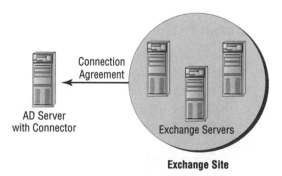

Exam Hint: Microsoft will probably add multiple servers to the graphic for questions regarding this model. Remember that every AD server within a domain and every Exchange server within a site hold the same directory database (for their environment). Unless you are asked to pick a bridgehead server, you can ignore the representation of servers—they are there to distract you.

In a Model 1 environment, you really have only one decision to make: Where do you want management to happen? You have three choices:

- Windows Active Directory only

- Exchange Server 5.5 Administrator only

- Both Windows 2000 and Exchange Server 5.5

In most cases, you will want the majority of object management to happen within Active Directory because it is the more flexible of the two directories. You might also want to limit your Exchange administrators to working within Exchange Administrator so that they do not need permissions within Active Directory.

Model 2: Single Windows 2000 Domain and Multiple Exchange Server Sites

This configuration will most likely be found in organizations with up to 20,000 users and/or multiple locations. In reality, from a design perspective, Model 2 is not much different from Model 1. Basically, you just set up a connector to each of the Exchange sites within the Exchange organization, as shown in Figure 9.9.

FIGURE 9.9 A Model 2 environment

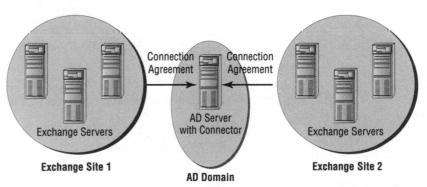

Once again, your only real design decision will be to consider where administration should take place. You have the same options as in Model 1 (Exchange or Active Directory only or both). You will, however, have to make this decision for each connection agreement.

Model 3: Multiple Windows 2000 Domains and a Single Exchange Server Site

It should be rare to encounter a set of circumstances in which you would have multiple Windows 2000 domains and only one Exchange Server site. In general, each AD domain can contain more objects than any single Exchange site, so the opposite (Model 4) is more likely. If, however, the original network started out with Windows NT and multiple domains *and* Exchange Server was added at a later date, it is conceivable that the Exchange Server organization would have been designed as a single site, whereas the NT environment (the older of the two) would have originally been set up with multiple domains.

Once again, this is a fairly easy environment to set up. Create an AD connector from each Active Directory domain to the Exchange Server site, as shown in Figure 9.10.

FIGURE 9.10 A Model 3 environment

Many people get confused at this point—they assume that if you synchronize the Exchange site to two different Windows 2000 domains, each Exchange object will be created in *both* domains. This is not the case. Earlier we mentioned that it was good design to place the AD connector either on or near a global catalog server. The reason that this is good design is that during the synchronization process, the connector searches for an Active Directory object with the same name as the Exchange object—using the global catalog. When it finds a match, it will synchronize changes from the Exchange side to the correct domain within the Windows 2000 environment.

Model 4: Multiple Windows 2000 Domains and Multiple Exchange Server Sites

Model 4 will be encountered only when working with very large companies. Because of the potential complexity of both the Active Directory structure and the Exchange Server organization, your connector strategy can become very complex. This is especially true if you did not follow Microsoft's recommendation (which we described earlier) of matching the two environments (having containers with the same function in both environments). You might end up creating multiple connection agreements between each Windows 2000 domain and each Exchange Server site. Your connectors have to be set up so that each Windows 2000 domain that needs to synchronize has a connector to each Exchange site with which it needs to synchronize. Sound complex? It should! Designing from a Model 4 environment can be like putting together a complex puzzle—it takes time, and you *have* to understand the relationships between the two directories. Figure 9.11 demonstrates how the connectors would be configured in a relatively small Model 4 environment.

FIGURE 9.11 A Model 4 environment

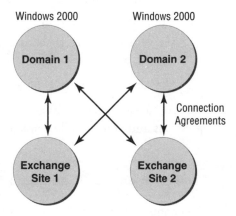

For your MCSE exam, there are a couple of points to remember:

- You do not need to install an AD connector in any Windows 2000 domains that do not have objects with corresponding objects in the Exchange directory.

- With multiple connectors, it is likely that there will be two paths through which a particular object could be synchronized. The AD connector will check the primary NT account server attribute of the Exchange Server object being synchronized. If the NT account exists in any domain to which the site has a connector, synchronization will occur with that Windows 2000 domain across the appropriate connector.

The Four Models in Review

After looking over the four models for the first time, many students are confused. In fact, we've had a few students decide to manage the two environments separately, hoping that Microsoft will make this easier in a later release of Windows 2000 or Exchange Server. After listening to our classroom lectures, though, most of these students see that this whole issue sounds complex but is, in reality, fairly straightforward.

You really have only three design decisions to make:

- Where should management take place—from the Active Directory side, the Exchange Server side, or both?

- Which Windows 2000 domains need to connect to which Exchange Server sites? (This is based upon the placement of user, distribution group, and contact objects within the AD domain hierarchy.)

- Are there any special configuration considerations for your connectors?

If you see a connector-based question on your exam, answer these three questions and you should be able to choose the correct answer!

Design Scenario: Planning a Connector Strategy

Your company has decided to upgrade its Microsoft Windows NT 4 network to Windows 2000. Your current NT network is based upon the multi-master domain model—you have two NT domains that contain user account information and six resource domains that do not contain user accounts. Your AD design team has determined that you will roll the objects from the resource domains into one of the two master domains (based upon the physical location of the resources) but that you will not merge the two master domains during the upgrade. In the end, your Windows 2000 network will consist of two domains named Orlando and Minneapolis.

Your company has also recently installed Exchange Server 5.5. The Exchange organization consists of one site (with Exchange servers in both offices).

You have been asked to create an AD connector plan for your company. Which of the Microsoft connector design models best describes your company?

This environment matches Model 3—Multiple Windows 2000 domains and a single Exchange Server site.

Draw a map of your connector strategy.

See Figure 9.10; change the names of the Windows 2000 domains to match your company.

List four pieces of information not given in the description that you would need before configuring your AD connectors.

The following information would be useful:

- The amount of available bandwidth at various times of day on the WAN link between Minneapolis and Orlando

- An estimate of the number of changes that will occur each day in your directories

- The acceptable delay in synchronization of changes between the two directories

- Where management should take place—in Active Directory, in the Exchange directory, or both

Summary

In this chapter, we have discussed the issues involved in synchronizing AD with a foreign directory. Although this appears to be a low-priority objective for your MCSE exam, you'll want to be comfortable with the concepts discussed.

Our discussion centered around the AD connector for Microsoft Exchange Server 5.5. The concept of synchronization should work with any X.500-compliant directory service, but this is the only viable connector available at this time. This connector will probably become obsolete with the release of Exchange 2000, but Microsoft is still very proud of it! Most of the AD connector–based questions you'll see on your examination will probably revolve around AD-to-Exchange synchronization.

Key Terms

Before you take the exam, be sure you're familiar with the following terms:

AD connector

connection agreement

directory synchronization

Review Questions

1. Which of the following best defines the function of an Active Directory connector?

   A. A software component used by the global catalog server to connect to AD servers in each domain

   B. A software component used to authenticate resource requests across domains within Active Directory

   C. A software component that allows synchronization between dissimilar directory services

   D. A software component used to configure a redundant network connection between domain controllers

2. Which of the following best defines directory synchronization?

   A. A process that keeps the information in two separate directories the same

   B. A process that ensures that the date and time match on all domain controllers within a domain

   C. A process that updates the information in the global catalog servers

   D. A process that ensures that changes made to the Active Directory database are applied in the correct chronological order

3. The relationship between two directories connected through an Active Directory connector is managed through which of the following?

   A. The ADC.ini file

   B. The connection agreement

   C. The translation manager component of Active Directory

   D. The Exchange Server directory replication process

4. The servers that receive and forward the changes between directories are known as _____ .

   A. S/F servers

   B. ADC management servers

   C. Bridgehead servers

   D. ADC domain controllers

5. Which of the following are recommended specifications for bridgehead servers? Choose all that apply.

   A. They should have adequate resources (CPU and memory) to support the overhead of handling synchronization traffic.

   B. They should be well connected to the network. In general, the bridgehead servers should be highly available; usually this means placing them on your backbone or in the center of the physical environment.

   C. If at all possible, the bridgehead server should also act as a global catalog server. If this is not possible, then the bridgehead server should at least be on the same network segment as a global catalog server.

   D. They must also act as the schema master for the Active Directory tree.

6. By default, which of the following actions takes place when an object is deleted within one of the directories connected through an AD connector?

   A. The object is automatically deleted in the other directory to ensure that the two databases are synchronized.

   B. A file that lists the objects that have been deleted is created on the server running the AD connector.

   C. An e-mail is sent to a specified account detailing the deletion and asking whether the action should be duplicated in the other directory.

   D. The object is flagged with a tombstone in the other directory, an e-mail is sent to the administrator account, and that individual has 30 days to remove the tombstone or the object will be deleted.

7. Which of the following is not a classification of events tracked by AD connector logging?

A. Replication

B. Attribute mapping

C. Synchronization

D. Service

E. Account management

8. In an environment with the AD Exchange connector installed and running, if an administrator changes the value of a user's telephone number attribute, which of the following actions will take place?

A. The entire object that represents that user will be sent across the connector to the other directory.

B. All objects within the user's home container will be updated in the other directory.

C. The user's new telephone number value will be sent across the connector.

D. The administrator will have to manually enter the user's new telephone number in the other directory.

9. When the AD Exchange connector is first installed, the user who installs it must _____ .

A. Create a new mailbox in Exchange to act as the recipient for all changes

B. Be a member of the Schema Admins group

C. Run the setup program in silent mode

D. Perform a backup and restore of all Exchange mailboxes to ensure that the format is correct for the connector

10. In a large environment with a lot of changes to the directories, Microsoft suggests which two of the following?

A. Configure multiple agreements that synchronize at different times.

B. Create one connector and have all traffic use that connector to take advantage of the compression capabilities built in to the connector.

C. If it is acceptable, you should configure your agreements so that synchronization occurs at night.

D. Manage all changes through the Exchange Administrator to take advantage of its more flexible nature.

11. Which of the following statements are true?

A. You do not need to install an AD connector in any Windows 2000 domain that does not have objects with corresponding objects in the Exchange directory.

B. Every Windows 2000 domain will have to have at least one connector installed and configured.

C. There is only one connector allowed per AD tree.

D. There is only one connector allowed per AD forest.

Answers to Review Questions

1. C. Active Directory connectors allow directories from different vendors or applications to communicate and share information.

2. A. Directory synchronization is a process that keeps the information in two separate directories synchronized; that is, changes made to information in one directory will be propagated automatically to the other.

3. B. Installing an AD connector adds a service within Windows 2000 Server. This service becomes a component of the AD subsystem. Once this software has been installed, you must build a relationship between AD and the target environment. A connection agreement defines this relationship. The connection agreement holds the communication configuration between the two environments.

4. C. Bridgehead servers receive and forward the changes between the directories.

5. A, B, C. There are certain conditions that you will have to consider when choosing which servers will act as the bridgeheads for any environment: They should have adequate resources (CPU and memory) to support the overhead of handling synchronization traffic, they should be well connected to the network, and they should also act as global catalog servers.

6. B. By default, an object that is deleted in one directory is not automatically deleted in any other directories to which a connector has been configured. Instead, a file that lists the objects that have been deleted is created on the server running the AD connector. This prevents accidental deletion of objects that need to be removed from only one directory or the other.

7. C. The five classifications of logged events are replication, attribute mapping, account management, service controller, and LDAP operations.

8. C. Only those attributes that have changed are replicated across the connector.

9. B. During the initial installation of the Active Directory connector (ADC), the process will make changes to the AD schema. For this reason, whoever installs the first connector must be a member of the Schema Administrators group.

10. A, C. Microsoft makes two suggestions that you should keep in mind during your design: (1) If you expect large numbers of changes, you should configure multiple agreements that synchronize at different times. (2) If it is acceptable, you should configure your agreements so that synchronization occurs at night.

11. A. Remember this fact for your MCSE examination: You do not need to install an AD connector in any Windows 2000 domain that does not have objects with corresponding objects in the Exchange directory.

Case Study: Persistent Image, LLC.

Take about 10 minutes to look over the information presented and then answer the questions at the end. In the testing room, you will have a limited amount of time—it is important that you learn to pick out the important information and ignore the "fluff."

Background

Persistent Image (PI) is a medium-size company headquartered in Orlando, Florida. In addition to its office in Orlando, it has a large facility in Minneapolis and branch offices in Chicago and Los Angles. It has recently acquired a company with a large office in Tampa.

PI's main product is a certification course for technical instructors—basically, instructors are taught how to present technical courses, how to set up classrooms efficiently, and how to improve retention in adult students. The company has recently branched out into managing the certification programs for a few companies that produce network-related software and hardware. It produces self-study kits, books, videos, and audiotapes for these certification programs as well as maintains a Web-based testing program.

Current System

Network PI's current network consists of 30 Windows NT 4–based servers spread out over its 5 locations. The NT network was originally designed as a multi-master environment with two master domains and two resource domains. The recent acquisition of a Web design company based in Tampa has added to the system another domain that has both user accounts and resources defined within it.

E-Mail PI's e-mail platform of choice is Exchange Server 5.5. The Exchange organization contains one site, named P-I. There are Exchange servers in both the Minneapolis and Orlando offices. Users in Chicago and Los Angeles access servers in Chicago and Orlando, respectively, to access their e-mail. The new office in Tampa is using Lotus Notes as its e-mail platform.

CASE STUDY

Current Issues

To reduce administrative overhead, PI would like to manage all of its directories (AD, Exchange Server 5.5, and if possible, Lotus Notes) through a single interface. With this in mind, you are to design a connector strategy for its environment.

Considerations in Design

CIO   "We'd like to have a single point of management for all directory accounts. We find that keeping track of multiple accounts for a single user is overtaxing our small IT staff."

Active Directory Design Team   "After the upgrade to Windows 2000, we plan to have two NT domains: one that contains resource records for Los Angeles, Chicago, and Minneapolis and another for Orlando and Tampa. We are not sure if we will force the Tampa office into switching their e-mail platform to Exchange Server. Although it would make life easier for us [the IT department], it would force the Web designers to change development platforms, and they aren't too keen on that idea!"

Questions

1. Which of the four connector design models best fits this environment?

    A. Model 1

    B. Model 2

    C. Model 3

    D. Model 4

2. Which of the following considerations should you take into account in your connector strategy?

   A. Finding a way to synchronize the Lotus Notes account information with AD

   B. How to best populate the new AD database with objects

   C. The bandwidth required for e-mail

   D. The structure of recipients containers within the Exchange directory

3. Draw your proposed solution. Consult the answers you provided above, and link elements using the proper connector. Remember that for us, implementation is not as important as a good plan. Don't worry about the physical aspects of the connectors—just decide which connector(s) you would implement to ensure a fully synchronized environment.

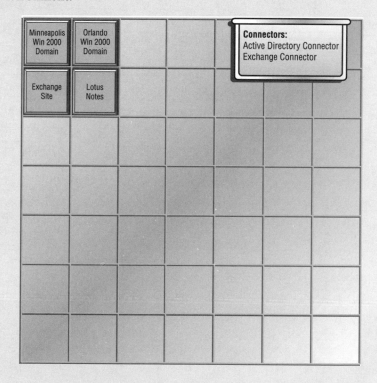

4. The CIO mentioned wanting a "single point of management for all directory accounts." Is this possible? (Select two answers.)

A. In theory, yes.

B. No, because Lotus Notes is not made by Microsoft.

C. Not currently, because all necessary technologies are not yet be available.

D. No, because Active Directory does not support this option.

5. From the list of objectives, decide whether each would be better served by converting the Tampa office to Exchange or leaving them on Lotus Notes.

Tampa Office Option	Objective
Convert to Exchange.	Provide for greater ease of administration.
Remain on Lotus Notes and use a connector.	Provide easier messaging collaboration.
	Maximize user efficiency (short term).
	Maximize user efficiency (long term).
	Simplify upgrades and third-party compatibility.
	Minimize IT training costs.
	Minimize user training costs.
	Minimize problems integrating Tampa users.

Answers

1. C. Model 3 is the best fit for Persistent Images. There are multiple Windows NT domains and only one Exchange Server site.

2. A, B, D. Rather than keeping the Lotus Notes environment as a separate point of management, you'll want to find a way to replicate between it and AD; you can use the existing Exchange accounts to populate AD through a connector; remember that the connector will try to place synchronized objects in a container of the same name.

3.

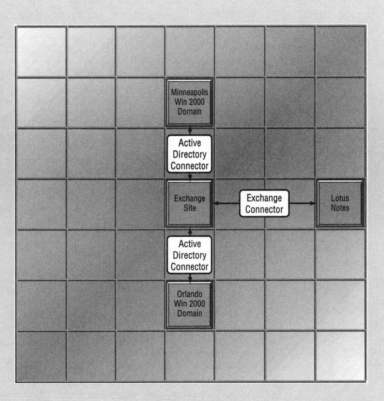

As you can see from the graphic, following a Model 3 design allows for a fully synchronized environment. The Active Directory connectors for both Windows 2000 domains can use the same Exchange site. Users from both domains can be created and authenticated in this site. The Lotus Notes directory also interfaces with Exchange, allowing the transfer of e-mail and user data.

CASE STUDY ANSWERS

4. A, C. Although you should be able to have a single point of management with Active Directory, it may be a while before certain connectors are created. Without these connectors, Active Directory will not be able to access and manage other directories, such as the one for Lotus Notes. Check carefully to find out about the availability and cost of connectors when you are planning an AD project using numerous directories.

5. See table.

Tampa Office Option
Convert to Exchange.
Minimize IT training costs.
Simplify upgrades and third-party compatibility.
Provide for greater ease of administration.
Provide easier messaging collaboration.
Maximize user efficiency (long term).
Remain on Lotus Notes and use a connector.
Minimize problems integrating Tampa users.
Minimize user training costs.
Maximize user efficiency (short term).

This really comes down to the age-old battle about forcing uniformity on the network. The question has nothing to do with whether Exchange is superior to Notes. Rather, it has to do with whether the IT staff will have to learn, support, upgrade, and troubleshoot one e-mail system or two. It also has to do with whether PI wants to annoy and possibly alienate staff in Tampa by coming in and making "unnecessary" changes to their environment. Long term, going with a single e-mail platform is almost certainly better for all involved, but in the short term, a connector may be the simplest and most politically expedient. It sure would be nice if network administration only involved understanding computers....

Chapter

10

Customizing the AD Schema

MICROSOFT EXAM OBJECTIVE COVERED IN THIS CHAPTER:

✓ Design a schema modification policy.

The standard AD schema that ships with Windows 2000 Server will probably be sufficient for most installations, but there might come a time when you need to add to or change the schema. Microsoft has included the ability to add new object classes, add new attributes to existing object classes, and disable object classes and attributes as needed. The goal is to create an AD database that is customized for the way in which a company does business.

Exam Hint: Although we have dedicated an entire chapter to this objective, the Microsoft MCSE exam does not test heavily on this subject. In reality, Microsoft does not expect many network administrators to modify the schema except through the installation of additional applications (those applications would automatically extend the schema to meet their needs). Although this is a low-priority objective, it does need to be covered (you just might see a question or two regarding schema customization). We've decided to add a bit of the mechanics of schema modification because you probably won't be exposed to it anywhere else in your MCSE studies.

Schema Basics

To review, the *schema* of the Active Directory database defines the objects that can be stored there. It is the formal definition of the object classes and attributes that exist in the database. The AD database is no different from any other database that you have worked with in the past. Before you can place information within it, you must lay out a structure to define how to store that data.

What's in a Schema?

Imagine that you were going to build a database to hold the telephone numbers and addresses of your business contacts. You wouldn't just start entering names and addresses, would you? The first step would be to decide exactly what information you would like to store. Your list might include the following:

- Company
- First name
- Last name
- Nickname
- Address
- City
- State
- Zip code
- Country
- Telephone number
- Pager/cellular phone number
- Fax number
- E-mail address

The next step would be to lay out the fields for each record, as shown in Table 10.1. You will need to decide the type of data each field will hold and the maximum size of each field, as well as add any special formatting requirements that are necessary for consistency.

TABLE 10.1 Contact Database Structure

Field	Type	Size (Characters)	Formatting
Company	Text	50	N/A
First name	Text	20	N/A

TABLE 10.1 Contact Database Structure *(continued)*

Field	Type	Size (Characters)	Formatting
Last name	Text	20	N/A
Nickname	Text	20	N/A
Address	Text	50	N/A
City	Text	25	N/A
State	Text	2	Should provide a pick list for consistent abbreviations
Zip code	Text	9	#####-####
Country	Text	2	Should provide a pick list for consistent abbreviations; use the two-letter abbreviations provided by the X.500 committee
Telephone number	Text	11	#-###-###-####
Fax number	Text	11	#-###-###-####
Pager/cellular phone number	Text	11	#-###-###-####
E-mail address	Text	25	username@domain_name

Once you have decided the structure of each record, you are ready to build your database—unless you decide to add a bit more functionality (to programmers, this is known as *feature creep*). You might also want to store records of each time you have been in touch with each of your contacts. You could do this by expanding the list in Table 10.1 to include a unique identifier, then using that unique field to relate to another database file. In the second file, you would then repeat the process of defining the fields that it would contain, as shown in Table 10.2.

TABLE 10.2   Related File

Field	Type	Size	Formatting	Related to
Unique ID	Numeric	3	N/A	Unique ID in contact list
Date	Date	N/A	US standard	N/A
Length of contact	Numeric	10	Number of minutes	N/A
Notes	Text	Variable length	N/A	N/A

The total description of your contacts database—including the description of each field, the relationships between files, any premade drop-down lists, and any other information about how the database is structured—is known as its *schema*. Every database has a schema, some more complex than others.

The Active Directory Schema

The schema of the Active Directory database is much more complex than that of our contact list database. Within the AD database, each different type of record defined is known as an *object class*. The fields, known as *attributes*, for each class might be different from those for other defined classes. The AD schema, for instance, must include definitions for the following database attributes:

Multiple record types in a single database   Traditional databases had one record type defined for each file in the related system of files. In the AD database, you must define a record type for each class of object that you wish to use in your environment.

Multivalue attributes   Certain characteristics of an object class need to store more than one value. A single user's telephone number attribute, for instance, might need to store multiple telephone numbers.

A definition of how the various pieces of the database fit together This is necessary due to the distributed nature of the AD database. Remember that this database is divided into partitions (domains), which are spread across multiple servers. Something in the schema must define how these partitions find each other, communicate, and share information as needed.

Attributes holding pointers to all other replicas of the same partition There might be multiple copies of a single partition; without these attributes, the replication of database changes could not take place.

A mechanism to track changes The replication process requires this of each object and each attribute of each object. This mechanism includes both the up-to-date vector and a time stamp.

Variable, rather than static, attribute lengths Some of the data that the database will hold might be textual and the database might grow quite large—over a million objects in a single partition. In other words, each record in the database should take up only as much disk space as necessary but should have the ability to grow as more information is added.

A hierarchy of object classes To reduce redundant design, the schema is built upon this hierarchy, with subordinate classes inheriting attributes from higher-level object classes.

To make matters even more complex, the Active Directory database schema must be fully—and easily— extensible so that it can grow to meet the changing needs of a dynamic business environment. In other words, the schema must be readily accessible so that changes to the database structure can be made. Make changes to the Active Directory schema by using the Active Directory Schema Manager included with Windows 2000 Server.

At the top of any LDAP-compliant directory service (such as Microsoft Active Directory), there is a special container known as rootDSE. When referring to this container, the appropriate syntax is to refer to LDAP:// rootDSE. The rootDSE container contains a number of entries, including the definition of the namespace of the LDAP structure and the schema of the database. The schema itself is stored in the subcontainer that follows this naming context:

```
CN=schema, CN=configuration, DC=domain_name, DC=domain_
root
```

For our purposes, we don't really even have to know where the actual schema is stored—the tools provided by Microsoft will find it. But it is interesting to note that Microsoft has used the industry-standard location so that other LDAP-compliant directory services can communicate (and perhaps synchronize) with AD.

Who Can Modify the Schema?

To make changes to the schema, a user must be a member of the Schema Admins group. By default, the Administrator user account is a member of this group. Although you can add other user accounts to the Schema Admins group, due to the nature of the task—which is complex and has far-reaching consequences—most companies will probably stick with the default. Whoever is going to perform the tasks associated with schema management *must* be knowledgeable in all aspects of Active Directory, the physical infrastructure of the network, and the business processes of the company.

We cannot stress this enough—the person or persons who take responsibility for schema change management must understand the technical aspects of the process, the business needs of the company, and how the two can best be integrated. There will be times when a decision must be made—whether to modify the AD schema to add functionality or to create a separate database to manage information. Take, for instance, our example of the King Technologies contact database. In reality, much of the information that we discussed is already stored within the AD database—in a couple of different object classes. We could, for example, create a user object for each of our clients. Because user objects include attributes such as telephone numbers and addresses, it would seem that this solution might be a great way to utilize the AD database to fulfill a business need. Of course, there are a few problems with this approach—first and foremost is the fact that creating a user account for each client opens a series of security issues that we would have to deal with! In some cases, perhaps even most cases, you will see more real business benefits by creating a separate database rather than adding to or modifying the Active Directory schema.

What Can Be Modified?

When modifying the directory schema, you may perform the following tasks:

- Create new classes
- Modify existing classes
- Create new attributes
- Modify existing attributes
- Deactivate classes
- Deactivate attributes

WARNING When you modify the schema, you are making a change that impacts the structure of the Active Directory database. This is not something that should be done lightly! Before you modify the schema, Microsoft suggests that you review the existing schema to determine if an existing object class or attribute can fulfill your needs.

Modifying Existing Classes or Attributes

Once you have determined that no existing class or attribute will fit your needs, consider modifying the schema. If at all possible, try to modify an existing object or attribute rather than creating a new one.

A user object, for example, has many attributes that might not be applicable to your environment. There are numerous tabs filled with attributes for a user object. You will probably not use all of these attributes in your environment.

NOTE Changing a display name for an existing attribute is one of the least-intrusive ways to modify the schema to meet your needs.

If schema modification becomes an AD design issue, modify an existing object class if all you need are new attributes. User objects are probably the best example of this situation. Many companies will want to store specific information about users in the directory. Often the generic definition of a user will not contain the additional attributes necessary. If your users do a lot of traveling, for instance, you might want to add attributes that store travel preferences, such as airline frequent-flyer information or smoking/nonsmoking preferences.

Creating an Auxiliary Class

An *auxiliary class* is really just an extension of an existing object class. For example, you might have two types of users: permanent and temporary. Although the normal user object might be perfect for your permanent employees, you might wish to create an auxiliary class for your temporary workers. The auxiliary class temp workers would be based upon the user class; it would inherit all of the attributes of the user class but could be modified to fit your needs. Basically, an auxiliary class acts as a shortcut—rather than starting from scratch to create a new class, you can start with an existing set of attributes and work from there.

Adding New Classes and Attributes

Add new attributes when no existing attribute meets your needs or can be modified to meet your needs. This can be an extensive change to the directory database, and you should think carefully before you do it.

The most intrusive and potentially dangerous change is to add a new object class. You should take this action only when no other option will fit the needs of your environment.

Can Classes and Attributes Be Deleted?

There is no way to delete an object class or attribute that is in the schema. You can, however, *deactivate* either a class or an attribute. We'll discuss deactivation in the next section.

As you can see, there are numerous types of modifications that can be made to the Active Directory database. Although the process is straightforward (albeit *not* exactly easy), modifying the schema is not something that you should do without prior planning. Anytime you change the structure of a database, you risk damaging it—not something you want to happen to your network's directory!

Deactivating Classes and Attributes

Classes and attributes are never removed from the schema. Instead, they are deactivated and marked as unused. This prevents irreversible mistakes and improves performance by not forcing a time-consuming cleanup of removed items.

Deactivating an item is functionally the same as deleting it, but deactivation leaves you the option of reversing your action at a later date.

Here is what happens when you deactivate an object class or attribute:

- That object class or attribute is no longer replicated throughout the network or to the global catalog server.

- You may no longer create objects that are part of the deactivated class or enter data into the attribute. Attempts to do so will return the same error that would be returned if the class or attribute had never existed.

- When an attribute is deactivated, you may no longer use it in definitions of new object classes or add it to an existing class.

- Objects created prior to the deactivation remain in the AD database and will appear in the various tools. You may not, however, change attributes of them; your only real management option is to delete them.

- Deactivated object classes and attributes still appear in searches for two reasons:

    - You can search for the deactivated information in order to clean up your directory.

    - You might not have deleted those objects that were created before the deactivation (which means that you might need to search for them at some point).

- You cannot create new objects or attributes with the same name, LDAP display name, or object identifier. This rule is based on common sense because the deactivated object class or attribute is still defined in the schema.

We'll discuss object identifiers later in this chapter.

What *Cannot* Be Modified?

The bulleted list at the end of the preceding section seems to imply that you can make just about any type of change to the directory that you desire. For the most part, this assumption is true. There are, however, a few notable exceptions.

There are certain attributes and object classes that cannot be disabled or changed. Any attribute whose name begins with the word *system* cannot be changed. This allows Active Directory to protect those attributes that are critical to its functioning.

This rule also applies to object classes that you create. If at the time of creation you list *any* attribute as *system*, that attribute cannot be changed later.

Modifying the Schema

Earlier, you read about the concepts of multiple-master and single-master environments. Both *multiple master* and *single master* refer to the process used to replicate changes throughout a distributed replicated database. In a multiple-master environment, all copies of the database can accept changes and can replicate those changes to all other copies. In a single-master environment, such as the PDC/BDC relationship used in earlier versions of NT, only one copy of the database can accept changes, and the server that holds the writable copy (the primary domain controller) is responsible for replicating them to all other domain controllers.

Windows 2000 Server is a multiple-master environment when it comes to replicating changes to the information stored within the directory database, but it is a single-master environment when it comes to replicating changes to the schema. In other words, there is only one domain controller, known as the *schema master*, on which schema modifications can be made at any given time. In Active Directory, these single-master operations are known as *Flexible Single Master Operations (FSMOs)*. The domain controller that is acting as the schema master is also known as the *schema FSMO*.

The term *FSMO* (pronounced "fizzmo") has recently been replaced with *operations master,* but we included it here because a lot of the older Microsoft documentation will still use it.

What Happens When the Schema Is Modified?

When the schema is modified, there is a delay before the changes take effect. This delay is incurred because there are actually two copies of the schema:

- One in memory
- One in the Active Directory

When a modification is made, the change is written to the Active Directory database. Active Directory waits for five minutes after the schema update before it commits the changes to the copy in memory. The copy in memory, known as the *cache schema*, is the schema that is current.

The copy of the schema used by various system processes and threads is the one stored in memory. This means that approximately five minutes will pass between the time you stop making changes to the schema and the time those changes become apparent.

The reason that the time is approximate is that there might be processes running at the time of the change. Rather than replace the old schema with the new one (in memory), the old and new schemas coexist until all current processes have ended. All new processes are pointed to the new schema, but any running processes continue to use the old. This prevents the introduction of a new schema from corrupting an active process.

During this five-minute interval, you cannot add objects that use a new or modified class or attribute. In other words, you must wait until the update has completed before making use of your changes.

Preparing for Schema Modifications

There are four preliminary steps you must complete before you can proceed with the task of modifying the Active Directory schema:

1. Obtain an OID (Object Identifier) for each new class or attribute you intend to create.

2. Verify your membership in the Schema Admins group.

3. Install Active Directory Schema Manager.

4. Set Registry settings that allow schema modifications.

So far, we've discussed the process of making modifications to the directory as if it were a common administrative practice. As you'll see, this is far from the case!

Microsoft
Exam
Objective

Design a schema modification policy.

Obtaining Object Identifiers

Object Identifiers (OIDs) are globally unique object identifiers. By global, we mean that these identifiers are used to define objects and attributes as they are applied to *any* directory service, from Microsoft Active Directory to Novell Directory Services. OIDs are registered with the International Standards Organization (ISO) issuing agency. By having a central group control how object classes and attributes are implemented, the industry can avoid incompatible network directories.

OIDs uniquely define data elements, syntaxes, and various other parts of distributed applications. ISO-issued OIDs are used in many standard technologies, including Open Systems Interconnection (OSI) applications, X.500 directories, Simple Network Management Protocol (SNMP), and many other applications in which a unique identifier is important. Each object class and attribute must have a unique OID if it is to exist in the AD schema. OIDs are organized in a hierarchical structure managed by the ISO.

You probably won't need to understand the entire OID naming process, but it is important to know that the OID represents a treelike structure much like the container/subcontainer structure of AD.

Lightweight Directory Access Protocol (LDAP) is an important protocol used for accessing information in network directories, such as Microsoft Active Directory. LDAP applications use the ISO-issued OIDs to identify the objects and attributes that are available in *any* directory to which they connect. In other words, to be LDAP accessible, every object and attribute within a directory must have an OID. (The OID itself becomes an attribute of each object defined.)

As stated earlier, the International Standards Organization acts as the issuing agent for new OIDs. To create a new object class or attribute within the AD schema, the first step is to apply to the ISO for an OID. The OID will be expressed as a string of numbers delimited by decimals, such as 1.2.840.*xxxxxx.w.y.z*. Table 10.3 describes the purpose of each piece of our sample OID.

TABLE 10.3   Decoding OID 1.2.840.*xxxxxx.w.y.z*

Number	Represents
1	This value acts as the root of the ISO hierarchy.
2	American National Standards Institute (ANSI).
840	United States.
xxxxxx	The organization applying for the OID is given a unique identifier.
w	A location within the organization.
y	A division within the location.
z	A group within the division.

Verifying Membership in the Schema Admins Group

Before anyone attempts to make any schema modifications, verify that the person who will perform the procedure is a member of the Schema Admins group. By default, the only member of this group is the Administrator account. (The Administrator account is automatically made a member of the Administrators, Domain Admins, Domain Users, Enterprise Admins, and Schema Admins groups.) The default membership list, consisting of only the Administrator account, will be sufficient for most organizations.

Modifying the directory schema is not something that many people should be doing, and there should *never* be multiple people performing modifications simultaneously!

Installing Active Directory Schema Manager

Administrators do not modify the schema as a matter of course, so Microsoft has not installed the Active Directory Schema Manager utility as part of the standard Windows 2000 installation. Follow these steps to add this tool:

1. On the Run command, type **MMC** (for Microsoft Management Console). The MMC will appear, as shown in Figure 10.1.

FIGURE 10.1   Microsoft Management Console

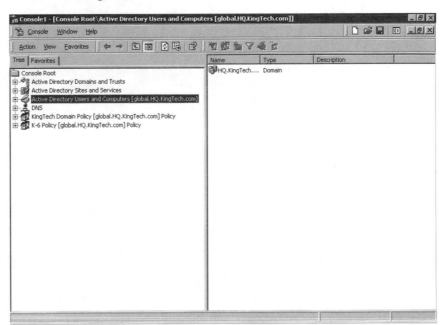

2. From the Console menu, choose Add/Remove Snap-in. The Add/Remove Snap-in dialog box, which you can see in Figure 10.2, will appear.

FIGURE 10.2 The Add/Remove Snap-in dialog box

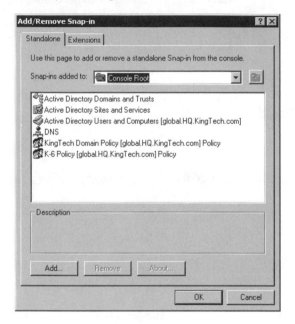

3. Click the Add button to access the Add Standalone Snap-in dialog box, shown in Figure 10.3.

FIGURE 10.3   The Add Standalone Snap-in dialog box

4. Highlight the Active Directory Schema Manager option and click Add.

 Notice that the Active Directory Schema Manager does not appear in our list in Figure 10.3. If you do not see an entry for Active Directory Schema in the Add Standalone Snap-in dialog box, you need to install the Schema Manager. The Schema Manager is part of the Windows 2000 Administration Tools Package in Add/Remove Programs in the Control Panel. The option pack is located on the Windows 2000 Server Installation CD as adminpak.msi.

5. Click Close, and the Active Directory Schema option will be added to your MMC.

The Active Directory Schema Manager utility must be connected to the current FSMO before modifications can take place. To ensure that the utility is pointing to the correct server, highlight the Active Directory Schema Manager option in the MMC, right-click, and choose Advanced. The Advanced Schema Manager Properties dialog box will appear. You can see this dialog box in Figure 10.4.

FIGURE 10.4 The Advanced Schema Manager Properties dialog box

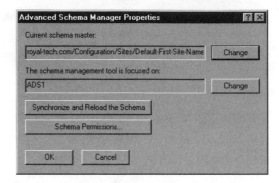

From here you can change the server that the Active Directory Schema Manager utility points to when making schema modifications. You can also access the dialog box used to set permissions to control which users and groups can perform certain functions in the AD database, as shown in Figure 10.5.

FIGURE 10.5 The Permissions for Schema dialog box

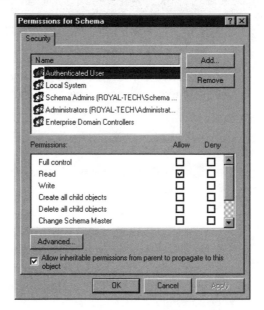

Here are the permissions available for the schema:

- Full Control
- Read
- Write
- Create All Child Objects
- Delete All Child Objects
- Change Schema Master
- Replicate Directory Changes
- Manage Replication Topology
- Synchronize Replication
- Update Schema Cache

The default permissions assignments are described in Table 10.4.

TABLE 10.4   Default Schema Permissions

User or Group	Permissions
Authenticated User	Read
Local System	All permissions
Schema Admins	All permissions except Full Control and Delete All Child Objects
Administrators	Replicate Directory Changes, Manage Replication Topology, Synchronize Replication
Enterprise Domain Controllers	Replicate Directory Changes, Manage Replication Topology, Synchronize Replication

Setting the Registry to Allow Schema Modifications

By default, all domain controllers have read-only access to the schema. To allow modifications, you must set a Registry setting on the domain controller that will act as the FSMO. The Registry parameter must be added to the Registry under the following key:

HKEY_Local_Machine\System\Current Control Set\ Services\ NTDS\Parameters

Add the parameter Schema Update Allowed with a data type of REG_DWORD. Set this value to anything other than 0 to enable modifications.

Only one domain controller can act as the FSMO, so setting this parameter in the Registry automatically promotes the current domain controller to the FSMO (and demotes the old one).

Because the Registry is a critical component of the Windows 2000 environment, be sure to back it up before making any changes. One wrong move and you'll end up having to reinstall NT because of a corrupted Registry!

The Five Types of Schema Modifications

As you read earlier, there are five types of modifications that you can make to the schema:

- Creating a new class
- Modifying an existing class
- Creating a new attribute
- Modifying an existing attribute
- Deactivating a class or attribute

The next few sections discuss the procedures for accomplishing each of these tasks. All of them are accomplished through the Active Directory Schema Manager (ADSM) snap-in to the MMC (discussed earlier in this chapter).

Creating a New Class

To create a new class, you create a *class-definition object*. In effect, this class-definition object becomes a container for the attributes that describe the object class. Within the ADSM utility, right-click the Class container and choose New ➢ Class. You will be presented with the Create New Class dialog box, shown in Figure 10.6.

FIGURE 10.6   The Create New Class dialog box

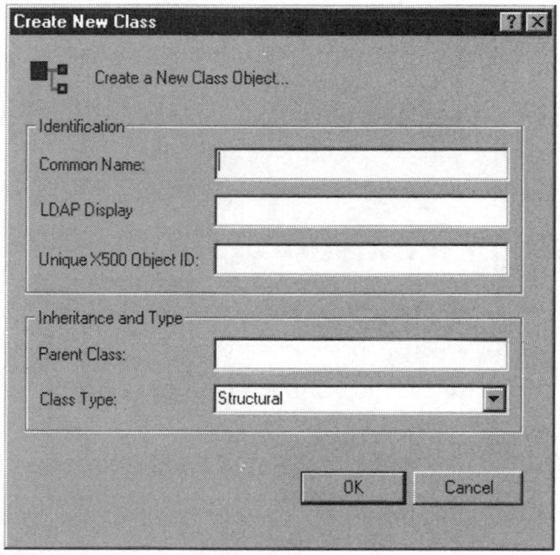

You will have to provide the following information:

Common Name   This field is mandatory and is used as the Common Name attribute for the object class. This is an indexed field; it is used for searches of the database.

LDAP Display   This is another mandatory field. LDAP tools will display the contents of this field to users when they access the directory.

Unique X500 Object ID   This is the OID you received from the ISO.

You will also have to determine whether the class you are creating should be a child to another class. Children inherit the attributes of their parents. This inheritance can be used to create a subtype of an object without having to apply for redundant OIDs or set up redundant attributes. An example would be our company's AD tree. Although we have "normal employees," we also have a subset known as "instructors." The instructors subclass inherits all of the properties of the user object class, but it also has attributes that are specific to the "instructor" type of user (vendor certifications, a list of courses taught, and so on).

There are also three types of classes:

Structural   Structural object classes are those from which AD objects can be created.

Abstract   Abstract object classes are templates used to build structural objects. An example of an abstract object class is the Top class. It contains all of the attributes that are mandatory for *every* other object class.

Auxiliary   Auxiliary objects are just lists of attributes that can be added to other object classes.

Modifying an Existing Class

To modify a class, expand the Class container within the ADSM. Right-click the appropriate class and choose Properties. You will see the class Properties dialog box shown in Figure 10.7

FIGURE 10.7   The class Properties dialog box

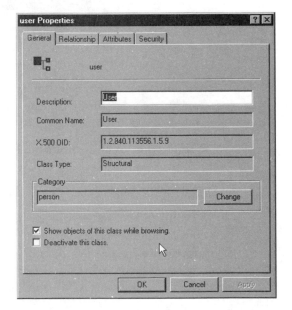

There are four tabs available:

- General

- Relationship

- Attributes

- Security

Each tab controls a different aspect of the object class.

Look back to Figure 10.7 to see the General tab. Here you can change items pertaining to how the class fits into the schema.

Figure 10.8 shows the Relationship tab. Here you can assign auxiliary object classes to this structural class.

FIGURE 10.8   The Relationship tab of the class Properties dialog box

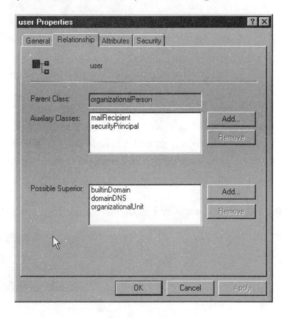

The Attributes tab is shown in Figure 10.9. Here you can add either mandatory or optional attributes to the object class.

FIGURE 10.9 The Attributes tab of the class Properties dialog box

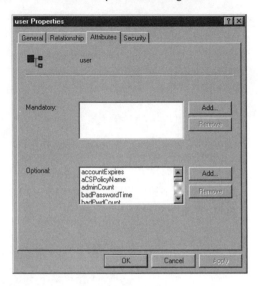

Finally, Figure 10.10 shows the Security tab. Here you can assign default permissions to this class of object. This can be useful if you need to apply special security to a class of objects but do not want to have to repeat the assignments each time you create an object. You might, for instance, want a certain type of object to be visible only to members of the Administrators group. By applying the permissions here, they would become the default for this class of object.

FIGURE 10.10 The Security tab of the class Properties dialog box

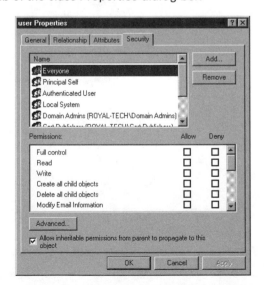

Creating a New Attribute

To create a new attribute, you create an *attribute-definition object*. The process is much like that of creating a new object class. Within the ADSM, right-click the Attributes container, then choose New ➤ Attribute. You will see the Create New Attribute dialog box, shown in Figure 10.11.

FIGURE 10.11 The Create New Attribute dialog box

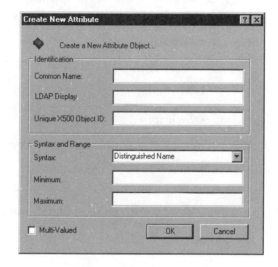

Here you enter the following information:

Common Name   This field becomes the Common Name attribute of the attribute.

Yes, attributes themselves have attributes—it can become confusing.

LDAP Display   This is the string that the LDAP utility will display to users when they access the directory.

Unique X500 Object ID   This is the OID you received from the ISO.

You must also configure the type of data that the attribute will hold. In the Syntax box, you will decide whether the property will hold a string of data, numeric data, a case-sensitive set of information, and so on. You may also set valid ranges for the data entered to avoid incorrect information. Finally, check the Multi-Valued box if the attribute will contain more than one value (such as the telephone number attribute).

Modifying an Existing Attribute

To modify an existing attribute, follow exactly the same process for modifying an existing object class, which was described earlier. Right-click the attribute and choose Properties. The same four tabs are available:

- General
- Relationship
- Attributes
- Security

These tabs offer the same set of configuration options offered for modifying an object class.

See "Modifying an Existing Class" earlier in this chapter for information about these tabs.

Deactivating Class or Attribute

In the ADSM, expand either the Class or the Attribute container, depending on what you want to deactivate. Within the container, find the item you wish to deactivate, right-click it, and choose Properties. On the General tab you will find a check box labeled Deactivate this <Class or Attribute>. Select this check box.

If you choose to deactivate an item that another object is dependent upon, AD will return an error describing the problem. This prevents you from deactivating an object that would interfere with the functionality of another class or attribute.

Considerations in Schema Management

So far, we've concentrated on the mechanics of schema management—the tools and techniques used to accomplish this task. Understanding how to accomplish a task, though, does not necessarily help you decide when it's appropriate to do so. Deciding whether or not to modify the AD schema is definitely something that should be considered during the design of any Active Directory environment. Although there are no explicit rules, there are a few suggestions that might help you make this choice.

Static Data Is Best

Because the AD database is replicated to multiple domain controllers within each domain, you must consider the impact of any schema modifications on replication traffic. The best information to store in the AD database will be static in nature. Things like telephone numbers, addresses, travel preferences—even items like insurance coverage—work well because they do not change on a regular basis. Avoid items such as inventory or price lists that change constantly.

Stand-Alone Facts Are Best

Don't add attributes or objects that require complex manipulation to make them useful. You wouldn't, for instance, want to add customer invoices to your AD database. Not only does this information change often, it must be related to multiple other items to be useful. With invoices, for example, you would have to relate the objects to client contacts, inventory, shipping, billing, and accounting functions. All of these relationships *are* possible, but there are probably more efficient ways to track such data.

Programming Might Be Required

To display objects and attributes in the management tools (specifically the MMC), you will have to write and maintain a snap-in that defines how your changes should be displayed. Although writing snap-ins is *supposed* to be fairly straightforward (we're not developers, so we can only guess), it is still programming. If you do not have someone with this skill on staff, you will have to outsource the effort—and that can eat up a large portion of your budget.

Make the Least-Intrusive Changes Possible

The most important suggestion (both in real life and for your exam) is to make the least-intrusive changes possible while still meeting the business needs of the environment. There is a definite order of preference for the types of changes that can be made:

1. If you can get by with changing the display name of an existing object class or attribute, do so! This is the least-dangerous type of change you can make and involves the fewest amount of change to the schema.

2. If existing attributes won't fulfill your need, then consider adding a new attribute to an existing object class.

3. If necessary, create an auxiliary class object, which is basically a copy of an existing object class with a new name. It is a fairly simple change to the schema—no new attributes or classes are defined.

4. As a last resort, define a whole new object class (complete with new attributes). This is the most dangerous change you can make!

Remember to make a complete backup of the AD database before attempting to modify the schema.

Design Scenario: Soft Shoe, Inc.

Your consulting firm has been hired to determine and implement solutions for a series of business needs for a nationwide distributor of designer shoes named Soft Shoe, Inc. You have been given a fairly complete description of its environment—both physical and business—and are required to make suggestions to meet a specific set of goals.

During your analysis of its network, you made the following notes:

- The network spans 5 locations, each of which acts as a central point of management for a region of the United States. The network supports a total of 750 users evenly spread out amongst the 5 facilities.

- The company has recently implemented Windows 2000 as its network operating system. It has 17 servers—3 in 4 of its locations and 5 at the corporate headquarters.

- It had an outside consulting firm perform an upgrade from Windows NT 4 to Windows 2000. The network consists of one domain, with domain controllers at each location. Network bandwidth does not appear to be an issue.

- The company has a small but competent IT staff.

- The company is currently using SQL Server databases to track inventory, sales, and account information and Exchange Server 5.5 as its messaging platform.

Your company has been given the task of accomplishing the following goals:

- The traveling sales staff is often rerouted unexpectedly. The local receptionist is responsible for making all travel changes. Soft Shoe, Inc. would like the travel preferences of traveling users to be available from any point on the network. This would include airline of preference and any frequent-flyer memberships, hotel of preference and any memberships, automobile rental preference and any memberships, and various other little facts such as window/isle or smoking/nonsmoking.

- The client would like to have a single repository for all customer contacts. This contact list should include some sort of automatic logging of customer communication.

- Each Soft Shoe employee is required to wear Soft Shoe brand shoes during any public appearance (during working hours). They would like to record the shoe size of each employee to ease distribution.

What, if any, schema changes would you recommend to Soft Shoe, Inc.?

Analyzing its business needs one at a time yields the following recommendations:

- Storing the travel preferences for the sales staff within the AD database is certainly feasible, but it is probably not the best solution for the customer. Given that the inclusion of so many new attributes would require multiple changes to the AD schema, the client would probably be better off creating a small database and replicating it throughout the WAN.

- Although we are not discussing the capabilities of Exchange Server 5.5, using Exchange Server 5.5 and Outlook can provide for a single repository for all customer contacts without resorting to schema modifications.

- Recommend that the client find an attribute of the user object class that they do not intend to use—such as the notes attribute. Mandate that this attribute be reserved for each user's shoe size. This allows you to store the information in AD without performing any schema modifications. (An industrious consultant would suggest that the display name be changed to Shoe Size and that an MMC snap-in be written to properly display this attribute's new name.)

Summary

Although you can make changes to the structure of the Active Directory database, this is not something you would do as part of the day-to-day administration of an AD environment. The modification process involves acquiring a valid OID for any new classes or attributes, and because it changes the schema, it could have a negative effect on your network—such as corrupting your AD database.

Microsoft offers the following suggestions for schema modifications:

- Modify the schema only when absolutely necessary.

- Use existing attributes when creating new object classes. This allows you to avoid the process of applying for numerous attribute OIDs.

- Avoid multivalued attributes as much as possible. Large attributes are costly to store (in terms of disk space) and to retrieve (in terms of network bandwidth) and therefore should be avoided.

- Use meaningful names for any new classes or attributes to avoid ambiguity.

At this point, we have really discussed the entire process involved in designing an Active Directory environment. In a real project, the next step would be to put your plan into action and start the rollout of your Windows 2000 servers. In the next chapter, we'll discuss the process of planning your Windows 2000 implementation with an eye toward avoiding potential problems and inconveniences for your users.

Key Terms

Before you take the exam, be sure you're familiar with the following terms:

attribute-definition object

attributes

auxiliary class

cache schema

class-definition object

Flexible Single Master Operations (FSMOs)

multiple master

object class

Object Identifiers (OIDs)

schema

schema FSMO

single master

Review Questions

1. Schema can best be described as _____ .

   A. The planning stage of operating system implementation

   B. The definition of a database design

   C. The plan used to control AD replication traffic

   D. The network security design

2. To modify the AD schema, a user must be a member of which of the following security groups?

   A. Domain Admins

   B. Forest Admins

   C. Schema Admins

   D. Tree Admins

3. At the top of any LDAP-compliant directory service (such as Microsoft Active Directory), there is a special container that contains a number of entries, including the definition of the namespace of the LDAP structure and the schema of the database. This container is referred to as _____ .

   A. HTTP://rootDSE

   B. FTP://rootDSE

   C. LDAP://rootDSE

   D. LDAP://SchemaDSE

4. Which of the following modifications can be made to the AD schema?

   A. Create a new class

   B. Modify an existing class

   C. Create new attributes

   D. Modify new attributes

   E. Delete an attribute

5. When a new object class is based upon an existing class of objects, what is the new object known as?

   A. A sub-class object

   B. An attribute object

   C. An auxiliary class object

   D. A pasted class object

6. The most drastic form of schema modification is to _____ .

   A. Create new classes

   B. Modify existing classes

   C. Create new attributes

   D. Modify existing attributes

   E. Deactivate classes

   F. Deactivate attributes

7. Which of the following actions take place when you deactivate an object class?

   A. That object class or attribute is no longer replicated throughout the network or to the global catalog server.

   B. You may no longer create objects that are part of the deactivated class or enter data into the attribute. Attempts to do so will return the same error that would be returned if the class or attribute had never existed.

   C. When an attribute is deactivated, you may no longer use it in definitions of new object classes or add it to an existing class.

   D. All instances of that object class are deleted from the AD database.

8. Object classes whose name begins with _____ cannot be modified.

    A. SYS

    B. Critical

    C. AD_SYSTEM

    D. SYSTEM

9. There are certain AD processes that can happen at only one server (either within a domain or within the entire forest). These processes are known as _____ .

    A. Single Server Operations (SSOs)

    B. Single Master Operations (SMOs)

    C. Fixed Server Operations (FSOs)

    D. Flexible Single Master Operations (FSMOs)

10. When the AD schema is modified, approximately _____ will pass between the time the change is made and the time the change takes effect.

    A. No time (The change is immediate.)

    B. 30 seconds

    C. 1 minute

    D. 5 minutes

11. Before modifications can be made to the schema, which of the following parameters must be added to the HKEY_Local_Machine\System\ Current Control Set\ Services\NTDS\Parameters Registry key?

    A. Schema Update = On

    B. Allow Schema Modify

    C. Schema Update Allowed = 1

    D. Allow Write to Schema

12. Place the following modification types in the order of preference.

   A. Changing the display name of an existing object class or attribute

   B. Adding a new attribute to an existing object class

   C. Defining a new object class

   D. Creating an auxiliary class object

Answers to Review Questions

1. B. The *schema* of the Active Directory database defines the objects that can be stored there. It is the formal definition of the object classes and attributes that exist in the database.

2. C. To make changes to the schema, a user must be a member of the Schema Admins group. By default, the Administrator user account is a member of this group.

3. C. At the top of any LDAP-compliant directory service (such as Microsoft Active Directory), there is a special container known as rootDSE. When referring to this container, the appropriate syntax is to refer to LDAP://rootDSE. The rootDSE container contains a number of entries, including the definition of the namespace of the LDAP structure and the schema of the database.

4. A, B, C, D. When modifying the directory schema, you may perform the following tasks: Create new classes, modify existing classes, create new attributes, modify existing attributes, deactivate classes, and deactivate attributes.

5. C. An auxiliary class is really just an extension of an existing object class.

6. A. The most intrusive and potentially dangerous change to the schema is to add a new object class. You should take this action only when no other option will fit the needs of your environment.

7. A, B, C. Deactivated object classes remain in the AD schema to ensure that data is not lost inadvertently. No class may be completely deleted from the schema once it is defined.

8. D. There are certain attributes and object classes that cannot be disabled or changed. Any attribute whose name begins with the word *system* cannot be changed. This allows Active Directory to protect those attributes that are critical to its functioning.

9. D . In Active Directory, single-master operations are known as Flexible Single Master Operations (FSMOs).

10. D . The time is approximate because there might be processes running at the time of the change. Rather than replace the old schema with the new one (in memory), the old and new schemas coexist until all current processes have ended. All new processes are pointed to the new schema, but any running processes continue to use the old. This prevents the introduction of a new schema from corrupting an active process.

11. C. Adding this entry removes the read-only attribute from the schema database. In reality, the value of this key can be set to any value other than 0 to allow modifications.

12. A, B, D, C. Always try to make the smallest change possible to the existing schema.

Case Study: Persistent Image, LLC

Take about 10 minutes to look over the information presented and then answer the questions at the end. In the testing room, you will have a limited amount of time—it is important that you learn to pick out the important information and ignore the "fluff."

Background

Overview   Persistent Image (PI) is a small company that teaches technical presenters how to properly present their companys' products. Although this is a niche market, PI has made a name for itself. It currently services more then 60 percent of the Fortune 500 companies and numerous overseas accounts.

CEO   "While we are not a large company in terms of employees, we do a lot of business with big companies. Basically, we are in the business of technical presentations. We offer three services to our customers—we can teach their internal staff how to design and deliver effective technical presentations, we can create the presentation for them and then teach their staff how to effectively deliver it, or we can write and deliver the presentations. Ninety percent of our business revolves around presentations for technical trade shows. Our staff spends a lot of time on the road, traveling from show to show and client to client."

CIO   "Since we don't really have a staff—we use contract instructors to present our seminars—we don't really have a lot of employees on our network. We do, however, support a lot of contractors who use our system sporadically—we provide e-mail, FTP sites, end-user applications (like Microsoft PowerPoint), and other peripheral support items as needed. Since most of our work is done across the Internet, security is a big concern."

CFO   "Most of our workers are contractors. We pay them for each job, so keeping track of who does what is critical! We also handle all travel arrangements and take care of billing our clients directly. We'd love to streamline the procurement of travel—I believe we could easily cut 30 percent of our total costs if we had a better handle on travel costs."

CASE STUDY

Current System

Network Operating System PI is currently using Windows 2000 Server and Active Directory as its network operating system. All company computers have been upgraded to Windows 2000 Professional. Contractors use their own computers to connect to the network, so PI has little control over the operating systems that they utilize. PI has a total of 52 staff employees and works with approximately 75 contractors. Each person has a corresponding user object within AD—including the contractors.

Windows 2000 Environment The Windows 2000 environment consists of one domain and two physical locations—Orlando and Minneapolis. Most of the administrative functions are handled in Minneapolis (such as accounting, sales, and marketing), and most of the production is handled in Orlando (such as Internet access, production of seminar materials, and management of the PI Web site).

User Programs Most administrative work is still done with a series of Excel spreadsheets and Word documents. In the early stages of the company, these tools were utilized to cut costs. Now they are beginning to add costs as management of the various documents uses more and more of the valuable time of the IT staff.

Internet Presence The company Web site—`www.persistent-image.com`—is divided into two areas, public and private. The public aspect is outsourced to a Web design firm in Orlando. The private area is managed by the staff in the Orlando office.

Current Issues

PI would like your consulting firm to look over its current network and suggest changes that will increase its efficiency and optimize its business processes. Gary and Bob, the founders of the company, are quite adept technically, but they do not have the time to perform an in-depth analysis of the company's needs. Because they both teach technical courses, however, they have handed you a complete description of PI's network and business models and have a specific set of goals in mind. You have two major goals: (1) Determine if the suggested solutions are feasible and reasonable. If there is a better way to accomplish a goal, you should present it to them. (2) Once you have determined the solution, you should detail an implementation plan for them. Based upon this information, PI will determine its course of action.

CASE STUDY

Goals

Travel Arrangements PI would like to shift the responsibility of travel arrangements from its own staff to that of a selected travel agency. The agency is willing if PI can make enough information available to them in a timely manner. All travel preferences for each internal and contract employee must be available at all times. If travel arrangements must be changed, there should be no delay caused by missing information.

Sales Staff The sales staff would like to build a shared client contact list but still have the ability to track customer contacts for the purpose of billing (and commissions).

Web Site PI has recently been given the contract to certify trainers for an outside training program. This means that PI will soon need to publish a schedule of courses on its Web site.

Considerations in Design

Security Because PI is a Web-based company, the two corporate offices both have direct connections to the Internet. Although this is necessary for its business, PI would like to ensure the highest level of security possible.

Fault Tolerance As mentioned earlier, travel preferences must be available at all times. It is not unusual for travel to be changed at the last minute.

Maintenance Although PI is in a technical field, its IT staff is small and overworked. Any solutions should be as maintenance free as possible.

Performance In general, performance is not an issue on the internal network. It is, however, important to preserve network bandwidth on PI's connections to the Internet.

Funding Funding is not an issue with PI. Like many technical companies, it is currently cash-rich and time-poor. To remain competitive, it must optimize its business practices.

Questions

1. Rank the following in order of importance to PI, from highest to lowest.

Objective	Objective
	Performance
	Security
	Availability
	Cost

2. You have proposed the following solution: Create a SQL database to track all travel preferences for each PI employee and consultant. Place this SQL database on a high-end server in Orlando and make it available through a secure Web browser–based application. Which of the following goals have you achieved?

   A. Management of information has been moved from separate documents to a central location.

   B. Data is available at all times.

   C. Travel arrangements are secure from unwanted access.

   D. Bandwidth is conserved for critical processes.

3. You have proposed the following solution: Extend the AD schema to include travel preference attributes for all users. Ensure that at least two domain controllers for the PI domain are located in each facility. Create a user account for the travel agency within the AD database and give that account the permission necessary to read these new attributes. Which of the following business goals have you accomplished?

   A. The travel information is available at all times.

   B. Network bandwidth usage has been optimized.

   C. Travel arrangements are secure from unwanted access.

   D. Costs have been controlled and ongoing maintenance has been minimized.

4. You need to propose a solution for securing PI's direct Internet links. PI is concerned about two issues: keeping its internal networks secure from outsiders and providing for secure communication between the offices. A previous consulting company recommended installing a firewall at each office. Which of the following best describes this solution?

   A. Solves both of PI's concerns

   B. Solves only the security concern

   C. Solves only the connectivity concern

   D. Solves neither of the concerns

5. You need to propose a solution for securing PI's direct Internet links. PI is concerned about two issues: keeping its internal networks secure from outsiders and providing for secure communication between the offices. A rival consulting company has recommended installing MS Proxy Server at each office and setting up a Microsoft Virtual Private Networking (VPN) connection between the sites. Which of the following best describes this solution?

   A. Solves both of PI's concerns

   B. Solves only the security concern

   C. Solves only the connectivity concern

   D. Solves neither of the concerns

6. You have been asked to reform PI's administrative system. Examine the following list of required tasks, and reorder them so as to provide for the best migration path.

Task	Task
	Train staff on how to use the new system.
	Discuss goals for the new system with management and staff.
	Back up old databases and files and remove them from the network.
	Examine current business processes.
	Create the new intranet system.
	Migrate all data to the new system and bring it online.

CASE STUDY

Answers

1. See table.

Objective
Security
Availability
Performance
Cost

Given the fact that most of the communication with staff utilizes the Internet, it is critical that the Internet connections be secure. Once they're secure, the next biggest issue is availability—user information must be available at all times. Performance comes in a distant third, and cost is barely an issue at all.

2. A, C. Although this solution might look good at first glance, it has certain limitations that must be considered. First, you have moved management of data from a series of Excel and Word documents to a single database. You have not, however, ensured that this database will be available at all times. If the Internet connection is down, then neither the Minneapolis office nor the outside travel agency will be able to access the information that it contains. Given the sophistication of Windows 2000 logon security, you can assume that the data is as secure as possible on the Internet. As far as bandwidth utilization goes, all access will have to cross a wide area link. This access will compete for bandwidth with other processes.

3. A, B, C. Because the travel preferences are now a part of the AD structure, this data is now available on each domain controller in the network—this provides a redundant copy in each location. Answer B would actually require more research—does data access produce more network traffic than AD replication? In general, though, you have more control over replication traffic, so it is usually the easiest to optimize. Because connections to the database will be made through an

NT logon, you can assume that the data is as secure as possible. The only goal you haven't achieved is that of controlled costs. Any changes to the schema will require a carefully designed implementation plan. You will also have to write a Microsoft Management Console snap-in and a custom application to access these new attributes.

4. B. The firewall is an excellent idea, but it is designed to protect the network from unauthorized access, not to provide secure access between sites.

5. A. It always hurts to admit that someone else had a good idea, but in this case, the competing consultant seems to have a pretty good idea. More important, this is a "Microsoft solution." In a Microsoft testing environment, nearly all correct answers will be accomplished using MS tools. Cisco- and Unix-based products generally need not apply.

6. See table.

Task
Examine current business processes.
Discuss goals for the new system with management and staff.
Create the new intranet system.
Train staff on how to use the new system.
Back up old databases and files and remove them from the network.
Migrate all data to the new system and bring it online

Your first objective should be to familiarize yourself with what the users need, what they like about the existing system, and what they would like to see improved. With this knowledge in hand, you can create a better system. After this, you will want to train the staff on how to use the new system, and once this is done, the old data can be brought in and the systems switched.

Chapter 11

Designing an Effective Rollout Plan

MICROSOFT EXAM OBJECTIVE COVERED IN THIS CHAPTER:

✓ Design an Active Directory implementation plan.

At this point in your design project, you should have a fairly good idea of what currently exists in your environment and what you would like your finished Active Directory structure to look like. You have poked and prodded, listened and suggested, monitored and analyzed every nook and cranny of the company. You should have an in-depth understanding of the following:

- The business management model in use

- The IT management model in use

- The network infrastructure

- The number of users, servers, and workstations

- The services currently being offered through the network

- The scope of the project

- How information and communication flow within the company

- How the IT department is structured, its personnel and their strengths and weaknesses, and the change-management processes currently in place

- The NT domain structure in place

- The types of containers you would like to create within AD

- How you plan to design your AD site boundaries to control bandwidth use on the network

- How you intend to manage the desktops within the network

- How you intend to connect to any foreign directories

- If any modifications to the AD schema will be required

The bottom line here is that you should now know more about the company as a whole than just about any employee (and that holds true whether you are an outside consultant or on staff). Most employees never know their company as well as you are now expected to. Once you are at this point, you need to consider the actual implementation of your AD design.

When you're planning the actual implementation of an upgrade or migration to Windows 2000, you'll often need to rely more upon your business sense than your technical skills. The reality is that all of the planning you have done up to this point has been to put together an ideal AD structure. Your job now is to decide the steps that will be taken to achieve this goal (or, as you'll see later in this chapter, a realistic version of your goal).

An Overview of Developing an Implementation Strategy

One of the most common mistakes made at this point in a design project is to lose sight of the goals of the process. Once the AD tree has been designed, the domain structure is agreed upon, the OUs have been planned, and all of the rest of the details have been worked out, many design engineers become engrossed in the technical details and forget to look at the big picture.

Before beginning to plan the implementation of an AD environment, it is best to reevaluate the reasons for the migration or upgrade. Review the interviews that were conducted during the analysis of the business needs, and if possible, interview key individuals again. Your objective here is to establish the overall goals of the migration. Many technologists will build a list of technical issues here: move to Windows 2000 to reduce the network traffic, or move to Active Directory because of the advances in policy management. In reality, technology itself is rarely enough of a reason to justify the expense and effort involved in a major upgrade. Your list should be made up of a series of business needs and proposed solutions, as shown in Table 11.1.

TABLE 11.1 Business Goals for the Move to Windows 2000

Business Goal	Windows 2000–Based Solution
Reduce connectivity costs and/or increase performance of the WAN.	Define AD site boundaries and set replication schedules to minimize the impact on wide area links.

TABLE 11.1   Business Goals for the Move to Windows 2000 *(continued)*

Business Goal	Windows 2000–Based Solution
Reduce desktop support costs.	Implement group policies to limit the amount of control users have over their desktop environment.
Decrease the overall IT administrative overhead.	Implement Active Directory to minimize the number of management arenas that exist.
Reduce network traffic overall.	Implement DDNS systemwide so that WINS can be removed from the system.
Reduce exposure to unwanted access to information.	Implement Windows 2000 security.
Control access to resources.	Implement Windows 2000 security.
Centralize management of application software.	Implement group policies to publish applications through Active Directory.
Improve security of confidential data.	Implement Windows 2000 encrypting file system.

Technology exists to meet business needs. If your list has needs that are not met or, worse, creates new business problems, then you will need to reevaluate the move to Windows 2000 or reevaluate the business needs of the company. In a successful design project, each business need will be met by some aspect of technology (or the redefinition of a business process).

Migration Considerations

Once you've determined that your proposed solution meets the business goals of the environment, you can begin to plan for the actual implementation. Here again, though, you will need to stop and evaluate another set of business needs—specifically, those needs that pertain to the process of migration. Your first list was really a set of goals to be achieved *by* the migration; this second list is a set of goals to be achieved *during* the process. You should build a table of these immediate goals and your proposed methods of achieving them, as shown in Table 11.2.

TABLE 11.2 Goals During Migration Process

Goal	Method
Minimize the impact of the migration on the business environment.	Servers should stay online during business hours; all upgrades and new installations will be implemented and tested during nonbusiness hours.
	A complete recovery plan will be in place and will be utilized in the event of lost productivity due to misconfiguration.
	All key servers will be migrated to new hardware so that the old server will be available in the event of problems.
	Group Policy changes will not be implemented until after the actual migration has been accomplished to avoid abrupt changes to the users' environment.
Security must be maintained throughout the process.	All changes will be tested in a lab environment before being implemented on the production system.
	Support personnel will monitor key access points (Internet connections, key files, etc.).
Minimize IT administrative overhead and intrusion into the workplace.	User accounts will be migrated (not re-created).
	Software distribution techniques will be used to minimize the number of visits to workstations.
Minimize immediate impact on users.	User accounts will be migrated, including security information, account restrictions, and passwords.

As you can see, Table 11.2 lists the possible pitfalls of any migration and the specific steps you intend to take to avoid them. Although this list will change from project to project, many of the same potential problems will occur in *any* major change to an IT environment.

Reevaluating Your AD Design

Once you have your list of business needs and a general list of technologies that will meet them, it is time to take another look at your proposed AD design. At this time, you need to determine if your proposed design will facilitate uses of technology to solve your business needs. To put this another way, compare your design with the business needs to ensure that they will be met. You would be surprised at the number of times the final suggestion does *not* fully meet the business needs of the environment! Taking the time to make this comparison at this point in the process helps to ensure that you do not implement a design that does not offer a complete business solution.

Once you have built your list of business needs and proposed solutions, it is often helpful to bring in an outside entity to look over your proposed Active Directory design. A disinterested party can often find flaws or alternative solutions that would not be apparent to someone who has worked on the project. There are many companies that offer this service—among them Persistent Image, the consulting firm of the authors.

You'll want to look at each portion of your proposed AD design with an eye on the business and migration goals that you have identified. You'll want to examine the following:

Current and planned domain structure   Windows NT 4 networks usually had more domains than are necessary in a Windows 2000 environment. You will need to plan for the consolidation of domains during your upgrade.

Plans for a single- or multi-tree design   Upgrading to single-tree AD design is much easier than upgrading to a multiple-tree forest environment. If your proposed design includes multiple AD trees, you will want to consider the long-term ramifications—if you need to merge the trees later, the only way to accomplish it is to restructure your entire organization.

Proposed site boundaries   Compare your proposed site strategy to the business goals of the migration. For example, if high availability is a goal, you will want to have multiple domain controllers at each site. Also, reevaluate your replication schedule to ensure that AD replication does not conflict with periods of high network usage.

Many companies use the migration to a new operating system as an excuse to upgrade WAN links. In this case, you will also want to compare the timing of the infrastructure upgrades with the schedule set for the overall upgrade process. If, for instance, you are given six months to upgrade to Windows 2000 but you expect the installation of new lines to take nine months, you will need to adjust your design accordingly (or pick up the pace of the WAN upgrades).

Administrative management model   At this point, it is a good idea to review your analysis of the IT management model—centralized or decentralized. Ensure that your proposed AD design is optimized for whichever model is in use.

Security strategies   Ensure that your proposed AD solution facilitates all of the security features that will need to be implemented. Also, define a migration plan that maintains security during the actual implementation process.

Recovery plans, both in the long and short term   Although a properly planned migration strategy should ensure that no problems are encountered, you should always have a plan for reversing the migration process if necessary. Your plan should include, at a minimum, a complete documentation of existing services and applications (of course, if you have been following the steps we have outlined in this book, you already have this documentation) and a complete backup of every server to tape, and Microsoft suggests that you find a BDC in each domain (or install a new one if none is available) that can be left offline during any upgrades. This ensures that your NT 4 SAM database is preserved intact.

Mixed vs. Native Mode

In an effort to preserve backward compatibility and to allow a more relaxed upgrade process, Microsoft has included components that allow a network to support both Windows 2000 and Windows NT 4 domain controllers working together within the same domain. Specifically, the first domain controller upgraded to Windows 2000 within a domain assumes the role of PDC emulator. Basically, the PDC emulator replaces the functionality of the original NT 4 PDC within the domain, replicating changes to the account database on all NT 4 BDCs still active in the domain. This allows for an incremental migration to Windows 2000—you can upgrade the PDC of your old NT 4 domain and then take your time upgrading the other NT 4 domain controllers to Windows 2000.

When a network is supporting domain controllers from multiple versions of Microsoft products (NT and Windows 2000), that network is said to be operating in *mixed mode*. Although this might sound like the perfect solution—especially for those companies with a limited upgrade budget, because it allows them to spread the costs of upgrading over a longer period of time—there are disadvantages to running in mixed mode. While in mixed mode operation, the domain cannot support universal or nested groups, and many of the advances made to group policies are not available.

Once all of the domain controllers within a domain have been upgraded to Windows 2000, Active Directory can be set to operate in *native mode*. An environment operating in native mode cannot have any Windows NT 4 domain controllers in operation. This allows the system to take full advantage of the features of Active Directory. The ultimate goal of any migration to Windows 2000 should be to move to native mode as soon as possible—either by upgrading all of the NT 4 domain controllers to Windows 2000 or by demoting them to member server status.

Technically, there is no easy way to demote a Windows NT 4 domain controller to member server status—Microsoft uses the word *demote* to soften the image. In reality, the only way to change an NT 4 domain controller into a member server is to reinstall NT 4.

Domain Upgrade Strategies

At this point, you have confirmed that your proposed Active Directory design is sound and that it will meet or exceed the business needs of the company. Now you need to consider each existing domain and the process that will be used to upgrade it to Windows 2000 and Active Directory.

Before we begin our discussion of upgrading domains, it is important that you understand the upgrade options available for your legacy NT servers. This information will impact your domain upgrade strategy and is, unfortunately, the kind of information that Microsoft traditionally tests on in the MCSE exams. Table 11.3 lists the upgrade paths available for older operating systems.

Operating systems that do not have a direct upgrade path to Windows 2000 can still be upgraded. You will have to upgrade them to an intermediate operating system that *does* have a direct path to Windows 2000. For instance, you could upgrade an NT 3.51 server to NT 4 and then upgrade the computer to Windows 2000 Server.

TABLE 11.3 Upgrade Paths Available for Windows NT Servers

Legacy Operating System	Can Upgrade to Windows 2000 Server	Can Upgrade to Windows 2000 Advanced Server
Windows NT 3.51	No	No
Windows NT 3.51 Advanced Server	No	No *Yes*
Windows NT 3.51 Workstation	Yes *No*	No
Windows NT 3.51 Server	No *Yes*	Yes *no*
Windows 95/98	Yes *No*	No

TABLE 11.3   Upgrade Paths Available for Windows NT Servers *(continued)*

Legacy Operating System	Can Upgrade to Windows 2000 Server	Can Upgrade to Windows 2000 Advanced Server
Windows NT 4 Workstation	No	No
Windows NT 4 Server	Yes	Yes *no*
Windows NT 4 Server Enterprise Edition	No	Yes

Exam Hint: Take a close look at Table 11.3. A few of the options are not what you would expect (for instance, NT 3.51 Server can upgrade to Windows 2000 Advanced Server but not Windows 2000 Server).

Designing an Upgrade Strategy

When upgrading an existing Windows NT environment, you will need to decide upon a strategy for upgrading your existing domain structure into your new Windows 2000 Active Directory domain structure. To create your plan, you will have to consider the following:

- The order in which domains will be upgraded

- The order in which servers will be upgraded

- When to move from a mixed- to a native-mode environment

- How many domain controllers will be required for each domain and at each site

You will also want to establish a checklist of actions to be taken after the upgrade to ensure that the process was successful.

Planning the Order of Domain Upgrades

Traditionally, the IT department was always the first area to be subjected to an upgrade. Given the fact that the user base in the IT department was usually the most technically savvy, they would work out any problems before the operating system was rolled out to end users. This philosophy of limiting the effect of changes to a select group was also applied to network operating systems. The first servers upgraded were often not mission critical. This reduced the effect of any problems on the productivity of the employees.

With Windows 2000, the rules change a bit. The first domain upgraded becomes the root domain for the forest. In other words, you must upgrade the most important domain *first* and then upgrade or restructure any additional domains. This does not mean that all servers within the domain must be upgraded immediately, but the PDC of what will be your root domain must be the first server in your new AD forest.

In general, you should upgrade your Windows NT account domains first because this provides the immediate benefit of management of user accounts through Active Directory. AD gives you much more latitude in the delegation of account administration, is much more scalable, and is able to support many more user accounts in a single domain than NT.

If you are not comfortable with the concept of account or resource domains, we suggest reading *Exam Notes: NT Server 4 in the Enterprise* (Sybex, 1999), by Robert King and Gary Govanus.

If you have multiple account domains, you will have to determine which should be upgraded first. Of course, the first one upgraded should be the domain that is going to act as your root domain. After that, though, there are a few guidelines to follow in choosing your order:

- Although you should have tested your upgrade process in a lab, it is still a smart idea to upgrade those domains to which you have easy physical access first. This ensures that you can easily implement your recovery plan without the delay of first traveling to the location of the domain controllers.

- Limit the impact of mistakes by upgrading the domain with the smallest number of accounts first. If you do have a problem, this will reduce the number of people affected.

- If you are going to merge or in some other way restructure domains, first upgrade those that will remain after the upgrade. Remember, if you intend to move users from one domain to another as part of your upgrade, the target domain needs to be in place *before* you move the accounts.

Once you have upgraded your account domains, the next step is to upgrade your resource domains. Because, by definition, resource domains do not contain user accounts, this should be a fairly straightforward process with little chance to make a negative impact on the workplace (famous last words if we ever heard them!). Here again, there are a few guidelines to help you choose the order of upgrade:

- Upgrade those domains in which AD-dependent applications are running. If, for instance, you plan to upgrade to Microsoft Exchange 2000 (an application that uses the AD database to store information) running on a server in a domain, then that resource domain should be among the first upgraded.

- Unlike user domains, you should upgrade large resource domains first. This gives you the immediate benefit of the many desktop-management features of Windows 2000.

- Once again, if you intend to restructure your domains, upgrade those that will remain after the upgrade is complete early in the process. Remember, you can't move a workstation into a domain unless the domain exists!

When you upgrade the first PDC in the first domain, that computer takes the roles of schema master, domain naming master, relative ID master, and infrastructure master for the root domain. Because this is, by definition, the first domain in the AD tree, it also assumes those roles (schema and domain naming masters) that are forestwide. For our discussion here, though, the most important role that the new AD server assumes is that of PDC emulator. This role allows the server to act as the PDC for any NT BDCs that are on the network. This role is so important that, if you upgrade a BDC first, it will assume the role of PDC emulator and the old PDC will be demoted.

When the Active Directory Installation Wizard is run, it installs all of the necessary components on the domain controller, such as the AD database and any protocols used in authentication (Kerberos v5, for example). The existing SAM is copied to the AD database, thus preserving user, group, and computer accounts. When a child domain is upgraded into an existing tree, transitive trusts are automatically created to the parent domain.

There is really no order of preference in upgrading the BDCs of the domain. The only consideration you will have to take into account is to ensure that any applications running on your BDCs are compatible with Windows 2000. If you have incompatible applications in use on your network, the correct Microsoft answer is to upgrade them to AD-enabled applications to take advantage of Windows 2000 capabilities. If this is not an option (either because no such version exists or because of lack of funding), you can move the applications to a member server so that all of the domain controllers can be upgraded to AD.

Exam Hint: Reread this section, "Planning the Order of Domain Upgrades." There are numerous rules to follow during an upgrade. Knowing these rules and suggestions will help when you are presented with a case study about upgrading an existing NT network!

Design Scenario: Kids First Toys

Kids First Toys is a national chain of retail stores specializing in educational toys for children. It has stores located in just about every major U.S. city, and each store is tied into a systemwide network. The primary purpose of the network is to facilitate inventory control—by ordering in bulk, Kids First can take advantage of large order discounts. From an administrative perspective, it has divided the U.S. into six regions: North Western, South Western, North Central, South Central, North Eastern, and South Eastern. Each region has at least one distribution center that controls inventory distribution for the region and houses regional management. Six major markets—New York, Atlanta, Chicago, Dallas, Seattle, and Los Angeles—have subregional distribution centers that distribute goods to the stores in their market.

The current network consists of Windows NT 4 servers, using Microsoft SQL Server for all company databases, Microsoft Exchange as the messaging platform, and Microsoft Internet Information Server for both its Internet Web site and its internal intranet. Each of the regional distribution centers is connected by T1 line to the corporate headquarters located in St. Paul, Minnesota. Each of the six subregional distribution centers is also directly connected to corporate headquarters and has a link to its regional center. All retail stores are connected to whichever distribution center ships to their location. The retail stores have 56K or faster dedicated lines. The company Exchange server is located in Atlanta and is scheduled to be upgraded to Exchange 2000 as part of this project.

The company's current Microsoft Windows NT 4 environment follows the single-master domain model. All user accounts are created and managed through the corporate domain in St. Paul. Each distribution center has at least one BDC for this domain to reduce the logon traffic on the T1 lines. No retail stores have servers locally—users log on to the network through the BDC located in the regional distribution center. Because of the small amount of traffic on the connections between the outlets and the distribution centers, this has not been considered a problem. Each distribution center (including the subregional ones) defines the boundaries for resource domains.

You must decide the order in which you will upgrade these domains to Windows 2000.

Although the overall network appears to be fairly complex, in reality, this is a straightforward upgrade project. There is only one account domain—St. Paul. Upgrade it first because it will become the root domain of your AD tree. If, after testing, you find no reason not to upgrade the BDCs located in each distribution center, upgrade them as soon as possible so that the domain can be configured to run in native mode. As for the resource domains, given that you haven't read the next section yet, upgrade the Atlanta resource domain first because it will be running an AD-aware application (Exchange 2000). After that, upgrade them based upon the number of resources in each domain, starting with the largest and working down.

Restructuring Domains

A domain upgrade maintains the existing domain structure, whereas a *domain restructure* is the process of redesigning your existing domains to match the business needs of your environment. Domain upgrades are the easiest and simplest form of migration, but domain restructuring allows for the creation of an environment that truly provides a business solution. Given the complex domain designs that were forced upon many networks due to the limitations of Windows NT 4, it is safe to assume that many of the migrations to Windows 2000 will include domain restructuring during implementation.

By the time you are ready to study for the Designing a Microsoft Windows 2000 Directory Services Infrastructure MCSE exam, you should already be familiar with the tools and techniques used to accomplish a domain restructure. For the exam, though, you will need to reinforce the rules of the game— what needs to be done to prepare (and in what order) to restructure, what can be accomplished, and what the results will be. You will also have to understand how domain security works in order to better plan a restructuring strategy.

Domain Security

The security systems of both Windows NT 4 and Windows 2000 rely upon *security identifiers* (SIDs) to determine which users or groups have permissions to resources. SIDs are domain-specific values that uniquely identify a security principal. Your user interface will display user-friendly names, such as Bking, but these names are mapped to the SID of the user for authentication purposes. During the logon process, users will identify themselves and provide whatever means of proof are necessary in the environment (the most common being a password, but many other types of proof can be used in Windows 2000). Once a user has proven their identity, the domain controller will return an *access token* to the user's workstation. This token contains the user's SID and the SIDs of any groups of which the user is a member.

For more information about other methods of identifying users, see *MCSE: Windows 2000 Network Security Design Study Guide*, by Gary Govanus and Robert King (Sybex, 2000).

When the user attempts to access a resource, the SIDs in the access token are compared with the SIDs in the resource's *access control list (ACL)* to determine if the user (or any groups of which the user is a member) has been granted permissions to the resource in question.

The process of using SIDs to authenticate to resources is fairly straightforward, but it does present a few problems when you are considering moving objects from one domain to another. Because the SID is domain specific (part of a user's SID is the domain SID for the domain in which the user exists), the SID generated for an object in one domain will not be valid for an object in another. In other words, if you were to move an object from one domain to another, the original SID would not be valid. In reality, the only way to move an object (such as a user) from one domain to another is to create a new object (thus generating a new SID) and then delete the old object. Unfortunately, this would result in a loss of permissions, because the ACL of resources would contain the old SID, not the new one. To eliminate this drawback to SID/ACL-based authentication, Active Directory security principal objects have an attribute not found in earlier Windows-based operating systems. Each security principal has the sIDHistory attribute. This attribute stores the former SIDs of restructured security principals. When a user attempts to authenticate to a resource, the sIDHistory information is also compared against the SIDs in the ACL. The sIDHistory information is automatically updated when an object is migrated from one domain to another. There is one caveat to the use of the sIDHistory attribute: it can be populated only in native-mode Windows domains. This means that the target domain (the domain to which the user is migrated) must be fully upgraded to Windows 2000 *before* any migration takes place.

Inter-Forest Restructuring

Inter-forest restructuring is the process of moving users, groups, and computer objects from either a Windows NT domain *or* a Windows 2000 domain in a separate AD forest to a new Windows 2000 domain. Figures 11.1 and 11.2 depict these two situations.

Inter-forest restructuring is a popular technique among consultants because it requires a new environment to act as the target for the moves. From an implementation perspective, this is the safest type of migration. In the event of problems, the old system is still up and available. You can easily reverse the migration process by unplugging the new servers and reattaching the old. You can then reevaluate your process and try again—all without even affecting productivity.

FIGURE 11.1 Moving accounts from NT to Active Directory

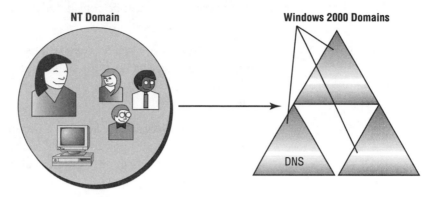

FIGURE 11.2 Moving accounts from one AD forest to another

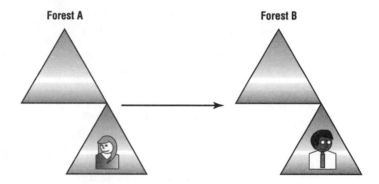

One popular method of migration is to create a complete AD forest in the lab, including all user, group, and computer accounts, and then cut and paste them into a production system. This approach allows for a complete test of the proposed AD design before it is implemented on the production network. Of course, this approach is also fairly expensive because you will need to have a fairly complete lab available. We've gone so far as to rent a lab from an education center (they usually have a few extra high-end computers that are used only for teaching resource-intensive applications), implementing and testing our design, and then cutting and pasting objects into our client's environment.

As with any other complex procedure, there are a few suggestions, requirements, and restrictions that must be considered before implementation. Here is a list of suggestions:

- Even though the original system will still be available after the restructuring, make a complete backup of the source environment before copying any objects. This way, an accidental deletion won't prevent you from reversing the process.

- Make a complete backup of the target environment *before* copying in new objects. This allows you to easily revert to the beginning of the process (without the hassle of re-creating any work configurations that you have already done).

- If you are combining multiple domains into a single Windows 2000 domain, back up the target after you finish copying in the objects from each source domain. Once again, this allows you to reverse your work back to a last-known-good status so you won't have to redo work that was successful the first time.

- If you wish to populate the sIDHistory attribute of the new accounts with its original SID, the target domain *must* be configured in native mode.

The requirements are as follows:

- The source domain controller's Registry must include the Registry entry HKEY_LOCAL_MACHINE\System\CurrentControlSet\ Control\LsaTcpipClientSupport: Reg_DWORD:0X1.

You must restart the domain controller after making this Registry edit.

- The user performing the restructuring operation must be a member of the Domain Admins group in the target domain and have administrative privileges in both the source and target domains.

- Account auditing *must* be enabled on both the source and target domains. (If the source is an NT 4 domain, you must enable both success and failure auditing of Group Management on the PDC.)

- Within the source domain, you must create a local group named *<source_domain_name>*$$$ (for example, Tampa$$$). This group should have no members.

And finally, there are some restrictions:

- The source domain controller must be either the PDC (in an NT 4 domain) or PDC emulator (in a Windows 2000 domain).

- All source objects must be security principals.

- The SID of the source object must be valid in the target domain. In other words, the SID must be unique. The SID must also not already be in use in the sIDHistory attribute of any existing object.

- Migration tools must be run on the target domain controller so physical access (or the ability to run the tools through a service such as Terminal Services) is possible.

The inter-forest migration strategy is the safest method of moving from a legacy NT environment or restructuring an existing Windows 2000 system. It is not only the preferred method used by consultants (because it reduces the risks involved in the process), it is also Microsoft's preferred method. If, on your MCSE exam, you are presented with a question in which an inter-forest restructuring is possible—it will be the correct Microsoft solution.

Intra-Forest Restructuring

Intra-forest restructuring involves moving security principals between domains within the same Active Directory forest. This type of restructuring will commonly be used by companies that are performing a two-phase migration to Windows 2000. In a two-phase migration, all legacy NT domains are first upgraded to Windows 2000. After this is accomplished, resource objects are moved from domain to domain to match the target AD design. Any unnecessary domains can then be eliminated and their servers migrated into an existing domain. This approach to migration offers the advantage of moving the entire company to Windows 2000 quickly—allowing the administrators and users to take advantage of the new features and benefits as soon as possible. Restructuring can then take place at a more leisurely pace.

Intra-forest restructuring might also take place if there are changes to the business environment. If, for instance, users need to move from one domain to another, perhaps because the company has been reorganized, the process of moving the objects will constitute intra-forest restructuring.

When you're performing any type of intra-forest restructuring, the only migration option available is a move. When an object is moved, a new object is created in the destination domain and the original object is deleted. Because this leaves no option for returning to your original configuration (putting the object back where it started), this form of restructuring is considered more of a risk than inter-forest structuring. Don't let this warning scare you, though—moving user objects from domain to domain within an AD forest is a normal part of Windows 2000 administration. It should, however, stress the importance of a good system recovery plan!

As with inter-forest restructuring, there are a few suggestions, requirements, and restrictions that must be considered before implementation.

The suggestions are as follows:

- Back up! Back up! Back up! Remember, the original object will be deleted after the new one is created (this is a move operation). If you are moving just a couple of users to a new domain, this is probably not a big issue, but if you are restructuring 1,000 users, you will want to be able to recover in the event of a problem.

- If available, it is a good idea to preserve a BDC of any domain that will be absorbed into Windows 2000 until you have determined that the restructuring process has been successful.

Here are the requirements:

- The target domain *must* be operating in native mode.

- The source domain controller's Registry must contain the entry HKEY_LOCAL_MACHINE\System\CurrentControlSet\Control\LsaTcpipClientSupport: REG_DWORD: 0X1.

- The user performing the move must have administrative privileges in both the source and target domains.

- Auditing must be enabled in both domains.

And the following restrictions apply:

- The source object cannot be a built-in account, such as the administrator account.

- The SID of the source object must not already exist in the target domain, including in the sIDHistory of any other security principal.

- You will use the Active Directory Migration Tool (ADMT) to perform the move. Administrative shares must be in existence on the computer upon which you run ADMT and on any computers upon which the ADMT must install an agent.

Restructuring Utilities

Although the Design exam does not test your ability to perform administrative tasks (that is tested in other MCSE examinations), it *does* test your ability to choose the right tool for the job. For that reason, we'll include a short description of the available domain restructuring utilities that are available. You should be aware of the function of each of the following tools:

- Active Directory Migration Tool (ADTM)

- ClonePrincipal

- Netdom

- Ldp

- MoveTree

Active Directory Migration Tool

ADMT is an MMC snap-in that allows both inter- and intra-forest restructuring through a graphical interface. Microsoft licensed the software from Mission Critical Software to facilitate the migration to Windows 2000. It includes a series of reporting functions (what is migrated, accounts referenced in ACLs, and any name conflicts that might occur), it populates the sIDHistory attribute, and it allows may of the operations to be reversed if a problem develops. It is available for download at the Microsoft Web site.

ClonePrincipal

ClonePrincipal is a series of Microsoft Visual Basic scripts that copy users and groups from a Windows NT 4 or Windows 2000 domain into a Windows 2000 native-mode domain. As such, it is used to populate the target domain in inter-forest structuring. You are not responsible for knowing the individual components that make up the scripts, but you should know that they are located on the Windows 2000 Server compact disc.

Netdom

Netdom is a command-line utility that is used to facilitate both intra- and inter-forest restructuring. Its primary use is to query a domain for a list of existing trusts and create new trust relationships automatically (when used in conjunction with an automated migration script).

Ldp

Ldp is a graphical utility that allows users to perform LDAP operations against any LDAP-compatible directory (such as Active Directory).

MoveTree

MoveTree is a command-line tool used to move objects—such as OUs, users, and groups—between domains within an AD forest (intra-forest restructuring). The target domain must be running in native mode.

Restructuring Strategy

Now that we have discussed the fundamentals of domain restructuring, we can begin our discussion of planning a restructuring strategy. At this point in the design process, you have a proposed domain structure in hand. You must now find the best way to implement that proposal—and therein lies the bulk of the Microsoft exam objective. *Best* is a relative term—what is best for one company might not be best for another. At the beginning of this chapter, we discussed reevaluating the business goals for the company—both the long-term goals *and* the short-term goals of the migration. You must now take those short-term migration goals and design a domain restructuring strategy that meets (or exceeds) them.

During your planning for the restructure process, you will need to perform the following:

- Determine what items need to be restructured.

- Determine the order in which domains should be restructured.

- Determine the order in which objects should be restructured.

- Choose a restructure method.

- Prepare the target domains.

- Test your results.

Determining What Items Need to Be Restructured

Because you have a model of what you would like your end result to look like, determining what changes have to occur should be a fairly straightforward process. Most of the time you will be reducing the number of domains during the migration process; legacy NT implementations often needed multiple domains to facilitate delegation of administration or to stay within the 40,000-object limit imposed upon NT account databases. With Windows 2000, and the large number of objects that the AD database can support (not to mention the ability to define AD sites to control replication traffic), most environments will require fewer domains than they did with earlier Microsoft networking products. Remember, the single-domain design will probably be the most common implementation. Do not create additional domains without justification.

Determining the Order in Which Domains Should Be Restructured

As we mentioned earlier, the first domain in an AD tree becomes the root domain. Because this domain defines the namespace of the tree, it is important that you consider your choice carefully. After that, many variables will come into play to determine the order in which domains should be upgraded or eliminated, including these:

- In most cases, account domains should be upgraded or eliminated before resource domains.

- If a particular group of users needs access to a feature of Windows 2000 (such as Group Policy objects), move them into a Windows 2000 domain early in the process.

- Many administrators prefer to experiment on a particular group of users (such as the IT department) before making changes to the rest of the user base.

- If you have an application that is not compatible with Windows 2000 running on an NT 4 domain controller, you might want to preserve that domain so that your Windows 2000 domains can run in native mode.

- Politics, as always, sometimes determines our course of action.

Determining the Order in Which Objects Should Be Restructured

Microsoft recommends the following order for migrating objects:

1. Restructure users and groups. This gives administrators the fastest access to the improved management capabilities of Windows 2000.

2. Restructure computer accounts. This allows administrators to begin using the software installation and management features of Windows 2000 quickly.

3. Restructure member servers. Because member servers do not hold a copy of the NT 4 accounts database, they can easily be moved from domain to domain. Migrating them before attempting to deal with domain controllers gives you experience (practice) before tackling the more intricate project of migrating domain controllers.

4. Move the domain controllers into the Windows 2000 domain.

Choosing a Restructure Method

There are two philosophies from which to choose when deciding upon the overall method of migration:

- Post upgrade
- Pristine install

Post Upgrade

The *post upgrade method* involves upgrading your legacy NT domains first and then shuffling your environment to match your proposed design. This method offers the benefit of Windows 2000 administration immediately, but it does entail some risk, and it can take longer to finish the overall migration with this method than with other methods. This method of migration is best used in the following situations:

- If a business need mandates a fast move to Windows 2000 to take advantage of one or more of its new features.

- If no new hardware will be purchased during the migration process.

- If the company expects to implement drastic changes to its internal organization in the near future. These changes should be severe enough to force major changes to business relationships, wide area links, or internal processes.

The major risk to using the post upgrade method of migration involves the fact that the environment is changed on a production system—any challenges that might develop can have a direct impact on the productivity of the business. Although a good recovery plan can alleviate many of these concerns, there is still a potential for unacceptable downtime.

Pristine Install

The *pristine installation method* involves creating a completely separate Windows 2000 Active Directory. This new system is usually implemented in a lab environment so that it can be adequately tested before implementation. Security principals can be migrated from your existing domains, or you can create new ones. This method offers the safest path to Windows 2000 because the old environment is never changed. If there are problems, the company can easily switch back to the legacy system and the process can be corrected. The major drawback to this migration method is cost—you must have enough equipment to implement a redundant domain structure. Many large firms utilize this form of migration to minimize the potential impact of the migration on their business. The pristine installation method of migration is best used in the following situations:

- When downtime due to the migration is unacceptable

- When funding is available for the additional hardware required

- When an immediate move to Windows 2000 is not mandated by business needs

Once again, the major advantage of the pristine installation method of migration is safety. The major drawback is cost. Most consultants will tend to suggest using the pristine installation method to reduce their liability if there are problems—everyone wants an "out" in the event of catastrophe.

Preparing the Target Domains

Before you can actually implement your AD design, there are certain issues that must be dealt with. Attention to detail during this preparation process can reduce problems during implementation. There are certain things you must do to prepare the target domains:

- Ensure that adequate hardware is in place to support Windows 2000 and Active Directory.

- Ensure that any namespaces you define will be unique.

- Ensure that DNS has been properly configured to support your new namespace.

- In the target domain (Windows 2000), ensure that OUs that are appropriate for your proposed design exist.

- Create an administrative transition plan that outlines the roles and responsibilities of each member of the IT department.

- Test your recovery plan in a lab environment, ensuring that you can re-create the existing environment in the event that something goes wrong.

Checking Your Results

After any restructuring has taken place, you will want to confirm the success of the process before eliminating any excess resources. You should test to ensure that security principals are functional and that their permissions are set correctly. Check group memberships. Check any applications to ensure that they are working properly and check your print environment.

When you have finished your test of the new environment, it is safe to decommission any domains that are no longer functional and reassign any remaining resources to your new environment.

One more time—Microsoft has recommended that you keep a domain controller from any decommissioned domain until you are satisfied that the migration process was successful!

Design Scenario: Royal Entertainment, Inc.

Royal Entertainment, Inc. is a national firm that sells and leases movies to local video rental outlets. It has a main office in Los Angeles, California, and regional distribution centers in Seattle, San Francisco, Dallas, Atlanta, Chicago, Minneapolis, Detroit, Boston, New York, Jacksonville, Orlando, and Cincinnati. Each of the regional offices is connected to the corporate headquarters by a T1 line with plenty of available bandwidth. All clients order inventory through a secure Web site (www.royal-entertainment.com), and all order processing is done at the regional distribution centers. The regional centers then order stock from the headquarters in California.

The current environment is configured following the complete trust domain model—each distribution center defines a domain and all domains have two-way trusts with all other domains. Each domain has been named after the city in which its office is located. Although Royal Entertainment wants to upgrade to Windows 2000, it has only a limited budget for the process. You have gotten the okay to purchase two new servers and, of course, any necessary software (and licenses).

Your proposed design includes only one domain, named Royal-Entertainment.com.

Describe your migration plan for Royal Entertainment, Inc.

Because you will want the root domain to be named Royal-Entertainment.com, and because you have the budget for a couple of new servers, rather than renaming and upgrading an existing domain, you should create a new domain on your new servers. Then upgrade each of the existing domains to Windows 2000, starting with the one that has the most user accounts. After all domains have been upgraded, move users from each of the regional domains to Royal-Entertainment.com, eliminating each of them as the objects are moved.

Designing to Reduce Impact

In every chapter of this book, we have stressed the importance of considering the business needs when making design decisions. In no other area is this as important as in the actual implementation of your design. A mistake made during implementation can bring an entire company to a halt. Bob has a sign hanging over his desk that reads, "Don't mess with the goose!" The sign reminds us of the importance of protecting our client's best interests—if they stop making money, we stop making money.

"Don't mess with the goose!" is a reference to the goose that lays the golden eggs—in this case, our "Golden Goose" is our client. Protecting the client's best interests is in *our* best interests!

We've all seen the math that goes into justifying the expense of a good backup strategy—take the average hourly salary times the number of employees and the result will equal the cost of an hour of downtime. We can take this a step further by calculating the lost revenue per hour of downtime and include that cost in our justification! This same cost analysis can be used to determine the cost of any downtime during your implementation of Windows 2000. Your goal during this process should be to minimize the impact of the migration upon the company's network, employees, and customers!

There are two distinct processes that can be involved in a migration to Windows 2000: upgrading domains and restructuring domains. Each of these processes can have an effect on the network. We'll look at methods to reduce these effects in the next couple of sections. From an exam perspective, you should be able to analyze a proposed solution to determine what its effect will be on the company's productivity. You should also be able to determine which migration strategy plans will have the least impact on productivity.

Controlling Impact During a Domain Upgrade

Any major change to an environment is bound to have some sort of impact. In the case of a domain upgrade, the impact can range from mild inconvenience (such as users calling to explain that something new has appeared on their screen) to catastrophic (such as an upgrade going sour and taking the data on the computer with it). This brings us back to the premise that our first responsibility is to set expectations. Many of the support calls that are generated by users during an upgrade can be avoided by providing information *before* changes are made.

Many years ago (more than we like to admit), we were involved in an upgrade from Novell 2.15 to Novell 3 (we know that this is a Microsoft-based book, but bear with us). Both versions of the Novell operating system had a tool known as Monitor. In both environments, the Monitor utility was often left on the server's screen because it provided useful information about the state of the server. Unfortunately, the Monitor interface was drastically changed in NetWare version 3—it now included a screen-saver "snake" that moved around the screen. After upgrading the servers, we left the office and went home, only to receive a frantic call about an hour later, "There's this thing on the server's screen moving around in a random manner! What did you guys do?" Had we bothered to provide a little information to the staff administrator, we could have avoided an after-hours phone call, but instead we were both paged, we both made a trip to the client site, and we both learned a valuable lesson.

The point of that old story is that the first rule for upgrades (or any type of change) is to anticipate problems and proactively prevent them. That's really the point of this entire chapter—the more issues you anticipate (and alleviate), the fewer problems you'll have to face after the upgrade. There are four major goals in an upgrade from Windows NT 4 to Windows 2000:

- Maintaining uninterrupted network services

- Maintaining security

- Maintaining the availability of applications

- Maintaining acceptable network performance

Failing to accomplish any one of these four goals can result in an upgrade process that is perceived as a failure. This might not be a literal truth, but we must remember that perception is often reality and a perception of failure can affect our future employability. We'll discuss each of the four goals in the next few sections. Once again, though, our discussion will stay at a fairly high level because they pertain to an AD implementation—knowledge of the installation, configuration, and management is prerequisite information.

Maintaining Uninterrupted Network Services

Windows NT 4 Server includes the ability to provide numerous network services through the operating system and add-on components. Many of these services were critical to a healthy NT network—some will still be important after you have upgraded to Windows 2000. Your upgrade strategy must ensure that all critical network services continue to function throughout (and after, if appropriate) the upgrade process. The following list includes some of the more important network services:

- DNS

- NetBIOS name resolution

- DHCP

- LAN Manager replication

- Remote access

- System policies

Each of these services will present a unique set of challenges during your implementation.

DNS

As we have mentioned before, Domain Name System (DNS) is a critical component of any Windows 2000 Active Directory environment. Windows 2000 uses DNS to locate network services, such as locating domain controllers during the logon process. In order for DNS to be used to find services, it must support SRV records, and unfortunately, the Windows NT 4 version of DNS does not! This means that it is imperative that your DNS services be migrated to a Windows 2000 server as soon as possible in the upgrade process.

Upgrading to Windows 2000 DNS is one way of providing support for SRV records. Because the use of SRV records is defined in an RFC, there are other implementations of DNS that will also suffice. But we are concerned with Microsoft solutions, so we can avoid complicating this issue with a discussion of them. For more information on third-party DNS solutions, see *Mastering Windows 2000 Server*, by Mark Minasi et al. (Sybex, 2000).

There are two methods of upgrading DNS to Windows 2000. The first and simplest method is to upgrade to Windows 2000 the Windows NT 4 server that currently acts as the master DNS server. Once it's upgraded, you can configure the zone to allow dynamic updates and you are set to go. The second method involves installing a new Windows 2000 server and configuring it to be a secondary DNS server for the existing zone. Once a zone transfer has occurred, you can then switch roles so that the new Windows 2000 server is the primary DNS server and configure it for dynamic updates.

There is actually a third option available for providing DNS support for a Windows 2000 environment, but it is a method that is not favored by many administrators. You *can* stay with the Windows NT version of DNS and add the appropriate SRV records to the zone file manually. Although NT 4 DNS services do not technically support SRV records, you can create them and queries for them will function. The problem, of course, is that if you choose this method, you will be forced to manage SRV records manually—a task that most administrators find onerous.

As you upgrade your NT domains, be aware that Windows 2000 Active Directory–enabled zones cannot be replicated between domains. If you need a zone to be hosted on DNS servers in other domains, you will have to configure those DNS zones to be secondary DNS zones.

Exam Hint: The bottom line is that DNS needs to be upgraded to Windows 2000 DNS services as soon as possible in the migration process.

NetBIOS Name Resolution

Windows NT 4 (and earlier) uses the Windows Internet Name Service (WINS) to resolve NetBIOS names into IP addresses. Although this service is not required in a Windows 2000 network, you need to ensure that no computers or applications are using it before you remove WINS from your environment. To determine if WINS is still required to support NetBIOS name resolution, you can track a few counters in Performance to see if it is still in use. The following counters are sufficient to check for uses of WINS:

Windows Internet Name Service Server: Total number of Registrations/ Sec   This is the total number of services that are registering with WINS each second. If this value is consistently zero, it is safe to assume that no WINS-dependent services still exist.

Windows Internet Name Service Server: Queries/Sec   This is the rate at which the WINS server is resolving NetBIOS names for client requests. Once again, a value of zero indicates that WINS is no longer being used.

DHCP

Because Active Directory requires TCP/IP, and because manually configuring TCP/IP addresses is inconvenient at best, it is likely that Dynamic Host Configuration Protocol (DHCP) will be utilized in most environments. Maintaining reliable DHCP services during a domain upgrade is not difficult, but it does require a little planning. The solution is to provide a backup DHCP server to renew leases that expire during the upgrade process.

Most upgrades will not be performed during normal business hours, so providing consistent DHCP services during the process will probably not be an issue in real-life implementations.

LAN Manager replication

In Windows NT 4, the LAN Manager replication (LMR) service is used to replicate logon scripts, system policies, and other types of data. In Windows 2000, this service has been replaced with the File Replication Service (FRS). The major difference between the two systems is that LAN Manager replication is a single-master replication scheme and Windows 2000's FRS is multi-master. In LMR, changes are made on the export server and replicated to import servers. In FRS, changes can be made at any domain controller and those changes will be replicated to all other domain controllers in the domain.

If you must live with a mixed (NT and Windows 2000) environment for a time, there are a couple of guidelines that can help to reduce the number of replication problems you will have:

- If the NT export server is the PDC, move the export services to another server in the domain. This allows the replication to continue to BDCs until the upgrade has been completed.

- The Windows 2000 Resource Kit contains a script file that builds a bridge between the export directory and the NetLogon share in Windows 2000. Basically, this allows files in the Windows 2000 NetLogon share to be replicated to the NT export server—allowing you to manage those files from a central location.

Remote Access

Windows NT 4 Routing and Remote Access Service (RRAS) is commonly used to provide users with dial-in access to the company network. After you upgrade an RRAS server to Windows 2000, it will continue to function as before. If, however, you have multiple RRAS servers and a mix of Windows NT and Windows 2000 servers acting as RRAS servers, you might encounter a few difficulties due to the different ways in which these two environments authenticate users to use RRAS services.

In NT 4, the RRAS service uses the LocalSystem account to log on and does so with NULL credentials (this means that the service logs on to the server without providing a username or password). By default, Active Directory does not allow a NULL session to access the attributes of objects. In other words, if a users dials in to an NT 4 RRAS server but is authenticated through a Windows 2000 server, the attempt to use dial-in services will be denied (RRAS won't be able to read the user's object to determine if they have permission to dial in). The only way to work around this issue is to ensure that the user authenticates through an NT BDC. Because there is no way to control which domain controller will authenticate a given logon attempt, it's best to use one of the following solutions:

- Upgrade all RRAS servers to Windows 2000.

- Place the RRAS service on NT BDCs. Users will then log on through the local account database.

System Policies

This is one of the more difficult (and often important) network services to control during an upgrade. The problem lies in the fact that NT 4 system policies are not migrated automatically during the upgrade. This is because system policies exist *only* as a file (Ntconfig.pol for NT clients), whereas Windows 2000 group policies are managed through Active Directory. In a mixed environment (NT and Windows 2000), if a client authenticates through an NT BDC, they will receive only NT system policies, and if they authenticate through a Windows 2000 domain controller, only AD group policies will apply. Also be aware that AD group policies can be applied only to Windows 2000 clients. If a user logs on at a computer running a legacy operating system but authenticates through a Windows 2000 domain controller, by default no policies will be applied. You can configure your environment to process both system policies and group policies, but this can get confusing if a user has had both applied to them.

Maintaining Security

This is probably the most far reaching of the potential problem areas in an upgrade. Almost every aspect of your security strategy will be affected by the move to Windows 2000, so you will have to plan carefully.

First the good news: Because both Windows NT 4 and Windows 2000 use access control lists (ACLs) to control access to resources, the upgrade to Windows 2000 should not affect your permissions structure. The upgrade process maintains the user and group SIDs (SIDs will change only if the object is moved to another domain, and even then the original SID will be preserved in the sIDHistory attribute if the target domain is running in native mode). Group memberships are also maintained, as are share and file permissions, Registry permissions, and trust relationships. Remember that the default trust configuration for Windows 2000 domains is that parent and child domains establish a two-way trust between themselves and that trusts are transitive. The upgrade process will convert any one-way trusts into two-way trusts automatically (if this is not what you desire, you will have to manually change them after the upgrade has completed).

Because all of the one-way trusts from your NT environment are automatically converted to two-way trusts by the upgrade process, you will have to review a few of your security strategies. Many administrators are concerned with this change to their environment. In reality, the two-way trusts and their transitive nature will not have any real effect on your security. What it does change, though, is your ability to place users from one domain into the ACLs of objects in all other domains. (The purpose of one-way trusts in NT 4 is to limit which users can be assigned permissions in which domains.) This means that you will have to carefully review the membership lists of each of your security groups to ensure that an incorrect addition has not been made.

Maintaining the Availability of Applications

The likelihood of an application being completely incompatible with Windows 2000 is extremely low. (So far, the only applications we've seen that wouldn't run on Windows 2000 were custom written—we've had great results with off-the-shelf software.) You should, however, test each server-based application in your lab before performing your domain upgrade. If for some reason an application will not run correctly on a Windows 2000 server, you should take action to correct the problem.

Check to see if an upgrade or service pack is available to fix the issue. Most application vendors have already released Windows 2000–compatible versions of their product (or they will soon). If no upgrade or fix is available (or will not be released in an acceptable amount of time), you might be wise to consider replacing the application with something that *is* Windows 2000 compatible.

That last statement might seem like we favor Windows 2000. Nothing could be further from the truth (we always try to suggest the best solution for our clients—no matter who makes it!). The truth of the matter, however, is that you (or your company) have made the decision to move to Windows 2000. If that is the case, it is in your best interest to work with Windows 2000–compatible software whenever possible.

If your application does not run on a Windows 2000 server, test the application on an NT 4 member server. Moving incompatible applications to member servers will allow you to switch your domain to native mode. You can then upgrade or replace the application in a more leisurely manner.

Maintaining Acceptable Network Performance

The key to maintaining acceptable network performance during (and after) an upgrade is to control network traffic. This is accomplished through proper placement of servers and an effective site boundary strategy. Careful planning of these issues will not only give you the best control of network traffic, it might actually decrease the amount of traffic on key networks to amounts below that generated in your Windows NT 4 network.

The first step is to define your AD sites as soon in the process as possible. After you have upgraded the first domain controller in your forest, define the sites you agreed upon earlier in the design process. Then as new servers are added to the system, they will automatically be placed in the appropriate site (remember, sites are tied to TPC/IP subnets, so as soon as you configure TCP/IP on the server, AD can decide which site the server should belong to). Implementing your site strategy early in the upgrade process will allow you to control when the domain data is initially replicated to new servers.

Another form of network traffic that needs to be controlled is traffic generated during client startup and authentication. Proper placement of Windows 2000 servers can help to keep this traffic off of your busy (and expensive) wide area links. The key to optimizing this traffic is to optimize the services that are involved. Placement of the following services can have a dramatic effect on network performance:

DHCP server   As each client initializes, it needs to receive an IP address (among other configuration parameters). These IP addresses will determine the AD site in which the client computer is located.

DNS server   As a client initializes, it obtains a list of available domain controllers by querying a DNS server for the appropriate SRV records. Those SRV records will direct a client to a domain controller within its own site if possible; if not, the process is completely random—with no control over which domain controller will be used for authentication.

Domain controller   The domain controller is accessed during the logon process. The most efficient placement of domain controllers allows users to be authenticated by a local server. Site membership is used to find local domain controllers.

Global catalog server   If the domain is configured in native mode, the domain controller will contact a global catalog server at logon to determine universal group membership.

If any of these services are not available locally, the result will be a failed authentication attempt, authentication over a wide area link, or authentication using cached credentials.

Microsoft recommends the following procedures for controlling authentication and initialization traffic:

- Deploy your site strategy as soon as the first PDC is upgraded to Windows 2000.

- Place a domain controller in each site that contains Active Directory clients.

- Place a global catalog server at each remote site.

- Provide WINS for legacy clients (until all clients have been upgraded).

Exam Hint: The list of suggestions for controlling authentication and initialization traffic will help solve many of the deployment questions found in the MCSE exam!

Documenting Your Plan

Microsoft *Exam* *Objective*	**Design an Active Directory implementation plan.**

This last objective is really a review of the entire design process up to this point. You'll want to document each of the steps outlined in earlier chapters and create an implementation plan based upon that information. When you are done, you should have a document that can be both used as a guide to implementation *and* presented to management to justify the time involved in an upgrade, the budget needed to implement, and even the business needs that an upgrade will fulfill. As consultants, we have created many of these documents—they help us sell our services. If you are a staff employee, this document can help both before the upgrade (providing justification for the upgrade) and after (acting as documentation of what was agreed upon). Your biggest challenge will be to remember that nontechnical personnel will probably end up reading this document (or portions of it, anyway). You must begin this document as you would any other business plan and not discuss technical details until the business needs and proposed solutions have been laid out.

Bob says, "I've taken a few business classes, and although most of the stuff didn't stick, the one thing I really tried to learn was the format for creating a business plan. Using this format to 'sell' our services has really opened doors for us. Most of the time we begin by talking to the IT department, but any large project will include discussions with upper management, and although they don't often understand the technical ramifications of what we do, they can always understand the business needs that we address."

There are two types of information that need to be included in your overall implementation plans: administrative and technical. Each has its purpose in the overall scheme of implementation.

Administrative Documentation

The administrative documents should describe any aspects of project management that would be considered business administration. This is the portion of your documentation that any manager should be able to read and understand—no matter what their technical level.

Mission Statement

Every good business proposal starts with a mission statement. The mission statement should, in broad terms, define the goal of the project. A mission statement should also emphasize the value of the move to Windows 2000. Mission statements should be concise and to the point, such as the following example:

> *The mission of our project is to upgrade our environment to a cost-effective, highly efficient operating system that meets the needs of our customers—reliable, efficient, stable, and easy to administer.*

Scope

The mission statement should be accompanied by documentation of the scope of the project. The scope of the project defines the beginning and end points of the project itself; here is an example:

> *The scope of our project is to investigate Windows 2000 and Active Directory to determine if they meet the qualifications put forth by our mission statement.*

Of course, you project might include more responsibilities:

> *The scope of our project is to design, implement, and configure a Windows 2000 Active Directory structure that meets or exceeds the criteria put forth in our mission statement.*

Notice the difference between the two statements? In the first, you are *not* responsible for creating an AD design or installing Windows 2000. In the second, you are responsible for every aspect of a migration to Windows 2000. Explicitly defining the limits and responsibilities of your project in a concise statement can help to both set expectations and reduce problems later. There is nothing worse than hearing someone in upper management say, "We never approved the actual purchase of Windows 2000 Server—you were just supposed to report back to us after you looked it over."

Budget Issues

You must also give an estimate of the total costs of the project. Although this is a preliminary set of figures, you need to be as accurate as possible. You will have to include the costs of a number of items:

- Hardware purchases
- Hardware upgrades
- Software purchases
- Employee salaries
- Communication costs
- Any outside consultants that might be required

Staffing

Your documentation should also include a complete list of the personnel you will need for the project, the level of their involvement, the amount of time they will be involved, and a description of their responsibilities. If you are using employees (as opposed to outside consultants), you should also include a description of their current responsibilities, who they currently report to, and what specific skills they possess that are required on the design team. If possible, provide two or three choices from different departments for each team position. This helps to avoid stripping a department of all of its technical personnel.

Communication

You should include a complete description of your plans for keeping upper management informed of the progress and problems being faced by the design team. Some companies prefer that all e-mail be cc'ed to someone in upper management, whereas others like a monthly report of project status.

Whatever communication strategy is agreed upon, live up to it! It is easier to justify additional time or dollars later if you have kept upper management apprised of your situation.

Technical Documentation

The technical documentation will grow as you move through the project. By the time you are ready to begin implementation, it should include the following:

- A complete description of the network infrastructure

- A complete description of the business analysis

- A complete description of the current IT environment

- A gap analysis (a list of the differences between what is currently in place and what will be required for a successful migration)

- A risk analysis that outlines that potential risks involved in each phase of implementation

- A complete description of your testing procedures

- A plan for a pilot rollout in a controlled environment

In fact, every piece of information that we have suggested you gather throughout the design process should end up in your documentation.

Many administrators use the final document as a piece of their résumé. It outlines their ability to analyze a business, suggest a solution, and implement a plan.

Summary

The point of this chapter was to utilize all of the information gathered in earlier phases of the design process to create an implementation plan that meets the business needs of the target company. Remember that there are two sets of needs that must be considered—business goals for after the migration and business needs during the process of migration. The former defines what you want to accomplish; the latter defines any limitations that might impact the path you choose to get there.

Well, that wraps up our discussion of designing an Active Directory structure. At this point in a real project, you would roll up your sleeves and start installing Windows 2000. Given that this book is designed to prepare you for both actual implementation *and* the MCSE test, your next move is to take the sample tests on the CD-ROM included with this book. Review this book a few times, and then take the test.

One last word of testing advice—*relax*! We've watched a lot of our students take tests over the years and have noticed that those people who come to a test relaxed and confident have a much better percentage of success then those who come in still trying to cram that last bit of information into their head. The Design tests are difficult, but not impossible. If you understand the concepts of a good design, you should do fine. Good luck from both of us—we hope we helped.

Key Terms

Before you take the exam, be sure you're familiar with the following terms:

access control list (ACL)

access token

domain restructure

inter-forest restructuring

intra-forest restructuring

mixed mode

native mode

post upgrade method

pristine installation method

security identifiers

Review Questions

1. A domain that supports both Windows 2000 and Windows NT domain controllers is said to be operating in _____ .

   A. Legacy mode

   B. Native mode

   C. Mixed mode

   D. Heterogeneous mode

2. A domain in which all domain controllers are running Windows 2000 *and* all features of Active Directory that are available is said to be running in _____ .

   A. Legacy mode

   B. Native mode

   C. Mixed mode

   D. Heterogeneous mode

3. You wish to upgrade a Windows 3.51 server to Windows 2000 Server. Which of the following will accomplish your goal?

   A. You must back up your data, format the hard disk, install Windows 2000, and recover your data from tape.

   B. Just run the upgrade wizard.

   C. First upgrade the 3.51 server to Windows NT 4, then upgrade to Windows 2000 Server.

   D. Run DCPROMO.EXE with the /351 switch.

4. You have decided to upgrade your desktop machine from Windows 98 to Windows 2000 Server. Which of the following will accomplish your goal?

   A. You must back up your data, format the hard disk, install Windows 2000, and recover your data from tape.

   B. Just run the upgrade wizard.

   C. First upgrade the 3.51 server to Windows NT 4, then upgrade to Windows 2000 Server.

   D. Run DCPROMO.EXE with the /Win98 switch.

5. The first domain controller upgraded to Windows 2000 defines
_____ .

    A. The version of Windows 2000 that will be maintained on all subsequent servers.

    B. Which domain will act as the root of the AD structure.

    C. The installation technique that will be used on all subsequent servers.

    D. Nothing—there is nothing special about the first upgrade.

6. Which of the following are suggestions for determining the order in which account domains will be upgraded to Windows 2000?

    A. Upgrade domains with small numbers of users first.

    B. Upgrade your largest domain first.

    C. Upgrade domains that will be eliminated after implementation early in the process.

    D. Upgrade domains that will be eliminated after the implementation later in the process.

7. Windows 2000 preserves permissions for objects that have been moved from one domain to another in which of the following ways?

    A. When an object is moved, a process is run that searches for the object's old SID in the ACL of all objects, replacing it with the object's new SID.

    B. The object's new SID is its old SID with the new domain identifier appended to the end, so all old security assignments will still work.

    C. Permissions are not preserved after a move operation.

    D. The object's old SID is placed in the sIDHistory attribute of the new object.

8. Inter-forest restructuring is _____ .

    A. The process of moving users, groups, or computer objects from either a Windows NT or Windows 2000 domain to another AD forest

    B. The process of moving users, groups, or computer objects from one domain to another within an AD forest

    C. The process of moving users, groups, or computer objects from one domain to another within an AD tree

    D. The process of moving users, groups, or computer objects from one OU to another in the same domain

9. Intra-forest restructuring is _____ .

    A. The process of moving users, groups, or computer objects from either a Windows NT or Windows 2000 domain to another AD forest

    B. The process of moving users, groups, or computer objects from one domain to another within an AD forest

    C. The process of moving users, groups, or computer objects from one domain to another within an AD tree

    D. The process of moving users, groups, or computer objects from one OU to another in the same domain

10. Which of the following are true about intra-forest domain processes?

    A. The target domain can be running in mixed or native mode.

    B. The user performing the move must have administrative privileges in both the source and target domains.

    C. Auditing must be enabled in both domains.

    D. You can move built-in accounts to facilitate customization.

(The answers to the questions begin on the next page.)

Answers to Review Questions

1. C. When a network is supporting domain controllers from multiple versions of Microsoft products (NT and Windows 2000), then that network is said to be operating in mixed mode.

2. B. An environment operating in native mode cannot have any Windows NT 4 domain controllers in operation. This allows the system to take full advantages of the features of Active Directory. The ultimate goal of any migration to Windows 2000 should be to move to native mode as soon as possible.

3. C. Because there is no direct upgrade available, you must first upgrade to an operating system that *does* have an upgrade path to Windows 2000 Server.

4. B. There is a direct upgrade available from Windows 95/98 to Windows 2000 Server.

5. B. The first domain upgraded becomes the root domain for the forest.

6. A, D. Upgrading small domains first limits the number of users who might be affected by mistakes, allowing you to refine your upgrade process on smaller groups of users. Upgrading domains that will be eliminated later in the process ensures that the target domains (where you will move objects) will be available.

7. D. During an authentication request, the ACL of the target resource is checked against the SID of the object requesting access. If this SID is not found in the ACL, the system will then perform this check with any SIDs in the sIDHistory attribute.

8. A. Inter-forest restructuring is the process of moving users, groups, and computer objects from either a Windows NT domain *or* a Windows 2000 domain in a separate AD forest to a new Windows 2000 domain.

9. B. Intra-forest restructuring involves moving security principals between domains within the same Active Directory forest.

10. B, C. The target domain must be in native mode, and built-in accounts cannot be moved from domain to domain (because each domain will have the same built-in accounts).

Case Study: Kodiak Wear

Take about 10 minutes to look over the information presented and then answer the questions at the end. In the testing room, you will have a limited amount of time—it is important that you learn to pick out the important information and ignore the "fluff."

Background

Overview   Kodiak Wear is a nationwide company that manufactures pet accessories. The company manufactures and sells training gear, a line of dog clothing, and miscellaneous other products for the discerning pet owner. The company headquarters is located in St. Paul, Minnesota. Kodiak Wear has recently merged with Feed Us Well, a manufacturer and distributor of special-needs dog foods. Both companies have developed a reputation for quality and value in their respective markets. Feed Us Well is stocked and sold by veterinarians across the country.

Kodiak Wear   Kodiak Wear has its headquarters in St. Paul; its manufacturing plants in White Bear Lake, Ladysmith, and Rolling Meadows; and its distribution centers in Chicago, Atlanta, Dallas, Reno, and Tampa.

Feed Us Well   Feed Us Well is headquartered in New Orleans; its manufacturing plants are in Denver, Seattle, Jacksonville; and its distribution centers are in New York, Los Angeles, and Detroit.

Problem Statement

CEO   "The high-end pet supply industry has grown by leaps and bounds as the baby boomers get older. While we don't foresee expanding into any new geographic areas, we do see our business continuing to grow with the market."

CIO   "Our existing network was designed before the Internet and Web access became the hot topic in business. We have 56Kbps lines to every Kodiak Wear facility and have just put 128 ISDN lines to every Feed Us Well location. We use VPNs on the Internet to connect each of our sites to the corporate headquarters here in St. Paul. The Feed Us Well locations are all directly connected to their headquarters in New Orleans, and that office is directly connected to our St. Paul office via a 256Kbps link. Most

CASE STUDY

of our links are currently running at more than 50-percent utilization, although that might change as we continue to merge the operations of the two companies."

Manufacturing Manager, Ladysmith "Staying in touch with the other sites is difficult. We pretty much manufacture to order, so I've got to be able to access order information from databases located in St. Paul, New Orleans, and each of the manufacturing sites. I'd love to see a central database of order, inventory, and sales data that I could use to plan my production runs."

CFO "Business has never been better! We do, however, see strong competition on the horizon from companies doing business on the Web. We've implemented a Web-based order system that allows retailers to access our inventory and place their orders online. We'd like to expand that to include the Feed Us Well line of products, since they have their foot in the valuable vet market."

Marketing Director "Since both companies have strong name recognition in the market, we'd like to be able to use both names after the upgrade. Right now, no one would buy dog food from someone at Kodiak Wear and no one would buy a doggy sweater from Feed Us Well—and our market research shows that changing those demographics would be extremely costly."

Customer Service Manager "Here at Kodiak Wear, we have a fairly static environment. Most of our customer service is in tracking ordering problems (either a lost order, an incorrect order, or an out-of-stock issue). At Feed Us Well, however, the customer support staff is constantly on the road talking to vets and retail stores. Those users are complaining that they can't get to their home resources from the Internet *or* when they sit down at a desk in one of our remote locations. I'd really love to have each salesperson's desktop follow them wherever they go."

IT Environment

Existing Operating Environment At this point in time, Kodiak Wear is a truly mixed environment—it has DOS/Windows, Windows 95/98, Windows NT Workstation, and even Macintosh clients. On the server side, it is currently using Unix to host its Web site and DNS services and Windows NT 4 servers for everything else.

CASE STUDY

DNS Issues   The version of DNS that is currently being used does not support SRV records.

Envisioned Operating Environment   Kodiak Wear would like to move to a Windows 2000–only environment (except for a few Macintosh computers that the people in marketing won't give up).

Network Operations Management

Overview   Kodiak Wear has a centralized administrative policy. There is a 24-7 help desk located in the corporate headquarters. Feed Us Well has always relied upon outside consultants for anything but minor technical issues. Each Feed Us Well facility has a dedicated IT employee who is responsible for supporting end-user issues and minor network administrative tasks. The goal is to move all of the IT support to the Kodiak Wear facility during the migration to Windows 2000.

Feed Us Well Network Management Needs   Because the user base in Feed Us Well is used to having on-site support, upper management is afraid that removing the on-site IT personnel will adversely affect productivity. They would like to continue to provide limited support on-site but remove their dependence on outside consultants (those tasks can be performed by the Kodiak IT staff).

Questions

1. Which two of the following recommendations would you suggest to Kodiak Wear?

    A. Replace the current DNS solution with Microsoft Active Directory–integrated DNS.

    B. Upgrade the 56Kbps links.

    C. Move to a decentralized IT management philosophy.

    D. Configure the internal network to use NetBIOS to increase security.

2. Which of the following would you propose?

   A. A single tree with the root domain named Kodiak.com.

   B. Build a forest with two trees—Kodiak.com and FeedUsWell.com.

   C. One tree with two branches, Kodiak and FeedUsWell. Each branch would represent a DNS zone.

   D. Name the root domain Kodiak.local and use outside DNS providers to access the company's public Web sites.

3. What would be the trust relationship between the Kodiak.com and FeedUsWell.com Active Directory trees?

   A. One-way trust.

   B. Two-way trust.

   C. Transitive trust.

   D. No trust would be established.

4. Which of the following best describes the Kodiak Wear forest *after* the upgrade?

   A. There will be one schema operations master, two RID managers, two PDC emulators, and one domain naming master.

   B. There will be one schema operations master, two RID masters, two PDC emulators, two infrastructure masters, and one domain naming master.

   C. There will be two schema operations masters, two RID masters, no PDC emulators, three infrastructure masters, and one domain naming master.

   D. There will be two schema operations masters, three RID masters, one PDC emulator, no infrastructure masters, and no domain naming master.

5. You are looking into using roaming profiles to allow users' settings to follow them. Determine whether each of the following objectives will be achieved through roaming profiles or whether another technology will be required. Note that not all objectives should be used because some fit neither option.

Options	Objectives
Can be accomplished using roaming profiles	Minimize LAN bandwidth usage.
Can be accomplished using RAS	Allow laptop users to access network resources while out of the office.
	Allow laptop users to browse Internet resources while out of the office.
	Allow users to have access to necessary shortcuts even when not at their own machine.
	Allow administrators to "lock down" user desktops.
	Allow users to take their network drive preferences with them.
	Allow laptop users to store Web pages locally for later use.

CASE STUDY

6. You have been given the project of upgrading both the Kodiak Wear and Feed Us Well networks to Windows 2000. Examine the following tasks and put them in the order that they should be performed to allow for a smooth transition.

Upgrade Path	Upgrade Path
	Upgrade BDCs in the Kodiak Wear domain to Windows 2000.
	Upgrade PDC in the Feed Us Well domain to a Windows 2000 domain.
	Configure all needed security and trust relationships between the domains.
	Upgrade all client machines to Windows 2000.
	Upgrade WAN links.
	Upgrade BDCs in the Feed Us Well domain to Windows 2000.
	Back up all machines that will be upgraded.
	Upgrade PDC in the Kodiak Wear domain to a Windows 2000 domain.
	Upgrade to Microsoft DNS.

Answers

1. A, B. Because the current DNS solution does not support SRV records, you will have to at least upgrade it to a later version. The best solution will be to move to Microsoft DNS to take advantage of other DNS benefits it supplies. Upgrading the 56Kbps links is indicated because they are currently running at better than 50-percent utilization.

2. B. Because both companies are currently managing their own Web sites, *and* because both companies are well known in their industry, it would be best to build an AD forest so that both companies can retain their own namespace.

3. B. The companies have merged and are continuing to consolidate management, so it would be best to provide access to both trees from either tree. This is also the default configuration in a forest, so no additional configuration will be needed after the upgrade.

4. A. Schema operations masters and domain naming masters are forest-wide roles (one per forest); RID masters and PDC emulators are domainwide roles (one per domain).

5. See table.

Options
Can be accomplished using roaming profiles
Allow users to take their network drive preferences with them.
Allow users to have access to necessary shortcuts even when not at their own machine.
Can be accomplished using RAS
Allow laptop users to access network resources while out of the office.
Allow laptop users to browse Internet resources while out of the office.

Roaming profiles are configured for the specific purpose of standardizing user desktops. Mandatory profiles are required for security, and either type of profile requires large amounts of data to be sent between the server and client during logon and logoff. RAS allows users to use a modem connection to access the network. The user's machine becomes a virtual part of the network, and they can access any network or Internet resources that they would be able to access in the office. RAS is not responsible for any sort of page caching or other offline access methods.

6. See table.

Upgrade Path
Upgrade WAN links.
Upgrade to Microsoft DNS.
Back up all machines that will be upgraded
Upgrade PDC in the Kodiak Wear domain to a Windows 2000 domain.
Upgrade PDC in the Feed Us Well domain to a Windows 2000 domain.
Configure all needed security and trust relationships between the domains.
Upgrade BDCs in the Kodiak Wear domain to Windows 2000.
Upgrade BDCs in the Feed Us Well domain to Windows 2000
Upgrade all client machines to Windows 2000.

Before any machines should be modified, the network infrastructure, including the WAN links and the DNS structure, should be upgraded to prepare for Windows 2000. Once this is done, you will want to upgrade the PDCs in each domain. Because it seems to be the central IT area, you will probably upgrade Kodiak Wear first so that it becomes the root tree of the new forest. Once both PDCs have been upgraded to Windows 2000, you should prepare any necessary trusts and other security. Other NT machines are compatible with Windows 2000, so the other NT domain controllers and the client machines can be converted as time permits.

Appendix

A

Practice Exam

1. Which of the following are valid Active Directory structural elements?

   A. Organizational units

   B. Domains

   C. Partitions

   D. Trees

2. Which of the following are used to define the boundaries of physical locations within the Active Directory environment?

   A. Locations

   B. Sites

   C. Facilities

   D. Domains

3. Company ABC has franchise locations in 15 cities. These facilities rely on ABC's IT staff for support of their internal networks. Which of the following classifications would best describe a franchise site?

   A. Corporate office

   B. Branch office

   C. Subsidiary office

   D. Information hub site

4. How many domains would you create for a manufacturing company that has 1 location, 250 users, and a limited budget?

   A. One

   B. Two

   C. Three

   D. One for each department

5. Which of the following are valid reasons for creating a multiple-tree environment?

    A. To control administrative privileges between departments

    B. To control network traffic between physical locations

    C. To support multiple namespaces

    D. When the AD environment will support multiple business entities

6. Which of the following is true of WINS?

    A. It is used for name resolution.

    B. It is not necessary in an environment that is made up strictly of Windows 2000 clients and Windows 2000–based applications.

    C. It is used for name registration.

    D. It resolves host names into IP addresses.

7. Company XYZ has offices in Minneapolis, Tampa, and Atlanta. Minneapolis and Tampa are connected by a 256Kbps link. Atlanta uses a dial-up connection to Tampa to access the company network. Which of the following scopes would apply to this environment?

    A. Simple

    B. Regional

    C. National

    D. International

8. Available bandwidth is best defined as _____ .

    A. The total bandwidth that the line is capable of carrying

    B. The amount of bandwidth available after current traffic has been accounted for

    C. How much bandwidth the connectivity provider is willing to sell you

    D. The cost per bit transferred on any given line

9. While interviewing staff members, you are told that the sales department is responsible for purchasing the next server out of their budget because it was their use of current resources that was driving the purchase. Which of the following business models would best describe this environment?

    A. Departmental

    B. Project based

    C. Product/service based

    D. Cost centers

10. Which of the following defines the phrase "business model"?

    A. A scale map of the location of resources within a facility

    B. The marketing strategy for a given product or service

    C. A description of the procedure used to manage the human resources database

    D. A definition of the management philosophy of a company

11. Buy From Us and We Sell It are two well-known companies that are in the process of merging. Both companies have been doing business successfully on the Internet for quite some time. Which of the following design strategies would be best for the AD structure?

    A. Your best design is probably a multiple-tree AD structure combined into a single forest.

    B. Your best design is probably a single AD tree with multiple NT domains.

    C. You should immediately merge the two Web sites into one, using the registered domain name of the larger company.

    D. You should design two AD trees with no consideration for interaction.

12. You are planning for the physical location of a database server. Which of the following should be taken into consideration for this decision?

    A. Which users will access the database

    B. Available bandwidth

    C. The hardware available for the server

    D. Training the personnel who will enter the data into the database

13. For a client with a low risk tolerance, which of the following migration strategies would be best?

    A. Initiate the implementation as quickly as possible to limit the time involved.

    B. Migrate to Windows 2000 in small steps.

    C. Migrate the PDC of all account domains immediately to take advantage of the management capabilities of Windows 2000.

    D. Do not migrate to Windows 2000.

14. After the analysis of your client's environment, you determine that they use a centralized IT management philosophy. Which of the following statements are true?

    A. The proposed AD structure will probably have numerous OUs.

    B. The proposed AD structure will have few OUs.

    C. You will need to design your AD structure to enable the delegation of IT responsibilities.

    D. You will need to design a training strategy for on-site support.

15. Covers, Inc. produces vinyl protective cases for various items—floppy disks, CD-ROMs, record albums, photographs, and so on. During your interviews with staff, you discovered that you couldn't get production information about the CD-ROM covers without talking to the production manager for CD-ROM covers. Which of the following business models would best describe this environment?

    A. Departmental

    B. Project based

    C. Product/service based

    D. Cost centers

16. How print drivers are maintained and updated is primarily an aspect of which of the following IT processes?

    A. Decision-making

    B. Centralized vs. decentralized management model

    C. Change-management

    D. Funding

17. The wide area link between Tampa and Orlando is currently running at 75-percent utilization. Which of the following statements are true?

    A. The line is overutilized and you should avoid placing more traffic on it.

    B. You need to upgrade the line immediately to avoid congestion.

    C. There is nothing to worry about—you can run at 75-percent utilization without problems.

    D. You need to determine what process is putting the traffic on the line.

18. The user account Sking is located in the Sales OU, which is within the KingTech.com domain of an Active Directory structure. Which of the following is the relative distinguished name of this object?

    A. CN=Sking.OU=Sales.O=KingTech.com

    B. CN=Sking

    C. CN=Sking, OU=Sales, DC=KingTech, DC=com

    D. Sking@KingTech.com

19. What is the suggested maximum number of zones that should be placed on a single Windows 2000 DNS server?

    A. 100

    B. 1,000

    C. 1 million

    D. There is no suggested limit.

20. Which of the following would be a properly formatted distinguished object name?

    A. CN=Sking\OU=Sales\O=Kingtech.com

    B. CN=Sking, OU=Sales, DC=Kingtech, DC=com

    C. DC=com, DC=Kingtech, OU=Sales, CN=Sking

    D. Sking@Kingtech.com

21. Which of the following server roles are forestwide?

    A. Schema master

    B. Domain naming master

    C. Infrastructure master

    D. PDC emulator

Answers to Practice Exam

1. A, B, D. Resource objects are organized into OUs, and OUs exist within domains. Domains are grouped into trees. See Chapter 6 for more information.

2. B. Sites are made up of a collection of IP subnets. All servers within a site should be well connected. See Chapter 7 for more information.

3. C. Subsidiary offices are not a part of the overall corporate resources. Usually, they will represent a partner company, a separate business division within the company, or franchise sites. The bottom line is that the corporate headquarters does not have complete control of the site. See Chapter 2 for more information.

4. A. This scenario is perfect for a single-domain environment—no WAN links, a small number of users, and a limited budget for domain controllers and other support peripherals. See Chapter 6 for more information.

5. C, D. Because all object names are derived from the name of the root domain, an AD tree defines a *single* namespace. You might also want separate trees if more than one distinct business will be involved in the structure. See Chapter 6 for more information.

6. A, B, C. Windows Internet Name Service is used to register and then resolve NetBIOS names into OU addresses. This function can be handled by DNS in an environment that is fully Windows 2000 based. Many students would believe that answer D, resolves host names into IP addresses, is also correct. With Microsoft questions, *never* read anything into them and never assume anything. The question only refers to the capabilities of WINS. When Microsoft DNS is configured to use the WINS database for resolution, DNS converts the host name into a NetBIOS name and submits it to WINS for resolution. The end result is that a host name is resolved, but WINS never receives it in host-name format! See Chapter 9 for more information.

7. C. The criteria for a national scope are different-speed dedicated lines (T1, 256K, 64K, etc.), dial-up connections, different network topologies (ATM, Frame Relay, etc.), different connectivity vendors, different hardware configurations (switches, routers, etc.), and different levels of available bandwidth. See Chapter 2 for more information.

8. B. Available bandwidth is the amount of bandwidth left after current traffic is accounted for. See Chapter 2 for more information.

9. D. Because a particular department is being "charged" for the expense of new hardware based upon their use of the current system, this is probably a cost center–based environment. See Chapter 2 for more information.

10. D. Business models define the relationships between groups within a company. See Chapter 2 for more information.

11. A. Whenever a merge occurs between two companies, you need to analyze the impact of changes to their environment or their existing customer relationships. In this case, because both companies have readily recognizable brand names, you should avoid changes without good reasons. See Chapter 6 for more information.

12. A, B, C. When planning for the placement of data sources, you must consider the network traffic that will be generated during access and the proximity of the data to the users who will actually access it. You must also consider the overhead that access will place on the server hosting the data source. See Chapter 2 for more information.

13. B. Although some people might argue for answer D, the Microsoft solution is to plan for a slow migration so as to limit potential problems. See Chapter 11 for more information.

14. B. In a centrally controlled IT environment, all IT decisions are made by a small group of individuals who are also responsible for implementation. Because there is less delegation of tasks, there are usually fewer OUs in the AD structure. See Chapter 6 for more information.

15. C. Given that there is a manager whose only responsibility seems to be managing CD-ROM cover production, you can assume that management is divided by product line. See Chapter 2 for more information.

16. C. Change-management refers to any updates, fixes, or other changes made to components of the IT environment. See Chapter 8 for more information.

17. D. Although this number *could* represent a problem, you will need to determine if this is a peak usage or if it is constant and what processes are placing this traffic on the wire. Without this knowledge, you cannot make any realistic assumptions about the line. See Chapter 2 for more information.

18. B. The *relative distinguished name* of any object is that portion of its name that uniquely identifies it in the container within which it resides. See Chapter 5 for more information.

19. B. Although placing more is possible, the additional overhead on the server would degrade server performance. See Chapter 5 for more information.

20. B. DNs identify the object by using its relative distinguished name and each of the containers to the top of the tree. Each component is separated with a comma. See Chapter 5 for more information.

21. A, B. There can be only one schema master and one domain naming master within an AD forest. See Chapter 7 for more information.

Case Study: Persistent Image

Take about 10 minutes to look over the information presented and then answer the questions at the end. In the testing room, you will have a limited amount of time—it is important that you learn to pick out the important information and ignore the "fluff."

Background

Persistent Image is a medium-sized provider of technical training supplies and services. The company creates course books, self-study books, and CD-ROM- and DVD-based training.

Persistent Image is in the process of acquiring Certified Users, a leading provider of online technical training. Certified Users has earned a reputation for providing quality training across the Internet but uses third-party materials. Persistent Image wishes to move into the online training market, and Certified Users would like access to consistent training materials. Both companies are looking forward to the merger.

As part of the merger, Persistent Image has decided to move both companies to a Windows 2000–based network.

Problem Statement

Persistent Image reports that support costs for its current network are too high. It also finds that there are too many people with administrative privileges. This problem stems from the time its network was created. The authors of the courseware all have technical backgrounds. In the early days of the company, before it had a dedicated IT staff, each of the authors would build whatever form of network they needed as a lab for their coursework. When the particular course was completed, the "lab" would be incorporated into the company network. At this point in time, just about every staff member has administrative privileges to some portion of the company network.

Persistent Image would like to incorporate Certified Users into its environment without forcing Certified Users to give up its autonomous management of its resources.

Organization

Headquarters   Persistent Image is headquartered in Orlando. All company-wide administrative staff work from this office: marketing, management, and IT staffs have offices there. The Orlando office has a total of 1,500 staff employees, all of whom use computers. There are also regional offices in Minneapolis, Denver, Dallas, and San Francisco.

Production Facilities   The company employs an additional 7,000 employees in 5 production facilities in the United States and another 750 in a facility in Mexico. Of these users, approximately 4,500 use computers. Each of the production facilities connects to the closest regional office by means of a 56Kbps line.

Persistent Image is opening offices in Europe. A sales office was recently opened in Paris. This facility connects to the Orlando office by means of a T1 line. The company is also planning to open manufacturing facilities in Europe.

Certified Users has an office in Tampa, with a total staff of 75 users.

Existing IT Environment

WAN   The WAN is designed as an extended start—each of the regional offices connects directly to Orlando, and each of the production facilities attaches to a regional office.

Client computers   All of the desktop client computers run Windows NT Workstation 4. The portable computers run Microsoft Windows, either 95 or 98.

Network   At this point, there are six Windows NT domains: one for Orlando, one each for the four regional offices, and one for the European facility. All domains trust all other domains in a complete mesh model.

For security reasons, management recently created a seventh domain named Persistent-Image.com. All of the intellectual property of the company is stored on servers within this domain. The Orlando IT staff is the only group that has administrative privileges to the Persistent-Image.com domain. They would like to use this domain as the root domain of their new Windows 2000 Active Directory environment.

Certified Users has one Windows NT 4 domain.

Network Roles   Persistent Image has begun to localize all IT support in the Orlando office. There are also IT staff members at each regional office who are responsible for lower-end support for their local office and any production facilities that are attached to it. The European office has one IT staff person who has little experience. Most of the support for Europe is taken care of through outside consultants. Given the specialized nature of Certified Users' industry, it has many high-tech employees on staff. It will continue to manage its own environment, but it will have access to the Persistent Image support staff as needed.

Envisioned IT Environment

WAN   Because current WAN bandwidth usage is minimal and there is plenty of available bandwidth, no changes to the current infrastructure are planned. The only addition will be a dedicated 256Kbps line to the Certified Users office in Tampa.

Network Roles   Persistent Image plans to centralize almost all IT support in two facilities: one in Orlando and another in Paris. It will continue to keep a small staff at each regional office, but their purpose will be limited to help desk–type issues—resetting passwords and account lockouts, maintaining printers and other devices, and application support.

Internet   Both Persistent Image and Certified Users have well-established Internet sites—Persistent-Image.com and CertifiedUsers.com, respectively.

Client Computers   Client computers will be upgraded to Windows 2000 Professional.

Questions

1. Which factors should you consider when designing the domain naming strategy for Persistent Image?

   A. The company has an Internet presence.

   B. Certified Users has an established Internet presence.

   C. Regional administrators will offer local support.

   D. The move into the European market.

2. You must design the site topology for Persistent Image. Which of the following will have the most impact on your decisions? (Choose two.)

   A. Available WAN bandwidth

   B. Current DNS implementation

   C. The location of the IT staff

   D. Number of locations

3. Certified Users should be able to administer its own resources after the upgrade to Windows 2000. Which of the following would be the best solution to accomplish this goal?

   A. (1) Create a domain for Certified Users, (2) create a Certified Users OU, (3) grant the Certified Users IT staff complete administrative control of its OU, and (4) move computer and user objects into the domain.

   B. (1) Create a separate OU for Certified Users, (2) locate this OU in the Persistent-Image.com domain, (3) grant the Certified Users administrators complete administrative control of its OU, and (4) move computer and user object into the OU.

   C. (1) Create a separate forest for Certified Users, (2) grant Certified Users complete administrative control of this forest, and (3) move computer and user objects into the forest.

   D. (1) Create two AD trees (one for Persistent Image and one for Certified Users), (2) tie the two AD trees into a forest, and (3) grant the IT staff of each company administrative privileges to their own tree.

4. Your design team is trying to decide if the European offices should be added to the Persistent Image Active Directory tree as an OU or as a domain. Which two of the following should be your main considerations?

   A. Available WAN bandwidth

   B. The proposed IT administrative plan for European facilities

   C. Geographic distances

   D. Expansion plans in the European market

5. In order to centralize Internet Web site administration, Persistent Image wants to host both the Persistent-Image.com and CertifiedUsers.com sites on the same machines. Which of the following options would make this possible?

   A. Host headers.

   B. URL redirection.

   C. Binding multiple IP addresses to the Web server.

   D. This cannot be done with Windows 2000. Only a Unix-based Web server has this capability.

6. Persistent Image has a number of existing domains that need to be upgraded and tied together with the move to Windows 2000. In what order would you recommend that the Persistent Image and Certified Users domains be upgraded?

Domains	Domains
	Regional Persistent Image offices
	European Persistent Image office
	Orlando Persistent Image office
	Persistent-Image.com domain
	Certified Users domain

CASE STUDY

7. In deciding to have a two-tiered network administration model, Persistent Image must define which regional office and production site administrative tasks need to be performed by local IT staffers and which are the responsibility of the central IT staff based in Orlando. Orlando staffers understand that they will need to work on-site at times, but they want to keep travel time to a minimum. Move the administrative tasks below to build a tree reflecting which IT group should perform a particular task.

Options	Tasks
Central IT staff responsibility	Plan Windows 2000 upgrade.
Local IT staff responsibility	Upgrade the domain controller to Windows 2000 Server.
	Manage WAN links.
	Install new desktop applications.
	Develop application standards.
	Deal with user account lockout and password problems.
	Create new user accounts.
	Install new network cards in client machines.
	Troubleshoot workstation hardware problems.
	Install service packs on server machines.
	Back up the server.
	Restore a crashed server from tape.
	Upgrade client machines to Windows 2000.

Answers

1. A, B. Because both companies have established Internet domains and both wish to keep their identities, you will need to consider these needs when creating a naming standard.

2. A, D. Site topology is generally concerned with traffic across wide area links.

3. D. Two separate AD trees would ensure that each company has control of its own resources, but creating a forest of them would allow shared resources.

4. A, D. Available bandwidth on an expensive trans-Atlantic wide area link will always be a design consideration. After that, the potential size of the environment (based upon projected expansion) will determine if an additional domain should be created.

5. A, C. Multi-hosting on Windows NT and Windows 2000 is very common and helps to consolidate updates and other Web tasks. Most modern browsers support host headers, which allow a machine to serve multiple DNS domains from a single IP address. Alternatively, multiple addresses can also be bound to a single network card, and each can host a separate site.

6. See table.

Domains
Persistent-Image.com domain
Orlando Persistent Image office
Regional Persistent Image offices
Certified Users domain
European Persistent Image office

Because it will be the root domain, the Persistent-Image.com domain must be first, after which upgrades probably should move from the center out. The upgrade of the Orlando headquarters first makes sense because most of the IT staff is there and they will be able to more easily monitor and troubleshoot any upgrade-related issues. After Orlando is stable, the regional offices can be brought in. The last two upgrades should be the new tree for Certified Users and the tricky upgrade of the European site. Because that site is just getting started and is very small, it is probably the lowest priority.

7. See table.

Options
Central IT staff responsibility
Restore a crashed server from tape.
Install service packs on server machines.
Create new user accounts.
Develop application standards.
Plan Windows 2000 upgrade.
Upgrade the domain controller to Windows 2000 Server.
Manage WAN links.
Local IT staff responsibility
Upgrade client machines to Windows 2000.
Back up the server.
Troubleshoot workstation hardware problems.
Install new network cards in client machines.
Install new desktop applications.
Deal with user account lockout and password problems.

Because travel between sites is to be kept to a minimum, day-to-day tasks should be assigned to local staff. These include dealing with all workstation issues, such as hardware and software problems. Local staff should also deal with most user support issues and daily tasks such as performing backups. The central IT staff, on the other hand, should deal with planning and initial network design, as well as most server support. Managing the WAN, upgrades, and disaster recovery all are issues that should involve the central IT staff.

Case Study: Show Trackers, Inc.

Take about 10 minutes to look over the information presented and then answer the questions at the end. In the testing room, you will have a limited amount of time—it is important that you learn to pick out the important information and ignore the "fluff."

Background

Show Trackers, Inc. is a national firm that specializes in providing registration and management services to trade shows across the United States. It has revolutionized the industry recently by adding smart cards to its services. Show attendees are issued a smart card that contains all of their relevant information on a small chip. The chip includes personal information (such as company specifics, addresses, and telephone numbers) as well as show-specific information (such as the schedule of events and any other information that might be relevant to the show's producers). The card can be read from a distance of up to 10 feet, so seminar attendance can be controlled without the congestion and confusion found in more traditional methods of attendee management. Once a customer has registered at any Show Trackers, Inc. production, their smart card can be used at any other show in which Show Trackers, Inc. is involved. Vendors attending a show are given a card reader that allows them to gather information regarding any attendee who stops at their booth or seminar.

Recent Partnership

Show Trackers, Inc. has recently partnered with a national marketing research firm, No Privacy Corp., to utilize the information gathered at the various shows to provide targeted lists for vendors. If, for instance, a customer were to attend a series of shows, the data describing which shows they attended, which hotel they stayed at, and even which vendors' booths they visited can easily be used to build an accurate profile of that customer's interests. These profiles, because they are so well defined, have the potential to become Show Trackers, Inc.'s biggest profit item.

The partnership with No Privacy requires that the two companies work together very closely. Although both companies will remain independent entities, they have decided to connect their IT resources into one large environment. This will make the exchange of data easier, more efficient, and more timely. The companies are so dedicated to this partnership that they have exchanged 25-percent ownership in each other; Show Trackers, Inc. owns 25 percent of No Privacy and vice versa.

Business Goals

Show Management   Show Trackers, Inc. wants to become an international show management firm. Currently, it provides management services for about 27 large trade shows a year in the United States, but it has had inquiries from trade shows in the European market.

Direct Marketing   Since it has included the smart card technology, Show Trackers, Inc. has been collecting data about both customers and vendors who attend each show. It recently ran a test mailing for a large networking convention held each year in Chicago. In exchange for 10 percent of any registrations it sold, Show Trackers, Inc. did a mass mailing to selected individuals based upon other shows that they had attended. Statistically, such a mailing should result in approximately a 3-percent "hit rate"— 3 percent of the recipients should register based upon the mailing. In its test, the hit rate was 12 percent with a 3-percent margin of error. In other words, the Show Trackers, Inc. mailing was approximately four times more effective than more traditional mailings.

New Facilities   Show Trackers, Inc., in conjunction with No Privacy, intends to continue to build its database of customer information by growing the show management side of the business. It has opened four regional offices in the United States, in addition to its corporate headquarters in Atlanta. It has also recently opened an administrative office in Frankfurt, Germany. This office is currently staffed by three salespeople and a receptionist.

Other Services   Show Trackers, Inc. expects to add quite a few new services over the next year or so. Some of these plans include providing an e-commerce site where show vendors can continue to sell products to show attendees online, a public database of show attendees, and automatically generated e-mail targeted to show attendees after the show has ended (these messages will be used to promote other shows and products being sold on the e-commerce site).

Current IT Environment

Show Trackers, Inc. Show Trackers, Inc. has an internal network that includes a small number of Windows NT 4 servers. In addition to hosting the company's messaging application (Microsoft Exchange Server 5.5) and its Web site (Microsoft Internet Information Server), these servers provide typical network services—DHCP, domain authentication, file, print, and WINS. The four new regional offices connect to Atlanta through a VPN over the Internet. The Frankfurt office has no real connection to the corporate network at this time. An RAS server has been installed in Atlanta, and Frankfurt dials in once a day to exchange e-mail and any files that need to be copied to either location.

No Privacy No Privacy has a medium-sized internal network located in its company headquarters in Chicago and is using Novell NetWare 4.*x* as its network operating system. It has only a few servers, but those servers store and manipulate large amounts of data. It has three IBM NetFinity 8500 servers that act as the database servers—running a large Oracle database on NetWare.

Domain Names Show Trackers has registered the DNS domain showtrack.com. No Privacy has registered the DNS domain nopriv.com. Neither company has established a strong presence on the Internet at this time. Both companies use an outside vendor to provide DNS services.

Envisioned IT Environment

Network Show Trackers, Inc. and No Privacy have decided to work together to build a network that can support their partnership. After doing some research, they have decided to rebuild using Windows 2000 and Active Directory. No Privacy will port its current Oracle database running on NetWare to an Oracle database running on Windows 2000 and will change messaging platforms to conform with Show Trackers' choice of Exchange Server.

Bandwidth They have ordered dedicated lines to Atlanta from each of the regional offices and No Privacy's headquarters. Because no one knows exactly what the bandwidth needs will be as they start to offer Internet services, each line has been leased with a bandwidth-on-demand option. Although this costs more than leasing a specific type of line (in most cases), their contract allows for each line to provide the equivalent of a T1 line if the demand warrants it.

Questions

1. Which of the following would you suggest to Show Trackers, Inc.?

   A. Create one AD domain and include all resources from both Show Trackers and No Privacy in it.

   B. Create two domains, forming one Active Directory tree. The root domain should be named showtrack.com and it should have one child domain named nopriv.com

   C. Create two domains, forming one Active Directory tree. The root domain should be named showtrack.com and it should have one child domain named nopriv.

   D. Create two AD trees. Name the root domains of these trees showtrack.com and nopriv.com. Tie the two trees into a single AD forest. The showtrack.com tree should have two domains: the root domain and a European domain.

2. You are designing a DNS strategy for Show Trackers, Inc. Which of the following would be the best solution?

   A. Continue using the outside vendor to provide DNS services.

   B. Install a copy of Unix and use its DNS services.

   C. Move to the Windows 2000 DNS service running in AD-integrated mode.

   D. Add DNS services to one of the new Windows 2000 servers and configure it to be a secondary server for the zone being managed by the outside vendor.

3. At a minimum, how many domain controllers should you install in this environment?

   A. 2

   B. 6

   C. 7

   D. 12

4. You are looking at how the VPN between the regional offices and Atlanta should be configured. Which of the following should be your primary concern?

   A. Transmission speed

   B. Security

   C. Authentication efficiency

   D. Ease of user access

5. Assuming that the Frankfurt office continues to grow, you may be asked to provide a more dependable and constant connection to the North American offices. Which of the following would provide a good combination of security, connection speed, and low cost?

   A. T1 leased line between Atlanta and Frankfurt

   B. 56K leased line between Atlanta and Frankfurt

   C. Dedicated dial-up connection between Frankfurt and Atlanta

   D. Dial-up to a Frankfurt ISP with a VPN connection to Atlanta

6. In order to transfer Show Trackers's DNS services from its outside vendor to its local network, a number of steps will need to be taken. Put the following steps into the order they need to be completed.

Tasks	Tasks
	Reconfigure all client machines to reflect the new DNS server.
	Request that the outside vendor remove the unused DNS information (and stop charging you for it!).
	Configure all needed DNS entries on the local server.
	Install local Windows 2000 DNS server.
	Request that the InterNIC entries for the primary and secondary DNS server for each domain be changed to the new DNS server's IP and host name.

CASE STUDY

7. You have been charged with developing a backup strategy for No Privacy's network. It has been determined that a full backup of the entire network will be performed each Friday night (Saturday at 1:00 AM), but due to the volume of data on the network, full backup of all data every night has been determined to be impractical. It has been decided that certain data will be scheduled to also be backed up nightly or hourly as needed. Build a tree and place each data type within its place in the tree by determining whether it should be backed up weekly, daily, or hourly.

Backup Options	Data Available on Network
Back up weekly	Customer data
Back up daily	Vendor data
Back up hourly	Corporate Web pages
	E-mail configuration files
	E-mail data files
	User configuration data (desktop profile information)
	User home directories
	Domain controller system files
	Active Directory information
	DNS, WINS, and DHCP server data files

Answers

1. D. Because both companies are to remain independent businesses, you will want to provide the best separation of resources while still maintaining the connection for sharing those resources. An AD forest with two AD trees is the best solution. Creating a European domain allows for easier growth into that market later.

2. C. DNS services are critical to the authentication process, so you will want DNS services that are local to the users. Moving to an AD-integrated design allows you to take advantage of all of the benefits of Microsoft's DNS implementation.

3. C. You will want to have at least one domain controller in the headquarters of both companies, a domain controller at each of the four regional offices, and one for the European domain.

4. B. When dealing with personal customer information such as the individual preferences reflected in the Show Trackers database, data security is of primary importance. The reason, of course, is twofold. First, people expect companies that collect this type data to protect it, and second, the information is the company's primary asset and has to be protected.

5. D. This is a tough decision, but phone connections between Europe and the U.S. are extremely expensive, as are leased lines. The best solution is therefore probably going to be a local dial-up to a Frankfurt ISP that leverages the Internet as its intercontinental backbone. Security shouldn't be an issue because VPNs are being used elsewhere on the network.

6. See table.

Tasks
Install local Windows 2000 DNS server.
Configure all needed DNS entries on the local server.
Request that the InterNIC entries for the primary and secondary DNS server for each domain be changed to the new DNS server's IP and host name.
Request that the outside vendor remove the unused DNS information (and stop charging you for it!).
Reconfigure all client machines to reflect the new DNS server.

Converting your DNS servers is actually a bit tricky, but if you are careful and give yourself time, it really isn't a problem. The first step is to install your new DNS server and duplicate all existing DNS information from the old server. Once the new server is available, you will need to change your Internet DNS records to reflect the new server. Once this change has occurred (it can take a couple of days), you can ask that the ISP discontinue serving your DNS information. Last, you probably will want to configure machines on the network to look to the local DNS server first, although this step is optional.

7. See table.

Backup Options
Back up weekly
DNS, WINS, and DHCP server data files
Domain controller system files
User configuration data (desktop profile information)
Back up daily
Active Directory information
User home directories
E-mail configuration files
Corporate Web pages
Back up hourly
Customer data
Vendor data
E-mail data files

Generally, application and system files don't change terribly often, and as such, a weekly backup of most files on the network is fine. Where this is not acceptable is where data is changing regularly, so your decision to back up more often should be based on looking at what is going to change and how important the safety of those changes is. There are three "mission-critical" network elements: the customer and vendor data and the corporate e-mail. These should be backed up as often as is practical. Other volatile files such as user home directory files and database configuration information should also be backed up nightly.

Appendix

B

Backing Up and Restoring Active Directory

Whenever one starts out to write a study aid for a professional certification exam, there is an ethical issue that must be considered. On the one hand, each of us knows the value of additional references to help us prepare for a tough test. On the other hand, though, is our concern over maintaining the value of our certification programs. If we provide all the answers, we achieve the goals for this manual, but we reduce the value of the overall certification.

We have both been certified technical instructors (for a variety of products) for quite some time. We both also feel that the true value of a certification program is the pertinent job skills that it provides. To write any kind of certification manual without covering those skills that are necessary in a real-world environment would be to ignore our responsibilities both as professional educators and as representatives of the MCSE program.

One of those critical job skills that *must* be covered in any Windows 2000 book is backing up and restoring your servers—both your valuable data and the AD database. In its first iteration of the course materials for its AD Design course, Microsoft included an entire chapter on backup and recovery. Based upon that course, our first table of contents for this book also included a chapter about backing up and restoring AD. As Microsoft refined the Windows 2000 course materials, that topic was moved to other courses and MCSE exams, and of course, we followed suit with our own materials.

Even though it isn't an actual test objective, backups are so important that both of us believed that this book should include a discussion of the process. Unfortunately, the goals of a study guide are well defined—cover the exam objectives only! A compromise was reached—we would include an appendix that covered the material.

The next step was to decide which of us would write it. Although we both thought it was important, we both were also neck deep in the actual chapters. In the end, we decided to include a section from another Sybex study guide: *MCSE: Windows 2000 Directory Services Administration Study Guide*, by Anil Desai (Sybex, 2000). Anil does a great job, both on this topic and in covering the Administrator's exam—we both give it two thumbs up! (Oh, and thanks Anil—we appreciate your help!)

Backup and Recovery of the Active Directory

If you have deployed the Active Directory in your network environment, there's a good chance that your users depend on it to function properly in order to do their jobs. From network authentications to file access to print and Web services, the Active Directory can be a mission-critical component of your business. Therefore, the importance of backing up the Active Directory data store should be evident.

There are several reasons to back up data, including the reasons that follow:

Protect against hardware failures   Computer hardware devices have finite lifetimes, and all hardware will eventually fail. Some types of failures, such as corrupted hard disk drives, can result in significant data loss.

Protect against accidental deletion or modification of data   Although the threat of hardware failures is very real, in most environments, mistakes in modifying or deleting data are much more common. For example, suppose a systems administrator accidentally deletes all of the objects within a specific OU. Clearly, it's very important to be able to retrieve this information from a backup.

Keep historical information   Users and systems administrators sometimes modify files but then later find that they require access to an older version of the file. Or, a file is accidentally deleted, but a user does not discover that fact until much later. By keeping backups over time, you can recover information from these prior backups when necessary.

Protect against malicious deletion or modification of data   Even in the most secure environments, it is conceivable that unauthorized users (or authorized ones with malicious intent!) could delete or modify information. In such cases, the loss of data might require valid backups from which to restore critical information.

Windows 2000 includes a Backup utility that is designed to back up operating system files and the Active Directory data store. It allows for basic backup functionality such as scheduling backup jobs and selecting which files to back up.

Figure B.1 shows the main screen for the Windows 2000 Backup utility.

FIGURE B.1 The main screen of the Windows 2000 Backup utility

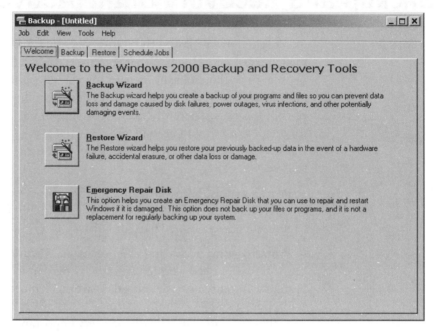

In this section, we'll look at the details of using the Windows 2000 Backup utility and how the Active Directory can be restored when problems do occur.

Overview of the Windows 2000 Backup Utility

Although the general purpose behind performing backup operations—protecting information—is straightforward, there are many different options that systems administrators must consider when determining the optimal backup and recovery scenario for their environment. Factors include what to back up, how often to back up, and when the backups should be performed.

In this section, we'll look at how the Windows 2000 Backup utility makes it easy to implement a backup plan for many network environments.

Although the Windows 2000 Backup utility provides the basic functionality required to back up your files, you may want to investigate third-party products that provide additional functionality. These applications can provide options for specific types of backups (such as those for Exchange Server and SQL Server), as well as Disaster Recovery options, networking functionality, centralized management, and support for more advanced hardware.

Backup Types

One of the most important issues when dealing with backups is keeping track of which files have been backed up and which files need to be backed up. Whenever a backup of a file is made, the Archive bit for the file is set. You can view the attributes of system files by right-clicking them and selecting Properties. By clicking Advanced, you will see the option File Is Ready for Archiving. Figure B.2 shows an example of the attributes for a file.

FIGURE B.2   Viewing the Archive attributes for a file

Although it is possible to back up all of the files in the file system during each backup operation, it's sometimes more convenient to back up only selected files (such as those that have changed since the last backup operation). There are several types of backups that can be performed:

Normal   *Normal backups* back up all of the selected files and then mark them as backed up. This option is usually used when a full system backup is made.

Copy   *Copy backups* back up all of the selected files but do not mark them as backed up. This is useful when you want to make additional backups of files to move off-site, when you want to make multiple copies of the same data, or for archival purposes.

Incremental   *Incremental backups* copy any selected files that are marked as ready for backup and then mark the files as backed up. When the next incremental backup is run, only the files that are not marked as having been backed up are stored. Incremental backups are used in conjunction with full (normal) backups. The general process is to make a full backup and then to make subsequent incremental backups. The benefit to this method is that only files that have changed since the last full or incremental backup will be stored. This can reduce backup times and disk or tape storage space requirements.

When recovering information from this type of backup method, a systems administrator will be required to first restore the full backup and then restore each of the incremental backups.

Differential   *Differential backups* are similar in purpose to incremental backups with one important exception: Differential backups copy all files that are marked for backup but do not mark the files as backed up. When restoring files in a situation that uses normal and differential backups, you only need to restore the normal backup and the latest differential backup.

Figure B.3 provides an example of the differences between the normal, incremental, and differential backup types.

Daily   *Daily backups* back up all files that have changed during the current day. This operation uses the file time/date stamps to determine which files should be backed up and does not mark the files as having been backed up.

Note that systems administrators might choose to combine normal, daily, incremental, and differential backup types as part of the same backup plan. In general, however, it is sufficient to use only one or two of these methods (for example, normal backups with incremental backups). If you require a combination of multiple backup types, be sure that you fully understand which types of files are being backed up. Figure B.4 shows the Backup Wizard's Type of Backup screen.

FIGURE B.3 Differences between the normal, incremental, and differential backup types

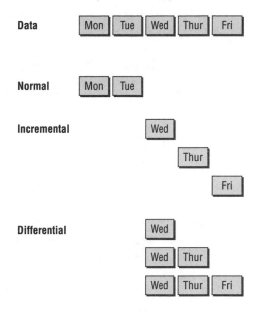

FIGURE B.4 Selecting the type of backup to perform

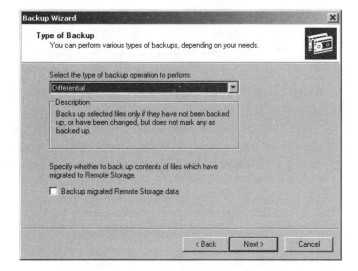

Another option is to create an Emergency Repair Disk (ERD). In the event that boot or configuration information is lost, the ERD and Windows 2000 Repair process can be used to restore a system.

Backing Up System State Information

When planning to back up and restore the Active Directory, the most important component is known as the *System State*. System State information includes the components that the Windows 2000 operating system relies on for normal operations. The Windows 2000 Backup utility offers the ability to back up the System State to another type of media (such as a hard disk, network share, or tape device). Specifically, it will back up the following components for a Windows 2000 domain controller (see Figure B.5):

Active Directory   The Active Directory data store is at the heart of the Active Directory. It contains all of the information necessary to create and manage network resources such as users and computers. In most environments that use the Active Directory, users and systems administrators rely on the proper functioning of these services in order to do their jobs.

Boot Files   These are the files required for booting the Windows 2000 operating system and can be used in the case of boot file corruption.

COM+ Class Registrations Database   Applications that run on a Windows 2000 computer might require the registration of various share code components. As part of the System State backup process, Windows 2000 will store all of the information related to Component Object Model+ (COM+) components so that this information can be quickly and easily restored.

Registry   The Windows 2000 Registry is a central repository of information related to the operating system configuration (such as desktop and network settings), user settings, and application settings. Therefore, the Registry is absolutely vital to the proper functioning of Windows 2000.

SysVol   The SysVol directory includes data and files that are shared between the domain controllers within an Active Directory domain. This information is relied upon by many operating system services for proper functioning.

FIGURE B.5   Backing up the Windows 2000 System State information

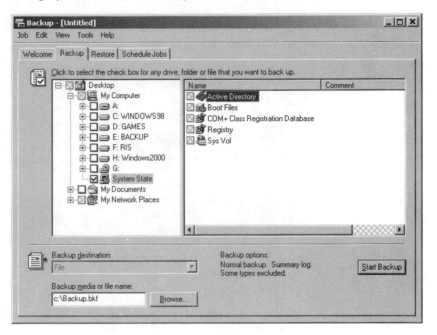

When you back up the System State information, the Windows 2000 Backup utility automatically backs up all of these types of files.

Scheduling Backups

In addition to the ability to specify which files to back up, you can schedule backup jobs to occur at specific times. Planning *when* to perform backups is just as important as deciding what to back up. Performing backup operations can reduce overall system performance; therefore, you should plan to back up information during times of minimal activity on your servers. Figure B.6 shows the Schedule functionality of the Window 2000 Backup utility.

FIGURE B.6 Scheduling jobs using the Windows 2000 Backup utility

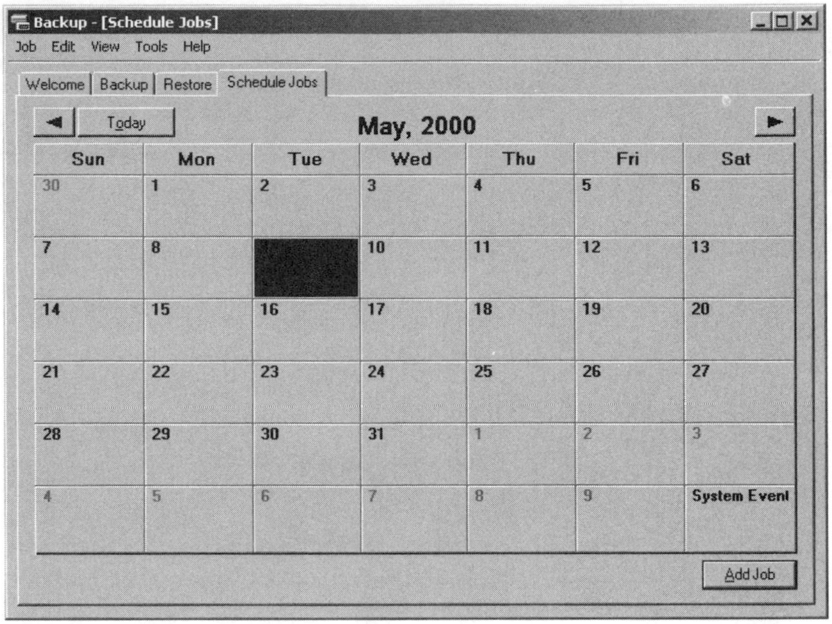

To add a backup operation to the schedule, you can simply click the Add Job button. This will start the Windows 2000 Backup.

Restoring System State Information

In some cases, the Active Directory data store or other System State information may become corrupt or unavailable. This could be due to many different reasons. A hard disk failure might, for example, result in the loss of data. Or, the accidental deletion of an OU and all of its objects might require a restore operation to be performed.

The actual steps involved when restoring System State information are based on the details of what has caused the data loss and what effects this data loss has had on the system. In the best case (relatively speaking, of course), the System State information is corrupt or inaccurate, but the operating system can still boot. If this is the case, all that must be done is to boot into a special *Directory Services Restore Mode* and then restore the System State information from a backup. This process will replace the current System State information with that from the backup. Therefore, any changes that have been made since the last backup will be completely lost and must be redone.

In a worst-case scenario, all of the information on a server has been lost or a hardware failure is preventing the machine from properly booting. If this is the case, there are several steps that you must take in order to recover System State information. These steps include the following:

1. Fix any hardware problem that might prevent the computer from booting (for example, replace any failed hard disks).

2. Reinstall the Windows 2000 operating system. This should be performed like a regular installation on a new system.

3. Reinstall any device drivers that may be required by your backup device. If you backed up information to the file system, this will not apply.

4. Restore the System State information using the Windows 2000 Backup utility.

We'll cover the technical details of performing restores later in this section. For now, however, you should understand the importance of backing up information and, whenever possible, testing the validity of backups.

Backing Up the Active Directory

The Windows 2000 Backup utility makes it easy to back up the System State as part of a normal backup operation. Exercise B.1 walks through the process of backing up the Active Directory.

Note that, although this book doesn't have exercises (instead, it has design scenarios), the book from which this appendix was taken does, so we decided to leave them in. For more exercises such as the two included in this appendix, see *MCSE: Windows 2000 Directory Services Administration Study Guide*, by Anil Desai.

EXERCISE B.1

Backing up the Active Directory

In this exercise, you will back up the Active Directory. In order to complete this exercise, the local machine must be a domain controller, and you must have sufficient free space to back up the System State (usually at least 300MB).

EXERCISE B.1 *(continued)*

1. Open the Backup utility by clicking Start ➤ Programs ➤ Accessories ➤ System Tools ➤ Backup.

2. To start the backup process using the Backup Wizard, click the Backup Wizard button.

3. Click Next to start the backup process.

4. In the What to Back Up dialog box, select Only Back Up the System State Data. Note that there are also options to back up all files on the computer and to back up only specific information. Click Next to continue.

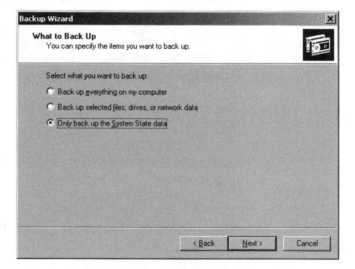

5. Next, you'll need to select where you want to back up this information. If you have a tape drive installed on the local computer, you'll have the option to back up to tape. Otherwise, the option will be disabled, and you can only select File. Select File for the backup media type, and then enter the full path and filename for the backup file. The default file extension for a Windows 2000 Backup file is .bkf. You should ensure that the selected folder has sufficient space to store the System State information (which is usually more than 300MB). Click Next to continue.

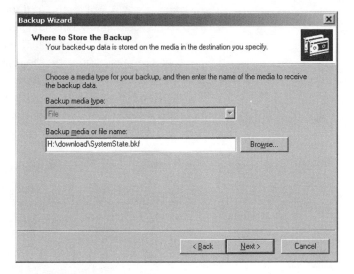

6. The Windows 2000 Backup Wizard will now display a summary of the options you selected for backup. Verify that the files to be backed up and the location information are correct. Note that by clicking the Advanced button, you can select from among different backup types (such as copy, differential, and incremental) and can choose whether remote storage files will be backed up. Click Finish to begin the backup process.

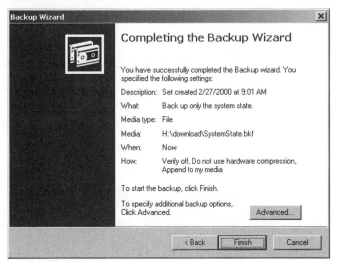

7. The backup process will begin, and the approximate size of the backup will be calculated. On most systems, the backup operation will take at least several minutes. The exact amount of time required will be based on server load, server hardware configuration, and the size of the System State information. For example, backing up the System State on a busy domain controller for a large Active Directory domain will take much longer than a similar backup for a seldom-used domain controller in a small domain.

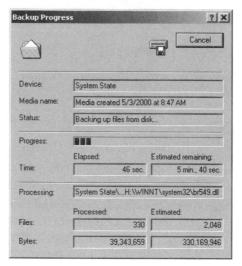

8. When the backup operation has completed, you will see information about the overall backup process. You can click the Report button to see information about the backup process (including any errors that might have occurred). Optionally, you can save this report as a text file to examine the information later.

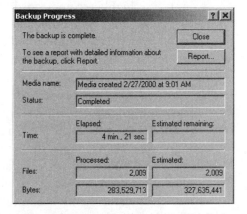

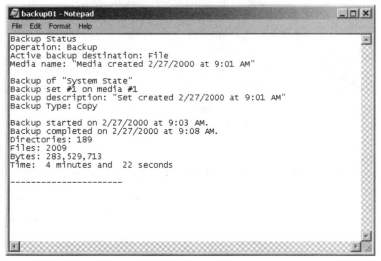

9. When finished, click Close and then close the Backup application.

Now that we've walked through the steps required to back up the Active Directory, it's time to look at methods for restoring System State information, should the need arise.

Restoring the Active Directory

The Active Directory has been designed with fault tolerance in mind. For example, it is highly recommended that each domain have at least two domain controllers. Each of these domain controllers contains a copy of the Active Directory data store. Should one of the domain controllers fail, the other one can take over the functionality. When the failed server is repaired, it can then be promoted to a domain controller in the existing environment. This process effectively restores the failed domain controller without incurring any downtime for end users.

In some cases, you might need to restore the Active Directory from backup media. For example, suppose a systems administrator accidentally deletes several hundred users from the domain. He does not realize this until the change has been propagated to all of the other domain controllers. Manually re-creating the accounts is not an option since the objects' security identifiers will be different (and all permissions must be reset). Clearly, a method for restoring from backup is the best solution.

 There are several features in Windows 2000 for solving boot-related problems and for reinstalling the operating system to fix corrupted files. These techniques are beyond the scope of this appendix (which focuses on restoring the Active Directory).

Overview of Authoritative Restore

Restoring the Active Directory and other System State information is an important process should system files or the Active Directory data store become corrupt or otherwise unavailable. Fortunately, the Windows 2000 Backup utility allows for easily restoring the System State information from a backup, should the need arise.

We mentioned earlier that in the case of the accidental deletion of information from the Active Directory, you may need to restore the Active Directory data store from a recent backup. But what happens if there is more than one domain controller in the environment? Even if you did perform a restore, the information on this domain controller would be seen as outdated and it would be overwritten by the data from another domain controller. And, this data from the older domain controller is exactly the information you want to replace.

Fortunately, Windows 2000 and the Active Directory allow you to perform what is called an *authoritative restore*. The authoritative restore process specifies a domain controller as having the authoritative (or master) copy of the Active Directory data store. When other domain controllers communicate with this domain controller, their information will be overwritten with that stored on the local machine.

Now that we have an idea of how an authoritative restore is supposed to work, let's move on to looking at the details of performing the process.

Performing an Authoritative Restore

When you're restoring Active Directory information on a Windows 2000 domain controller, the Active Directory services must not be running. This is because the restore of System State information requires full access to system files and the Active Directory data store. If you attempt to restore System State information while the domain controller is active, you will see the error message shown in Figure B.7.

When using Windows 2000 Backup to recover System State information, you have the option of restoring data to an alternate location. However, this operation will only copy some components from the System State backup, and it will not restore the Active Directory.

FIGURE B.7 Attempting to restore System State while a domain controller is active

In general, restoring data and operating system files is a straightforward process. It is important to note that restoring a System State backup will replace the existing Registry, SysVol, and Active Directory files. Exercise B.2 walks you through the process of restoring System State and Active Directory information. This process uses the ntdsutil utility to set the authoritative restore mode for a domain controller after the System State is restored but before the domain controller is rebooted.

Warning: Any changes made to the Active Directory since the backup performed in Exercise B.1 will be lost after the completion of Exercise B.2.

EXERCISE B.2

Restoring the System State and the Active Directory

In this exercise, you will restore the Active Directory. In order to complete this process, you must have first completed the steps in Exercise B.1.

1. Reboot the local machine. During system startup, press the F8 key to enter the Windows 2000 Server boot options.

2. From the boot menu, choose Directory Services Restore Mode (Windows 2000 Domain Controllers Only) and press Enter. The operating system will begin to boot in safe mode.

3. Log on to the computer as a member of the *local* Administrators group. Note that you cannot log on using any Active Directory accounts since network services and the Active Directory have not been started.

4. You will see a message warning you that the machine is running in safe mode and that certain services will not be available. For example, a minimal set of drivers has been loaded, and you will not have access to the network. Click OK to continue.

5. When the operating system has finished booting, open the Backup utility by clicking Start ➢ Programs ➢ Accessories ➢ System Tools ➢ Backup.

6. On the main screen of the Backup utility, click the Restore Wizard icon.

7. Click Next to begin the Restore Wizard.

8. Expand the File item by clicking the plus sign. Expand the Media item, and then click the plus sign next to the System State icon.

9. Enter the path and filename of the backup file that you created in Exercise B.1. The Backup utility will scan the file for the appropriate backup information.

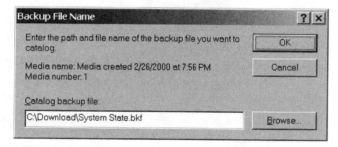

10. Place a check mark next to the System State item, and then click Next.

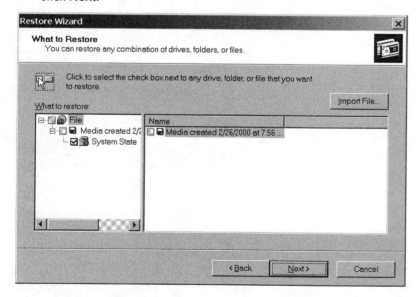

11. The Restore Wizard will display a summary of the recovery options that you selected.

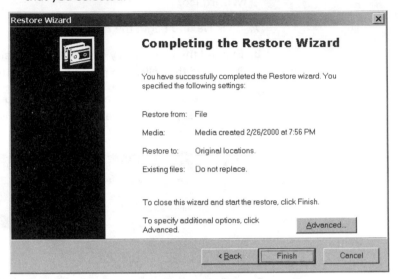

12. Click the Advanced button to specify the location for the restored files. The options include the original location, an alternate location, or a single folder. Verify that the original location option is selected, and then click Next.

13. You will then be prompted to specify how you want files to be restored. Select the Always Replace the File on Disk option, and click Next.

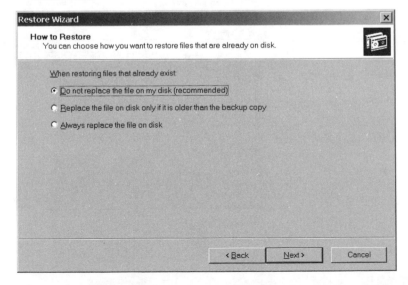

14. For the Advanced Restore Options dialog box, use the default settings (none of the boxes checked). Click Next.

15. To begin the Restore operation, click Finish. Windows 2000 Backup will begin to restore the System State files to the local computer.

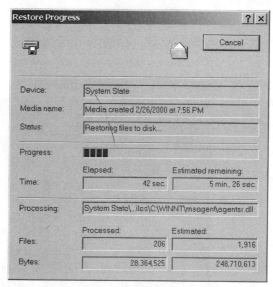

16. Once the System State information has been restored, you will see statistics related to the recovery operation. To view detailed information, click the Report button. When you are finished, click Close.

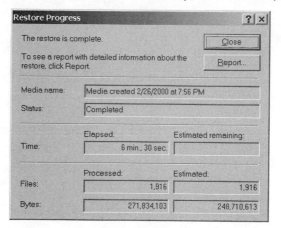

EXERCISE B.2 *(continued)*

17. You will be prompted to choose whether or not you want to restart the computer. Select No. Close the Windows 2000 Backup application.

18. Now, you will need to place the domain controller in authoritative restore mode. To do this, click Start ➢ Run and type **cmd**. At the command prompt, type **ntdsutil** and press Enter. Note that you can type a question mark and press Enter to view help information for the various commands available with the ntdsutil application.

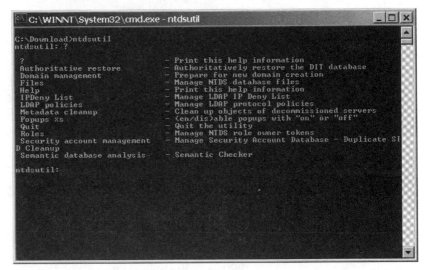

19. At the ntdsutil prompt, type **authoritative restore** and press Enter.

20. At the authoritative restore prompt, type **restore database** and press Enter. You will be asked whether or not you want to perform an authoritative restore. Click Yes.

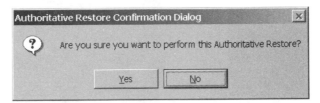

EXERCISE B.2 *(continued)*

21. The ntdsutil application will begin the authoritative restore process. When the process has completed, type **quit** twice to exit the ntdsutil. Then, close the command prompt by typing **exit**.

```
C:\WINNT\System32\cmd.exe - ntdsutil                              _ □ ×
Help                          - Print this help information
Quit                          - Return to the prior menu
Restore database              - Authoritatively restore entire database
Restore database verinc %d    - ... and override version increase
Restore subtree %s            - Authoritatively restore a subtree
Restore subtree %s verinc %d  - ... and override version increase

authoritative restore: restore database

Opening DIT database... Done.

The current time is 02-28-00 22:25.03.
Most recent database update occured at 02-26-00 20:01.14.
Increasing attribute version numbers by 300000.

Counting records that need updating...
Records found: 0000001422
Done.


Found 1422 records to update.

Updating records...
Records remaining: 0000000000
Done.


Successfully updated 1422 records.

Authoritative Restore completed successfully.

authoritative restore:
```

22. Finally, click Start ➢ Shut Down, and restart the computer. Following a reboot of the operating system, the Active Directory and System State information will be current to the point of the last backup.

In addition to restoring the entire Active Directory database, you can also restore specific subtrees within the Active Directory by using the restore subtree command. This allows you to restore specific information and is useful in the case of an accidental deletion of isolated material.

Following the authoritative restore process, the Active Directory should be updated to the time of the last backup. Furthermore, all other domain controllers for this domain will have their Active Directory information overwritten by the results of the restore operation. The end result is an Active Directory environment that has been recovered from media.

Glossary

A

Accelerated Graphics Port (AGP)   A type of expansion slot supported by Windows 2000. AGP is used by video cards and supports high-quality video and graphics performance.

access control entry (ACE)   An item used by the operating system to determine *resource* access. Each *access control list (ACL)* has an associated ACE that lists the permissions that have been granted or denied to the users and groups listed in the ACL.

access control list (ACL)   An item used by the operating system to determine *resource* access. Each object (such as a folder, network share, or printer) in Windows 2000 has an ACL. The ACL lists the *security identifiers (SIDs)* contained by objects. Only those identified in the list as having the appropriate permission can activate the services of that object.

access token   An object containing the *security identifier (SID)* of a running *process*. A process started by another process inherits the starting process's access token. The access token is checked against each object's *access control list (ACL)* to determine whether or not appropriate permissions are granted to perform any requested service.

Accessibility Options   Windows 2000 Professional features used to support users with limited sight, hearing, or mobility. Accessibility Options include special keyboard, sound, display, and mouse configurations.

Accessibility Wizard   A Windows 2000 Professional Wizard used to configure a computer based on the user's vision, hearing, and mobility needs.

account lockout policy   A Windows 2000 policy used to specify how many invalid *logon* attempts should be tolerated before a user account is locked out. Account lockout policies are set through *account policies*.

account policies   Windows 2000 policies used to determine password and *logon* requirements. Account policies are set through the *Microsoft Management Console (MMC) Local Computer Policy* snap-in.

ACE   See *access control entry*.

ACL   See *access control list*.

ACPI   See *Advanced Configuration and Power Interface*.

Active Desktop   A Windows 2000 feature that makes the *Desktop* look and work like a Web page.

Active Directory   A directory service available with the Windows 2000 Server platform. The Active Directory stores information in a central database and allows users to have a single user account (called a *domain user account* or *Active Directory user account*) for the network.

Active Directory user account   A user account that is stored in the Windows 2000 Server *Active Directory's* central database. An Active Directory user account can provide a user with a single user account for a network. Also called a domain user account.

adapter   Any hardware device that allows communications to occur through physically dissimilar systems. This term usually refers to peripheral cards that are permanently mounted inside computers and provide an interface from the computer's bus to another medium such as a hard disk or a network.

AD connector   A software component that allows synchronization between dissimilar directory services.

Administrator account   A Windows 2000 special account that has the ultimate set of security permissions and can assign any permission to any user or group.

Administrators group   A Windows 2000 built-in group that consists of *Administrator accounts.*

Advanced Configuration and Power Interface (ACPI)   A specification that controls the amount of power given to each device attached to the computer. With ACPI, the operating system can turn off peripheral devices when they are not in use.

Advanced Power Management (APM)   A Windows 2000 feature designed to reduce the power consumption of a computer, which is especially important for laptops that are running on battery power.

AGP   See *Accelerated Graphics Port.*

alert   A system-monitoring feature that is generated when a specific *counter* exceeds or falls below a specified value. Through the *Performance Logs and Alerts* utility, administrators can configure alerts so that a message is sent, a

program is run, or a more detailed log file is generated.

Anonymous Logon group   A Windows 2000 *special group* that includes users who access the computer through anonymous logons. Anonymous logons occur when users gain access through special accounts, such as the IUSR_*computername* and TsInternetUser user accounts.

answer file   An automated installation script used to respond to configuration prompts that normally occur in a Windows 2000 Professional installation. Administrators can create Windows 2000 answer files with the *Setup Manager* utility.

APM   See Advanced Power Management.

Application layer   The seventh (top) layer of the *Open Systems Interconnection (OSI)* model that interfaces with application programs by providing high-level network services based on lower-level network layers.

Application log   A log that tracks events that are related to applications that are running on the computer. The Application log can be viewed in the *Event Viewer* utility.

assigned application   An application that is propagated through a group policy. An assigned application will appear as an icon on the user's desktop and will automatically install when the user accesses the icon.

attribute   Each object within the AD structure represents a record in the AD database. The fields of each record are known as attributes.

attribute definition object An object within the *schema* that holds a description of an attribute.

audit policy A Windows 2000 policy that tracks the success or failure of specified security events. Audit policies are set through *Local Computer Policy*.

Authenticated Users group A Windows 2000 *special group* that includes users who access the Windows 2000 operating system through a valid username and password.

authentication The process required to log on to a computer locally. Authentication requires a valid username and a password that exists in the local accounts database. An *access token* will be created if the information presented matches the account in the database.

automated installation The process of installing Windows 2000 using an unattended setup method such as *Remote Installation Services (RIS)*, *unattended installation*, or *disk images*.

auxiliary class A object class that is an extension of an existing class.

available bandwidth The amount of additional traffic that a network segment can handle once current traffic has been taken into account (total bandwidth – used bandwidth = available bandwidth).

B

backup The process of writing all the data contained in online mass-storage devices to offline mass-storage devices for the purpose of safekeeping. Backups are usually performed from hard disk drives to tape drives. Also referred to as archiving.

Backup Operators group A Windows 2000 built-in group that includes users who can back up and restore the *file system*, even if the file system is *NTFS* and they have not been assigned permissions to the file system. The members of the Backup Operators group can access the file system only through the *Windows 2000 Backup* utility. To be able to directly access the file system, the user must have explicit permissions assigned.

backup type A *backup* choice that determines which files are backed up during a backup process. Backup types include *normal backup*, *copy backup*, *incremental backup*, *differential backup*, and *daily backup*.

Backup Wizard A Wizard used to perform a *backup*. The Backup Wizard is accessed through the *Windows 2000 Backup* utility.

baseline A snapshot record of a computer's current performance statistics that can be used for performance analysis and planning purposes.

Basic Input/Output System (BIOS) A set of routines in firmware that provides the most basic software interface drivers for hardware attached to the computer. The BIOS contains the boot routine.

basic storage A disk-storage system supported by Windows 2000 that consists of *primary partitions* and *extended partitions*. Drives are configured as basic storage after an operating system has been upgraded from Windows NT.

Batch group A Windows 2000 *special group* that includes users who log on as a user account that is only used to run a batch job.

binding The process of linking together software components, such as network *protocols* and *network adapters*.

BIOS See *Basic Input/Output System*.

boot The process of loading a computer's operating system. Booting usually occurs in multiple phases, each successively more complex until the entire operating system and all its services are running. Also called bootstrap. The computer's *BIOS* must contain the first level of booting.

BOOT.INI A file accessed during the Windows 2000 *boot* sequence. The BOOT.INI file is used to build the operating system menu choices that are displayed during the boot process. It is also used to specify the location of the *boot partition*.

Boot Normally A Windows 2000 Advanced Options menu item used to boot Windows 2000 normally.

boot partition The *partition* that contains the system files. The system files are located in C:\WINNT by default.

BOOTSECT.DOS An optional file that is loaded if the user chooses to load an operating system other than Windows 2000. This file is only used in *dual-boot* or *multi-boot* computers.

bottleneck A system *resource* that is inefficient compared with the rest of the computer system as a whole. The bottleneck can cause the rest of the system to run slowly.

branch office A wholly controlled facility that does not meet the criteria to be a *corporate office*.

bridgehead server A server that is designated as the preferred domain controller to replicate directory services information between defined sites.

broadcast packet A network packet that is addressed in a manner that identifies its destination as being all computers.

business model A description of the business relationships within a company.

C

cache schema The copy of the AD *schema* that is stored in memory.

caching A speed-optimization technique that keeps a copy of the most recently used data in a fast, high-cost, low-capacity storage device rather than in the device on which the actual data resides. Caching assumes that recently used data is likely to be used again. Fetching data from the cache is faster than fetching data from the slower, larger storage device. Most caching algorithms also copy data that is most likely to be used next and perform *write-back caching* to further increase speed gains.

canonical name An object's name using a notation that lists all container objects in the path to the object, starting from the top of the AD tree and working down.

CD-based image   A type of image configured on a *Remote Installation Services (RIS)* server. A CD-based image contains only the Windows 2000 Professional operating system.

CDFS   See Compact Disk File System.

central processing unit (CPU)   The main *processor* in a computer.

centralized management   A management model in which all IT *resources* are managed by a small group of people in a single location.

change management   The process of managing changes to an environment, such as keeping print *drivers* up-to-date or installing new software.

Check Disk   A Windows 2000 utility that checks a hard disk for errors. Check Disk (chkdsk) attempts to fix file-system errors and scans for and attempts to recover bad sectors.

CIPHER   A command-line utility that can be used to encrypt files on *NTFS volumes*.

cipher text   Encrypted data. Encryption is the process of translating data into code that is not easily accessible. Once data has been encrypted, a user must have a password or key to decrypt the data. Unencrypted data is known as plain text.

class-definition object   An object within the AD *schema* that holds a description of a class of objects.

clean install   A method of Windows 2000 Professional installation that puts the operating system into a new folder and uses its default settings the first time the operating system is loaded.

client   A computer that is on a network and subscribes to the services provided by a server.

communication flow   A description of the sharing of information and the free flow of ideas within a company. As such, it is both a physical aspect (who talks to whom) and a philosophical aspect (how much freedom of information exists) of AD design.

COM port   Communications port. A serial hardware interface conforming to the RS-232C standard for low-speed, serial communications.

Compact Disk File System (CDFS)   A *file system* used by Windows 2000 to read the file system on a CD-ROM.

compression   The process of storing data in a form that takes less space than the uncompressed data.

Computer Management   A consolidated tool for performing common Windows 2000 management tasks. The interface is organized into three main areas of management: System Tools, Storage, and Services and Applications.

computer name   A *NetBIOS* name used to uniquely identify a computer on the network. A computer name can be from 1 to 15 characters in length.

connection agreement   A connection agreement defines the relationship between two directories connected through an AD connector.

connection-oriented service   A type of connection service in which a connection (a path) is established and acknowledgments are sent. This type of communication is reliable but has a high overhead.

connectionless service A type of connection service that does not establish a connection (path) before transmission. This type of communication is fast, but it is not very reliable.

Control Panel A Windows 2000 utility that allows users to change default settings for operating system services to match their preferences. The *Registry* contains the Control Panel settings.

CONVERT A command-line utility used to convert a *partition* from *FAT16* or *FAT32* to the *NTFS* file system.

copy backup A *backup type* that backs up selected folders and files but does not set the archive bit.

corporate office A location in which the company has invested heavily in facilities, information services staff, and hardware or is heavily staffed.

cost center model Usually a hybrid of all of the other business models. In this model, the functions of business are once again divided into groups—based on projects, products/services, or traditional departments—just as they are in the other models. The big difference is in how those groups interact. Each group is seen as a separate business entity within the company. Groups charge each other for the services they provide.

counter A performance-measuring tool used to track specific information regarding a system resource, called a performance object. All Windows 2000 system resources are tracked as performance objects, such as *Cache, Memory,*

Paging File, Process, and *Processor.* Each performance object has an associated set of counters. Counters are set through the *System Monitor* utility.

CPU See *central processing unit.*

Creator group The Windows 2000 *special group* that created or took ownership of the object (rather than an individual user). When a regular user creates an object or takes ownership of an object, the username becomes the *Creator Owner.* When a member of the *Administrators group* creates or takes ownership of an object, the Administrators group becomes the Creator group.

Creator Owner group The Windows 2000 *special group* that includes the account that created or took ownership of an object. The account, usually a user account, has the right to modify the object but cannot modify any other objects that were not created by the user account.

D

daily backup A *backup type* that backs up all of the files that have been modified on the day that the daily backup is performed. The archive attribute is not set on the files that have been backed up.

DAP See *Directory Access Protocol.*

data compression The process of storing data in a form that takes less space than the uncompressed data.

data encryption The process of translating data into code that is not easily accessible to increase security. Once data has been encrypted, a user must have a password or key to decrypt the data.

Data Link layer In the *Open Systems Inter-connection (OSI) model*, the layer that provides the digital interconnection of network devices and the software that directly operates these devices, such as *network adapters*.

Debugging Mode A Windows 2000 Advanced Option menu item that runs the Kernel Debugger, if that utility is installed. The Kernel Debugger is an advanced trouble-shooting utility.

decentralized management A management model in which *resources* are managed locally.

default gateway A *TCP/IP* configuration option that specifies the gateway that will be used if the network contains routers.

departmental model The traditional method of managing a business. The basics of the departmental model are quite simple—look at the tasks that make up the business processes of a company, group them according to function, and manage each group.

Desktop A directory that the background of the Windows Explorer shell represents. By default, the Desktop includes objects that contain the local storage devices and available network *shares*. Also a key operating part of the Windows 2000 graphical interface.

device driver Software that allows a specific piece of hardware to communicate with the Windows 2000 operating system.

Device Manager A Windows 2000 utility used to provide information about the computer's configuration.

DHCP See *Dynamic Host Configuration Protocol*.

DHCP server A server configured to provide *DHCP* clients with all of their *IP* configuration information automatically.

dial-up networking A service that allows remote users to dial into the network or the Internet (such as through a telephone or an ISDN connection).

Dialup group A Windows 2000 *special group* that includes users who log on to the network from a dial-up connection.

differential backup A *backup type* that copies only the files that have been changed since the last *normal backup* (full backup) or *incremental backup*. A differential backup backs up only those files that have changed since the last full backup, but does not reset the archive bit.

Digital Versatile Disc (DVD) A disk standard that supports up to 4.7GB of data. One of DVD's strongest features is backward compatibility with CD-ROM technology, so that a DVD drive can play CD-ROMs. Formerly known as Digital Video Disk.

directory A database used to organize information.

Directory Access Protocol (DAP)   The X.500 protocol designed to allow access to X.500-compliant directories. Its major failing was that it was proprietary in nature—any given implementation would work only with a specific brand of directory. For this reason, it is not used much in today's world.

directory replication   The process of copying a directory structure from an export computer to an import computer(s). Anytime changes are made to the export computer, the import computer(s) is automatically updated with the changes.

directory synchronization   A process that keeps the information in two separate directories synchronized; that is, changes made to information in one directory will be propagated automatically to the other.

Disk Cleanup   A Windows 2000 utility used to identify areas of disk space that can be deleted to free additional hard disk space. Disk Cleanup works by identifying temporary files, Internet cache files, and unnecessary program files.

disk defragmentation   The process of rearranging the existing files on a disk so that they are stored contiguously, which optimizes access to those files.

Disk Defragmenter   A Windows 2000 utility that performs *disk defragmentation.*

disk image   An exact duplicate of a hard disk, used for *automated installation.* The disk image is copied from a reference computer that is configured in the same manner as the computers on which Windows 2000 Professional will be installed.

Disk Management   A Windows 2000 graphical tool for managing disks and *volumes.*

disk partitioning   The process of creating logical *partitions* on the physical hard drive.

disk quotas   A Windows 2000 feature used to specify how much disk space a user is allowed to use on specific *NTFS volumes.* Disk quotas can be applied for all users or for specific users.

distinguished name   The relative distinguished name of an object plus the names of the containers that make up the path to that object.

distribution server   A network server that contains the Windows 2000 distribution files that have been copied from the distribution CD. Clients can connect to the distribution server and install Windows 2000 over the network.

DNS   See *Domain Name System.*

DNS server   A server that uses *DNS* to resolve domain or host names to *IP addresses.*

DNS zone   The portion of the DNS *namespace* that is contained in a single file.

domain   In Microsoft networks, an arrangement of client and server computers referenced by a specific name that shares a single security permissions database. On the Internet, a domain is a named collection of hosts and subdomains, registered with a unique name by the InterNIC.

domain name   The textual identifier of a specific Internet host. Domain names are in the form of server organization type (`www.microsoft .com`) and are resolved to Internet addresses by *DNS servers.*

domain name server   An Internet host dedicated to the function of translating fully qualified domain names into *IP addresses*.

Domain Name System (DNS)   The *TCP/IP* network service that translates textual Internet network addresses into numerical Internet network addresses.

domain naming master   A Windows 2000 server that is responsible for adding or removing domains from the *forest*.

domain restructure   The process of redesigning your existing domains to match the business needs of your environment.

domain user account   A user account that is stored in the Windows 2000 Server *Active Directory's* central database. A domain user account can provide a user with a single user account for a network. Also called an Active Directory user account.

drive letter   A single letter assigned as an abbreviation to a mass-storage *volume* available to a computer.

driver   A program that provides a software interface to a hardware device. Drivers are written for the specific devices they control, but they present a common software interface to the computer's operating system, allowing all devices of a similar type to be controlled as if they were the same.

driver signing   A digital imprint that is Microsoft's way of guaranteeing that a driver has been tested and will work with the computer.

Dr. Watson   A Windows 2000 utility used to identify and troubleshoot application errors.

DRWTSN32   The command used to access the *Dr. Watson* utility.

dual-booting   The process of allowing a computer to *boot* more than one operating system.

DVD   See *Digital Versatile Disc.*

dynamic disk   A Windows 2000 disk-storage technique. A dynamic disk is divided into dynamic *volumes*. Dynamic volumes cannot contain *partitions* or *logical drives*, and they are not accessible through DOS. You can size or resize a dynamic disk without restarting Windows 2000.

Dynamic Host Configuration Protocol (DHCP)   A method of automatically assigning *IP addresses* to client computers on a network.

dynamic storage   A Windows 2000 disk-storage system that is configured as *volumes*. Windows 2000 Professional dynamic storage supports *simple volumes*, *spanned volumes*, and *striped volumes*.

E

EB   See *exabyte.*

effective rights   The rights that a user actually has to a file or folder. To determine a user's effective rights, add all of the permissions that have been allowed through the user's assignments based on that user's username and group associations. Then subtract any permissions that have been denied the user through the username or group associations.

EFS   See *Encrypting File System.*

Emergency Repair Disk (ERD)   A disk that stores portions of the *Registry*, the system files, a copy of the partition boot sector, and information that relates to the startup environment. The ERD can be used to repair problems that prevent a computer from starting.

Enable Boot Logging   A Windows 2000 Professional Advanced Options menu item that is used to create a log file that tracks the loading of *drivers* and *services*.

Enable VGA Mode   A Windows 2000 Professional Advanced Options menu item that loads a standard VGA driver without starting the computer in *Safe Mode*.

Encrypting File System (EFS)   The Windows 2000 technology used to store encrypted files on *NTFS partitions*. Encrypted files add an extra layer of security to the *file system*.

encryption   The process of translating data into code that is not easily accessible to increase security. Once data has been encrypted, a user must have a password or key to decrypt the data.

ERD   See *Emergency Repair Disk*.

Error event   An *Event Viewer* event type that indicates the occurrence of an error, such as a driver failing to load.

Ethernet   The most popular Data Link layer standard for local area networking. Ethernet implements the Carrier Sense Multiple Access with Collision Detection (CSMA/CD) method of arbitrating multiple computer access to the same network. This standard supports the use of Ethernet over any type of media, including wireless broadcast. Standard Ethernet operates as 10Mbps. Fast Ethernet operates at 100Mbps.

Event Viewer   A Windows 2000 utility that tracks information about the computer's hardware and software, as well as security events. This information is stored in three log files: the *Application log*, the *Security log*, and the *System log*.

Everyone   A Windows 2000 *special group* that includes anyone who could possibly access the computer. The Everyone group includes all of the users (including *Guests*) who have been defined on the computer.

exabyte   A computer storage measurement equal to 1,024 *petabytes*.

extended partition   In *basic storage*, a *logical drive* that allows you to allocate the logical partitions however you wish. Extended partitions are created after the *primary partition* has been created.

extensible   Used to refer to a database whose *schema* can be modified.

F

Failure Audit event   An *Event Viewer* event that indicates the occurrence of an event that has been audited for failure, such a failed logon when someone presents an invalid username and/or password.

FAT16   The 16-bit version of the *File Allocation System (FAT)*, which was widely used by DOS and Windows 3.*x*. The file system is used to track where files are stored on a disk. Most operating systems support FAT16.

FAT32   The 32-bit version of the *File Allocation System (FAT)*, which is more efficient and provides more safeguards than *FAT16*. Windows 9*x* and Windows 2000 support FAT32. Windows NT does not support FAT32.

fault tolerance Any method that prevents system failure by tolerating single faults, usually through hardware redundancy.

fax modem A special modem that includes hardware to allow the transmission and reception of facsimiles.

File Allocation Table (FAT) The *file system* used by *MS-DOS* and available to other operating systems such as Windows (all versions), OS/2, and Macintosh. FAT, now known as *FAT16*, has become something of a mass-storage compatibility standard because of its simplicity and wide availability. FAT has fewer fault-tolerance features than the *NTFS* file system and can become corrupted through normal use over time.

file attributes Bits stored along with the name and location of a file in a directory entry. File attributes show the status of a file, such as archived, hidden, and read-only. Different operating systems use different file attributes to implement services such as *sharing*, *compression*, and *security*.

file system A software component that manages the storage of files on a mass-storage device by providing services that can create, read, write, and delete files. File systems impose an ordered database of files on the mass-storage device. Storage is arranged in *volumes*. File systems use hierarchies of directories to organize files.

File Transfer Protocol (FTP) A simple Internet protocol that transfers complete files from an FTP server to a client running the FTP client. FTP provides a simple, no-overhead method of transferring files between computers but cannot perform browsing functions. Users must know the *URL* of the FTP server to which they wish to attach.

Flexible Single Master Operation (FSMO) server A server that has the AD responsibilities that are handled in a single-master manner. Although this term is no longer used, it still appears in much of Microsoft's documentation.

forest A collection of AD trees.

format The process of preparing a mass-storage device for use with a *file system*. There are actually two levels of formatting. Low-level formatting writes a structure of sectors and tracks to the disk with bits used by the mass-storage controller hardware. The controller hardware requires this format, and it is independent of the file system. High-level formatting creates file system structures such as an allocation table and a root directory in a *partition*, thus creating a *volume*.

frame A data structure that network hardware devices use to transmit data between computers. Frames consist of the addresses of the sending and receiving computers, size information, and a checksum. Frames are envelopes around packets of data that allow the packets to be addressed to specific computers on a shared media network.

frame type An option that specifies how data is packaged for transmission over the network. This option must be configured to run the *NWLink IPX/SPX/NetBIOS Compatible Transport* protocol on a Windows 2000 computer. By default, the frame type is set to Auto Detect, which will attempt to automatically choose a compatible frame type for the network.

FTP See *File Transfer Protocol*.

G

GB See *gigabyte*.

GDI See *Graphic Device Interface*.

geographic model A description of the number of physical locations that make up the network and the connectivity between them.

gigabyte A computer storage measurement equal to 1,024 *megabytes*.

global catalog server A Windows 2000 server that holds a partial replica of the entire *forest*. This replica is most commonly used to facilitate searches of the AD database.

GPO See *Group Policy object*.

GPO nodes Within the group policy configuration tool, options are separated into nodes, each node representing a specific set of options.

Graphics Device Interface (GDI) The programming interface and graphical services provided to *Win32* for programs to interact with graphical devices such as the screen and printer.

Graphical User Interface (GUI) A computer shell program that represents mass-storage devices, directories, and files as graphical objects on a screen. A cursor driven by a pointing device such as a mouse manipulates the objects.

Group Policy object (GPO) An object that is within the AD database and used to store security or configuration information for users, groups, and computers.

groups Security entities to which users can be assigned membership for the purpose of applying the broad set of group permissions to the user. By managing permissions for groups and assigning users to groups, rather than assigning permissions to users, administrators can more easily manage security.

Guest account A Windows 2000 user account created to provide a mechanism to allow users to access the computer even if they do not have a unique username and password. This account normally has very limited privileges on the computer. This account is disabled by default.

Guests group A Windows 2000 built-in group that has limited access to the computer. This group can access only specific areas. Most administrators do not allow Guest account access because it poses a potential security risk.

GUI See *Graphical User Interface*.

H

HAL See *Hardware Abstraction Layer*.

hard costs Costs that can be easily identified and quantified, such as the cost of hardware and software.

hard disk drive A mass-storage device that reads and writes digital information magnetically on discs that spin under moving heads. Hard disk drives are precisely aligned and cannot normally be removed. Hard disk drives are an inexpensive way to store *gigabytes* of computer data permanently. Hard disk drives also store the software installed on a computer.

Hardware Abstraction Layer (HAL) A Windows 2000 service that provides basic input/output services such as timers, interrupts, and multiprocessor management for computer hardware. The HAL is a *device driver* for the motherboard circuitry that allows different families of computers to be treated the same by the Windows 2000 operating system.

Hardware Compatibility List (HCL) A list of all of the hardware devices supported by Windows 2000. Hardware on the HCL has been tested and verified as being compatible with Windows 2000.

hardware profile A file that stores a hardware configuration for a computer. Hardware profiles are useful when a single computer (a laptop that can be docked or undocked) has multiple hardware configurations.

HCL See *Hardware Compatibility List.*

hibernation The storage of anything that is stored in memory on the computer's hard disk. Hibernation ensures that none of the information stored in memory is lost when the computer is shut down. When the computer is taken out of hibernation, it is returned to its previous state.

hierarchical naming A method of naming objects in which a layered structure, often referred to as a tree, is built to organize resources.

home folder A folder where users normally store their personal files and information. A home folder can be a local folder or a network folder.

host An Internet server. Hosts are constantly connected to the Internet.

hot swapping The ability of a device to be plugged into or removed from a computer while the computer's power is on.

HTML See *Hypertext Markup Language.*

HTTP See *Hypertext Transfer Protocol.*

hyperlink A link within text or graphics that has a Web address embedded in it. By clicking the link, a user can jump to another Web address.

Hypertext Markup Language (HTML) A textual data format that identifies sections of a document such as headers, lists, hypertext links, and so on. HTML is the data format used on the World Wide Web for the publication of Web pages.

Hypertext Transfer Protocol (HTTP) An Internet protocol that transfers HTML documents over the Internet and responds to context changes that happen when a user clicks a *hyperlink*.

I

IEEE See Institute of Electrical and Electronic Engineers.

IIS See Internet Information Services.

incremental backup A *backup type* that backs up only the files that have changed since the last normal or incremental backup. It sets the archive attribute on the files that are backed up.

incremental zone transfer A *DNS zone* transfer in which only changed information is sent to secondary DNS name servers.

Indexing Service A Windows 2000 service that creates an index based on the contents and properties of files stored on the computer's local hard drive. A user can then use the Windows 2000 Search function to search or query through the index for specific keywords.

Industry Standard Architecture (ISA) The design standard for 16-bit Intel-compatible motherboards and peripheral buses. The 32/64-bit *PCI* bus standard is replacing the ISA standard. Adapters and interface cards must conform to the bus standard(s) used by the motherboard in order to be used in a computer.

Information event An *Event Viewer* event that informs you that a specific action has occurred, such as when a system shuts down or starts.

information flow A description of the traffic generated on the network, its point of origin, its purpose, and the amount of bandwidth it uses.

infrastructure The physical aspects of a network such as the wiring, network links (LAN, MAN, WAN), and connectivity devices such as routers, hubs, and switches.

infrastructure master A Windows 2000 server that is responsible for updating group-to-user references when group members are renamed or relocated. It updates the group object so that it knows the new name or location of its members.

inherited permissions Parent folder permissions that are applied to (or inherited by) files and subfolders of the parent folder. In Windows 2000 Professional, the default is for parent folder permissions to be applied to any files or subfolders in that folder.

initial user account The account that uses the name of the registered user and is created only if the computer is installed as a member of a workgroup (not into the *Active Directory*). By default, the initial user is a member of the *Administrators group*.

Institute of Electrical and Electronic Engineers (IEEE) A professional organization that defines standards related to networks, communications, and other areas.

Institute of Electrical and Electronic Engineers (IEEE) 1394 standard A standard that supports data transfer at speeds up to 400Mbps. Some of the trademark names for this standard are FireWire, I-link, and Lynx.

Integrated Services Digital Network (ISDN) A direct, digital, dial-up connection that operates at 64KB per channel over regular twisted-pair cable. ISDN provides twice the data rate of the fastest modems per channel. Up to 24 channels can be multiplexed over two twisted pairs.

intersite replication AD replication between domain controllers that are located in different AD sites.

InterSite Topology Generator (ISTG) A Windows 2000 server that generates the connection objects between sites within an AD *forest*.

Intel architecture   A family of microprocessors descended from the Intel 8086, itself descended from the first microprocessor, the Intel 4004. The Intel architecture is the dominant microprocessor family. It was used in the original IBM PC microcomputer adopted by the business market and later adapted for home use.

Interactive group   A Windows 2000 *special group* that includes all the users who use the computer's resources locally.

interactive logon   A *logon* when the user logs on from the computer where the user account is stored on the computer's local database. Also called a local logon.

interactive user   A user who physically logs on to the computer where the user account resides (rather than over the network).

inter-forest restructuring   The process of moving users, groups, and computer objects from either a Windows NT domain *or* a Windows 2000 domain in a separate AD forest to a new Windows 2000 domain.

internal network number   An identification for *NetWare* file servers. An internal network number is also used if the network is running File and Print Services for NetWare or is using IPX routing. This option must be configured to run the *NWLink IPX/SPX/NetBIOS Compatible Transport* protocol on a Windows 2000 computer. Normally, the internal network number should be left at its default setting.

international model   A business model that crosses international borders.

Internet connection sharing   A Windows 2000 feature that allows a small network to be connected to the Internet through a single connection. The computer that dials into the Internet provides network address translation, addressing, and name resolution services for all of the computers on the network. Through Internet connection sharing, the other computers on the network can access Internet resources and use Internet applications, such as Internet Explorer and Outlook Express.

Internet Explorer   A World Wide Web browser produced by Microsoft and included with Windows 9*x*, Windows NT 4, and now Windows 2000.

Internet Information Services (IIS)   Software that serves Internet higher-level protocols like *HTTP* and *FTP* to clients using Web browsers. The IIS software that is installed on a Windows 2000 Server computer is a fully functional Web server and is designed to support heavy Internet usage.

Internet Print Protocol (IPP)   A Windows 2000 protocol that allows users to print directly to a *URL*. Printer and job-related information are generated in *HTML* format.

Internet printer   A Windows 2000 feature that allows users to send documents to be printed through the Internet.

Internet Protocol (IP)   The Network layer protocol upon which the Internet is based. IP provides a simple connectionless packet exchange. Other protocols such as TCP use IP to perform their *connection-oriented* (or guaranteed delivery) services.

Internet service provider (ISP)   A company that provides dial-up connections to the Internet.

Internet Services Manager   A Windows 2000 utility used to configure the protocols that are used by *Internet Information Services (IIS)* and *Personal Web Services (PWS)*.

internetwork   A network made up of multiple network segments that are connected with some device, such as a router. Each network segment is assigned a network address. *Network layer protocols* build routing tables that are used to route packets through the network in the most efficient manner.

InterNIC   The agency that is responsible for assigning *IP addresses*.

interprocess communications (IPC)   A generic term describing any manner of client/ server communication protocol, specifically those operating in the *Application layer*. IPC mechanisms provide a method for the client and server to trade information.

interrupt request (IRQ)   A hardware signal from a peripheral device to the microcomputer indicating that it has input/output (I/O) traffic to send. If the microprocessor is not running a more important service, it will interrupt its current activity and handle the interrupt request. IBM PCs have 16 levels of interrupt request lines. Under Windows 2000, each device must have a unique interrupt request line.

intra-forest restructuring   The process of moving security principals between domains within the same Active Directory *forest*.

intranet   A privately owned network based on the *TCP/IP* protocol suite.

intrasite replication   AD replication between domain controllers within the same AD site.

IP   See *Internet Protocol*.

IP address   A four-byte number that uniquely identifies a computer on an IP *internetwork*. InterNIC assigns the first bytes of Internet IP addresses and administers them in hierarchies. Huge organizations like the government or top-level *ISPs* have class A addresses, large organizations and most ISPs have class B addresses, and small companies have class C addresses. In a class A address, InterNIC assigns the first byte, and the owning organization assigns the remaining three bytes. In a class B address, InterNIC or the higher-level ISP assigns the first two bytes, and the organization assigns the remaining two bytes. In a class C address, InterNIC or the higher-level ISP assigns the first three bytes, and the organization assigns the remaining byte. Organizations not attached to the Internet are free to assign IP addresses as they please.

IPC   See *interprocess communications*.

IPCONFIG   A command used to display the computer's *IP* configuration.

IPP   See *Internet Print Protocol*.

IRQ   See *interrupt request*.

ISA   See *Industry Standard Architecture*.

ISDN   See *Integrated Services Digital Network*.

ISP   See *Internet service provider*.

K

kernel The core process of a preemptive operating system, consisting of a multitasking scheduler and the basic security services. Depending on the operating system, other services such as virtual memory drivers may be built into the kernel. The kernel is responsible for managing the scheduling of *threads* and *processes*.

Knowledge Consistency Checker (KCC) A process that, among other things, generates the intrasite topology for AD replication.

L

Last Known Good Configuration A Windows 2000 Advanced Options menu item used to load the configuration that was used the last time the computer was successfully booted.

LDAP See *Lightweight Directory Access Protocol*.

Lightweight Directory Access Protocol (LDAP) An industry-standard method used to access and manage LDAP-compliant directories (such as AD).

LLC sublayer See *Logical Link Control sublayer*.

Local Computer Policy A *Microsoft Management Console (MMC) snap-in* used to implement account policies.

local group A group that is stored on the local computer's accounts database. These are the groups that administrators can add users to and manage directly on a Windows 2000 Professional computer.

Local Group Policy A *Microsoft Management Console (MMC) snap-in* used to implement local group policies, which include computer configuration policies and user configuration policies.

local logon A *logon* when the user logs on from the computer where the user account is stored on the computer's local database. Also called an interactive logon.

local policies Policies that allow administrators to control what a user can do after logging on. Local policies include *audit policies*, *security option policies*, and *user rights policies*. These policies are set through *Local Computer Policy*.

local printer A printer that uses a *physical port* and that has not been shared. If a printer is defined as local, the only users who can use the printer are the local users of the computer that the printer is attached to.

local security Security that governs a local or interactive user's ability to access locally stored files. Local security can be set through *NTFS permissions*.

local user account A user account stored locally in the user accounts database of a computer that is running Windows 2000 Professional.

local user profile A profile created the first time a user logs on, stored in the Documents and Settings folder. The default user profile folder's name matches the user's logon name. This folder contains a file called NTUSER.DAT and subfolders with directory links to the user's *Desktop* items.

Local Users and Groups   A utility that is used to create and manage local user and group accounts on Windows 2000 Professional computers and Windows 2000 member servers.

locale settings   Settings for regional items, including numbers, currency, time, date, and input locales.

logical drive   An allocation of disk space on a hard drive, using a *drive letter*. For example, a 5GB hard drive could be partitioned into two logical drives: a C: drive, which might be 2GB, and a D: drive, which might be 3GB.

Logical Drives   A Windows 2000 utility used to manage the logical drives on the computer.

Logical Link Control (LLC) sublayer   A sublayer in the *Data Link layer* of the *Open Systems Interconnection (OSI)* model. The LLC sublayer defines flow control.

logical port   A port that connects a device directly to the network. Logical ports are used with printers by installing a network card in the printers.

logical printer   The software interface between the physical printer (the *print device*) and the operating system. Also referred to as just a *printer* in Windows 2000 terminology.

logoff   The process of closing an open session with a Windows 2000 computer or network.

logon   The process of opening a session with a Windows 2000 computer or a network by providing a valid authentication consisting of a user account name and a password. After logon, network resources are available to the user according to the user's assigned *permissions*.

logon script   A command file that automates the *logon* process by performing utility functions such as attaching to additional server resources or automatically running different programs based on the user account that established the logon.

M

MAC (media access control) address   The physical address that identifies a computer. *Ethernet* and Token Ring cards have the MAC address assigned through a chip on the network card.

MAC sublayer   See *Media Access Control sublayer*.

Magnifier   A Windows 2000 utility used to create a separate window to magnify a portion of the screen. This option is designed for users who have poor vision.

MAKEBT32.EXE   The command used to create *Windows 2000 Professional Setup Boot Disks*.

mandatory profile   A *user profile* created by an administrator and saved with a special extension (.man) so that the user cannot modify the profile in any way. Mandatory profiles can be assigned to a single user or a group of users.

mapped drive   A shared network folder associated with a drive letter. Mapped drives appear to users as local connections on their computers and can be accessed through a drive letter using My Computer.

Master Boot Record (MBR)   A record used in the Windows 2000 *boot* sequence to point to the active partition, which is the partition that should be used to boot the operating system. This is normally the C: drive. Once the MBR locates the active partition, the boot sector is loaded into memory and executed.

MB   See *megabyte.*

MBR   See *Master Boot Record.*

Media Access Control (MAC) sublayer   A sublayer in the *Data Link layer* of the *Open Systems Interconnection (OSI)* model. The MAC sublayer is used for physical addressing.

megabyte   A computer storage measurement equal to 1,024 kilobytes.

member server   A Windows 2000 server that has been installed as a non-domain controller. This allows the server to operate as a file, print, and application server without the overhead of account administration.

memory   Any device capable of storing information. This term is usually used to indicate volatile *random-access memory (RAM)* capable of high-speed access to any portion of the memory space, but incapable of storing information without power.

Microsoft Disk Operating System (MS-DOS)   A 16-bit operating system designed for the 8086 chip that was used in the original IBM PC. MS-DOS is a simple program loader and file system that turns over complete control of the computer to the running program and provides very little service beyond file system support and that provided by the *BIOS.*

Microsoft Installer (MSI)   A standard that is used to automatically deploy applications with *Windows Installer packages.*

Microsoft Management Console (MMC) The Windows 2000 console framework for management applications. The MMC provides a common environment for *snap-ins.*

mixed mode   When a domain is supporting domain controllers from multiple versions of Microsoft products (NT and Windows 2000), that network is said to be operating in mixed mode.

MMC   See *Microsoft Management Console.*

modem   Modulator/demodulator. A device used to create an analog signal suitable for transmission over telephone lines from a digital data stream. Modern modems also include a command set for negotiating connections and data rates with remote modems and for setting their default behavior.

MS-DOS   See *Microsoft Disk Operating System.*

MSI   See *Microsoft Installer.*

multi-booting   The process of allowing a computer to *boot* multiple operating systems.

multi-master environment   An environment in which multiple servers hold replicas of the same database (or portions thereof) and in which each of these servers can accept changes to the data and replicate those changes to the other servers.

My Computer   The folder used to view and manage a computer. My Computer provides access to all local and network drives, as well as *Control Panel*.

My Documents   The default storage location for documents that are created. Each user has a unique My Documents folder.

My Network Places   The folder that provides access to shared resources, such as local network resources and Web resources.

N

namespace   An environment in which every object has certain aspects in common with every other object. If, for instance, you were to create a domain named KingTech.com, each object in the structure would have that (KingTech.com) as a part of their name.

Narrarator   A Windows 2000 utility used to read aloud on-screen text, dialog boxes, menus, and buttons. This utility requires some type of sound output device.

national model   A business model that covers an entire nation. Best identified by a complex *infrastructure*, multiple time zones, locations with different local laws and regulations, complex services, and large numbers of users.

native mode   A domain that is supporting only Windows 2000 domain controllers is said to be running in native mode.

NDS   See *Novell Directory Services*.

NetBEUI   *See NetBIOS Extended User Interface*.

NetBIOS   See *Network Basic Input/Output System*.

NetBIOS Extended User Interface (NetBEUI)   A simple *Network layer transport protocol* developed to support *NetBIOS* installations. NetBEUI is not routable, and so it is not appropriate for larger networks. NetBEUI is the fastest transport protocol available for Windows 2000.

NET USE   A command-line utility used to map network drives.

NetWare   A popular network operating system developed by Novell in the early 1980s. NetWare is a cooperative, multitasking, highly optimized, dedicated-server network operating system that has client support for most major operating systems. Recent versions of NetWare include graphical client tools for management from client stations. At one time, NetWare accounted for more than 70 percent of the network operating system market.

network adapter   The hardware used to connect computers (or other devices) to the network. Network adapters function at the *Physical layer* and the *Network layer* of the *Open System Interconnection (OSI) model*.

Network Basic Input/Output System (NetBIOS)   A client/server *IPC* service developed by IBM in the early 1980s. NetBIOS presents a relatively primitive mechanism for communication in client/server applications, but its widespread acceptance and availability across most operating systems makes it a logical choice for simple network applications. Many of the network IPC mechanisms in Windows 2000 are implemented over NetBIOS.

network directory   A directory used to organize and secure network *resources*.

Network group   A Windows 2000 *special group* that includes the users who access a computer's resources over a network connection.

Network layer   The layer of the *Open System Interconnection (OSI) model* that creates a communication path between two computers via routed packets. *Transport protocols* implement both the Network layer and the *Transport layer* of the OSI stack. For example, *IP* is a Network layer service.

network printer   A *printer* that is available to local and network users. A network printer can use a *physical port* or a *logical port*.

New Technology File System (NTFS)   A secure, transaction-oriented file system developed for Windows NT and Windows 2000. NTFS offers features such as *local security* on files and folders, *data compression*, *disk quotas*, and *data encryption*.

normal backup   A *backup type* that backs up all selected folders and files and then marks each file that has been backed up as archived.

Novell Directory Services (NDS)   The brand name for Novell's network directory.

NTBOOTDD.SYS   A file accessed in the Windows 2000 *boot* sequence. NTBOOTDD.SYS is an optional file (the *SCSI* driver) that is used when the computer has a SCSI adapter with the onboard *BIOS* disabled.

NTDETECT.COM   A file accessed in the Windows 2000 *boot* sequence. NTDETECT.COM is used to detect any hardware that is installed and add information about the hardware to the *Registry*.

NTFS   See *New Technology File System*.

NTFS permissions   Permissions used to control access to *NTFS* folders and files. Access is configured by allowing or denying NTFS permissions to users and groups.

NTLDR   A file used to control the Windows 2000 *boot* process until control is passed to the *NTOSKRNL.EXE* file.

NTOSKRNL.EXE   A file accessed in the Windows 2000 *boot* sequence. NTOSKRNL.EXE is used to load the *kernel*.

NTUSER.DAT   The file that is created for a *local user profile*.

NTUSER.MAN   The file that is created for a *mandatory profile*.

NWLINK IPX/SPX/NetBIOS Compatible Transport   Microsoft's implementation of the Novell IPX/SPX protocol stack.

O

object   A record in the Active Directory database.

object class   A definition of a specific type of record in the AD database.

Object Identifiers (OIDs)   Identifiers that are used to define objects and attributes as they are applied to *any* directory service, from Microsoft Active Directory to Novell Directory Services. OIDs are registered with the International Standards Organization (ISO) issuing agency. By having a central group control how object classes and attributes are implemented, the industry can avoid incompatible network directories.

offline files and folders A Windows 2000 feature that allows network folders and files to be stored on Windows 2000 clients. Users can access network files even if the network location is not available.

OID See *Object Identifiers*.

On-Screen Keyboard A Windows 2000 utility that displays a keyboard on the screen and allows users to enter keyboard input by using a mouse or other input device.

Open Systems Interconnection (OSI) model A reference model for network component interoperability developed by the International Standards Organization (ISO) to promote cross-vendor compatibility of hardware and software network systems. The OSI model splits the process of networking into seven distinct services, or layers. Each layer uses the services of the layer below to provide its service to the layer above.

operations master A server that is responsible, in a single-master manner, for a particular process.

optimization Any effort to reduce the workload on a hardware component by eliminating, obviating, or reducing the amount of work required of the hardware component through any means. For instance, file caching is an optimization that reduces the workload of a hard disk drive.

organizational unit (OU) A container within an X.500-complaint directory structure. OUs are used to organize resource records.

originating write An attribute of an object, it identifies the domain controller at which a change to that object was first implemented.

OSI model See *Open Systems Interconnection model*.

OU See *organizational unit*.

outsourcing Using an outside individual or firm to provide some ongoing service.

owner The user associated with an *NTFS* file or folder who is able to control access and grant permissions to other users.

P

page file Logical memory that exists on the hard drive. If a system is experiencing excessive paging (swapping between the page file and physical RAM), it needs more memory.

partition A section of a hard disk that can contain an independent *file system volume*. Partitions can be used to keep multiple operating systems and file systems on the same hard disk. For our purposes, a partition is a portion of the overall AD database. Partitions are more commonly known as domains.

password policies Windows 2000 policies used to enforce security requirements on the computer. Password policies are set on a per-computer basis, and they cannot be configured for specific users. Password policies are set through *account policies*.

PB See *petabyte*.

PC Card   A special, credit-card-sized device used to add devices to a laptop computer. Also called a PCMCIA card.

PCI   See *Peripheral Connection Interface*.

PCMCIA card   See *Personal Computer Memory Card International Association card*.

Peer Web Services (PWS)   Software that acts as a small-scale Web server, for use with a small *intranet* or a small Internet site with limited traffic. Windows 2000 uses PWS to publish resources on the Internet or a private intranet. When you install *Internet Information Services (IIS)*, on a Windows 2000 Professional computer, you are actually installing PWS.

Performance Logs and Alerts   A Windows 2000 utility used to log performance-related data and generate *alerts* based on performance-related data.

Peripheral Connection Interface (PCI)   A high-speed, 32/64-bit bus interface developed by Intel and widely accepted as the successor to the 16-bit *ISA* interface. PCI devices support input/output (I/O) throughput about 40 times faster than the ISA bus.

permissions   Security constructs used to regulate access to resources by username or group affiliation. Permissions can be assigned by administrators to allow any level of access, such as read-only, read/write, or delete, by controlling the ability of users to initiate object services. Security is implemented by checking the user's *security identifier (SID)* against each object's *access control list (ACL)*.

Personal Computer Memory Card International Association (PCMCIA) card   A special, credit-card-sized device used to add devices to a laptop computer. Also called a PC Card.

Personal Web Manager   A Windows 2000 utility used to configure and manage *Peer Web Services (PWS)*. This utility has options for configuring the location of the home page and stopping the Web site, and displays statistics for monitoring the Web site.

petabyte   A computer storage measurement that is equal to 1,024 *terabytes*.

Physical layer   The first (bottom) layer of the *Open Systems Interconnection (OSI)* model, which represents the cables, connectors, and connection ports of a network. The Physical layer contains the passive physical components required to create a network.

physical port   A serial (COM) or parallel (LPT) port that connects a device, such as a printer, directly to a computer.

Ping   A command used to send an Internet Control Message Protocol (ICMP) echo request and echo reply to verify that a remote computer is available.

Plug and Play   A technology that uses a combination of hardware and software to allow the operating system to automatically recognize and configure new hardware without any user intervention.

policies   General controls that enhance the *security* of an operating environment. In Windows 2000, policies affect restrictions on password use and rights assignments, and determine which events will be recorded in the *Security log*.

policy inheritance   Each policy that is processed will override those settings made in policies applied earlier in the process. In other words, if a parameter is set to "true" in the local policy, the site policy could change it to "false," the domain policy could change it back to "true," and then various OU policies could change it back.

POST   See *Power On Self Test*.

post upgrade method   A method of upgrading to Windows 2000 in which existing NT domain controllers are upgraded first and any modifications to the domain structure are implemented afterward.

Power On Self Test (POST)   A part of the Windows 2000 *boot* sequence. The POST detects the computer's *processor*, how much memory is present, what hardware is recognized, and whether or not the *BIOS* is standard or has *Plug-and-Play* capabilities.

Power Users group   A Windows 2000 built-in group that has fewer rights than the *Administrators group*, but more rights than the *Users groups*. Members of the Power Users group can perform tasks such as creating local users and groups and modifying the users and groups that they have created.

Pre-Boot Execution Environment (PXE)   A technology that allows a client computer to remotely boot and connect to a *Remote Installation Service (RIS)* server.

Presentation layer   The layer of the *Open Systems Interconnection (OSI) model* that converts and translates (if necessary) information between the *Session layer* and *Application layer*.

primary DNS server   In a traditional DNS environment, the primary servers for any zone is the server that can accept changes to the zone and transfer those changes to other DNS servers.

primary domain controller (PDC) emulator master   A Windows 2000 server that emulates an NT 4 PDC to provide backward compatibility in a mixed environment. Each domain within an AD forest will have one, and only one, PDC emulator.

primary partition   A part of *basic storage* on a disk. The primary partition is the first partition created on a hard drive. The primary partition uses all of the space that is allocated to the partition. This partition is usually marked as active and is the partition that is used to *boot* the computer.

print device   The actual physical printer or hardware device that generates printed output.

print driver   The specific software that understands a *print device*. Each print device has an associated print driver.

print processor   The process that determines whether or not a print job needs further processing once that job has been sent to the *print spooler*. The processing (also called *rendering*) is used to format the print job so that it can print correctly at the *print device*.

print queue   A directory or folder on the *print server* that stores the print jobs until they can be printed. Also called a *print spooler*.

print server   The computer on which the printer has been defined. When a user sends a print job to a *network printer*, it goes to the print server first.

print spooler   A directory or folder on the *print server* that stores the print jobs until they can be printed. Also called a print queue.

printer   In Windows 2000 terminology, the software interface between the physical printer (see *print device*) and the operating system.

printer pool   A configuration that allows one printer to be used for multiple *print devices*. A printer pool can be used when multiple printers use the same *print driver* (and are normally in the same location). With a printer pool, users can send their print jobs to the first available printer.

priority   A level of execution importance assigned to a *thread*. In combination with other factors, the priority level determines how often that thread will get computer time according to a scheduling algorithm.

pristine installation method   A method of upgrading to Windows 2000 in which a new Windows 2000 domain controller is installed and configured (including Active Directory) and the business is moved to this environment after it is set up.

process   A running program containing one or more *threads*. A process encapsulates the protected memory and environment for its threads.

processor   A circuit designed to automatically perform lists of logical and arithmetic operations. Unlike microprocessors, processors may be designed from discrete components rather than be a monolithic integrated circuit.

processor affinity   The association of a *processor* with specific *processes* that are running on the computer. Processor affinity is used to configure multiple processors.

product/service-based model   A business model in which *resources* are dedicated to the support of whatever products or services the company sells.

project-based model   A business model in which the company is broken into small groups, or teams (to use the vernacular). Each team contains all of the *resources* necessary to support a company project.

propagation dampening   An algorithm used to prevent unnecessary replication of directory changes.

properties   The fields of a record in the Active Directory database.

protocol   An established rule of communication adhered to by the parties operating under it. Protocols provide a context in which to interpret communicated information. Computer protocols are rules used by communicating devices and software services to format data in a way that all participants understand.

PXE   See *Pre-Boot Execution Environment*.

published application   An application that is propagated through a group policy. A published application will appear in the list of applications that can be installed through the Add/Remove Programs applet in Control Panel.

PWS   See *Peer Web Services*.

R

RAM See *random-access memory*.

random-access memory (RAM) Integrated circuits that store digital bits in massive arrays of logical gates or capacitors. RAM is the primary memory store for modern computers, storing all running software processes and contextual data.

RAS See *Remote Access Service*.

real-time application A *process* that must respond to external events at least as fast as those events can occur. Real-time *threads* must run at very high priorities to ensure their ability to respond in real time.

Recovery Console A Windows 2000 option for recovering from a failed system. The Recovery Console starts Windows 2000 without the graphical interface and allows the administrator limited capabilities, such as adding or replacing files and starting and stopping services

Recycle Bin A folder that holds files and folders that have been deleted. Files can be retrieved or cleared (for permanent deletion) from the Recycle Bin.

REGEDIT A Windows program used to edit the *Registry*. It does not support full editing, as does the *REGEDT32* program, but it has better search capabilities than REGEDT32.

REGEDT32 The primary utility for editing the Windows 2000 *Registry*.

regional model A business model with well-defined geographic boundaries, a simple *infrastructure*, and no complex setup issues.

Regional Options A *Control Panel* utility used to enable and configure multilingual editing and viewing on a localized version of Windows 2000 Professional,

Registry A database of settings required and maintained by Windows 2000 and its components. The Registry contains all of the configuration information used by the computer. It is stored as a hierarchical structure and is made up of keys, hives, and value entries.

relative distinguished name The portion of an object's name that is an attribute of the object itself.

relative ID master A Windows 2000 server that controls the creation of security IDs for new objects created in the domain. Each object has a security ID that is made up of a domain identifier (the same for every object in the domain) and a unique relative ID that differentiates the object from any other in the domain. To ensure that these IDs are unique, only one server in each domain generates them.

Remote Access Service (RAS) A service that allows network connections to be established over a modem connection, an *Integrated Services Digital Network* (*ISDN*) connection, or a null-modem cable. The computer initiating the connection is called the RAS client; the answering computer is called the RAS server.

remote installation Installation of Windows 2000 Professional performed remotely through *Remote Installation Services (RIS)*.

Remote Installation Preparation (RIPrep) image A type of image configured on a *Remote Installation Services (RIS)* server. An RIPrep image can contain the Windows 2000 operating system and applications. This type of image is based on a preconfigured computer.

Remote Installation Services (RIS) A Windows 2000 technology that allows the remote installation of Windows 2000 Professional. An RIS server installs Windows 2000 Professional on RIS clients. The RIS server can be configured with a *CD-based image* or a *Remote Installation Preparation (RIPrep) image*.

Removable Storage A Windows 2000 utility used to track information on removable storage media, which include CDs, DVDs, tapes, and jukeboxes containing optical discs.

rendering The process that determines whether or not a print job needs further processing once that job has been sent to the spooler. The processing is used to format the print job so that it can print correctly at the *print device*.

replication The process of updating a copy of a directory database. For AD, replication refers to the process of maintaining the copies of the SAM database stored on domain controllers.

replication latency The amount of time it takes for a change to the AD database to be replicated to another domain controller.

Replicator group A Windows 2000 built-in group that supports *directory replication*, which is a feature used by domain servers. Only *domain user accounts* that will be used to start the replication service should be assigned to this group.

Requests for Comments (RFCs) The set of standards defining the Internet protocols as determined by the Internet Engineering Task Force and available in the public domain on the Internet. RFCs define the functions and services provided by each of the many Internet protocols. Compliance with the RFCs guarantees cross-vendor compatibility.

resource Any useful service, such as a *shared folder* or a *printer*.

Restore Wizard A Wizard used to restore data. The Restore Wizard is accessed through the *Windows 2000 Backup* utility.

return on investment (ROI) The amount of time that a new technology will take to pay for itself in reduced costs.

RFC See *Request For Comments*.

RIPrep image See *Remote Installation Preparation image*.

RIS See *Remote Installation Services*.

roaming profile A *user profile* that is stored and configured to be downloaded from a server. Roaming profiles allow users to access their profiles from any location on the network.

ROI See *return on investment*.

root domain   The first domain installed into an AD tree.

router   A *Network layer* device that moves packets between networks. Routers provide *internetwork* connectivity.

S

Safe Mode   A Windows 2000 Advanced Options menu item that loads the absolute minimum of *services* and *drivers* that are needed to start Windows 2000. The drivers that are loaded with Safe Mode include basic files and drivers for the mouse (unless a serial mouse is attached to the computer), monitor, keyboard, hard drive, standard video driver, and default system services. Safe Mode is considered a diagnostic mode. It does not include networking capabilities.

Safe Mode with Command Prompt   A Windows 2000 Advanced Options menu item that starts Windows 2000 in *Safe Mode*, but instead of loading the graphical interface, it loads a command prompt.

Safe Mode with Networking   A Windows 2000 Advanced Options menu item that starts Windows 2000 in *Safe Mode*, but it adds networking features.

schema   The definition of the structure of the AD database.

schema FSMO   The operations manager that holds the master copy of the directory *schema*. In other words, the schema FSMO is the only server that can write to the schema.

schema master   A Windows 2000 server that controls the structure of the AD database. Any updates or modifications made to the database structure must be made on this server first. It will then replicate these changes to the rest of the AD servers in your forest. This ensures that all AD servers are "speaking the same language." There should never be a case in which one server knows about a new object class or property but another server does not. Also known as the *schema FSMO*.

scope   A description of the complexity of a project. The scope can be used to estimate the time and costs involved in competing the project.

SCSI   See *Small Computer Systems Interface*.

secondary DNS server   In a traditional DNS environment, secondary servers hold a copy of the zone data but are unable to process changes to that information. Secondary servers receive updates to the zone file from *primary DNS servers*.

security   The measures taken to secure a system against accidental or intentional loss, usually in the form of accountability procedures and use restriction, for example through *NTFS permissions* and *share permissions*.

security identifier (SID)   A unique code that identifies a specific user or group to the Windows 2000 security system. SIDs contain a complete set of *permissions* for that user or group.

Security log   A log that tracks events that are related to Windows 2000 auditing. The Security log can be viewed through the *Event Viewer* utility.

security option policies   Policies used to configure security for the computer. Security option policies apply to computers rather than to users or groups. These policies are set through *Local Computer Policy*.

security principal   Any object within the AD database that can be granted rights to another object.

separator page   A page used at the beginning of each document to identify the user who submitted the print job. When users share a printer, separator pages can be useful for distributing print jobs.

serial   A method of communication that transfers data across a medium one bit at a time, usually adding stop, start and check bits to ensure quality transfer.

service   A *process* dedicated to implementing a specific function for another process. Most Windows 2000 components are services used by user-level applications.

Service group   A Windows 2000 *special group* that includes users who log on as a user account that is only used to run a *service*.

service pack   An update to the Windows 2000 operating system that includes bug fixes and enhancements.

Session layer   The layer of the *Open Systems Interconnection (OSI) model* dedicated to maintaining a bi-directional communication connection between two computers. The Session layer uses the services of the *Transport layer* to provide this service.

Services   A Windows 2000 utility used to manage the *services* installed on the computer.

Setup Manager (SETUPMGR)   A Windows 2000 utility used to create automated installation scripts or unattended *answer files*.

SETUPMGR   See *Setup Manager*.

share   A *resource* such as a folder or printer shared over a network.

share permissions   Permissions used to control access to shared folders. Share permissions can only be applied to folders, as opposed to *NTFS permissions*, which are more complex and can be applied to folders and files.

shared folder   A folder on a Windows 2000 computer that network users can access.

Shared Folders   A Windows 2000 utility for managing *shared folders* on the computer.

shortcut   A quick link to an item that is accessible from a computer or network, such as a file, program, folder, printer, or computer. Shortcuts can exist in various locations including the *Desktop*, the *Start menu*, or within folders.

SID   See *security identifier*.

Simple Mail Transfer Protocol (SMTP) An Internet protocol for transferring mail between Internet hosts. SMTP is often used to upload mail directly from the client to an intermediate host, but can only be used to receive mail by computers constantly connected to the Internet.

simple volume   A *dynamic disk* volume that contains space from a single disk. The space from the single drive can be contiguous or noncontiguous. Simple volumes are used when the computer has enough disk space on a single drive to hold an entire volume.

single-master environment   An environment in which multiple servers hold replicas of the same database (or portions thereof) and in which only one of these servers can accept changes to the data and replicate those changes to the other servers.

site link   The connection between sites. A site link is usually a representation of the wide area connection between two locations, although it can also represent a backbone that connects multiple locations.

site link bridges   Site links are considered transitive in nature—that is, if three sites are connected by site links, a replication path exists between all of the sites. In the event that your entire network is not fully routed, you can turn off the transitive nature of site links and configure all replication paths manually. Once the transitive nature of site links has been disabled, you will have to configure *site link bridges* between sites that are not physically connected. Site link bridges are the logical path followed by the replication process.

slipstream technology   A Windows 2000 technology for *service packs*. With slipstream technology, service packs are applied once, and they are not overwritten as new services are added to the computer.

Small Computer Systems Interface (SCSI) A high-speed, parallel-bus interface that connects hard disk drives, CD-ROM drives, tape drives, and many other peripherals to a computer. SCSI is the mass-storage connection standard among all computers except IBM compatibles, which use SCSI or IDE.

SMTP   See *Simple Mail Transfer Protocol.*

snap-in   An administrative tool developed by Microsoft or a third-party vendor that can be added to the *Microsoft Management Console (MMC)* in Windows 2000.

soft costs   Costs that are incurred during a project and cannot be easily quantified, such as lost productivity due to unfamiliarity with new tools, employee turnover, or downtime due to server problems.

software package   A software package contains all of the files necessary to install an application along with a description of all system changes needed (Registry changes, file locations, etc.).

software publishing   One of the services that can be offered through *GPOs*. Software publishing allows an administrator to assign an application to a user, group, or computer. (The application can appear either as an icon that will install the program when accessed or as an additional option in the Add/Remove Programs applet.)

spanned volume   A *dynamic disk* volume that consists of disk space on 2 to 32 dynamic drives. Spanned volume sets are used to dynamically increase the size of a dynamic volume. With spanned volumes, the data is written sequentially, filling space on one physical drive before writing to space on the next physical drive in the spanned volume set.

special group   A group used by the system, in which membership is automatic if certain criteria are met. Administrators cannot manage special groups.

spooler   A service that buffers output to a low-speed device such as a printer, so the software outputting to the device is not tied up waiting for the device to be ready.

SRV resource records   DNS records that provide the *IP address* of a service rather than a device.

Start menu   A Windows 2000 *Desktop* item, located on the *Taskbar*. The Start menu contains a list of options and programs that can be run.

stripe set   A single *volume* created across multiple hard disk drives and accessed in parallel for the purpose of optimizing disk-access time. *NTFS* can create stripe sets.

striped volume   A *dynamic disk* volume that stores data in equal stripes between 2 to 32 dynamic drives. Typically, administrators use striped volumes when they want to combine the space of several physical drives into a single logical volume and increase disk performance.

subnet mask   A number mathematically applied to *IP addresses* to determine which IP addresses are a part of the same subnetwork as the computer applying the subnet mask.

subsidiary office   Sites that are part of the overall business but are not controlled by the company.

Success Audit event   An *Event Viewer* event that indicates the occurrence of an event that has been audited for success, such as a successful logon.

synchronization   Directory *synchronization* occurs between dissimilar implementations of a directory service. For example, because both Active Directory services and Novell Directory Services follow an industry-standard method of access, it is possible for each environment to update the other with information from its own database.

Sysprep   See *System Preparation Tool.*

System group   A Windows 2000 *special group* that contains system processes that access specific functions as a user.

System Information   A Windows 2000 utility used to collect and display information about the computer's current configuration.

System log   A log that tracks events that relate to the Windows 2000 operating system. The System log can be viewed through the *Event Viewer* utility.

System Monitor   A Windows 2000 utility used to monitor real-time system activity or view data from a log file.

system partition   The active *partition* on an Intel-based computer that contains the hardware-specific files used to load the Windows 2000 operating system.

system policies   Policies used to control what a user can do and the user's environment. System policies can be applied to all users or all computers, or to a specific user, group, or computer. System policies work by overwriting current settings in the *Registry* with the system policy settings. System policies are created through the *System Policy Editor*.

System Policy Editor   A Windows 2000 utility used to create *system policies*.

System Preparation Tool (Sysprep)   A Windows 2000 utility used to prepare a *disk image* for disk duplication.

System Tools   A Computer Management utility grouping that provides access to utilities for managing common system functions. The System Tools utility includes the *Event Viewer*, *System Information*, *Performance Logs and Alerts*, *Shared Folders*, *Device Manager*, and *Local Users and Groups* utilities.

T

Task Manager   A Windows 2000 utility that can be used to start, end, or prioritize applications. The Task Manager shows the applications and *processes* that are currently running on the computer, as well as *CPU* and *memory* usage information.

Task Scheduler   A Windows 2000 utility used to schedule tasks to occur at specified intervals.

Taskbar   A Windows 2000 *Desktop* item, which appears across the bottom of the screen by default. The Taskbar contains the *Start menu* and buttons for any programs, documents, or windows that are currently running on the computer. Users can switch between open items by clicking the item in the Taskbar.

TB   See *terabyte*.

TCO   See *total cost of ownership*.

TCP   See *Transmission Control Protocol*.

TCP/IP   See *Transmission Control Protocol/Internet Protocol*.

TCP/IP port   A *logical port*, used when a printer is attached to the network by installing a network card in the printer. Configuring a TCP/IP port requires the IP address of the network printer to connect to.

terabyte (TB)   A computer storage measurement that equals 1,024 *gigabytes*.

Terminal Server User group   A Windows 2000 *special group* that includes users who log on through Terminal Services.

thread   A list of instructions running in a computer to perform a certain task. Each thread runs in the context of a *process*, which embodies the protected memory space and the environment of the threads. Multithreaded processes can perform more than one task at the same time.

total cost of ownership (TCO)   TCO is the costs involved in purchasing and maintaining a PC; it includes the cost of support, updates, upgrades, connecting those PCs, supporting the network—every cent spent to acquire, configure, and maintain your IT environment. Most of the experts agree that the ongoing costs far outweigh the initial purchase price of hardware and software.

transitive   For our purposes, this term refers to trust relationships. In Windows 2000, trusts are transitive in nature. In other words, if A trusts B, and B trusts C, then A trusts C.

Transmission Control Protocol (TCP) A *Transport layer* protocol that implements guaranteed packet delivery using *IP*.

Transmission Control Protocol/Internet Protocol (TCP/IP) A suite of Internet protocols upon which the global Internet is based. TCP/IP is a general term that can refer either to *TCP* and *IP* used together or to the complete set of Internet protocols. TCP/IP is the default protocol for Windows 2000.

Transport layer The *Open Systems Interconnection (OSI) model* layer responsible for the guaranteed serial delivery of packets between two computers over an *internetwork*. *TCP* is the Transport layer protocol in *TCP/IP*.

transport protocol A service that delivers discreet packets of information between any two computers in a network. Higher-level, *connection-oriented services* are built on transport protocols.

U

unattended installation A method of installing Windows 2000 Professional remotely with little or no user intervention. Unattended installation uses a *distribution server* to install Windows 2000 Professional on a target computer.

UNC See *Universal Naming Convention*.

Uniform Resource Locator (URL) An Internet standard naming convention for identifying resources available via various *TCP/IP* application protocols. For example, `http://www.microsoft.com` is the URL for Microsoft's World Wide Web server site, and

`ftp://gateway.dec.com` is a popular FTP site. A URL allows easy hypertext references to a particular resource from within a document or mail message.

uninterruptible power supply (UPS) An emergency power source that can provide a limited amount of power to a computer in the event of a power outage.

Universal Naming Convention (UNC) A multivendor, multiplatform convention for identifying shared resources on a network. UNC names follow the naming convention `\\computername\sharename`.

Universal Serial Bus (USB) An external bus standard that allows USB devices to be connected through a USB port. USB supports transfer rates up to 12Mbps. A single USB port can support up to 127 devices.

update sequence number (USN) When a change is made to the database stored on a domain controller—either through a user action or through replication from another domain controller—the domain controller assigns the change an update sequence number (USN). Each domain controller keeps its own USNs and increments the value for each change that occurs. With respect to a single domain controller, you can think of the USN as a change counter. Each domain controller will have different values for changes that occur on its copy of the directory database. These values are not synchronized between domain controllers within a domain.

upgrade A method for installing Windows 2000 that preserves existing settings and preferences when converting to the newer operating system.

upgrade pack   Software in the form of a migration DLL (dynamic link library) used with applications that need to be upgraded to work with Windows 2000.

Upgrade Report   A report generated by the Setup program that summarizes any known compatibility issues that you might encounter during the upgrade. The Upgrade Report can be saved as a file or printed.

UPS   See *uninterruptible power supply*.

USB   See *Universal Serial Bus*.

user principal name   An object's relative distinguished name combined with the name of the domain tree in which it exists.

user profile   A profile that stores a user's Desktop configuration. A user profile can contain a user's Desktop arrangement, program items, personal program groups, network and printer connections, screen colors, mouse settings, and other personal preferences. Administrators can create *mandatory profiles*, which cannot be changed by the users, and *roaming profiles*, which users can access from any computer they log on to.

user rights policies   Policies that control the rights that users and groups have to accomplish network tasks. User rights policies are set through *Local Computer Policy*.

username   A user's account name in a *logon-authenticated* system.

Users group   A Windows 2000 built-in group that includes end users who should have very limited system access. After a *clean installation* of Windows 2000 Professional, the default settings for this group prohibit users from compromising the operating system or program files. By default, all users who have been created on the computer, except *Guest*, are members of the Users group.

USN   See *update sequence number*.

Utility Manager   A Windows 2000 utility used to manage the three accessibility utilities: *Magnifier*, *Narrator*, and *On-Screen Keyboard*.

V

video adapter   The hardware device that outputs the display to the monitor.

virtual memory   A *kernel* service that stores memory pages not currently in use on a mass-storage device to free the memory occupied for other uses. Virtual memory hides the memory-swapping process from applications and higher-level services.

virtual private network (VPN)   A private network that uses links across private or public networks (such as the Internet). When data is sent over the remote link, it is encapsulated, encrypted, and requires authentication services.

volume   A storage area on a Windows 2000 *dynamic disk*. Dynamic volumes cannot contain *partitions* or *logical drives*, and they are not accessible through DOS. Windows 2000 Professional dynamic storage supports three dynamic volume types: *simple volumes*, *spanned volumes*, and *striped volumes*.

VPN   See *virtual private network*.

W

Warning event   An *Event Viewer* event that indicates that you should be concerned with the event. The event may not be critical in nature, but it is significant and may be indicative of future errors.

Web browser   An application that makes *HTTP* requests and formats the resultant *HTML* documents for the users. Most Web browsers understand all standard Internet protocols.

well-connected computers   Computers that are connected over highly reliable, fast connections with adequate available bandwidth.

Win16   The set of application services provided by the 16-bit versions of Microsoft Windows: Windows 3.1 and Windows for Workgroups 3.11.

Win32   The set of application services provided by the 32-bit versions of Microsoft Windows: Windows 95, Windows 98, Windows NT, and Windows 2000.

Windows 9x   The 32-bit Windows 95 and Windows 98 versions of Microsoft Windows for medium-range, Intel-based personal computers. This system includes peer networking services, Internet support, and strong support for older DOS applications and peripherals.

Windows 2000 Backup   The Windows 2000 utility used to run the *Backup Wizard*, the *Restore Wizard*, and create an *Emergency Repair Disk (ERD)*.

Windows 2000 boot disk   A disk that can be used to *boot* to the Windows 2000 Professional operating system in the event of a Windows 2000 Professional boot failure.

Windows 2000 Multilanguage Version   The version of Windows 2000 that supports multiple-language user interfaces through a single copy of Windows 2000.

Windows 2000 Professional   The current version of the Windows operating system for high-end desktop environments. Windows 2000 Professional integrates the best features of Windows 98 and Windows NT Workstation 4, supports a wide range of hardware, makes the operating system easier to use, and reduces the cost of ownership.

Windows 2000 Professional Setup Boot Disks   Floppy disks that can used to boot to the Windows 2000 operating system. With these disks, you can use the *Recovery Console* and the *Emergency Repair Disk (ERD)*.

Windows Installer packages   Special application distribution files used to automate the installation of applications. Windows Installer packages work with applications that are in *Microsoft Installer (MSI)* format or *ZAP file* format. The use of Windows Installer packages requires a Windows 2000 Server computer with the *Active Directory* installed.

Windows Internet Name Service (WINS)   A network service for Microsoft networks that provides Windows computers with Internet numbers for specified *NetBIOS* computer names, facilitating browsing and intercommunication over *TCP/IP* networks.

Windows NT   The predecessor to Windows 2000 that is a 32-bit version of Microsoft Windows for powerful Intel, Alpha, PowerPC, or MIPS-based computers. This operating system includes peer networking services, server networking services, Internet client and server services, and a broad range of utilities.

Windows Update   A utility that connects the computer to Microsoft's Web site and checks the files to make sure that they are the most up-to-date versions.

WINS   See *Windows Internet Name Service.*

WINS server   The server that runs *WINS* and is used to resolve *NetBIOS* names to *IP addresses.*

WMI Control   A Windows 2000 utility that provides an interface for monitoring and controlling system resources. WMI stands for Windows Management Instrumentation.

workgroup   In Microsoft networks, a collection of related computers, such as those used in a department, that do not require the uniform security and coordination of a domain. Workgroups are characterized by decentralized management, as opposed to the centralized management that domains use.

write-back caching   A caching optimization wherein data written to the slow store is cached until the cache is full or until a subsequent write operation overwrites the cached data. Write-back caching can significantly reduce the write operations to a slow store because many write operations are subsequently obviated by new information. Data in the write-back cache is also available for subsequent reads. If something happens to prevent the cache from writing data to the slow store, the cache data will be lost.

write-through caching   A caching optimization wherein data written to a slow store is kept in a cache for subsequent rereading. Unlike *write-back caching*, write-through caching immediately writes the data to the slow store and is therefore less optimal but more secure.

X

X.500 recommendations   A set of industry-accepted guidelines that define how a network directory should be defined.

Z

ZAP files   Files that can be used with *Windows Installer packages* instead of *Microsoft Installer (MIS)* format files. ZAP files are used to install applications using their native Setup program.

Index

Note to the Reader: Page numbers in **bold** indicate the principal discussion of a topic or the definition of a term. Page numbers in *italic* indicate illustrations.

G

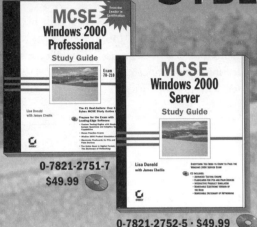
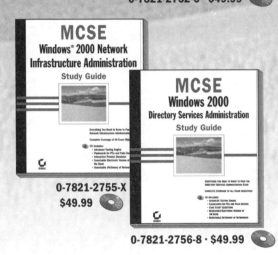

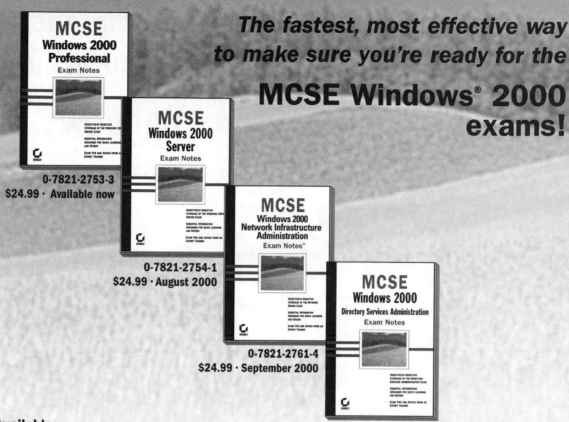